THE ART OF ARTS

Anita Albus

THE ART
OF ARTS

Rediscovering Painting

TRANSLATED BY MICHAEL ROBERTSON

UNIVERSITY OF CALIFORNIA PRESS
Berkeley · Los Angeles · London

University of California Press
Berkeley and Los Angeles, California

University of California Press, Ltd.
London, England

First Paperback Printing 2001

Originally published in Germany as *Die Kunst der Künste* by
Vito von Eichborn GmbH & Co. Verlag KG, Frankfurt, in 1997.

Library of Congress Cataloging-in-Publication Data
Albus, Anita, 1942–
  [Kunst der Künste, English]
  The art of arts : rediscovering painting / Anita Albus ; translated
by Michael Robertson.
     p.   cm.
  Originally published: New York : A.A. Knopf, 2000.
  Includes index.
  ISBN 0-520-22964-9 (alk. paper)
  1. Eyck, Jan van, 1390–1440—Contributions in oil painting.
2. Painting, Renaissance—Europe, Northern.   3. Visual perception.
4. Color in art.   I. Title.
  ND673.E9 A8413 2001
  750'.1—dc21

Printed in the United States of America

08   07   06   05   04   03   02   01   00

9   8   7   6   5   4   3   2   1

The paper used in this publication meets the minimum requirements
of ANSI/NISO Z39.48-1992 (R 1997) (*Permanence of Paper*). ∞

For Franziska and Isabel

Grammar provides painting with its concordances, dialectics its consequences, rhetoric its persuasiveness, poetry its inventiveness, public speaking its energy, arithmetic its numbers, music its consonances, symmetry its measures, architecture its proportions, sculpture its forms, perspective and optics its enlargements and reductions, and finally astronomy and astrology its signs for recognizing the constellations; who, then, can doubt that as the sum of all arts, it is the principal art, which encompasses all the others?

CALDERÓN DE LA BARCA

Contents

Part One

THE VISIBILITY OF
THE INVISIBLE

Thou art clothed with honor and majesty, who coverest thyself with light as with a garment, who hast stretched out the heavens like a tent, who hast laid the beams of thy chambers on the waters, who makest the clouds thy chariot, who ridest on the wings of the wind, who makest the winds thy messengers, fire and flame thy ministers. Thou didst set the earth on its foundations, so that it should never be shaken. Thou didst cover it with the deep as with a garment.

PSALM 104.1–6

Only through maps of heaven can maps of earth be made; only viewed from above . . . does the whole sphere of heaven appear, and the sphere of earth itself will swim therein, small perhaps, but round and shining.

JEAN PAUL

I
Earth, Apple, and Fly

ive hundred and thirty years before the Lunar Orbiter sent back from the icy, lifeless reaches of space the first images of the shining earth rising into the sky above the moon, Jan van Eyck painted a cosmic panorama, an image of the world as seen from flight, from the bird's-eye view. No bird could have flown so high that its gaze would encompass the three continents in van Eyck's painting, and as one looks out of an airplane window, the landscape shrinks gradually into geometric patterns, before even this patchwork vanishes from sight beneath the endless, barren banks of cloud. Van Eyck, the Duke of Burgundy's court painter and valet, depicted mountain ranges, hills, forests and oceans, cities, rivers, streets, and lakes with a topographical exactitude that produced an impossible visual effect of simultaneous close-up and distance. It was still several hundred years before either the telescope or the microscope was to be invented.[1] But an awareness that the earth is round had

[1] "The first compound microscope consisted of a combination of a biconvex lens and a biconcave lens, with the former serving as the objective lens and the latter as the ocular, or eyepiece . . . Today's compound microscopes are, of course, constructed differently. They consist of two convex lenses or two lens systems, each of which functions as a single convex lens . . . However, this design emerged only later, and it is not found before the second decade of the seventeenth century. The first telescope design, which according

been handed down since antiquity—and every traveler who carefully observed the stars on the horizon could confirm it from experience. The oldest German geographical treatise, dating from the twelfth century, compares the earth surrounded by the seas to the yolk floating in the white of the egg.[2] A century later, in his poem *Mappemonde, ou image du monde,* Gautier de Metz wrote that a man could walk round the globe like a fly around an apple. In the Middle Ages, Jerusalem was regarded as the navel of the earth's apple—the place of pilgrimage, the battlefield of the lost Crusades. To the east of the Holy Land, world maps depicted Paradise. With the earthly sphere sufficiently far off for the Deluge not to have touched it, Paradise, with its four rivers—the Ganges, Nile, Euphrates, and Tigris—lies filled with the scent of flowers and the song of birds, concealed from the human race behind walls of mist and impenetrable wildernesses.

On this side of the lost Paradise, the world beneath the moon is the center of a cosmos of hierarchic order, the realm of mutability, to which the sublunary elemental spheres of water, air, and fire also belong. The immutable structure above the moon reaches from the courses of the planets to the sphere of the fixed stars in the firmament,

---

to credible sources was produced by the Dutch spectacle-maker Franz [Hans] Lippershey, also consisted of a combination of a convex lens serving as the objective lens and a concave lens as the ocular. This assembly is still known as the Dutch telescope today, and in its binocular form it provides the basis for today's opera glasses." (Friedrich Dannemann, *Die Naturwissenschaften in der Entwicklung und in ihrem Zusammenhange* [Leipzig, 1921; rptd. Vaduz, 1971], vol. 2, pp. 12-13.) In the fall of 1608, Lippershey is said to have invented the telescope in Middelburg; the origins of the microscope are obscure. The first reliable evidence is that of Constantijn Huygens (1596-1687), who saw the instrument in use by the court inventor Cornelis Drebbel (1572-1633). Cf. Ilse Jahn, *Grundzüge der Biologiegeschichte* (Jena, 1990), p. 187.

[2] Cf. Renate Hilsenbeck, "Mittelalterliche Weltkunde und Behaim Globus," in *Behaim-Globus,* exhib. cat., Germanisches Nationalmuseum (Nuremberg, 1992), vol. 1, pp. 223-237.

with its ultimate boundary lying in the primum mobile, which contains the divine spark of creation and communicates its movement to the other spheres.

The earth had not yet been surveyed by geodesy. The only gauge in medieval world maps is the sacred history of salvation. Until the end of the fourteenth century, exact measurements were available only in portulan charts— sailing directions for coastal shipping.

At the behest of Philip the Good, the Duke of Burgundy, Jan van Eyck took part in voyages to various countries between 1426 and 1436. In 1427, he was the portraitist accompanying a delegation to Spain whose task was to court the niece of King Alfonso V of Aragon on the Duke's behalf. The delegates negotiated in Valencia for two months, in vain. Isabella d'Urgel was not to become duchess of Burgundy, and the princess was never to be immortalized in a portrait by the painter from Bruges.

The father of countless bastards, but lacking a legitimate heir, Philip the Good sent his envoys and his court painter to Lisbon a year later, again to court a bride. It was an age devoted to splendor, and one can imagine the two ships, magnificently decorated, setting sail from the port of Sluis in Zeeland on 19 October 1428. It was a stormy day, and the long swallowtailed pennants, decorated with Philip's coat of arms, would be flapping wildly from the top of the gold-plated mast. After spending several weeks in England to repair storm damage, the ships reached Lisbon in mid-December. It was almost a month before the Burgundian nobles were received at the court of King John I in Aviz, but after four more weeks Jan van Eyck had painted two portraits of Isabella, the King's eldest daughter, on whom the choice had fallen. For safety, the small portraits of the thirty-two-year-old beauty were sent to Philip the Good by two different routes—one overland, the other by sea. The portrait confirmed the Duke's resolve to extend his influence through a marriage to the Portuguese princess. In regal fashion, he celebrated his wedding by founding the chivalric Order of the Golden Fleece. Its emblem was a flintstone with steel whetter and spark, and its motto was "*Aultre n'au, ray*"—I shall have no other. In fact, Isabella was his third and last spouse, and she had to share him with thirty, three mistresses. "What his eyes desired delighted his heart, and with the greed that was in his heart, his offenses multiplied. Whatever he desired, that came to pass," commented his chronicler, Chastellain.[3] Playing the troubadour was only a minor role for him, however. He preferred his chroniclers to style him the last Alexander, a second Hector, a Hercules. The Grand Duc d'Occident hoped for recognition as the savior of Christendom. He planned to liberate Jerusalem, to reconquer Constantino, ple, to drive the Hussites from Bohemia. Long in prepa, ration and loudly proclaimed, these crusades were later abandoned without further ado. The more distant the likelihood of the project's being fulfilled, the more elabo, rate the pomp and splendor with which the sacred vow to undertake the expedition was celebrated. Ships were commandeered, magnificent fleets assembled, banners of the Cross were unfurled in solemn processions, and diplomats reconnoitered the terrain on secret missions.

Jan van Eyck joined two of these clandestine journeys. Certain motifs in his paintings—snow,covered moun, tain ranges, cliffs, a depiction of the Mosque of Omar (the Dome of the Rock) in Jerusalem—have been regarded by one art historian as indicating that the painter crossed the Alps to Italy, and made a pilgrimage from

[3] Georges Chastellain (1405–1475). The chronicle written by the ducal historian, which covers the period 1420–1474, is the most detailed record of Burgundian his, tory. Cf. Christa Doricum, *Burgund und seine Herzöge in Augenzeugen, berichten* (Düsseldorf, 1966), and Johan Huizinga, *The Autumn of the Middle Ages,* trans. Rodney J. Payton and Ulrich Mammitzsch (Chicago, 1996).

there to the Holy Land.[4] But no lost paintings or documents, suddenly rediscovered, were produced to support this assertion, and it was not long before it was contradicted; the two sides have been passing the burden of proof back and forth ever since. No matter where the painter traveled, it seems likely that his covert journeys were connected with Philip's chimerical crusades, and that he turned cosmographer for reasons of strategy. The measurable distances on his world map show an awareness of the Ptolemaic network of parallels and meridians, coordinate lists, and projection procedures, which had only been discovered in Byzantium shortly before, in 1400.

Eyck's *mappa mundi* has been lost. We know of the painting only because it was described by a Genoese humanist, Bartolomeo Fazio, who was chronicler and secretary to the King of Naples, Alfonso V of Aragon. In 1456, in a small volume entitled *De Viris Illustribus*, Fazio described van Eyck's world map as the most perfect work of its age.[5]

[4] Charles Sterling, "Jan van Eyck avant 1432," and "La Mappemonde de Jan van Eyck," *Revue de l'Art* 33 (1976), pp. 7–82. While envoys were taking Isabella's portrait to Philip the Good, the Burgundian delegation itself traveled on in 1429 from Aviz to various cities on the Iberian peninsula, including a visit to Granada. Van Eyck would therefore have been familiar with the view from the Alhambra toward the Sierra Nevada. It would be more natural to regard his "Alps" as a visionary, idealized image of the snow-covered Sierra.

[5] The full text of Fazio's description in Latin of the paintings of van Eyck and Rogier van der Weyden is given by Erwin Panofsky in his *Early Netherlandish Painting: Its Origins and Character* (Cambridge, Mass., 1953), pp. 361–362.

*The forms of all visible things are
enfolded in the sense of sight.*

NICHOLAS OF CUSA

II
The Leaping Guest

he conquest of the third dimension, anticipated during the thirteenth and fourteenth centuries, reached its completion in
the fifteenth. A new relationship to the
world proclaims itself. It is no longer a
matter of reproducing traditional patterns, an ideal image
in the soul, as envisaged in the Middle Ages. The eyelids
have opened, and the eyes are now returning the world's
gaze. In the light of the infinite continuum of space, the
multiplicity of things attains unprecedented unity.

In van Eyck's paintings, the dissolution of the
medieval cosmos—with the application of geometry to
space leading to a discarding of theology—is both visible
and at the same time suspended. The immense audacity of
his use of perspective, in which near sight and far sight
concur, is not at once apparent to the modern viewer. It
cannot be gauged except in its historical context.

To grasp a perspective to which the mortal eye has no
access, since no one can focus on what is nearby and far
off simultaneously, one has to transcend the boundaries of
perception. Erwin Panofsky was a master of this skill.[1]
The art historian was particularly gifted in this respect,
since he not only was a fearless thinker of great sensitivity

[1] The word "skill," which in the
sixteenth and seventeenth centuries
was also used to mean "an art or science," comes from an Old Norse
word that in English originally
meant "reason, the power of dis-
crimination" before developing
today's sense of "cleverness, expert-
ness." Cf. *Oxford English Dictionary*,
2nd ed. (Oxford, 1989).

and immense learning, but also happened to have a slight handicap: he was nearsighted in one eye and farsighted in the other.[2] In ophthalmology, the condition is known as anisometropia. There can be few better examples than this unusual characteristic of the way in which perception can be incomparably more complex than the mechanical processes of photography.[3]

Provided the sizes of the orbits of the two eyes remain within a certain range, the brain can compensate for the difference easily. Nerve cells recognize the discrepancies between the visual interpretations produced by the two retinas, transfer the information at the correct scale to the "maps" of the different visual fields contained in the two cerebral hemispheres, and in this way create an accurate image. In these circumstances, the interplay between the eyes and the optic nerves during the first five years of life produces a particularly dense neural network—it needs to compensate in order to provide what normally sighted people take for granted. Ideally, the visual capacity of someone with compensated anisometropia will be the same as that of someone with good isometric sight. If the difference between the two eyes is substantial, however, the result is a conflict between the two retinas in which the brain favors the better eye (usually the more frequently exercised nearsighted one), leading to increasing weakening of the neural connections of the other eye. Before this happens, glasses have to be used to promote compensation. In unfavorable conditions, if the handicap is not recognized in childhood and corrected using a patch to cover the "good" eye temporarily, the disparity between the two eyes becomes so great that compensation becomes

[2] Cf. William S. Heckscher, "Erwin Panofsky: A Curriculum Vitae," in Erwin Panofsky, *Three Essays on Style* (Cambridge, Mass., 1995), p. 185.

[3] On the neurobiology of vision, see David H. Hubel, *Eye, Brain, and Vision* (New York, 1988).

impossible. In this case, the incompatible images create what ophthalmologists term *horror fusionis*—the terror produced by a state in which the difference can no longer be interpreted, resulting in helpless chaos. In this desperate situation, there is only one solution: the brain abandons one of the eyes, even though it is basically healthy. The sufferer now sees an accurate image—but at the expense of the inevitable flattening caused by monocular vision.

Sight is always already interpretation, a complex and many-layered process of interaction between the eye and the brain. Strictly speaking, the "sense of sight" constructs images that we have never actually seen quite *thus*.[4] As the gaze fixes on different points in tiny jumps, or "saccades," the world paints itself on the concave retina, initially in two-dimensional spherical images distorted at the edges. Including the eye's blind spot and the outline of the nose at the center of the field of vision, these images are also reversed back to front and upside down. At the end of a process of comparative and differentiating interpretation in the brain—a process that becomes increasingly abstract at each successive stage—the world is reconstructed in its perceptual dimensions: the images from the retinas fuse with spatial depth to form an immaculate, consistently colored image, linked to the other senses and to memory.

In a talented child, a latent danger of *horror fusionis* might promote this ability to differentiate, since coherence would be perceived as pleasant, and this preference for clarity, transparency, and distinctness would be further encouraged by each successful perception. Of course, Panofsky's visual disability was not the reason for his mental acuity; in fact, he was so rich in intellectual gifts

[4] Cf. Claude Lévi-Strauss, *The Naked Man*, vol. 4 of *Mythologiques*, trans. John and Doreen Weightman, University of Chicago Press ed. (Chicago, 1981), p. 678.

that his thirst for knowledge was capable of turning even deficiencies to advantage. In the context of van Eyck's painting, Panofsky's anisometropia was a stroke of luck: he was able, as it were, to look through a microscope and a telescope simultaneously. He could calmly select a standpoint in front of a painting, remove his glasses, and focus first with one eye and then with the other, as if looking through a monocular. But to achieve perfect depth focus, he had to put his glasses back on again in order to transcend the boundaries of perception as a normally sighted person would do. "The beholder is compelled to oscillate between a position reasonably far from the picture and many positions very close to it."[5]

As Panofsky recognized in the early 1920s,[6] the audacious discoveries of the "great Jan van Eyck" included finding out how to liberate "three-dimensional space from its ties with the front plane of the picture." The outstanding works of the Italian painters of the period depict the spatial world as if seen through a window, as a detail whose coherence is grasped from a geometrically fixed standpoint; but the viewer of a van Eyck is conceived as part of the painting itself—as a guest leaping from point to point at the same visual banquet.

Panofsky trained his eye to distinguish between the original and reproductions.[7] Neither the finest print screen nor a collotype using the largest number of colors conceivable is capable of presenting the hidden meaning of a work of art without the interpreter's memory of the actual painting. In printing processes, none of the material quality of the painting is communicated, the quality that at every level of observation—from the physical

[5] Erwin Panofsky, *Early Netherlandish Painting*, p. 182.

[6] Erwin Panofsky, *Perspective as Symbolic Form,* trans. Christopher S. Wood (New York, 1991), pp. 59–60.

[7] Erwin Panofsky, "Original und Faksimilereproduktion," *Der Kreis* 8 (Hamburg, 1930), p. 160.

body consisting of layers of fixed pigment to the spatial illusion created by the portrayal on a two-dimensional surface—must be perceived as a living whole.

The greater the number of layers used to build up a painting, the more the painting loses in color reproduction. Van Eyck's illusionism is incapable of being reproduced photomechanically. Responding to the embarrassment of this situation by resorting to enlargement is the latest triumph of the "imaginary museum." Intimate portraits are blown up to life size in massive illustrated books; landscapes and interiors are dismembered and monumentally swollen to the limits of what the screen process will bear—as if sheer quantity could compensate for the lack of quality. But this does not bring us a single millimeter closer to the open secret of a density that surpasses the capacity of human sight.

III
View from Paradise

 o matter what process is used, *The
Madonna of Chancellor Rolin* is not photo-
genic. In print, it seems to differ little from
any of the other great paintings of the
period. The impression on seeing the orig-
inal in the Louvre is thus all the more overwhelming. Facing the incomparable vividness of the "true appearance,"
you have to rub your eyes. The reverse of the Magritte title
Ceci n'est pas un tableau springs to mind—because this
painting is a *cosmos*.[1]

In a space of less than 65 × 62.3 cm, the artist has captured the fullness of an entire world. The scene is the cool,
airy hall of a Romanesque-looking palace, set on a hill
overlooking a town, countryside, and a river. The principal figures: the work's patron, Nicolas Rolin, chancellor
to Philip the Good, is kneeling with his hands clasped
over a book of hours before the Virgin, who is presenting
her son to him. Above her head, with its parted hair,
floats the Virgin's imposing crown, decorated with jewels
and pearls and held by an angel whose rainbow-colored
wings are studded with peacock-feather eyes. The many-
eyed angel is perhaps gazing at the artist's *repentance*[2] at a
deeper level in the painting—the purse, later deleted,

---

[1] Cf. below, p. 175, note 9.

[2] "Pentimenti"—literally,
"touches of repentance"—is the
term used for corrections and dele-

tions of underpainted layers in the
painting; these can be revealed
using X-ray processes or infrared
photography.

which at first hung from the belt of the powerful and unscrupulous upstart Rolin.

According to Chastellain, Chancellor Rolin was a man who tried

> to govern everything entirely by himself, to have everything passing through his own hands and at his own discretion, whether it concerned war, peace, or financial matters. The Duke counted on him in every respect, depending on him entirely as his principal advisor, and there was no office and no sinecure, either in the city or the country, through-out his whole realm, not one gift or loan, that was not effected by him and executed by him and dependent on him as the one person who had charge of every matter. The confidence with which the whole world honored him brought him profits so inestimably great that none could name the fig-ure, guess at it, or so much as believe it, so astound-ing was its size . . . This man was very wise in worldly matters, but his path did not seem to encompass both maxims of wise conduct. For the more he devoted himself to things that pass away and are fallible, the further he departed from that which is certain and worthy of consideration. He was forever reaping his harvest on this earth as if earthly life were eternal for him, and in this his mind strayed from the path and his wisdom led him into foolishness, since he could never keep himself within measure and could not set for himself the limit in that next stage of existence that his advanc-ing years might have suggested to him. His nature was such that he would let no one rule in his place so that he might pass into retirement peacefully, but strove to climb ever higher and multiply his wealth

to the very end—dying sword in hand, in triumph over fortune.[3]

There is no guardian angel to mediate between this embodiment of absolute earthly power and the incarnation of divine wisdom. The viewer of the painting clearly sees things that escape the person being portrayed; the Chancellor does not perceive what surrounds him. He is as large as the Virgin, and the chamber is too small in relation to him to be a *real* hall. His refined hands are suitably clasped, and he is posing with Stoic seriousness in a heavy gold brocade coat trimmed with mink, which gives his figure a massive quality. In his features, with his deeply furrowed brow and directionless, quite unreverential gaze, one suspects a touch of impatience over the length of the sitting required of him for the portrait. Clearly he was a man of action, not of contemplation. A minor pentimento at the back of his neck reveals a late correction of a certain thickheadedness. History records a man obsessed with power, indomitable, filled with greed; yet the painting shows a human being in all his contradictory and enigmatic uniqueness. No other painter could have made him more Rolin-like. Van Eyck's contemporaries and successors might vie with the artist in reproducing costly materials—fabrics or furs that look as if the brush must have reconstructed them thread by thread and hair by hair. But depicting human skin so that it gives a living, breathing effect was a different matter. In this, van Eyck was unrivaled.

Compared with the child's delicate skin and the Madonna's girlish bloom, Rolin's complexion is coarse.

[3] Georges Chastellain, *Grande Chronique des Ducs de Burgoyne,* in *Oeuvres,* ed. M. le baron Kervyn de Lettenhove (Brussels, 1836–1866), vol. 3, pp. 330–331, cited after Heinz Roosen-Runge, *Die Rolin-Madonna des Jan van Eyck* (Wiesbaden, 1972), p. 17.

The painter has studied the various textures of the epidermis with the eye of a geologist exploring the history of the earth's crust. "To him, what is smooth and straight is emptiness and desolation."[4] The living quality derives from small irregularities. Each special characteristic, no matter how ephemeral, is recorded. There is a vein bulging under Rolin's shaven temple, his cheek is marked by a small wart, there is one curl resisting his circular hairstyle.

The peak of Rolin's glittering career was the Treaty of Arras. The cross on the bridge in the distance is a reference to a clause in this peace treaty, which was intended to bring Burgundy's torments to a close. The cross was erected on the bridge of Montereau to symbolize atonement for the killing of John the Fearless,[5] who had himself turned murderer. The date of the peace treaty is recorded on the tile at the very front of the painting: twenty-one light and dark squares correspond to the day, and the nine at the center is the month. The painting must therefore date from after 21 September 1435.[6]

[4] Max J. Friedländer, *Die Altniederländische Malerei* (Berlin, 1924), p. 136.

[5] John the Fearless (1371–1419), the father of Philip the Good, was involved in the murder of his cousin Louis of Orleans in Paris in 1407. On 10 September 1419, on the bridge of Montereau and in the presence of the Dauphin (later King Charles VII), the latter's followers split open John's skull with an ax. "A century later, a monk would accompany King Francis I on a visit to the crypt at Champmol. The monarch would pause for a moment before a skull with a gaping cleft—the skull of John the Fearless. And the monk would say, 'Sire, this

is the breach through which the English penetrated France.' " (Jean Markale, *Isabeau de Bavière* [Munich, 1994], p. 350.)

[6] Cf. Emil Kieser, "Zur Datierung und Deutung der RolinMadonna des Jan van Eyck," in *Städel-Jahrbuch* (Munich, 1967), pp. 73–95. Kieser's interpretations are today dismissed as "unconvincing conjectures" (Hermann Kamp, *Memoria und Selbstdarstellung* [Sigmaringen, 1993], p. 158). The dendrochronological study of the panel carried out in 1983, however, confirms Kieser's conjecture based on a reading of the tile: the painting was made *after* the Peace of Arras. Cf. note 6 on p. 108 below.

The panorama between the columns of the open arcade, extending from the little Garden of Paradise in front of the palace as far as the firmament, occupies all of 32 × 28 cm. All over the nearby town, on the shining banks of the river, the rampart with its battlements, the arching bridge with its tower, on the stairways, squares, streets, and roads, there are tiny people busily going about; some are on foot, others are on horseback or row-ing in small barques across the river's gleaming mirror. It seems to be a Sunday; houses, gardens, fields, and vine-yards have all been tidied and arranged, all the work of man is done. Now one can wander along the riverbank walk, alone or in company, admiring the mill boats, peeping down through the battlements to the colorful bustle below or gazing into the bluish distance, where far-off towns are shimmering like mirages below a range of snow-covered mountains. Or one can stroll with one's partner along the winding path between the vineyards up to the wood on the hill, or chat to a neighbor under the lime-tree in a suburban square and visit friends and rela-tions on the opposite bank, who are looking out of win-dows or standing in doorways ready to receive their guests. The many churches beckon to silent prayer—it is not the hour for sermons. On the bend of the river, behind the island's enchanted castle, there are children on the shore skimming flat stones across the smooth surface of the crystal-clear water, while high above, in the azure firmament, a flock of birds[7] is tracing its wedge-shaped course.

[7] Philippe Lorentz, curator of Dutch Old Masters at the Louvre, describes the birds as being wild geese (Micheline Comblen-Sonkes and Philippe Lorentz, *Corpus des Primitifs Flamands, Musée du Louvre,* vol. 2 [Paris, 1995], p. 15). The tiny birds are barely visible in reproduc- tions, and even in the original it is not possible to determine whether they are wild geese or cranes. The latter migrate each fall across Bur- gundy toward Spain, flying in a wedge-shaped formation day and night. When the leading crane, exhausted from its strenuous posi-

In the farthest distance, faintly, in the glowing yellow part of the sky near the capital on the first arcade, floats the disk of the moon, almost full, with zones of shadow and light.

The miracle of the painting draws its life from the depiction of what is invisible—the shimmering air filled with light, which seems to interfere with the air the viewer is breathing. The atmosphere in the painting transforms itself as lighting conditions in the museum change, and it has consequently been interpreted at various times as showing a morning scene, a midday scene, or an evening one.[8] The book of hours on the prayer stool draped in blue velvet does not provide any hints regarding the time of day, since under the magnifying glass the text proves to be merely trompe-l'oeil lettering. However, on the hem of the Madonna's gown there are words embroidered in gold thread among the pearls and jewels; sometimes visible on the madder-red silk, sometimes concealed within the deep folds of the material, they are taken from the Office of the Virgin. This matins prayer praises the Virgin Mary using verses taken from the twenty-fourth chapter of the book of Ecclesiasticus (Sirach),[9] in which Wisdom sings

tion, is replaced by the hindmost, the wedge formation collapses amid loud screeching, before being re-established in accordance with the saying in St. Matthew, "But many that are first shall be last; and the last shall be first." The significance of the crane in Christian iconology as a symbol of intelligence and vigilance seems to me to suggest that in the Rolin Madonna, the flock of birds—like those in the Ghent altarpiece and in the small portrait of St. Barbara—consists of cranes. On the symbolism of the crane, see Donat de Chapeaurouge, *Ein-*

führung in die Geschichte der christlichen Symbole (Darmstadt, 1984; 1991 ed.), p. 88.

[8] Cf. Comblen-Sonkes and Lorentz, *Corpus des Primitifs,* p. 40.

[9] "Ecclesiasticus, or the Wisdom of Jesus the Son of Sirach" is one of the apocryphal or deuterocanonical books of scripture. The author, Joshua ben Sira, is "the last canonical representative of Jewish wisdom in Palestine. He is an outstanding example of those *hasidim* (the devout) of Judaism ... who were soon to defend their faith against the persecutions of Antiochus Epipha-

its own praises in the midst of its people: "In the beloved city likewise he gave me a resting place, and in Jerusalem was my dominion."

This matins prayer belongs to the eighth hour of the night, and is sung at two o'clock in the morning. Eight arms are also seen on the star on the marble tiles of the hall, in eight rows of eight columns, sometimes visible and sometimes concealed by the figures. The Pythagoreans regarded the square of eight as being related to the celestial wisdom that arranged the whole universe so purposefully. The Wheel of Fortune has eight spokes; eight human beings were saved in Noah's Ark; the Sermon on the Mount contains eight beatitudes; eight is the number of rebirth through baptism, resurrection, and eternal life—and on the eighth day, a new era begins.[10]

The sun-drenched day is at the same time an "overbright night," which is why the moon is also seen in the sky. Its visibility is owed to a supernatural conjunction. The Arcadian light in which all things, no matter how distant and tiny they may appear, maintain their special form comes from a sun that never sets: the orientation of the cathedral shows that the source of the light lies on this

nes, and preserve little islands of faith in Israel . . . Though Ecclesiasticus was not accepted into the Hebrew canon, it is frequently cited in the rabbinical writings; in the New Testament, the Epistle of St. James borrows many expressions from it, and it is, next to the Psalms, the Old Testament book most frequently quoted in the Christian liturgy." (*The Jerusalem Bible* [London, 1966], p. 1035.)

[10] The recumbent figure of eight—the symbol of infinity in mathematics—also belongs to this metaphorical series. "The fact that Christ rose from the dead on the eighth day, namely the eighth day after the Sabbath, forms the basis for most interpretations of the number eight." (Heinz Meyer, *Zahlenallegorese im Mittelalter* [Munich, 1975], p. 139.) Augustine also describes the number eight as "eternal blessedness" and as "the Kingdom that has no end, so that eternity is signified both temporally and spatially." Cf. Chapeaurouge, *Symbole*, pp. 75–77.

side of the painting in the northwest, on the eighth arm of the compass.[11]

The Rolin Madonna shows the world from the perspective and in the light of God, who sees that it is good that every thing and every being enjoys its own uniqueness. There are shadows, certainly, but there is no total darkness. Darkness is not a black pigment, but is produced by numerous transparent layers of paint that trap the light in mysterious depths. In this world, everything is familiar but at the same time different from real life. In real gardens, iris, columbine, and lily of the valley have already faded by the time the white trumpets of the Madonna lily open. In the garden of the Virgin in front of the palace, roses, peonies, lilies of the valley, irises, columbines, and lilies are all flowering simultaneously.

The painting is a view from the heavenly Jerusalem,[12] in which all opposites are resolved; biblical and Burgundian history, vicinity and distance, day and night, light and shadow form a perfect unity, in which no mediation is needed between redeemed humanity and a mortal God.

Well might these thoughts arise and spread through all the fullness of the sphere of thought—similarities corresponding to one another, contrasts disclosing and resolving themselves, the miracle of clarity

---

[11] Another indication that the light is coming from the northwest is provided by the shadow of the rod that is the distinguishing mark of the little man on the rampart.

[12] With its countless churches, the city belongs to the Messianic world, but is not itself the heavenly Jerusalem, the holy city of which the book of Revelation says, "I saw no temple in the city." The palace represents the heavenly Jerusalem, in which "the Lord God the Almighty and the Lamb" are the temple, as Revelation declares.

[13] Paul Valéry, Oeuvres, ed. Jean Hytier, Pléiade ed. (Paris, 1957), vol. 1, p. 206. Shortly before his death in May 1945, the poet describes in this passage the appear-

incessantly enacting itself, and all the Ideas glittering in the gentle radiance of each like gems—for
that is what they are—in the crown of unifying
cognition.[13]

It is not heaven on earth that Van Eyck is depicting, but a
world that has ascended into heaven, and that is almost
indistinguishable from the real one. Here, however, the
city's "gates shall never be shut by day—and there shall
be no night there."[14]

Reminiscences of the expulsion from the Garden of
Eden, the murder of Abel, the Flood, and the drunkenness of Noah are consigned to the capital above the
Chancellor's head; on the Virgin's side, the capital shows
the justice of Trajan.[15]

At the center of the visual square,[16] between the world
and the palace, at the crosshairs of the artist's gaze, there is
a man in a fur-trimmed blue coat, with a red turban and
red socks, standing at the battlements. His figure casts a

ance of "a kind of angel" in human
form who sits weeping on the edge
of a fountain. He is living in an age
in which it is only through despair
that even angels are able to hold fast
to the image of wisdom. It is an
image in which the angel of the
Rolin Madonna seems to find voice,
five hundred years after its creation.

[14] Revelation 21.25.

[15] According to the interpretation given by Panofsky in *Early
Netherlandish Painting*. Roosen-
Runge interprets the scene as a
depiction of the Queen of Sheba
before Solomon—each art historian
has his own interpretation. Cf.
Roosen-Runge, *Rolin-Madonna.*

[16] "The city lies foursquare, its
length the same as its breadth" is

the description of the heavenly
Jerusalem given in the book of
Revelation (21.16). In order to
give the effect of squareness, a picture has to be taller than it is wide.
Since it appears as a square to the
eye, without actually being one, it
is termed "visual square." Eber-
hard Schenk zu Schweinsberg has
reconstructed the geometrical design of van Eyck's picture for-
mats. The visual square in the
Rolin Madonna is constructed on
the formula $h = h\,2 + g/2$: "two elements in a relationship of immediate interaction with one another,
such as half the width plus the
height of a triangle of that width
on one side, add up to produce the
height of the painting." (*Bildformat*

shadow on the wall,[17] from which his striking profile stands out. He is holding a rod in his hand, showing his status as a court official,[18] and he seems to be waiting for his brother, with the black turban and black stockings, who is peering endlessly downward, to turn back to him again. It is Van Eyck standing at the center of the picture he has painted, risking a glance back at the viewer out of the corner of his eye.

der Brüder van Eyck [Limburg, 1952], p. 12.)

[17] If the sun were just setting in the west, as some art historians have thought, then the shadows of the figures on the rampart would have to be much longer and at a greater angle to the wall. Cf. Roosen-Runge, *Rolin-Madonna,* and Elisa-

beth Dhanens, *Jan van Eyck* (Antwerp, 1980).

[18] The court painter has here taken the place of the angel in Revelation, who "had a measuring rod of gold to measure the city and its gates and walls." On the interpretation of the rod in Christian iconography, see Chapeaurouge: "In addition to

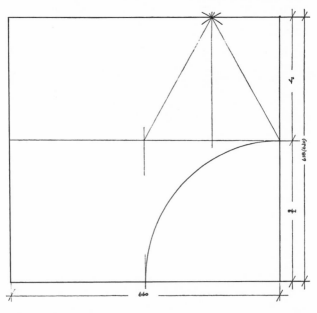

Rolin Madonna (Paris)

His painting has thrown up a great many puzzles for art historians. They have tried in vain to explain the two magpies on the garden path.[19] Why should there be two birds of misfortune, known for their thieving and talkative ways, in a garden whose flowers glorify the virtues of the Virgin Mary? Admittedly, magpies are among the birds that remain faithful to a single partner throughout their lives; apart from that, however, nothing Christian is known about these nest-robbers. A medieval morality tale records the story of a magpie that steals a guilder from a rich man in order to bring good cheer to its poor master.[20] The birds' fascination with glittering objects, and their motley plumage, suggest a role in restoring equality between rich and poor—at least in fairy tales. Infrared photography[21] of the Rolin painting has revealed two pentimenti involving alterations that affect its composition. Who, other than Rolin himself, can have requested that the purse at his belt be deleted from the picture, or can have had the arm of the Christ Child, which was

the crown of laurels as a sign of eternal victory, it is above all the rod that gives a person importance" (*Symbole*, p. 56).

[19] Cf. Roosen-Runge, *Rolin-Madonna*. The peacocks on the rampart and parapet seem to be easier to decipher. In the fifteenth century, the peacock was considered to be a bird of Paradise, and was a symbol of resurrection and eternal life. The ancients regarded its magnificent tail as reflecting the starry sky, and Augustine mentions in the *City of God* the legend that its flesh was imperishable. Cf. also Manfred Lurker, *Wörterbuch der Symbolik* (Stuttgart, 1991). According to a French legend, magpies are metamorphosed peacocks: they once had a golden bush of feathers on their heads, their feathers reflected the light shimmering in every color, and their tails were even longer than the peacock's. They arrogantly mocked the dying Savior on the cross, landing on him and laughing and playing the fool. In punishment for this, God transformed their glorious costume into black and white, and turned their formerly splendid song into a hoarse croaking. Cf. Ernst and Luise Gattiker, *Die Vögel im Volksglauben* (Wiesbaden, 1989), p. 179.

[20] Albert Wesselski, *Märchen des Mittelalters* (Berlin, 1925), p. 114.

[21] J. van Asperen de Boer, "La Vièrge au Chancelier de Rolin de Van Eyck: Examen au moyen de la réflectographie à l'infrarouge," *Revue du Louvre* 15 (1990), 37–49.

originally lowered, raised in benediction of the Chancel/
lor? There was to be nothing in the portrait that might
recall its patron's notorious greed. Among his fulsome
compliments to the artist when inspecting the underdraw/
ing for the portrait on its chalk ground, the cunning
strategist must therefore have included a couple of small
"buts" expressing his reservations. "But the purse!" "But
the benediction!" The first had to be removed and the sec/
ond had to be painted in. Rolin wanted to present an
immaculate image of his own sanctity to an ungrateful
world, which had eyes only for his purse, ignoring the
blessings of his statesmanship, his charitable works, his
countless donations.[22] The artist would probably have

[22] The historian Hermann Kamp regards Rolin's overpainted purse as indicating the patron's desire to conceal how recently he had been elevated to the aristocracy: "The purse was a symbol mainly worn by counselors working in the administration . . . By request/ ing the removal of the purse, the Chancellor was deliberately elimi/ nating a symbol that would have suggested a similarity with portraits of nonaristocrats or recent aristo/ crats. Rolin was simply behaving as if he had always belonged to the aristocracy." Cf. H. Kamp, *Memo/ ria,* p. 259. Without questioning Kamp's method, Philippe Lorentz in 1994 proved that the interpreta/ tion of the purse as symbolizing a court official was incorrect. Lorentz presents, among other evidence, that of a contemporary witness who describes the Duke of Burgundy as wearing such a purse in 1461. Cf. Philippe Lorentz, "Les Rolins et les 'Primitifs Flamands,' " in the catalog of the Rolin exhibition *La bonne Étoile des Rolins* (Autun, 1994),

pp. 23–29. Kamp presupposes a rigid interpretative scheme: purse = symbol of court official. However, symbols can alter their meaning in context; their significance can never be stated a priori, but can only be deciphered from their re/ lationship with other symbols. On the belt of the traitor Judas, the purse signifies treachery; St. Matthew the Evangelist wears one since he is a former tax collector; St. Louis wears one to symbolize a stable currency. In depictions of the Vices, the purse hangs on the coat of the cardinal sin of greed, while in images of the humors it hangs heavily on the melancholic's belt. As an age/old symbol of wealth and greed, the purse became in the fifteenth century a constant feature of Saturnian images. Cf. Raymond Klibansky, Erwin Panofsky, and Fritz Saxl, *Saturn and Melancholy: Studies in the History of Natural Philosophy, Religion, and Art* (London, 1964), p. 285. In an illustration in Hennegau's chroni/ cle, Rolin is seen with his purse at

been subjected to a long-winded tirade; he may have voiced objections to altering the composition—to the annoyance of his patron, who would have dismissed him with a half-jesting threat to withdraw the commission; he had heard of one Rogier de la Pasture[23] who wasn't a bad painter, either.

Studies of the background in the painting have shown that its numerous details were not included in the under-drawing. Perhaps the magpies flew into the painting unexpectedly, once Rolin's request had been complied with? If this were the case, then the enigma of the two thieves in the little Garden of Paradise would be solved.

Van Eyck's learning, his knowledge of ancient authors, is attested to by various sources.[24] Some of his paintings contain references to Ovid, so it would be no surprise if the wily birds here had been transformed in the manner described in the *Metamorphoses:* "Nine magpies, birds who can imitate any kind of sound, had settled on the boughs, and were lamenting their fate." The nine daughters of the *rich* landowner Pierus, "proud that they were nine in number," challenge the Muses to a singing

---

the Burgundian court. The context of the heavenly Jerusalem is completely different. In Paradise, the *absent* purse only works if the *presence* of its bearer is not to be called into question. The needle's eye through which the Kingdom of God is reached is, of course, fashioned in such a way that it is easier for a camel with two humps to get through it than a rich man with a purse . . .

[23] This was the French name of the painter Rogier van der Weyden, whom Rolin commissioned a decade after the van Eyck painting to paint the triptych for the hôtel-Dieu at Beaune that he had endowed. The reverse of the altar wings shows the elderly Rolin with his third wife, Guigone de Salins. "*Il est bien juste que Rolin, après avoir fait tant de pauvres pendant sa vie, leur laisse un asile après sa mort,*" Louis XI is said to have remarked on the foundation of the hospital. ("It is very just that Rolin, having created so many paupers during his life, should leave a refuge for them after his death.") Cf. M. G. Abord, *Nicolas Rolin* (Dijon, 1958), p. 28.

[24] Cf. Dhanens, *Jan van Eyck,* p. 181.

contest. "Though it was shameful to contend with them," as Urania, the Muse of astronomy, tells Pallas Athene, "there was more shame—we thought—in turning down their challenge." The Pierides begin with a loud song of falsehoods belittling the gods and praising the hundred-armed titan Typhoeus, "who dared to hope for heaven as his kingdom." When they lose the contest, they even revile the goddesses who have defeated them. At this, Calliope, the Muse of poetry, says, "You challenged us: for that alone, you merit punishment. But now you dare to add your rude abuse. Our patience is not endless: you would test our anger, and our wrath will rage—unchecked." At once, the rich man's mocking daughters find their nails turning to claws, their arms becoming covered in down and plumage, and their faces narrowing into horny beaks; all that is left of their laughter is a clacking noise. "Yet, though they now are winged, their endless need for sharp, impulsive, harsh derisive speech remains: their old loquacity—they keep."[25]

Arrogance is thus transformed into a bird that steals from the nests of *songbirds*. The two "daughters" of the wealthy Rolin, his two little "buts" of reservation, may have suffered a similar fate.[26] As embodiments of Rolin's croaking criticism, the two magpies with their notorious greed, with their doubts about salvation, may have been a witty touch of revenge at a deeper mental level, through which the artist consciously gave wings to the touches of

[25] Ovid, *Metamorphoses* 5. 294–678 (*The Metamorphoses of Ovid*, trans. Allen Mandelbaum [New York, 1993]).

[26] On the personification of abstractions in ancient rhetoric and *descendants* of the technique in the Middle Ages, Renaissance, and Baroque, cf. Ernst Robert Curtius, *European Literature and the Latin Middle Ages*, trans. Willard R. Trask (New York, 1953), pp. 131–134; p. 132: "In medieval didactic poems on the virtues and vices, we find the rudiments of a 'genealogy of morals.' These genealogical relationships are not always clear. Is desire for fame the sister, the granddaughter, or the daughter of Pride?"

"repentance" he had been forced to add. This interpretation of the magpies had to be hidden from contemporaries, but a shrewd observer might still have said to himself, "If a man like Rolin can dwell in the heavenly Jerusalem, then even magpies can live in a garden of virtues . . ."

Rolin himself would hardly have been concerned about the trivial birdlife in the background, once he had been portrayed without a purse, and receiving God's benediction in "a home in heaven." After all, the plumage of the unlucky birds[27] fitted the picture mimetically as a continuation of the black-and-white stars in the tiling.

[27] The only case in which the magpie apparently does not bring bad luck is when it accompanies Arithmetic in depictions of the seven liberal arts; cf. G. Heinz-Mohr, *Lexikon der Symbole* (Düsseldorf, 1971), p. 172. The magpie's motley plumage sometimes accompanies paintings of "Lady" Rhetoric: in ca. 1493 in a woodcut, "Cicero and Rhetoric," in *Katalog der deutschsprachigen illustrierten Handschriften des Mittelalters*, ed. N. H. Ott et al. (Munich, 1991), vol. 1, no. 10. In paintings, the magpie is often seen perching on gallows, or on the cross of the thief at the Crucifixion. In depictions of the Vices, it represents vanity and extravagance. In Wolfram von Eschenbach's *Parzival,* it is compared with doubt concerning salvation: "If vacillation dwell within the heart the soul will rue it. Shame and honour clash where the courage of a steadfast man is motley like the magpie. But such a man may yet make merry, for Heaven and Hell have equal part in him" (trans. A. T. Hatto [Harmondsworth, 1980], p. 15). According to one legend, the magpie has a motley coat because it laughed at Christ's crucifixion. Cf. Lurker, *Wörterbuch,* and Hannelore Sachs, Ernst Badestübner, and Helga Neumann, *Christliche Ikonographie in Stichworten* (Munich, 1994). The Latin name for the magpie, *Pica pica,* is related to the root for "pitch," "pitch-black." In French, the bird is called *pie,* and there is also a dialect word *agace* (*agacer* originally meant "to screech" like a magpie, with the senses "irritate," "aggravate," "pester" later deriving from it). Up to the nineteenth century, *pie* (from the Latin root *pius*) in refined speech was an adjective meaning "pious, charitable, merciful"; *faire oeuvre pie* meant "to do a pious work." The magpies might also therefore be taken to refer to Rolin's charitable endowments. In French, *pie* is only used today as the adjective meaning "pied, particolored." Superimposing the two senses of the word in *oeuvre pie,* the pious/particolored deed might seen as a "white lie." This is exactly the sense in which the

The magpies' coat is chiaroscuro, but the peacock shimmers in the colors of the rainbow. Ambivalent like many of the birds and animals in Christian iconography, the peacock's significance varies according to its surroundings. It is sometimes good, sometimes evil. In Paradise, it symbolizes immortality,[28] but in the secular world it is the first of the Vices, Superbia (arrogance, pride). Its seraphic plumage is a feast for the eyes, but its shrill cry is a cacophony to the ears. Ever since the *Physiologus,* the bird's shrill cry has been linked to its scratching claws and interpreted as a complaint:

> For the peacock is a quite delightful bird, above every other fowl under heaven, having splendid plumage and delightful wings, striding about here and there, regarding itself with admiration and ruffling its feathers, and contorting itself and turning to look at itself.

magpie is regarded in the *Wyngaerden der Sele,* a tractate formerly attributed to Johannes Veghe (1431/32–1504), which may be of Dutch origin. In this text, magpies are described as worldly-wise people who are trying to atone for evil deeds on earth by doing as many good deeds in compensation. (*Wyngaerden der Sele des Johannes Veghe,* ed. Rademacher [Hiltrup, 1940], p. 428. On the question of its authorship, see Dietrich Schmidtke, "Bemerkungen zum 'Wyngaerden der Sele' des Ps.-Veghe," in *Verbum et Signum: Festschrift für Friedrich Ohly,* ed. Hans Fromm et al. [Munich, 1975], vol. 2, pp. 413–436.)

[28] The peacock symbolizes resurrection in two different time periods. It can instantaneously raise its tail into a fan, while its tail feathers, lost in the fall, grow back again in spring after the intervening winter. In the tenth book of his *Natural History,* Pliny writes that the peacock sleeps perched in trees in the dense forests because it feels shame on losing its feathers in the fall, and it only reemerges in spring. This is probably the source of the legend that its flesh is imperishable, allowing feathers to be instantaneously or cyclically resurrected from it. The bird's negative associations surely derive from its behavior: "The most outstanding characteristic of the peacock is its arrogant thirst for domination, which it manifests not only toward its mate, but also toward human beings—often making it intolerable on a poultry farm" (*Brehms Tierleben* [Leipzig, 1911], vol. 7, p. 49).

But when its gaze falls upon its feet, it cries out in loud complaint; for its feet do not match the rest of its form at all.

The moral of the allegory:

You too, wise human being, when you consider your destiny and the good things that God has given you, rejoice and be glad and exult in your heart; but when you look at your feet—which is to say, at your sins—then cry out and weep to God, and scorn the injustice of it, just as the peacock scorns its feet.[29]

The peacock is simultaneously attractive and repul-sive. Its screech is the link between its ability to produce a glorious fan and its sinfully ugly feet; it offends the human ear, but placates the divine one.[30] Once it reaches Par-adise, the screecher has nothing more to reproach itself with.

The painting shows three[31] peacocks in the first arcade on Rolin's side of the painting. Concealed by his sleeve,

---

[29] *Physiologus,* trans. and com-mentary by Otto Seel (Zurich, 1960; 1992 ed.), p. 78. "An old Ital-ian proverb says that the peacock has the plumage of an angel, the voice of a devil, and the gait of an assassin." (*Brehms Tierleben,* vol. 7, p. 49.)

[30] The change in the peacock's significance seems to have begun in the late Middle Ages, when the sense of sight began to vie with the sense of hearing for predominance. See the excellent study by Donat de Chapeaurouge, *Das Auge ist ein Herr, das Ohr ein Knecht* (Wiesbaden, 1983). In symbolism, the peacock falls gradually silent as time goes

on. Its feet receive hardly any atten-tion anymore, and the contradictory interpretations both involve the fan. The peacock came to be regarded as the vainest of all the birds only after the belief in immortality became a self-serving one. This was when the peacock's puffed-up courtship dis-play entered the symbolism of Van-ity. The feet and the screech are forgotten, although the physical examples of the species are still heard to complain.

[31] The symbolism of the num-ber three here refers to the three days that Christ spent in the tomb before the Resurrection.

the body of one of the birds seems to have been separated from its head, like Argus Panoptes in Greek mythology. In the ancient world, the peacock was honored as the bird of Juno, the Queen of Heaven. Jupiter's jealous wife transformed the hundred eyes of her herdsman Argus, who was tricked by Mercury and beheaded, into "jewels that glittered like the stars,"[32] which she set on the tail of her favorite bird. In Christian interpretations of Ovid, Argus was seen as representing secular princes and the shepherds of the Church, who practice wise foresight with a hundred eyes, but can still be deceived. "One who has lost his prudence is like a peacock without a tail."[33]

None of the peacocks in the Rolin portrait has fanned out its feathers. With its tail of eyes turning toward the curios in the space above, one of the peacocks is standing on the battlements and peering in the direction of Rolin. Its clumsy feet are clearly visible; as the *Physiologus* shows, these are no obstacle on the path to eternal life. Its own screeching complaint follows swiftly on its heels, just as forgiveness follows the complaint—provided that the sinner will part with his purse.

The anniversary of the Treaty of Arras was the annual feast day of the apostle and evangelist St. Matthew, whose symbol is his purse.[34] "Matthew sinned by avarice by seeking ill-gotten gains, since he was a tax gatherer, a keeper of the customs."[35] Speedily converted by Christ,

---

[32] Ovid, *Metamorphoses* 1.720–724.

[33] Gudrun Schleusener-Eich-holz, *Das Auge im Mittelalter* (Munich, 1985).

[34] In the case of the Evangelist, the presence of the purse reveals the vanquishing of greed, while the absence of the purse in Rolin's case conceals the vanquishing of greed

only in *effigie*. September 21 had been celebrated as St. Matthew's Day, a public holiday, since the early Middle Ages. I am grateful to K. Ferrari d'Occhieppo for this observation.

[35] Jacobus de Voragine, *The Golden Legend: Readings on the Saints*, trans. William Granger Ryan (Princeton, 1993), vol. 2, p. 187.

Matthew has his greed for profit transformed into generosity. He humbly confesses the baseness of his origins: "Following the prescription that the just man is his own first accuser, he called himself Matthew the publican."[36] The evil dragons that fell asleep at his feet are seen decorating the arch of the central arcade. His sermon after overcoming the dragons also fits the picture:

> Now the apostle began to preach a great sermon to the people about the glory of the earthly paradise, telling them that it had stood above all the mountains and had been close to heaven; that in it there were no thorns or brambles, and lilies and roses did not wither; that old age never came, and people always stayed young; that there the angels played upon their instruments, and that when the birds were called, they obeyed at once. The apostle went on to say that mankind had been expelled from this earthly paradise, but that through the birth of Christ they had been recalled to the paradise of heaven.[37]

Thus, even the tiniest detail in the painter's cosmos contains hidden significance.

> Jan van Eyck evolved a technique so ineffably minute that the number of details comprised by the total form approaches infinity. This technique achieves homogeneity in all visible forms as calculus achieves continuity in all numerical quantities. That which is tiny in terms of measurable magnitude yet is large as a product of the infinitesimally

The Golden Legend was the most popular religious book of the Middle Ages.

36 Ibid., p. 186.
37 Ibid., p. 184.

small; that which is sizable in terms of measurable magnitude yet is small as a fraction of the infinitely large.[38]

Panofsky makes reference to Nicholas of Cusa, whose theological and mathematical speculations prepared the way for the modern spatial concept of quantum continuum, and whose philosophy parallels van Eyck's art.

[38] Panofsky, *Early Netherlandish Painting* (Cambridge, Mass.), p. 181.

D oes not all philosophy ultimately con-
sist of this: behaving as if it did not know what we know with
certainty—and as if, on the contrary, it knew precisely what
we certainly do not know?   PAUL VALÉRY

IV
A Cosmographer's Conjectures

 toic, Platonic and Neoplatonic, nominalist, and mystical currents fuse together in
the philosophy of Nicholas of Cusa to
form a single, unique structure. If we were
to regard the collapse of the foundations of
medieval philosophy as a fall from grace—and at the end
of the twentieth century there might be good reason to do
so—then the Franciscan William of Ockham might be
seen as the serpent on the Tree of Knowledge, and
Nicholas of Cusa would be among those who devoured
the fruit. In contrast to other students of the serpent, however, Nicholas never lost sight of Paradise, in spite of
the rupture caused by the forbidden fruit. The Invincible
Teacher—one of the honorifics by which Ockham
was addressed[1]—challenged the Aristotelian distinction
between celestial and earthly matter, and ascribed the
same nature to celestial bodies as to ephemeral earthly
bodies. Here below and there above, there was not the
slightest difference. Everything in the world and everything above it must be contingent, for God could have
created everything quite differently.

[1] Another term of praise was Venerabilis Inceptor—the Admirable
Initiator.

Ockham was an astute logician, a skeptical philoso-pher, and a fundamentalist theologian. The unification of worlds that had formerly been distinct—the perfect, unique, harmonious, and immutable sphere above the moon, and the intrinsically finite, contingent, and impre-cise earth—led this antithetic thinker to generate a multi-tude of distinctions. He stood for a rigorous distinction between church and state, between philosophy and theol-ogy, reason and faith, knowledge and experience, logic and metaphysics, objects and concepts, intuitive and abstract knowledge. The unity of composites of form and matter was difficult to reconcile with his system, since he was as impatient of contradiction as his God, whom he absolutized into sheer will. He even transferred the category of relation to the realm of transcendence. His principle of economy, known as Ockham's razor—the requirement that simpler explanations must be preferred to more complex ones—is still a valid axiom of scientific procedure today. He did not recognize general concepts or universals as having any reality beyond thought; reality could be ascribed only to sensory perceptions and intu-itively perceived individual objects—a position that sparked off the twelfth century's dispute over universals, which continues to smolder to this day. This long-running contention between the "ancients" and the "moderns," realists and nominalists, can be traced right down to the present century, in which the "knights of the razor"[2] have exalted logic and economy in thought into the central maxim of modern life.

[2] William James, *The Will to Believe, and Other Essays in Popular Philosophy,* ed. Frederick H. Burk-hardt et al. (Cambridge, Mass., 1979), p. 105; cf. Edgar Wind, *Art and Anarchy,* 3rd ed. (London, 1985), p. 87. The most succinct appreciation and critique of Ock-ham's method is by Ernst Cassirer: "Ockham's 'razor' is certainly a valuable instrument, and one that is indispensable for epistemology as a whole; but if it is applied in the wrong place, we run the risk of cut-ting through the natural bands and ligaments that hold together the

Nicolas of Cusa went his own way. He observed the commandment not to reduce the plenitude of the world unnecessarily. It would have been inconceivable to him that the dissection of parts might one day mean losing sight of the whole. Turning his back to the modern age,[3] he invoked the unfolding of divine harmony, order, and proportion in the abundance of sublunary forms with so much urgency that he seems to have had a presentiment of approaching conflicts. His magic word was *nexus,* his touchstone was *beryl,* his method was *coincidentia oppositorum,* and the term by which he described his art was *conjecture*—a word that originally meant the casting together of apparently disconnected items. What Ockham, a century before, had mercilessly divided, Nicholas of Cusa transformed into a "play of the world"[4] in the face of an infinite referential horizon.[5] He followed the *via moderna* in his view of the unified nature of the universe and the individual essence of things, but diverged from it in regarding objects as not being sufficient unto themselves. Reason is one thing, intellect is another. This Cusanian distinction contains the potential reconciliation between the two paths. Reason analyzes and divides, but intellect

organs of perception" (*Zur modernen Physik* [Darmstadt, 1994], p. 191).

[3] See the outstanding interpretation by Hans Blumenberg, *Aspekte der Epochenschwelle: Cusaner und Nolaner* (Frankfurt am Main, 1976), and Ernst Cassirer's superb *The Individual and the Cosmos in Renaissance Philosophy,* trans. Mario Domandi (New York, 1963; Philadelphia, 1972)—which among other things emphasizes Nicholas of Cusa's tolerance, "which is anything but indifference. The multiplicity of forms of faith is not tolerated as a mere empirical juxtaposition, but rather is speculatively required and epistemologically founded" (p. 30).

[4] The "play" of the globe is its rotation.

[5] Cf. Stephan Otto on Nicholas of Cusa, in *Klassiker der Philosophie* (Munich, 1985) and in *Geschichte der Philosophie in Text und Darstellung* (Stuttgart, 1984), vol. 3 (Renaissance), and the lucid explanation of Nicholas of Cusa's philosophy from the medieval point of view by Kurt Flasch, ibid., vol. 2 (Middle Ages). See also *Nicholas of Cusa: Selected Spiritual Writings,* trans. H. Lawrence Bond, pref. Morimichi Watanabe (New York, 1997).

conceives perceptible phenomena within itself. There *is* no immediate image of the world. Seeing is knowing, and "knowing is measuring":[6] but since the world is characterized by its imprecision, truth in the earthly realm is possible only with qualifications. Anything that is free of qualification can only be in God. The Cusanian conception of God is as abstract as could be: idea of ideas, form of forms, absolute unity and eternity, origin and principle of all being. Beyond all that is comparable, he can only be described using the superlative polyptoton[7] or oxymoron. "There is in him, therefore, the nonbeing of all that can be."[8] We overlook the One if we regard it as a conceptual contradiction of multiplicity and nonbeing. God is beyond all that is either single or multiple, "beyond all definition and infinitude, entire, everywhere and nowhere, having every possible form and at the same time formless and completely inexpressible, all in all, in no thing nothing, all and nothing in itself, intact, undivided, even in the smallest thing, and at the same time in nothing at all."[9] He is the invisibility of visible things, just as the world is the visibility of invisible contents, the *not—other* from which difference originally emerges, just as becoming emerges from the *can—is* and development from the *greatest-and-smallest-at-once,* or accident from what may not *not* be: absolute necessity, since the world does not come from God by accident.[10]

Between 24 November 1437 and 8 February the fol-

---

[6] Nicholas of Cusa (1401–1464), *Über den Beryll* (Hamburg, 1987), p. 91.

[7] The *superlative polyptoton* (the Book of Books, the Song of Songs, etc.) is not derived from classical rhetoric, but is a stylistic figure of hyperbole belonging to the Hebrew language. Cf. Jorge Luis Borges, "From Someone to Nobody," in *Selected Non-Fictions,* ed. Eliot Weinberger (New York, 1999), pp. 341–343.

[8] Nicholas of Cusa, *Gespräch über das Seinkönnen* (Stuttgart, 1990), p. 59.

[9] Loc. cit.

[10] The words in italic are Cusanian terms for God.

lowing year, returning from Constantinople to Venice as an escort of the Byzantine Emperor and the Patriarch of the Eastern Church, along with twenty-eight archbishops, to conduct negotiations on church unity with the Pope in Ferrara, Nicholas of Cusa had the coincidence of opposites personally revealed to him on a stormy sea. Whether from East or West, high dignitaries and ship's boys alike, all were equally distant both from their own world and the foreign one, all equally delivered up to the fury of elements on the swaying decks of the ship. "God is recognized in ignorance, i.e., in what is inconceivable, in shadow, in darkness and in the unknown . . . as that in which opposites coincide, movement and stillness, so that they are not separate concepts, but beyond all duality and difference."[11]

That which does not differ from Nothingness, because it is everything that *can* be, cannot be grasped by the understanding. The existence of the Cusanian Creator encompasses his nonexistence: the hidden God *cannot be perceived.*[12] "Accidentally," unity has unfolded into a certain plurality. The plurality of things arises from the fact that

> God is in nothing. Take away God from the creature and you are left with nothing; take away the substance from a composite being, the accidents also disappear and nothing remains. Is it possible for the human mind to grasp this? The accident ceases to exist when the substance is removed . . . Yet it cannot be said that an accident is nothing, for while it inheres in its substance it confers something on it.[13]

[11] Nicholas of Cusa, *Seinkönnen,* p. 60.

[12] *Ex(s)istere* means literally "to stand out, to be perceptible."

[13] Nicholas of Cusa, *Of Learned Ignorance,* trans. Germain Heron (London, 1954), p. 78.

As the origin of all things, God is not in proportion with the world. The word of words, the absolute origin of language, to which no other word refers, is set in what is meaningless. Eternal being is incapable of becoming, and since "all possibilities whatsoever" are subjected to limitation once they are accomplished in reality, in an "infinite reality" there can be no possibility whatever. The Cusanian speculation can therefore be read in reverse: if creation is subtracted from God, nothing will remain but the origin of nothing.

Without reference to his creations, God can be grasped only through negation. All affirmative names express

> what the one ineffable Name implies; and since the proper Name is Infinite it includes all the numberless names that denote particular perfections. Numerous as such names may be they are never so many or so great that they could not be added to, for each of them is to the proper and ineffable Name what the finite is to the infinite.[14]

The infinite cause of creation is without essence. It should be remembered that

> the concept of infinite being is much poorer than that of the finite. If one tries to imagine a "God" of infinite gifts, one will find that—like Locke's ape—he recites identical sentences. There can be no real knowledge for him, since in his omniscience every insight is merely a reflection. Nor can there be any real action for him, since in his omnipotence every act is a metamorphosis. A god of this kind can only be conceived of as constantly playing— but not even playing seriously in the manner of an

[14] Ibid., p. 58.

artist, because even beauty could never be realized for him, since the perfection of a shape would always be certain to him in advance, just as an artist looks inside a piece of marble, and he would not need to hew it out of the stone as the artist does. This divine being, which is supposed to be more than human, proves on closer inspection to be only half human—a fiction created by subtracting from man that aspect of him that constitutes the seriousness of his existence. For human beings, decisions have consequences, since they involve intervening in reality and falling victim to the fate of everything that is real—becoming historical . . . "Experience" is for God a meaningless concept; for an animal, which does not know the ambitions and embarrassments of intelligence, it is a biological process of habituation. But for human beings, experience means testing by realization, i.e., history. This is why only human beings possess "memory"—in the strict sense of the word.[15]

It is only in an unfinished world with no final truth that memory can exist; and where nothing is lacking, there can be no desire. In an audacious move, Nicholas of Cusa equates God's incomprehensibility with the structure of the universe. His heresy went far beyond the pantheism of which he was unjustly accused,[16] and it was perfectly accommodated by the depth of his faith. Between the lines, the heresy can be read as saying: God has emerged from creation as the principle, and as the *unattainable* measure, of perfection.

The precondition for the abundance of nature lies in what is restless, limited, changeable, and composite.

[15] E. Wind, *Das Experiment und die Metaphysik* (Tübingen, 1934), pp. 35–36.

[16] The Cusanian world is pantheistic; God is both present in it and absent from it, as in a mirror.

Nothing living is one, it is always many. In the best Heraclitean tradition, Nicholas of Cusa regarded pure presence, perfect stillness, and identical being as utter impossibilities in a world of flux. Even in the tranquility of death there is no standstill. Thus, we can never

> pronounce any one thing to be pure, irredeemable corruption. Stellar influences when focused upon an individual may sometimes cause it to fall away into its constituent elements, so that one or other mode of existence disappears; and therefore, it were better to regard corruption as different modes of being, and to pronounce with Virgil that there is no room for death anywhere. For death would appear to be no more than the resolution of a composite into its elements.[17]

The *nunc,* too, regarded as the being of time, cannot lie in the earthly realm. Just as everything that we see already lies in the past, we can never say "now" of the future. Being as such, however, travels ahead of thinking, just as light travels ahead of seeing. Everything *is* before it becomes perceptible. "What is grasped is therefore not the thing itself, but its resemblances, images, and signs. Thus, there is no knowledge of its way of being, although it can be seen with great certainty that this way of being exists."[18]

Nicholas of Cusa would not have been true to himself if he had complained about the unattainability of being. For him, the Creator is not Ockham's tyrant, who is even capable of deception, but a mathematician and artist, whose gifts unfold themselves in all beings, as permanence within the instant, calm within movement, unity within multiplicity, identity within difference. "Who

[17] Nicholas of Cusa, *Learned Ignorance,* p. 116.

[18] Nicholas of Cusa, *Kompendium* (Hamburg, 1982), p. 3.

could help admiring this craftsman who in spheres and stars and in the vast stellar spaces employs such skill that, with no discontinuity, achieves in the widest diversity the highest unity?"[19] Since absolute precision and stability have no place in reality, the earth can be neither perfectly round nor motionless. It lies no longer in the center of space, but has been raised to the status of a star, the equal of the sun and the fixed stars. The limitless universe has its center everywhere and its boundaries nowhere. It is regulated by the same laws of finite infinity everywhere, laws that are based not in the things themselves, but in their referential context.

Ultimate precision befits neither stars nor man. "For the comprehension of truth can always be increased, but never exhausted."[20] The capacity to think is exercised in the art of speculation, and produces "quasi-truths." Each creature is given its own world: "Different perceptual images are created by the ant, the lion, the spider, the cow, just as different trees draw different nutrients from the same soil, each according to its nature."[21] Everything consists of opposed components in gradations of diversity. Nicholas of Cusa regarded each individual being as a single unfolding of God, as a living mirror of the universe. All is in all and each is in each—"*quodlibet in quodlibet.*"[22] The tender links between each various thing, unity in multiplicity, are astounding, deserving of admiration. The incomparable perfection of the Creator is revealed

---

[19] Nicholas of Cusa, *Learned Ignorance*, p. 120.

[20] Nicholas of Cusa, *Mutmassungen* (Hamburg, 1988), pp. 3 and 5.

[21] Nicholas of Cusa, *Kompendium*, p. 21.

[22] Nicholas of Cusa, *Learned Ignorance*, pp. 83–85: "Everything in Everything." As a noun, *quodlibet*, meaning "what you wish," also refers to a humorous musical form in which various songs are sung simultaneously or in parts while observing the rules of counterpoint. A quodlibet is therefore like an interplay of musical unfolding and enfolding. It is an image that suits a philosophy which regards Nature as God's *composed* opera.

everywhere in the same variable way. "The inference from this is that every creature, as such, is perfect, though by comparison with others it may seem imperfect."[23]

Just as the Creator has unfolded himself in nature, man can become an artist-god by imitating nature.

> Man is thus microcosm, or a human world. The field of human nature encompasses within its human potentiality God and space. Man can there-fore be a human god, and just as he can be a god in human fashion, so he can also be a human animal, a human lion, or bear, or any other. Everything exists in its own way within human nature. In human nature, therefore, everything is unfolded, just as it is in space in a general fashion.[24]

What is general is not itself an object of perception; it is a figure of thought, certainly, but generality in objects does not differ from generality in thought. Mind and world correspond in their structure. "By creating, human nature does not reach out beyond itself, but rather by unfolding its power it attains to itself. Nor does it effect anything new, but rather all that it creates in its unfolding, it experiences thereby as already having been within it."[25]

The foundation for the existence of all things may remain ungraspable, but the soul is a mirror designed for truth. All cognition may be asymptotic; but using our senses, imagination, and intelligence, we can recon-struct the manifold phenomena of the world. Every form

---

[23] Nicholas of Cusa, ibid., p. 21. All that is divisible has a spark of indivisibility enfolded in it, and that is its resemblance to God. Everything grasps a not-other within it, and unfolds its meaning only by referring to another. The enfolded similarity produces the differences during the process of unfolding. "All forms are similar, and none is identical to the others," Goethe was to write four hundred years after Nicholas of Cusa.

[24] Nicholas of Cusa, Mutmas-sungen, p. 171.

[25] Loc. cit.

of art is based in the observation of nature, and produces resemblance. In Nicholas of Cusa's philosophy
of the Creator, vision is the assimilative power that
makes cognition possible. In an allegory for a perfect
creature endowed with sense and insight, he describes a
cosmographer

> who possesses a city with five gates, namely the
> senses, through which messengers from the whole
> world enter and report on the whole structure of the
> world, in the following order: the messengers bring-
> ing news of light and color in the world enter
> through the gate of the sense of sight; those with
> news of sounds and voices enter through the gate of
> hearing; those with news of smells enter through the
> gate of the sense of smell; those with news of taste
> through the gate of the sense of taste; and those with
> news of warmth, cold, and other tactile matters
> enter through the gate of the sense of touch. The
> cosmographer sits recording all these reports, so that
> he can compile a description of the whole sensory
> world. But if one of the gates of his city, for exam-
> ple that of the sense of sight, were to remain forever
> shut, the description of the world would seem
> defective to him, since the messengers of what is vis-
> ible would find no entrance. And then the descrip-
> tion would mention nothing of the sun, the stars,
> light and color, nothing of the human figure, ani-
> mals, trees, and cities, and nothing of the greater
> part of the beauty of the world . . . The same
> would apply to the other senses. The cosmographer
> therefore eagerly endeavors to ensure that all these
> gates are kept open, so that he can constantly receive
> information from ever new messengers, and render
> his description more and more true.
> When he has finally finished a complete descrip-

tion of the sensory world in his city, he copies it onto a map in proper order and in the correct proportions, so that none of it will be lost. He then turns to this map, dismisses the messengers for the ensuing time, and closes the gates. Now he turns his inward eye to the Creator of the world—who is none of that which the cosmographer has understood and recorded from the information received from his messengers, but rather the master of works and cause of it all. In the cosmographer's view, the Creator is related to the entirety of the world in the same way that the cosmographer himself is related to the map as a cosmographer; and in accordance with the relation between the map and the true world, he contemplates the Creator of the world within himself, as the cosmographer, and thus within his spirit looks upon the truth that is in the image, and sees the signified within the sign.[26]

Mathematics is the net in which the works of God can be captured. If we were to imagine the Cusanian cosmographer as being a master not only of geometry and geography but also of the techniques of oil painting, it might provide an allegory for Jan van Eyck, following his motto *"Als ich chan,"*[27] with its mixture of pride and humility, and condensing all the fullness of the world into his *mappa mundi.*

[26] Nicholas of Cusa, *Kompendium,* pp. 31 and 33.

[27] "As I can," in the sense of "as best I can." Van Eyck often gave this Flemish motto in Greek lettering.

> There is, it would seem, in the dimensional
> scale of the world a kind of delicate meeting place between
> imagination and knowledge, a point, arrived at by diminishing
> large things and enlarging small ones, that is intrinsically
> artistic.   VLADIMIR NABOKOV

V

The Infinite Chamber

he process of perceiving van Eyck's paintings repeats the process by which they
were created. One needs to hold open
the gates of all the senses if one is to measure the fullness of being in the Rolin
Madonna. But as soon as one steps back to grasp the unity
in the painting's variety, the details withdraw—necessarily, just as the whole cannot be perceived when one is lost
in the detail. The disjunction between proximity and distance requires the gates to be closed. It is only in "inward
recollection, not in direct observation, that the structure of
the world reproduced in this painting reveals itself to us
completely."[1]

Among the lost paintings by van Eyck, known to us
only through Fazio's enthusiastic descriptions, is a depiction of a bath chamber in which women of extraordinary
beauty are stepping out of the water, the more intimate
parts of their bodies modestly hidden by delicate linen,
while a little dog laps up the spilt water from the floor.
The beads of sweat on the shriveled skin of an old
woman, and the flame of a lantern that seems to be actually burning, are painted with beguiling skill; a window
offers a glimpse of the outside world, with horses and tiny

[1] Heinz Roosen-Runge, *Rolin-Madonna*, p. 21.

people, and in the distance there are mountains, woods, villages, and castles, "painted with such art that one might think each was fifty miles distant from the next."[2] What Fazio praises as the finest part of the work, however, is a mirror that reflects not only the back of one woman whose face and breast are turned toward the viewer, but also the whole chamber, with everything that is in it.

In the interior seen in the Arnolfini Betrothal,[3] the same type of convex mirror also allows the depiction of the room, with everything that is in it, from a hidden side. The mirror dissolves the boundaries of pictorial space like a real mirror, and the boundaries of time like a magical one. The presence of the painter and another witness at the wedding is reflected as if they were on this side of the painting; they are seen entering through the door. The viewer is thus virtually reflected within the painting itself—although he may not recognize himself in the figures in the anteroom. On the frame of the mirror, ten colored miniatures under convex glass recall the Passion of Christ. In a reflecting eye set in a frame,[4] the artist has thus summed up the past, the present, and the future. His paintings show the world as if seen through beryl—the eyeglass described by old Nicholas of Cusa, polished into a simultaneously concave and convex form, a gleaming white, clear crystal through which one sees that the largest things coincide with the smallest.[5]

It is not impossible that Nicholas of Cusa, on one of his numerous journeys, whether in Burgundy or Italy, may have seen paintings by van Eyck. His speculations in

[2] See p. 7 above, note 5.
[3] The painting known as the Arnolfini Betrothal, dating from 1434, is in the National Gallery, London.

[4] The convex mirror in the frame has a diameter of two inches.
[5] Cf. Nicholas of Cusa, *Über den Beryll*.

The Vision of God, written in 1453, are based on a painting by Rogier van der Weyden,[6] which he knew from Brussels. In this late work, the Cardinal describes the eye of God as a spherical mirror, which sees everything around it and at the same time each individual distinctly. "Now I contemplate eternal life in a mirror, in an icon, in an enigma."[7]

When this was written, van Eyck's mortal remains had long since been interred—the exact date of his death given on the memorial slab was worn away by churchgoers' feet after a few decades. Parish documents indicate that he died at some time during June 1441.

Nicholas of Cusa completed the writing of his *On Learned Ignorance* in Cusa (Kues, on the Moselle River in Germany), after returning from Constantinople and Ferrara in February 1440. His teachings first reached a wider audience decades later, with the advent of printing.

Historians and art historians have often tried to assign van Eyck's art to a philosophical category. Some have regarded him as a pupil of the *doctor christianissimus* Jean Gerson,[8] who attempted to mediate between the various currents of medieval thought; others have emphasized nominalist influences. Although one can hardly imagine a thinker less interested in reconciling the senses with reason than William of Ockham, the "great Jan" has even been regarded as an Ockhamist.[9] From the medieval

---

[6] Rogier van der Weyden's selfportrait has not survived. Cf. Chapeaurouge, *Das Auge,* chapter 3.

[7] Nicholas of Cusa, *The Vision of God,* in *Nicholas of Cusa: Selected Spiritual Writings,* trans. H. Lawrence Bond (New York, 1997), p. 240. On this point, see also Blumenberg, *Cusaner,* p. 98.

[8] Jean Gerson (1363–1429) taught in Bruges and as chancellor of the University of Paris. A

restrained mystic and "enlightened intellectual," he was surprised at the predominant immorality of his age: "I don't know what I can say; sermons are given all the time, but always in vain" (Huizinga, *Autumn of the Middle Ages,* p. 281).

[9] On this point, I must regretfully disagree with the historian Georges Duby, *Grundlegung des neuen Humanismus, 1280–1440* (Geneva, 1966), p. 211; see also Blumenberg,

ist's point of view, Gerson and Nicholas of Cusa are kindred spirits; a Renaissance researcher might point out that Gerson, as a French defender of the *devotio moderna,* would have regarded any comparison between the artist and the Creator as mere pride of spirit.[10]

Art does not illustrate thought, and it was only when there was nothing more to see that art began to depend on philosophy. The light and the perspective used in van Eyck's paintings are farther ahead of the discoveries of his own time than he himself would have been capable of gauging—as were the audacious speculations of Nicholas of Cusa, which point far beyond his own century, their influence being fully felt only when his name was long forgotten.[11] To approach his philosophy in the light of van Eyck, even though the painter and the Cardinal knew nothing of one another, could appear misguided only to those determined to cling to Descartes's *cogito*—a momentous seventeenth-century fallacy undreamed of in Nicholas of Cusa's and van Eyck's view of cosmos,

whose assessment of nominalism differs from Duby's: "Although the general lost its constitutive significance, the value of the concrete realm was not thereby in any way enhanced, but instead became an amorphous sea of details, upon which conceptual understanding was obliged to set identification marks" (*Cusaner,* p. 76). The most obvious misassessment of fifteenth-century Flemish painting is found in Huizinga; in his melancholy eyes, the van Eyck brothers represent a decadent "proliferation of form over the Idea"; his misjudgment went so far that he writes of their "failure" at the macroscopic level (*Autumn of the Middle Ages,* pp. 319, 375–376).

[10] Ibid., pp. 187–188 and 224–225.

[11] The physicist, natural philosopher, and historian of science Pierre Duhem (1861–1916) compared Nicholas of Cusa's writings with Leonardo da Vinci's, and concluded that, in his work as a *naturalist,* Leonardo had been influenced by Nicholas of Cusa's philosophy. However, he ignores Leonardo as a *painter* in this comparison. (Pierre Duhem, *Études sur Léonard de Vinci: Ceux qu'il a lus et ceux qui l'ont lu* [Paris, 1906, rptd. 1984]). Dürer's self-portrait of 1500 has also been linked with Nicholas of Cusa. Cf. Werner Beierwaltes, *Visio Facialis— Sehen ins Angesicht* (Munich, 1988). See also Dieter Wuttke, *Dazwischen. Kulturwissenschaft auf Warburgs Spuren* (Baden-Baden, 1996), index.

logos, and humanity, although potentially contained within it.[12]

The wounding recognition that the earth is not the center of the universe was compensated for by the enhanced status of the individual. "No matter where a person were he would believe he was at the centre," Nicholas of Cusa writes in the second book of *Learned Ignorance*.[13] The equivalence of every point of view corresponds to the continuum of space. "The discovery of the

[12] "A painter who knows his grammar and who pushes his sentence structure to the extreme of perfection without breaking it, who copies it most accurately from what he sees, is transferring into his painting, whether he likes it or not, what the most enlightened minds of his time have thought, or are beginning to think." (Paul Cézanne, *Über die Kunst* [Hamburg, 1957]), p. 28.) Neither the zeitgeist nor mysticism are required to explain the correspondences between the greatest painter of the time and the greatest thinker. Van Eyck and Nicholas of Cusa stand in the same tradition, rooted in classical antiquity. In the work of both, *reflectiveness* is a virtue wrested out of dark times to offer a guiding light. Jean Paul (the pseudonym of the German novelist Jean Paul Friedrich Richter, 1763–1825) regarded "divine reflectiveness" as one of the essential forces of genius. "The inner freedom of reflectiveness is secured and granted through the alternation and movement of great faculties, so that no single faculty can by dominating become an inferior self." (*The Horn of Oberon: Jean Paul Richter's School for Aesthetics*, trans. Margaret R. Hale [Detroit, 1973], p. 36.) In the work of Lewis Carroll, the equivalent of prudence is the "perfectly balanced mind"; the mathematician and writer recognized this as the "rarest of gifts." The turmoil and disjointedness of his life shows that "a perfectly balanced mind" by no means corresponds to what is known as a balanced existence. It is only through a seismographic sensitivity to minimal fluctuations that a sense of balance can develop. Jean Paul therefore distinguishes between "ordinary active reflectiveness ... directed only outward" and the "higher" reflectiveness, inwardly directed, which benefits the work alone. The life of Nicholas of Cusa, as a German cardinal in the service of the Roman Curia, was also anything but harmonious. At his death, this great conciliator's inner turmoil and disjointedness were given physical form: at his own request, his bones were laid to rest in Rome and his heart in Cusa. Cf. Lewis Carroll, "Preface to *The Hunting of the Snark*," in *The Penguin Complete Lewis Carroll* (Harmondsworth, 1982), p. 678, and Erich Meuthen, *Nikolaus von Kues* (Münster, 1992).

[13] *Learned Ignorance*, p. 110.

vanishing point, as 'the image of the infinitely distant points of all the orthogonals,' is, in a sense, the concrete symbol for the discovery of the infinite itself,"[14] and is directly linked to the empowerment of the individual subject. Because perspective

> is by nature a two-edged sword: it creates room for bodies to expand plastically and move gesturally, and yet at the same time it enables light to spread out in space and in a painterly way dissolve the bodies. Perspective creates distance between human beings and things . . . but then in turn it abolishes this distance by, in a sense, drawing this world of things, an autonomous world confronting the individual, into the eye. Perspective subjects the artistic phenomenon to stable and even mathematically exact rules, but on the other hand, makes that phenomenon contingent upon human beings, indeed upon the individual: for these rules refer to the psychological and physical conditions of the visual impression, and the way they take effect is determined by the freely chosen position of a subjective "point of view." Thus the history of perspective may be understood with equal justice as a triumph of the distancing and objectifying sense of the real, and as a triumph of the distance-denying human struggle for control; it is as much a consolidation and systematization of the external world, as an extension of the domain of the self. Artistic thinking must have found itself constantly confronted with the problem of how to put this ambivalent method to use.[15]

[14] Erwin Panofsky, *Perspective as Symbolic Form,* trans. Christopher S. Wood (New York, 1991), p. 57.

[15] Ibid., pp. 67–68.

As was seen in the case of anisometropia, the constancy and homogeneity of our visual experience is due to cortical interpretations that ultimately fuse our episodic perceptions into a unit. We do not actually see, as central perspective implies, with a single, fixed eye, but with two eyes that are constantly jumping about; and the other senses provide support for this view of the world.[16] A mathematically incorrect construction can therefore create an optical illusion; equally, a correct one can create an impression of visual error. A correct depiction can *appear* to be correct only if it is constructed from a distance corresponding to human sight. A wide field of vision seen from the immediate vicinity must therefore have an effect that seems all the more erroneous the more accurate the geometrical structure of the image is. Only a peep-box can cancel out the deceptive effects—the rising floors, falling ceilings, and distorted edges of exaggerated close-up—by fixing the observer firmly to the only valid viewpoint. But the "rational" distance that would allow a correspondence to emerge between objective construction and subjective visual impression simultaneously reduces the painting's power of illusion. The distanced observer shares the artist's standpoint, but is not part of his vision—as he is in the Dutch artists' foreground.

A form of optics capable of grasping proximity and distance with the same foveal acuity would not be restricted to a single vanishing point. A divine standpoint is not possible using central perspective. Van Eyck's perspective transcends the boundaries of human perception,

[16] "Despite any efforts we may make, the eyes do not hold perfectly still but make constant tiny movements called *microsaccades;* these occur several times per second and are more or less random in direction and about 1 to 2 minutes of arc in amplitude." In 1952, researchers discovered that "if an image is optically artificially stabilized on the retina, eliminating any motion relative to the retina, vision fades away after about a second and the scene becomes quite blank!" (David H. Hubel, *Eye, Brain, and Vision,* p. 81.)

and thereby necessarily breaches the laws of geometry. The impression of perfect spatial truth is owed to artistic illusion: all of van Eyck's paintings have several vanishing points.[17] The art historian G. J. Kern was hardly able to disguise his disappointment on reaching this conclusion in his research. If the history of art is conceived as a progression, it seems unimaginable that the "pioneer" could have worked with several horizons and left it to his imitators to focus spatial depiction on a single point. Since Kern, the view has been that van Eyck arrived at his conception of space empirically. He may have devoted himself to geometry, as Fazio explicitly states, but his interest in the study of Euclid and Vitello was concerned less with perspective and more with the natural laws governing the way in which a mirror image is produced on a convex surface. According to this view, he arranged his depth lines simply by eye. In the Rolin painting, an almost mathematically correct solution must therefore have occurred to him more or less accidentally. The diagonals in the central squares of the floor in the foreground of the painting correspond precisely to the distance. But Kern considered that this clear evidence of construction using "compass and ruler" was undermined by the fact that the remaining squares on the edges and toward the background lead to a higher vanishing point, so that in these areas the distance decreases. The correct version of

[17] In almost all of the paintings, the orthogonal perspective is *essentially* determined by two points that lie vertically above one another on two horizons. Between the two *perspective regions* lies a discontinuous area in which two or more vanishing points of the less significant orthogonals are concealed. The mirrored room in the Arnolfini painting also displays several horizons, which deviate from those of the main room. The horizons of the window and ceiling are staggered against one another, and they cut through the mirror image, which within its small circle displays a larger part of the room than the immediate depiction. Cf. G. Josef Kern, *Grundzüge der linear-perspektivischen Darstellung in der Kunst der Gebrüder Van Eyck und ihrer Schule* (Leipzig, 1904). See the illustration on p. 376.

the tiled floor reconstructed by the art historian deviated, in his eyes, so little from the one actually painted that he considered these different distances to have been an "over-sight."[18] Neglecting the content by concentrating on the formal level, Kern failed to notice the qualitative impov-erishment of van Eyck's meaning-laden cosmos that would necessarily result from a correction entirely quanti-fying its space. Not only would the floor have a tendency to rise when seen from any deviating point of view, but the number of the squares would increase from sixteen to seventeen, so that the hall's symbolic dimension, with its eight by eight stars, would be lost. The changes in the background of the painting would be even more serious. The tremendous foreshortening would deepen the hall behind the figures, so that they would have to move back-ward in order to maintain a balanced spatial position. In the painting as it is, the figures are as inordinately large in relation to the architecture as the viewer is in relation to the image. To enter the painting physically, the viewer would have to drink a magic shrinking potion like Alice

[18] A vital contribution to the understanding of van Eyck's per-spective was made by David L. Carleton, in "A Mathematical Analysis of the Perspective of the Arnolfini Portrait and Other Sim-ilar Interior Scenes by Jan van Eyck," *Art Bulletin* 64, no. 1 (1982), pp. 118–124. Carleton con-cluded that the perspective used in the Arnolfini Betrothal and similar interiors in van Eyck's late work corresponds to a coherent mathematical concept, which he terms "elliptical perspective." Pho-tographs of three-dimensional mod-els are used to illustrate the difference between central and elliptical per-spective. The effects of the latter are similar to the gentle wide-angle optics of a slightly curving convex mirror, confirming Kern's conjec-ture that Jan van Eyck, after study-ing Euclidean geometric optics, "occupied himself with the theory of reflection and its laws" (Kern, *Grundzüge,* p. 28). Taking Panof-sky's approach, Carleton interprets the *hidden* element of discontinuity in the spatial continuum as seen from the elliptical perspective as a "disguised optic" corresponding to the "disguised symbolism." Art historians objected to the mathemati-cian's hypothesis with predictable vehemence, but Carleton responded with perfect composure. Cf. *Art Bulletin* 65, no. 3–4 (1983), pp. 680–692, and *Art Bulletin* 73, no. 1–2 (1991), pp. 53–62.

in Wonderland. "The figures in van Eyck's paintings cannot exist in the spaces surrounding them in the normal human way," Kern reasoned. "The relationship between the figures and the architecture in the center and background of the paintings is more correctly structured. The two little men on the terrace in the Rolin painting, the countless people appearing on the town's streets and squares, appear to have a natural size."[19]

In *rational* terms, the figures in the hall would have to be reduced to their normal scale. They would then be able to exist in the palace "in the normal human way"—and even in all too human a way, as transient beings in an overwhelming space. With their complete balance between body and space—an equivalence of indifference—they would have lost the paradisal dimension of their existence: the suspension of time. The painting would thus have lost its visionary effect.

In *divine* terms, the figures and their abode form a unity. It is their "unnatural" relationship to the space that makes their allegorical attachment *as* wisdom *within* wisdom possible at all.[20] As a *symbolic animal*,[21] man is bound to

[19] Kern, *Grundzüge*, p. 21.

[20] We have already encountered the superlative polyptoton—a rhetorical figure and metaphor for infinity—in Nicholas of Cusa, above. The significance of rhetoric, the second of the seven liberal arts, in the Middle Ages and the modern period was also investigated by Ernst Robert Curtius. "In the Florentine quattrocento L. B. Alberti advised painters to familiarize themselves 'with the poets and rhetoricians,' who could stimulate them to discover (*inventio!*) and give form to pictorial themes." (Curtius, *European Literature and the Latin Middle Ages*, p. 77.) Perhaps there is a rhetorical figure underlying the Rolin painting and the Berlin *Virgin and Child in a Church*. What else is the wisdom within wisdom than the wisdom of wisdom, and what else does the small Berlin portrait depict than the church within the church? Cf. Panofsky, *Early Netherlandish Painting*, p. 145.

[21] The definition of the human species as "symbolic animal" derives from Ernst Cassirer, *An Essay on Man: An Introduction to a Philosophy of Human Culture* (New Haven, 1944), p. 26.

space in the symbolic realm in the same unchanging fashion as mollusks are bound to the mother-of-pearl shell in
which they are embodied; and the interior in van Eyck,
whether church, palace, or chamber, resembles this
shell—at once constricted and infinite.[22]

[22] The spirals of shells, like that of the *Nautilus* and similar forms, grow according to the law of the logarithmic spiral. The essential characteristic of this curve is its continual similarity: in spite of its *asymmetrical growth,* the spiral shell maintains its proportions at every instant. "We may at once illustrate this curious phenomenon by drawing the outline of a little *Nautilus* shell within a big one. We know, or we may see at once, that they are of precisely the same shape; so that, if we look at the little shell through a magnifying glass, it becomes identical with the big one. But we know, on the other hand, that the little *Nautilus* shell grows into the big one, not by growth or magnification in all parts and directions, as when the boy grows into the man, but by *growing at one end only."* D'Arcy Wentworth Thompson, *On Growth and Form: The Complete Revised Edition* (Cambridge, 1942; rptd. New York, 1992), p. 758. Mathematically, the logarithmic spiral always remains the same spiral, whether it is revolved, stretched, or scaled down in size. If one follows the spiral from outside inward, one arrives over a finite distance at an infinite number of spirals. Jakob Bernouilli (1654–1705), who carried out systematic research on the logarithmic spiral, termed it *spira mirabilis.* He wanted his gravestone to show an image of this spiral encircled with the motto EADEM MUTATA RESURGO ("Though changed, I shall rise again the same"). But instead of the logarithmic spiral, the mason used the Archimedean one, which revolves unchanged, like a coiled rope.

Imagination can easily stoop to wit, like a giant to a dwarf, but the latter cannot rise to the former.

JEAN PAUL

VI
Sins of Indulgence

he expertise of the court painter was not limited to the fine art of panel painting. His tasks included illuminating manuscripts; decorating sculptures in polychrome; embellishing royal palaces; painting, gilding, and equipping ships; designing tapestries, costumes, and banners; providing ornamentation for tombs; and inventing fantastical contraptions for banquets and celebrations. Even a painter of the stature of Melchior Broederlam[1] was not too proud to decorate the armchairs for the house of the Count of Flanders; Hugo van der Goes[2] painted coats of arms on shields; and Gerard David[3] delighted Maximilian by painting the railings or shutters of the chamber in which the King was held captive in Bruges in 1488.[4] Even the mechanical marvels in the château of Hesdin—designed as an enchanted palace of the Orient—were fabricated by painters. Colard le Voleur was the name of one of these wonderworkers in the service of the Burgundian duke, Philip the Good. He produced a ballad book that spouted forth soot, and as a counterfeiter and deceiver of the eyes (as his name suggests), he invented a distorting mirror in which

---

[1] Melchior Broederlam (1381–1409).

[2] Hugo van der Goes (ca. 1440–1482).

[3] Gerard David (ca. 1460–1523).

[4] Cf. Huizinga, *Autumn of the Middle Ages*, p. 299.

it was said that various deceitful tricks could be seen even before they were played.[5] He was also involved in decorating a room with murals relating the tale of Jason, the Greek hero who succeeded in stealing the Golden Fleece through Medea's cunning. The story's protagonists were shown in robes of the most extravagant fashion conceivable—Medea with a Gothic bonnet shaped liked a sugar loaf, Jason with a narrowly belted waist and multicolored pointed shoes, like those worn by knights (they had to cut off the tips to flee from lost battles). The illusionistic effect of the painting was enhanced by mechanical contrivances. The viewer was allowed to escape Medea's magic spells and pass on to fresh amusements only after being dazzled, deafened, drenched, and dusted by contraptions for creating lightning, thunder, rain, and snow.

The centerpieces of the living pictures known as *entremets,* which were displayed by competing aristocrats at banquets, were also developed in the workshops of artists. At a celebration in 1430 in honor of the new duchess, Isabella, a vol-au-vent was presented, out of which a blue sheep with golden horns and a big wild animal leapt, tussling with each other in front of the astounded guests. The sheepskin contained "Madame d'Or," the golden-haired dwarf, and hidden in the wild animal was Hans the giant—these were two of Philip the Good's favorite court jesters. We could barely imagine the bizarre magnificence of this vanished form of art if chroniclers had not described the quite lunatic splendor with which Philip the Good staged the taking of crusade vows at a banquet in Lille on 17 February 1454. The vow was sworn on a living pheasant, wearing a gem-studded golden chain around its neck and over its fine

[5] Cf. Linda Seidel, *Jan van Eyck's Arnolfini Portrait: Stories of an Icon* (Cambridge, 1993), pp. 1, 168.

plumage. All the expense of the ceremonies was paid for by the Duke, right down to the costumes of the guests, who were dressed in black, white, and gray, with the knights in damask and the squires in silk. At the gargan-tuan meal, each dish contained forty-eight different food-stuffs, and the roasts arrived in carriages turned out in blue and gold. Before sitting down to eat, one could admire the *entremets*—the showpieces and living alle-gories, which were set out on one large, one medium, and one small table: a gigantic vol-au-vent, in which twenty musicians played alternately on various instruments; a glass church, with a crucifix, a bell that rang, and four singers inside; a full-rigged carrack (a belly-shaped trad-ing ship with three masts), with crew and heavy cargo; a spring of water with little shrubs made of glass, with leaves and flowers, in a small meadow, surrounded by cliffs of sapphire and other rare gems, with St. Andrew and his cross at the center; the castle of Lusignan with Melusine in the shape of a serpent on the main tower and orange-water springing from two smaller towers into the surrounding moats; a windmill on a hill with a magpie on its roof, and people of each estate shooting at it with bows and crossbows; a desert with a living depiction of a tiger fighting with a snake as a man on a camel rides past, while another uses a stick to beat a bush full of little birds as a knight sits with his lady in a garden surrounded by rose hedges; a marvelous strange forest with animals seemingly alive; a fool riding on a bear past peculiar mountains and cliffs covered in glass dust and mirrors to feign a winter landscape; Dame Église enthroned in a tower on the back of an elephant, which is being led by a giant disguised as a Turk—Hans the court jester as the Grand Turc. The walls of the banqueting hall were hung with splendid new tapestries showing scenes from the life of Hercules, clad as a Burgundian knight challenging apple-breasted Amazons in gold brocade robes to a tournament.[6]

When the company sat down to the repast, a shepherd stepped forth from the vol-au-vent and played on the bag-pipes, and an unsaddled horse caparisoned in vermilion silk with two masked trumpeters sitting on it back-to-back blowing a fanfare went round the hall backward, before the feast began. The chronicler also reports an apocalyptic monster, half griffin, half man, riding on a wild boar and carrying in turn a clown, whose ludicrous posture with his legs in the air was described as a *posture savante.*

The vision Olivier de la Marche conjures up in this description is like a picture puzzle, in which it is pointless to look for the line at which kitsch ends and art begins. Small things appear large (the vol-au-vent), and large things tiny (meadow and forest, windmill and ship), as if a child were delighting in a game of pretend and indulging in dreams of omnipotence. This crazy juxta-position of crude jokes and pious allegory, choice materi-als and barbaric pomp, brazen foolishness and fairy-tale sophistication speaks of a riotous delight in extremes that meet.

Comical figures romp about in the margins of the illuminated manuscripts in a similar fashion. A wild boar comes along disguised as a bishop riding on a drom-edary, a single leg with a face on its hairy thigh is wearing a crown of tendrils, and countless apes, hares, bears, and hybrid creatures clowning about and playing musical instruments accompany the pious images of the Bible story. Sometimes a grotesque figure looks like a herald

[6] Cf. Wolfger A. Bulst, "Das Olympische Turnier des Hercu-les mit den Amazonen. Flämische Tapisserien am Hofe der Este in Fer-rara," in Joachim Poeschke, ed., *Italienische Frührenaissance und nordeu-ropäisches Mittelalter* (Munich, 1993).

announcing Bosch-like visions, while fools—like the peasant with a wooden spoon riding the wrong way round on a donkey whose tail he is using to stroke his chin—anticipate the living proverbs of a Bruegel. In the margins of manuscripts, the artists' imagination had free rein. Long before the still life developed into a genre in its own right, illuminators using gouache and watercolor had developed all the magic of trompe-l'oeil painting in their books of hours—depicting flowers, mussels, insects, and small animals, in niches and pillars or as if simply scattered across the page, casting soft shadows on the parchment.

Perhaps it is only "frontier-police prejudice"[7] that prevents us from regarding the forest with live animals

[7] The dictum stems from Aby Warburg. "An artistically poor picture fascinated him just as much as a good one, and often even more, for a reason that he himself explicitly stated—because there was more to learn from it . . . And why? Because at the fracture points that are, so to speak, the advantages that the bad work has over the good one, the analytical problem the artist was struggling with becomes clear. This is a problem the complex structure of which is much more difficult to notice in the face of a great work of art, because in this case the artist has dealt with the solution so effortlessly." (Edgar Wind, "Warburgs Begriff der Kulturwissenschaft und seine Bedeutung für die Ästhetik," in *Aby M. Warburg, Ausgewählte Schriften und Würdigungen,* ed. Dieter Wuttke [Baden-Baden, 1979], pp. 401–417.) No comparison without differentiation: Warburg's parallel between works "of the freest and most applied type of art" is based on the different evaluations of their artistic rank. "Enthusiastic astonishment in the face of the mysterious event of artistic genius can only increase in its intensity when we recognize that genius is a gift, and at the same time a conscious analytical energy." (A. Warburg, "Italienische Kunst und internazionale Astrologie im Palazzo Schifanoja zu Ferrara" [1912], in Wuttke, p. 185.) The "influential frontier-police attitude in art history" that Warburg fought against has in the meantime swept the field. The modern dilettante regards the distinction between low and high art as obsolete, and it was thus inevitable that the "vanguard" of art historians would follow suit. Today it is no longer the frontier policeman from whom Warburg's method faces scolding, but the night watchman—to whom all cats are proverbially gray. Quite naively, and in truly blind admiration, Vermeer's *View of Delft* has been described, for example, by

shown at the pheasant banquet in Lille as being a precur-
sor of landscape painting. No matter whether the
entremets were artistic or tasteless, producing them must
have offered outstanding training for the eye. It is impossible to reconstruct a ship, a cathedral, a castle, and a windmill on a smaller scale unless you know them inside out.
A model of a church in which there is space for a crucifix, a ringing bell, and four singers presupposes some
degree of reflection on the relationship between body and
space, and shows how naive it is to think that the painters
of the period had no conception of "correct" proportions.
What could make the rule clearer than the exceptions to it
seen in the topsy-turvy world of the *entremets*? And there
is no better way of studying the effects of light and shade
than in a small model. Following the Gothic tradition,
the seventeenth-century painter Nicolas Poussin still
made little wax figures that he draped with wet paper or
fine taffeta, using threads to pull them back and forth
across the stage of a box with a perforated backdrop for
lighting, in order to try out composition, color effect, perspective, and light and shadow *en miniature* before putting
the scene into the picture on the canvas.[8]

As court painter and valet, van Eyck would certainly

saying that painting has never
approached color photography as
closely as in this unique work of
art—cf. Kenneth Clark, *Landscape
into Art* (1949; New York, 1976), p.
65. Panofsky spoke as long ago as
1925 of the dangers "threatening the
parallelizing method, which is perhaps all too often used today, in
practice (because the wish to discover analogues will easily lead to
arbitrary and even forced interpretations of given phenomena)" ("Über
das Verhältnis der Kunstgeschichte
zur Kunsttheorie," in *Grundfragen*, p.

66). For Panofsky, the attempt to
grasp the "immanent meaning of
a phenomenon" is the boundary
line at which interpretive violence
and "wild arbitrariness" begin. On
misunderstandings of Warburg's
method in our time, see also Dieter
Wuttke, *Aby M. Warburgs Methode
als Anregung und Aufgabe* (Wiesbaden, 1990).

[8] Nicolas Poussin, *Lettres et pro-
pos de l'art* (Paris, 1989), and Claude
Lévi-Strauss, *Look, Listen, Read*,
trans. Brian C. J. Singer (New
York, 1997).

have taken part in the banqueting arrangements.[9] Compared with the allegorizing sins of indulgence, the ele-
phantine trumpery of the *entremets,* his own showpieces
must have seemed diminutive and precious. But if he
adjusted the diffusing glass of his imagination and the
collecting lens of his mind to the level of the Burgundian
banqueting circus, then even a dwarf and a giant might
have combined—if only as a tussle between a blue sheep
and a big wild animal.

[9] In 1432, van Eyck was reim-
bursed for the expenses of a journey
to Hesdin. The reason why he had
returned to Bruges from the Duke's
summer residence is not evident
from the account books. In 1434, six
statues were gilded and painted in
his workshop, and at one time these
decorated the town hall in Bruges.
They have not survived the centuries, and all the works the painter
created at the behest of Philip the
Good have also been lost.

Three epochs are seen in the formation of the world:

1. Desire for crystallization; urge to move together, to join together, to force a way through, to take shape.

2. Epoch of isolation; the elements stand on their own, turn others away, are independent, maintain their purity.

3. The elements become indifferent, mingle with one another, stand alongside each other.

Inorganic nature keeps all of these characteristics alive throughout the ages. GOETHE

VII
The Devil in the Tube

ot a trace of painting technique betrays the fact that van Eyck's pictures are created artifacts. It is only a glance through the microscope that reveals the painter's hand. This is what gives van Eyck's paintings their illusory effect: they are as perfect as if they had not been painted, but had *grown*. According to the Aristotelian definition of *techné*, adopted also by Nicholas of Cusa,[1] the artist reconstitutes the world by imitating the

[1] "Art, as far as possible, imitates nature, but it will never be able to reproduce it precisely as it is." (Nicolas of Cusa, *Of Learned Ignorance,* trans. Germain Heron [London, 1954], p. 69.) "For the observations that the wise men who serve science found in nature, they sought through the similarity produced by reason to transfer to a general art ... Every form of art is therefore based on an observation that the wise man has made in nature." (*Kompendium,* pp. 37–39.)

"It is easy to see that intelligence, so far as it flows from divine reason, has a share in art; on the other hand, we recognize it as nature, so far as it develops art out of itself; for art is as it were an imitation of nature." (*Mutmassungen,* p. 155.) "Art arises, when from many notions gained by experience one universal judgement about similar objects is produced." (Aristotle, *Metaphysics* 1.1, trans. W. D. Ross, *Complete Works of Aristotle: The Revised Oxford Translation,* ed. Jonathan Barnes [Princeton,

workings of nature. Jean Paul (a painter in words) asks in his *Horn of Oberon*,[2] "But is it then all one, whether you imitate *nature* or imitate *according* to nature?" He gives reasons why it is not possible to reproduce nature without imitating in *accordance* with it. "Actually the principle of copying nature faithfully hardly has any meaning. Since it is impossible to exhaust her individuality with any one copy, and since a copy must always choose which traits it leaves out or includes, the question of imitation becomes the new question: following what law, by the hand of what artist, is nature raised into the realm of poetry?"[3]

The materials that painters use to imitate the workings of nature are called pigments. Appearing to the naked eye as colored dust, they are not soluble in a liquid painting medium. In a glass of pigmented water, the paint gradually settles to the bottom after a time, like sand. If it is stirred up again and spread onto a sheet of paper with a brush, then once the water has evaporated the paint simply lies on top of the paper, without adhering to it.

Loose pigments are used only in pastels, which have to be protected by glass, since the color grains are captured by the roughened base on the flesh side of parchment or by the layer of size on paper, but remain as sensitive to touch as the colored dust on the wing of a butterfly. The

1984], p. 1552.) The idea of a structural similarity between the works of man and the shapes of nature leads Aristotle back to Heraclitus. Nature's way of perfecting itself by unifying opposites is imitated by art using its own means. Cf. *Historisches Wörterbuch der Philosophie* (Basel, 1971–1995), vol. 4, p. 1359.

[2] Jean Paul Richter, *The Horn of Oberon: Jean Paul Richter's School for Aesthetics,* trans. Margaret R. Hale (Detroit, 1973). Warburg, Panofsky, Wind, and Heckscher all attended Jean Paul's "school for aesthetics." In the meantime, the poet's teachings have ceased to be read by art historians. Today the field of aesthetics is dominated by cryptic philosophers, who give a prophetic appearance to Jean Paul's words about the "night . . . of men born blind, which truly annihilates the opposition between light and darkness in the higher equation of nonseeing." Cf. Jean Paul, *Horn of Oberon,* p. 287.

[3] Ibid., p. 18.

butterfly's brilliant colors are created by a system built up in layers, in which iridescent effects are produced by the interplay between the pigment and the various physical structures of the scales. Painters used to imitate this process from nature. Although there were one or two pigments they could obtain ready-made from the apothecary or from a monastery, they were also familiar with the material from which their paintings were made in its raw form. In front of their very eyes they had the metals, minerals, earths, plants, woods, bones, lice, shells, and snails needed, and they knew the processes by which to transform these into pigments. They knew which materials could be sublimated, calcined, smelted, eluted, ground, pounded, precipitated, boiled, dried, and distilled, and in their apprenticeships they had all spent endless hours grinding pigments with the muller against the slab. Compared with today, only a few colors were available—but the complex systems for using them in the fifteenth century make today's techniques look like child's play. We have forgotten what every butterfly "knows": that the visual effect of colors is created by the interplay between tone and body. The color *tone* is one thing, and the shape and structure of the color are another. Each pigment has a different body, which refracts, reflects, and absorbs light in a different way. The blue tone of artificial ultramarine, produced industrially since 1830, is apparently indistinguishable from that of natural ultramarine, laboriously obtained from the semiprecious stone lapis lazuli. A glance through the microscope reveals the difference, which emerges so clearly in the painting that it is visible even to the untrained eye. The synthetic pigment, with its small, homogeneous round crystals, produces a uniformly consistent blue surface, while genuine ultramarine—the most expensive of all the pigments, with its large, irregular crystals of varying transparency and with naturally embedded particles of calcite, pyrite, mica, and quartz—appears like a glittering firmament. Above all, the transparent splinters of the calcite crystals embedded in lapis lazuli sparkle like stars within the deep blue. The *astronomical* difference between the old and the new pig/ment is not as marked with other colors as it is with ultra/marine, but the same principle always applies. The oxides precipitated from ferrosalt solutions in the laboratory in the space of a few hours differ from ochre earths in their spotless purity and in the absolute constancy of their com/position and tint. By contrast, brown, red, and yellow ochre earths, products of the weathering of iron/bearing rocks over thousands of years, have nuances that vary depending on their location of origin and method of extraction. Under the microscope, one can see why: the extremely fine, transparent crystals that predominate in each case have more or less differently colored, colorless, opaque, and coarser particles intermingled with them. Under the microscope, even the most finely colored yel/low ochre proves to be a composite.

The perceptual properties of natural mineral pig/ments can be appreciated even without the help of enlargement, from their original form. In nature, mala/chite crystals, for example, sometimes form pale green tufts of needles, and at other times dense, dark green kidney/shaped cushions. Concave fractures in them have an oily sheen, fibrous fractures have a silky one, and the crystal surfaces are diamantine. Pounded, crushed, and ground, the hard rock produces a heavyish, coarse pow/der of sharp/edged, relatively large fibrous prismatic crys/tals, which have the same combination of dense coloring and transparency as the original form of the malachite.

Genuine malachite was replaced by artificially pro/duced copper carbonate. This synthetic malachite, known as verditer, proved to be as treacherous as the natural form when used carelessly, and consequently also fell into oblivion.

In van Eyck's time, green was the greatest problem in painting. The pigments derived from plant juices were intensely colored, but unstable in light; the green parts of green earths were too weak to hold their own among other colors; and even the coloring capacity of malachite and chrysocolla was limited, while the artificially produced mineral colors verdigris and copper resinate were unstable and incompatible. A great deal of skill and resourcefulness was needed to use these limited materials in a panel painting[4] to produce the brilliant green of a meadow, a parrot, a coat, or a dress.

Since the eighteenth century, more and more green pigments have been invented, with a stability when exposed to light that leaves nothing to be desired. With the exception of the quickly abandoned Schweinfurt green, a brilliant but highly poisonous copper arsenite compound, most of them are nontoxic, in contrast to the older green pigments. The intensity of their color is undoubtedly beyond criticism—not only that, but they are also inexpensive. Kurt Wehlte, the most influential writer on painting technique since Max Doerner, praised chromium oxide green and other modern pigments as products far excelling the materials used by the old masters.[5] This much is true: a genuine ultramarine costing its own weight in gold is not as hyperblue and pure as the cheapest artificial blue, and no malachite rock, no matter how fine, will produce a color capable of competing in brightness with chromium oxide green and helio genuine

---

[4] Different rules apply to illuminated manuscripts and *Tüchleinmalerei* (cloth painting), with their glowing watercolors. (*Tüchleinmalerei* was a form of painting on linen cloth in the late Gothic period in Germany; cf. Rolf E. Straub, "Tafel- und Tüchleinmalerei des Mittelalters," in Hermann Kühn, Heinz Roosen-Runge, Rolf E. Straub, and Manfred Koller, *Reclams Handbuch der künstlerischen Techniken* [Stuttgart, 1984], vol. 1, p. 152.)

[5] Kurt Wehlte, *The Materials and Techniques of Painting*, trans. Ursus Dix (New York, 1975), pp. 127–128.

green. And for those not satisfied by the nuances of these, there is a choice of twelve more green tones available. But the variety is deceptive. What Karl Löwith saw as the fatal cost of progress applies to modern paints; the cost lies precisely in the success that apparently justifies it.[6] As mechanically created products of the chemical industry, the paints are defined in an utterly quantitative fashion, and their advantages mainly serve the dye and paint industries, in which producing paints for artists plays only a marginal role. Improvements in color nuances, brightness, and stability were purchased at the cost of a loss of body. Tone is only one aspect of color, and its beauty lies hidden in the structure and shape of its individual particles. From a purely chromatic point of view, velvet and silk, cotton and linen, parchment and paper have exactly the same color if they are identically dyed. The play of light in the different textures of the materials, however, gives each color a different appearance. The same phenomenon is involved in the body of paints. It is not by chance that the language of color nuances is always connected with bodies: sky blue, lavender blue, turquoise blue, gentian blue, violet blue, cornflower blue, reed green, apple green, grass green, bottle green, olive green, almond green, sea green, emerald green, straw-colored, honey yellow, lemon yellow, maize yellow, mustard yellow, sand-colored, quince yellow, wheat yellow, amber-colored, rose red, fire red, crab red, strawberry-colored, cherry red, ruby-colored, scarlet, blood red, brick red, salmon pink, wine red, ruby red, cinnabar red, rust red, ginger, pear-colored, chestnut brown, hazelnut brown, coffee brown, cocoa brown, cognac-colored, ash gray, mouse gray, pearl gray, dove gray, oatmeal gray, raven black, jet black, soot black, lily white, snow white,

[6] Karl Löwith, *Der Mensch inmitten der Geschichte* (Stuttgart, 1990), p. 334.

eggshell-colored, ivory-colored, milk white. Each name associates a color with a variety of textures—transparent or opaque, smooth, rough, dense, or friable bodies that shine, sparkle, reflect, or shimmer softly or harshly in the light and thereby elicit a luminous or refracted, tired or fiery, cheerful or gloomy impression, like the crystalline scales, leaves, lenses, needles, splinters, grains, spheres, and rhombi of the historical pigments. Although modern paints also have a variety of bodies, these have simpler structures, and even in the laboratory are smaller and more uniform than their heterogeneous predecessors. Many of them are amorphous, and all are poorer in visual properties. The light has easier work with them: many of them are too fine to be able to refract it twice, and not a single pigment discovered since the nineteenth century is capable of producing interference colors.

It is not merely that the body of each individual color is more homogeneous than that in the older pigments; the individual particles also differ less from one another. The smaller they turn out in the laboratory, the more they tend to clump together. These agglomerates are then ground to the primary grain size, or even smaller—often to a size so fine that their color appearance is absorbed into the tone, as in inks that have no body. This is what gives the final touch to the notorious uniformity of modern pigments: along with the degree of fineness, the mechanical grinding also increases the powder's homogeneity. The result is not perfection, but sterility. This is what makes the colored powder so marketable. Its characteristics are adapted to the needs of the painting, decorating, and printing ink industries in every respect. The less the effort in time and energy required to produce them, the cheaper paints become. The greater the saturation of the tone, the less pigment is needed, and consequently the paints can hardly be colorful enough. The more stable, homogeneous, and proof against separation they are, the more

durable the product is in the can, and its unvarying composition satisfies the requirements of industry standards.

Necessary though it is to produce durable and inexpensive goods, it is commensurately absurd for artists'
paints to be produced from the same pigments as paint for
automobiles and other mass-produced products. However, paints in tubes and pans for artists' purposes are
bound in a different way from those intended for auto
painting, printing, and decorating. The binder that
envelops the colored bodies varies the refraction. An
aqueous medium favors covering properties, an oily or
resinous one favors transparency, while the airy quality of
pastels gives each pigment an opaque appearance. Since
the colored bodies only develop within the medium that
holds them together, a good way of using the binder
would be to make it relieve the sterile quality of modern
pigments slightly. But the opposite is the case. The same
applies to tubes and pans of paint as to any kind of
canned food: the priority is on durability, to which taste
takes second place, and as a result people come to feel dis-
gusted by genuine fresh peas, tomatoes, and beans, and
instead cultivate vegetables that look spotless and taste of
nothing. The laws that rule the market and production
are no less compelling for the manufacturers of artists'
paints than for the chemical companies that supply them
with their pigments. Even a small company has to keep
prices low, meet the standard, guarantee stability and
durability, and favor materials that are suitable for
mechanical filling of containers. Once their own requirements have been met, the manufacturers then give some
thought to the needs of painters, which they have to lump
together. No matter which methods the artists may use to
create their works—whether linear or painterly, two-
dimensional or sculptural, abstract or figurative—the
manufacturer wants them all to be reaching for the same
tubes.

In the nineteenth century, reaching for a can of paint became the norm, and today it has become so natural that no one notices how peculiar it is that painting is the only one of the fine arts that has submitted to the economic pressures of industrial production in the choice of its materials. One might have thought that the ordinary products of the quantitatively determined industrial world would have no place in the qualitative cosmos of art. Whether it is the violin, viola, or cello, instruments for producing sounds are still made by hand, no matter how "modern" the compositions being played on them. No one would dream of asking a composer to adapt his works to the stereotyped sound of factory-made instruments—and if he did so, not a single soloist or orchestra of note would play them. Even in an applied art such as cookery, it is customary for the artists to produce their own meat juices, even though the industrial production of Liebig's Extract is as old as that of tube paints.

When it became redundant to have any physical knowledge of the materials of which paintings are made, much more of the spirit of their work was lost than painters might have dreamed. Goethe recognized at an early stage that an estrangement from concrete elements was the greatest opportunity for coarse mediocrity. He wrote to Karl Friedrich Zelter in June 1825,

> Everything, my dear friend, is now ultra, everything has become inexorably transcendent, in thought as well as in action. No one is aware of himself any-more, no one understands the element within which he moves and works, no one grasps the material he is processing. There can be no question of mere simplicity; there is quite enough simple stuff. Young people are stirred up far too early and then swept away in the whirl of time; riches and speed are what the world admires and what everyone strives for;

railways, fast mails, steamships, and every possible facility for communication are the fields in which the cultured world is bent on outdoing itself, overdeveloping itself, and thereby obstinately per-sisting in mediocrity.[7]

The old ultramarine received its name from the origin of the stone: lapis lazuli came from beyond the sea, from Asia—*outre mer.* The new one comes from the laboratory and is *ultra*-blue, just as all the paints are now *ultra.* God is hidden in details, while the devil simulates God *en gros et en détail.* The devil of the painters lies in the tube. Being a nihilist, he abhors bodies, and promises totality in their stead. In this way, along with the use of preserves, the dia-bolical stupidity of preferring to "paint ether upon ether with ether"[8] entered into painting. The triumph of this stupidity has whitewashed over the lamentations con-cerning lost craft skills that course through the table talk, journals, and letters of the great painters of the nineteenth century. None of the salon painters ever perceived the incomparability of the old paints, while Cézanne admit-ted that with his brush in his hand, his tube paints made him sweat blood.[9] He admired the *iridescence* and the rich-ness of Veronese's colors, the method of constructing a painting in layers, and what he called the "secret soul of grounds."[10] He regarded Jacques-Louis David as the last to have understood his craft—although David's idealiz-ing attitude went against the grain with him, and he went so far as to assert that David had killed painting. It had to

[7] Johann Wolfgang von Goethe, *Gedenkausgabe der Werke, Briefe und Gespräche* (Zurich, 1965), pp. 633–634.

[8] Jean Paul Richter, *Horn of Oberon,* p. 17.

[9] Paul Cézanne, *Über die Kunst,* p. 28.

[10] Ibid., p. 38.

have been somebody. Only salon painters were capable of doubting that painting was in a mortal condition. Fast painters tried to use an impasto application to compensate for the paints' lack of body. "Nowadays people lay it on thick at once," Cézanne grumbled about this sudden fit of bricklaying technique, complaining that the "science of preparations" was being lost, "this liquid power that comes out of the underpaintings . . . Nowadays people paint over, scratch off, scratch off again, make the layer thick. It is like mortar."[11]

In the generation before Cézanne, Delacroix had reached quite similar conclusions regarding the "true" technique of painting: "The greater the master, the more perfect it is: Rubens, Titian, Veronese, the Dutch masters; their particular care, rubbed paint, grounding, letting the various layers dry . . . This tradition has been completely lost among modern painters. Bad products, careless grounding, poor canvas, brushes, repulsive oils."[12]

With the vast, slick paintings of the salon artists of the nineteenth century before our eyes, it is easy to understand the artists' abhorrence of contemporary glaze and the fact that they soon condemned painting in layers completely. "I believe the fellow is glazing," Wilhelm Leibl said contemptuously of Hans Thoma.[13] It is one of the ironies of history that the doctrine of painting *alla prima* emerged from an admiration for the old masters' perfect glazing, which was impossible to achieve with the new materials. Renoir gave this its clearest expression: "Because the Old Masters knew their craft, they possessed this wonderful

[11] It would be interesting to trace the topos of murdered painting back in history. In Ingres's eyes, Rubens was the murderer; Poussin thought it was Caravaggio—"he came into the world to annihilate painting." Cf. Claude Lévi-Strauss, *Look, Listen, Read,* p. 34.

[12] Cézanne, *Über die Kunst,* p. 37.

[13] Cited after Max Doerner, *Malmaterial und seine Verwendung im Bilde* (Stuttgart, 1976), p. 201.

material and these transparent paints, whose secrets we try to fathom in vain."[14]

Unwaveringly, patiently, and with eyes wide open, a single painter approached the secret of the glaze: Philipp Otto Runge. He expounded his thoughts about color in a letter that Goethe included in his *Theory of Colours.* Forgotten by artists, who now paint only *alla prima,* Runge's letter to Goethe is quoted here in full. His ideas, and the words he found for them, have in the course of nearly two hundred years lost nothing of their brilliance, freshness, and transparency. Anachronistic as they are, they point beyond our own times.

[14] Ibid., p. 206.

VIII
Letter Concerning Transparency

Wollgast, 5 July 1806

fter a short walk over our delightful island of Rügen, where the quiet solemnity of the sea is interrupted diversely by pleasant peninsulas and valleys, hills and cliffs, I found, not only a friendly welcome from my family, but also the favor of your letter; and it is most encouraging to me to see that my earnest wish has been fulfilled, and that my works may indeed be well received, in whatever way. I am keenly aware that you have been able to appreciate endeavors lying out of the path which you yourself might wish for in art; and to explain to you my reasons for working in this way would be as foolish as trying to declare my own way the correct one.

Although art in practice brings great difficulties for all those entering into it, this is so to the greatest possible degree in our own times. But for someone who has reached an age at which the intellect has already come to predominate to begin exercises in the initial stages, it must surely be impossible—without destroying himself—to pass forth from his own individuality toward more general endeavors.

He who loses himself in the boundless abundance of the life unfolding around him, and is thereby irresistibly prompted to copy it—and who thus feels so powerfully moved by the total impression—will surely seek to penetrate into the proportions, nature, and strengths of the great masses in precisely the same fashion in which he enters into the characteristic quality of the details.

He who considers the great masses—with a constant sense of the way in which all things are alive, down to the tiniest detail, affecting everything else——cannot conceive of them without a particular connection or affinity, far less depict them without being drawn to consider their fundamental causes. And when he does so, he cannot return once again to his initial freedom without working his way through to the pure ground, as it were.

To clarify what I mean: I believe that the old German artists, if they had known something of form, would have lost the immediacy and naturalness of expression in their figures, until they had reached a certain stage in this science.

There have been those who have built bridges and suspension work and other such technical things simply by eye. That is certainly possible for a time, but once a certain height has been reached and one naturally hits upon mathematical conclusions, his whole talent will be for nothing unless he works his way through the science and back into freedom.[1]

In the same way, ever since I was first astounded by the particular phenomena seen in the mixing of the three colors, I had no peace until I had attained a certain picture of the whole world of color that would be broad enough to enclose within it all the transformations and phenomena concerned.

When a painter sees a fine landscape, or any kind of effect in nature appeals to him, it is a very natural idea for him to wish to discover which materials might be mixed to reproduce the effect. This led me at least to study the peculiarities of colors and whether it might be possible to penetrate deeply enough into their powers for it to be plain to me what they do, what is effected by them, or what has effects on them. I hope you will look considerately on an attempt I have merely noted down here to clarify to you my views, which——I believe——can only be stated as a whole. However, I hope that for painting it will not be worthless or vain to look at colors from this standpoint; nor will this view either contradict or render unnecessary the efforts of physical science to discover something general concerning colors.

---

[1] Emphasis added by A. A.

Since, however, I am unable to present you here with incontro-vertible evidence—as such evidence would have to be based on exhaustive experiments—I beg you merely to confine yourself to your own instincts in order to understand what I mean by saying that a painter can deal with no other elements than those here declared.

1. *As is well known, there are only three colors, yellow, red, and blue; only, if we take these in their full strength and conceive of them as a circle, e.g. (see the plates)*

Red

Orange   Violet

Yellow   Blue

Green

then from the three colors, yellow, red, and blue, three transitions are formed, orange, violet, and green (I term everything orange that lies between yellow and red, or what inclines toward these sides from yellow and red), and at their midpoints these are at their most bril-liant and are the pure mixtures of the colors.

2. *If one tries to conceive of a bluish orange, a reddish green, or a yellowish violet, it is rather like trying to imagine a southwest wind from the north. But if one wishes to explain a warm violet, the following may perhaps provide some material for the purpose.*

3. *Two pure colors such as yellow and red produce the pure mixture orange. But when blue is added to this, it becomes sullied, in such a way that if this is done in equal proportions, all the color is canceled into a dull gray.*

Two pure colors can be mixed, but two middle colors cancel each other out or sully one another, since part of a third color has been added.

If the three pure colors cancel one another out into gray, then the three mixtures, orange, violet, and green, will do the same at their midpoints, since the three colors will again be equally strong therein.

Now, since only the pure transitions of three colors lie in this whole circle, and they only receive the addition of gray when they are mixed, white and black are also available in addition, for greater variation.

4. White renders all colors duller when it is added, and if they also become lighter, they lose their clarity and fire.

5. Black sullies all colors, and if it also makes them darker, they lose both their purity and clarity.

6. White and black mixed together produce gray.

7. It is easily perceived that the range of the three colors together with white and black does not exhaust the impression of nature in its elements that is perceived by our eyes. Since white makes the colors dull, and black sullies them, we are inclined to assume that there is brightness and darkness. However, the following considerations will show to what extent this view can be upheld.

8. In addition to the difference between lighter and darker in the pure colors, another important difference is observed in nature. For example, if we consider red cloth, paper, taffeta, satin, or velvet, the red of a sunset or transparent glass at a single brightness and purity, there is a difference present that lies in the transparency or opacity of the material.

9. If we mix the three colors, red, blue, and yellow, together opaquely, a gray is produced that is the same as the gray that can be mixed from white and black.

10. If one mixes these three colors transparently, in such a way that none predominates, one obtains a darkness that cannot be produced by any of the other parts.

11. Both white and black are opaque, or dense. One should not be distracted by the expression "white glass," for all that is meant by the expression is clear glass. White water is inconceivable, if it is pure, just as clear milk is inconceivable. If black merely made things dark, it could also be clear; but since it sullies, this is not possible.

12. The opaque colors lie between white and black; they can never be as light as white, and never as dark as black.

13. The transparent colors are limitless in their lightening and darkening, and fire and water can be seen as their height and depth.

14. The product of the three opaque colors, gray, cannot recover its purity either through the light or by admixture; it either pales to white or darkens to black.

15. Three pieces of glass in the three pure colors, if laid one over another, would produce a darkness deeper than that of each color alone, namely as follows: three transparent colors together produce a colorless darkness that is deeper than any one of the colors. Yellow, for example, is the brightest and most brilliant of the three colors, but when one mixes enough yellow with very dark violet that they cancel each other out, the darkness is increased to a high degree.

16. If one takes a dark transparent glass, such as is best found among optical glasses, and a piece of polished coal of half the thickness, and lays both on a white ground, the glass will appear brighter; but if two more of each are added, the coal will remain the same, due to its opacity; the glass, however, will darken infinitely, even though this is not visible to the eye. A darkness of this sort can equally be achieved by the individual transparent colors, so that black by contrast appears merely like a dirty spot.

17. If we dilute such a transparent product of the three transparent colors in this way and allow the light to shine through it, a kind of gray is produced, but one that is very different from the mixture of the three opaque colors.

18. The brightness of a clear sky at sunrise directly around the sun, or going before the sun, can be so great that we can hardly bear it. If we were now to draw conclusions concerning the three colors from this colorless clarity as it advances there, as a product of the three, they must be so bright and so far removed from our capacities that they would remain as much of a mystery to us as those engulfed in darkness.

19. But we can now see that brightness or darkness cannot be set in comparison or proportion to the transparent colors in the way that black and white are to the opaque ones. Rather, it is a property

itself, and is as one with clarity and color. One might imagine a pure ruby: thick or thin though it might be, the red is one and the same, and it is therefore only a transparent red that becomes bright or dark depending on whether it is aroused by the light or deserted by it. In this way, the light naturally ignites the product of these colors in its depth and elevates it to a brilliant clarity that allows every color to shine through. This illumination, of which color is capable because the light ignites it to ever more intense fire, means that it often surges round us unnoticed and in a thousand transformations reveals objects that would be impossible with a simple mixture, leaving everything in its clarity and even intensifying it. Thus, we can often find that the most indifferent objects are cloaked with a charm that usually lies more in the illumination of the air lying between us and the object than in the lighting of its forms.

20. Once one has become absorbed in it, the relationship of the light to transparent color is of an infinite delight; and the igniting of the colors, the blending of them one into another, their rebirth, and their vanishing is like breath being drawn at great pauses from eternity to eternity, from the highest light down to the lonely and eternal silence that lies in the deepest tones.

21. The opaque colors are, by contrast, like flowers that dare not measure themselves against the heavens, but that are nevertheless still bound to the weakness of one side (the white) and the evil of the other (the black).

22. But it is precisely these colors that are capable—if they are not mixed with either white or black, but are thinly spread across them—of producing such graceful variations and such natural effects that the practical application of the ideas described here must hold fast to them particularly; in the end, the transparent colors are merely like spirits playing over them, and only serve to raise them up and intensify their power.

A firm belief in a certain spiritual bond in the elements can ultimately provide the painter with great consolation and cheer, which he is unable to attain in any other fashion, since his own life becomes so lost in his work; and the material, methods, and goal *together ultimately bring forth that perfection in him which surely must be brought forth by ever diligent and faithful efforts, so that it cannot remain without beneficial effects on others as well.*

When I consider the materials with which I work, and hold them against the yardstick of these qualities, then I know precisely where and how I should apply them, since none of the materials we work with is entirely pure. I cannot go into practical matters in detail here—firstly because it would be too lengthy, and also all I had in mind was to show you the standpoint from which I consider color.[2]

[2] *Goethe's Werke, vollständige Ausgabe letzter Hand* (Stuttgart and Tübingen, 1833), vol. 52, pp. 360–371; Philipp Otto Runge, *Briefe und Schriften,* ed. Peter Bethausen (Berlin, 1981), pp. 182–186. The letter from Runge is not included in the English translation of Goethe's *Theory of Colours.*

IX
Diffusing Glasses, Collecting Lenses, and a Chameleon in Puff Pastry

he painters of the fifteenth century were immune to the arrogance of total uniformity. When they instructed their apprentices to pulverize pigments in the mortar, to grind them on the stone or elute them in water, it was the greatest possible brilliance and purity that they had in mind; but absolute purity was an impossibility, even with the greatest care and patience. Most of the pigments are mineral. Created by the transformations of the earth's crust, all minerals include foreign elements. Whether they are formed from volcanic ejecta, weathered rock, inflorescence, metamorphism, precipitation, or sedimentation, the diversely shaped stones and colored earths are never perfectly pure. Assembled by nature and processed by hand, no paints are identical to one another. Each apprentice has a different knack with the materials, and in every lapis lazuli stone from across the seas, the golden veins of pyrite and the glittering calcite crystals form different markings. They grow within a space that has been left free to chance, but they contribute to the color's beauty in a way that is not accidental. Embedded particles, foreign elements, and minimal deviations from the symmetry of the crystal are the subtle watermarks of its natural quality. As remnants of the discontinuity in the environment that caused the crystallization,[1] they preserve a memory of the mineral's growth. It is not the ideal crystal, but the realities of its "defects" and "impurities" that tell the story of its origin. Even if we lack the knowledge enabling us to read the geological book of nature, the tiny irregularities in the crystalline shape confide something of the mystery present in every creation of form, which even the natural sciences cannot utterly decipher. It is not from what is smooth, but from what is *rough* that enigmas renew themselves. "The great field for new discoveries is always the unclassified residuum."[2]

Even the artificial mineral pigments that have been derived since antiquity from lead, tin, copper, quicksilver, sulfur, and arsenic were *rougher* in the fifteenth century than their modern counterparts. The fine irregularity that produces their visual effect is similar to that of natural pigments. The incomparable beauty of the old syntheses was no miracle. Today, pigments are produced in sterile laboratories at lightning speed, because time is money, and the materials used have to be as uniform as possible. By contrast, the old pigments crystallized in primitive conditions, incorporating all sorts of *rough* elements. They had time to grow to perfection, and chance was

[1] "Let us examine a snowflake. If it consists of spherical crystals, we can conclude that it arose in more or less balanced conditions. The molecules had time to spread across the whole surface. By contrast, if the snowflake has marked branching, then it arose far out of balance: the crystallization took place much faster. Nowadays we no longer study ideal crystals, but real ones that preserve a record of their origin in the defects (dislocations, etc.) of their structure." (Ilya Prigogine and Isabelle Stengers, *Das Paradox der Zeit* [Munich, 1993].)

[2] William James, *The Will to Believe, and Other Essays in Popular Philosophy,* ed. Frederick H. Burkhardt et al. (Cambridge, Mass., 1979), p. 222.

always in play. Crystals become all the more beautiful the more slowly they form. Rougher in the grain, mature in shape, and more irregular in their particle sizes, the paints were both more regular and more irregular at one and the same time. Writings about painting techniques in our time have fallen entirely under the spell of statistics, and are dominated by the idée fixe that there is a valid optimal grain size for every pigment, guaranteeing the maximum gain for all the visual properties. This imaginary size is said to lie between 0.4 and 2 microns—an ideal never found in older paintings. A scientific study of the particle size of azurite and ultramarine in early Netherlandish paintings has shown that the most finely ground paint is in the Ghent altarpiece, with an average size of 4.9 microns.[3]

The painter measures his time by the stimulus of grinding and mingling tiny prisms of paint. Van Eyck brought the art of imitating nature to perfection, producing the greatest variety of effects with small and limited means. From the very beginning, his renown was linked to his *techné*. Fazio's description is a cautious one. The painter, he wrote, was well versed in the sciences and arts concerned with the materials of painting, and it might therefore be assumed that he had made many discoveries relating to the properties of paints, derived from reading Pliny and other authors of antiquity. A hundred years later, this conjecture had encapsulated itself into a legend. Giorgio Vasari declares "Giovanni da Bruggia in Fiandra" to have been the inventor of oil painting, and in the preface to his *Lives of the Most Eminent Painters, Sculptors, and Architects* praises this glorious invention as a "great

[3] J. R. J. van Asperen de Boer, "An Examination of Particle Size Distributions of Azurite and Natural Ultramarine in Some Early Netherlandish Paintings," *Studies in Conservation* 19 (London, 1974), pp. 233–243.

facilitation of the art of painting."[4] Today, Vasari's assertion is tirelessly consigned to the realm of legend; oil painting was discovered long before van Eyck. As with every legend, however, Vasari's contains a grain of truth. And in the case of van Eyck, the grain in question can be taken perfectly literally.

The secret of his technique has been sought in the medium—in vain. The precise composition of the binder he used is not known even to the present day, despite all the scientific analyses that have been carried out. Almost every year, a new solution to the puzzle is triumphantly announced, only to be sheepishly revised shortly afterward. Sometimes the binder is thought to have been a fatty emulsion, sometimes oil on tempera, sometimes an oil-resin mixture. The most fruitful research work was carried out in the early 1950s by Paul Coremans's team in Brussels. This investigation of the Ghent altarpiece, *L'Agneau mystique au laboratoire,* describes the binder as a "drying oil + x." Coremans identified the principal constituent as linseed oil, and he suspected that the "x" factor might be a substance similar to "certain natural resins," as they bind with oil so closely that the film of paint shows a perfectly homogeneous structure. In the meantime, analytical methods have become more sophisticated. The successors of Coremans identified protein in the binder, and there has been a renewed tendency to accept the emulsion theory dismissed by Coremans. It is still doubtful which protein the oil was emulsified with. Is it egg white, egg yolk, vegetable gum, or animal glue? When they are fresh, the various proteins used in a painting are easy to identify. After more than half a millennium, however, a substance is never what it was originally. No method of investigation, no matter how

[4] G. Vasari, cited in E. Berger, *Quellen für Maltechnik während der* *Renaissance und deren Folgezeit* (Munich, 1901), p. 27.

precise, is capable of compensating for this time factor. Light, climate, and *atmospherics* influence the natural aging process, microorganisms such as fungi and bacteria can colonize a picture, and it is only extremely rarely that a painting can survive the centuries without being repeatedly cleaned, overpainted, and varnished. Scientific investigation itself requires the most drastic alterations to the object of study: removing a sample and embedding it in Canada balsam, or separating layers of paint that have fused together (an operation it is impossible to carry out flawlessly) in order to analyze the binder. Fungi and bacteria also show up as proteins in a chromatographic analysis. Finding chemical evidence of proteins in the film of paint is one thing; interpreting it is another. "Merely looking at a thing cannot benefit us," Goethe wrote in the preface to his *Theory of Colours.* "Each glimpse merges into contemplation, contemplation into thinking, and thinking into association—and in this way, we can say that in every attentive glance at the world, we have already begun to theorize."[5] Without a theory capable of encompassing the painter's entire cosmos, scientifically deduced facts cannot be meaningfully interpreted. What applies to all the techniques of painting applies no less to research into them: "Ultimately, it is only the mind of the artist that can breathe life into any technique."[6]

While the analysis by Coremans and his colleagues[7] may be controversial in its details, the theory on which it

[5] Cf. J. W. von Goethe, *Theory of Colours,* trans. Charles Lock Eastlake (London, 1840; rptd. Cambridge, Mass., 1970), p. xl (translation revised here).

[6] Ibid., p. 350 (translation revised here).

[7] Scientists from a wide variety of disciplines were involved in Coremans's research on the Ghent altarpiece. The results were published in Antwerp in 1953 under the title *Les Primitifs flamands, III. Contributions à l'étude des primitifs flamands, 2. L'Agneau mystique au laboratoire,* and were the product of an entente cordiale between the natural sciences and the humanities. Among the "laboratory assistants" was Panofsky, who counted his experiences as an assistant on Coremans's staff in Brussels as among the

is based is correct, and they were therefore able to penetrate deeper into the secret of van Eyck's technique than
any other researchers before or since.

Fazio was close to the mark in speaking not of invention but of *discoveries* made by van Eyck relating to the
properties of colors. The "great Jan" did not revolution-
ize the traditional methods of painting. The novel,
incomparable aspects of his technique are derived from a
systematic development of all the potential inherent in the
simple layered structure of oil painting handed down by
Theophilus and Cennini—in the same way that the
complex form of a plant is contained in the seed.[8]

Van Eyck "multiplies the number of layers, refines the
play of transparency that is raised into a basic principle,"[9]
and by overlaying increasingly differentiated modeling
achieves a density and plasticity in the depiction that were
unknown in painting before his time. The light penetrates a multitude of "geological" layers right through to
the ivory-colored polished chalk ground, which enhances
the brilliance and radiance of the colors from the depths.

happiest in his life as a scholar.
"Interrupted by occasional visits to
Ghent, [the group's discussions]
took place in a kind of glass cage,
the transparent walls of which were
festooned with the original X-ray
films, so that one had the impression
of being a tiny insect living and
crawling about between the wood
panel and the topmost layer of varnish, inside the actual substance of
the Ghent altarpiece." The rapport
within the group was so good that
afterward none of them was able to
say who was responsible for which
observation. "It delighted me in
equal measure to find some of the
opinions I had brought with me
being disproved, while others were

confirmed," Panofsky wrote in 1965
in his obituary of Coremans, "who,
more than anyone else, has encouraged the lamb of art history to lie
down with the wolf of the natural
sciences" (E. Panofsky, "The Pro-
moter of a New Co-operation
between the Natural Sciences and
the History of Art," *Bulletin de l'Institut Royal du Patrimoine Artistique* 8
[1965], pp. 62–67).

[8] The tractate *Schedula diversarum
artium* by Theophilus Presbyter
dates from the first half of the
twelfth century; Cennini's *Trattato
della pittura* was written ca. 1390.

[9] P. Philippot, "Vision et exécu-
tion eyckiennes," in *L'Agneau mystique,* p. 96.

The principle of abstraction and increasing differentiation that determines the complex layered structure recalls
the way in which images arise in the brain. The completed panel painting is the synthesis of an *analytical*
vision. Before the painter can begin executing it, he sepa-
rates the image in his imagination into its components,
layer by layer. At the beginning comes the sketch, transferring the composition into flowing lines and shadings.
Underdrawing in black in an aqueous medium, laid on
the smooth chalk ground *alla prima* with a fine brush, provides light and shadow, outline and volume, without
establishing any details. It is here, and only here, in the
hidden sphere, that the artist's *manner* receives direct
expression, his characteristic play of line and the specific
rhythm of his hand.[10] The potential for modification
without retouching is exploited in the flow of the drawing. An initial pair of eyes over the corrected pair in an
angel's face, the sixth finger on a hand, the double line of
a cheek are disregarded in the later painting process, just
like the purse that Rolin disapproved of. Beforehand, a
colorless film of oil is laid on, which impregnates the
ground with the underdrawing—without being isolated,
the strongly absorbent chalk would draw the oil out of the
paint layers and make the colors dull.

Now the staging of the "deeds and sufferings of
light"[11] commences. Color by color and layer by layer, the

[10] In the early twentieth century,
the musicologist Gustav Becking
investigated the specific rhythmic
curves of artists of the spoken word,
of the written word, and of music.
He identified three curves, which
are known as Becking curves, after
their inventor:

Main beat	Minor beat	Type
Sharp	Sharp	Heine type
Sharp	Round	Goethe type
Round	Round	Schiller type

Van Eyck's Becking curves correspond to the Goethe type. On
this topic, see Roman Jakobson,
"Linguistics in Relation to Other
Sciences," in his *On Language*,
ed. Linda R. Waugh and Monique Monville-Burston (Cambridge, Mass., 1990), pp. 479–480.

[11] On the "sufferings" of light
in the depths, see Hermann Kühn,
"Farbmaterialien, Pigmente, und
Bindemittel," in *Reclams Handbuch*

absorption, penetration, refraction, diffusion, reflection, and mirroring are varied. The common principle is the transition from near-opacity to complete transparency—a path that can be faster or slower, depending on the color and tone. Usually it courses from light to dark, from cold tones to warm ones.

The first layer is the most two-dimensional image, separated into chromatic fields corresponding to the analysis of the visual structure of the individual paints. With the exception of lead-tin yellow, vermilion, and black, all of the paints are mixed with white lead, which compensates for the weakening of the light in the depths.[12] This layer is distinguished from a local *imprimatura,* or veil, by the modeling element involved: the division of the chromatic fields into bright, medium, and dark parts, which the painter achieves by using more or less white lead. The underdrawing still shimmers through the various densities of the colored veil. Its pattern is communicated to the second layer, in which less white lead is used to bar the light. "In all of the paint areas, the addition of white lead decreases toward the top, until in the top layer, or even in the second last layer, it ceases altogether. The topmost layer is usually a glaze in the pure, unadulterated color tone."[13]

Layer by layer, the depiction acquires greater color and plasticity; light is modeled with white lead, shadows with color, until a middle tone arises—the physical basis of the glazes. Black, gray, white, and the pastel tones of flesh have the simplest structure: a single layer, sometimes thicker, sometimes thinner, on the ground. The rare yellow parts receive brown or red underpainting. The lack

der künstlerischen Techniken (Stuttgart, 1984), vol. 1, p. 12.

[12] Lead-tin yellow and vermilion can manage without the addition of white, as they already possess the properties required: brightness, body, and covering power.

[13] Rolf E. Straub, "Tafel- und Tüchleinmalerei des Mittelalters," in *Reclams Handbuch,* vol. 1, p. 219.

of coloring power in the green pigments malachite and copper resinate demands the most complex substructure. All green tones are based on grisaille painting, which Doerner incorrectly attributed to the whole of van Eyck's palette. But grisaille is not always simply grisaille. In Doerner, all of the colors receive the same tyrannical underpainting in matching tones, while in van Eyck's flexible system, there are three different pathways into green. Sometimes the modeling is produced by variously thick layers of copper resinate on a whitish or blackish ground, and sometimes malachite and white lead over a gray ground tone creates the sculptural basis for the copper resinate glazes.[14]

The medium tone of the enamel-like sketch is followed by a play of glazing and overpainting. These more transparent layers

are in no sense corrective repetitions; planned *ab initio* as integral components of the whole process, they are the normal means of producing a certain tone, a transparency, a density. Ultimately, these too undergo modeling, until they acquire a considerable density in certain shadowed areas, which necessarily arises through the difficulty of creating dark values using transparent materials . . . And now we come to the final phase. Just as the lights and shadows of the large composition are superimposed on a medium ground tone, in order to relieve or deepen the chiaroscuro, it is now the turn of the details—through an identical process of superimpositions—to find their place on this side and that side of the level that they bring to life.[15]

[14] Researchers now believe it is not a natural malachite that is involved, but an artificial one. See pp. 320–326 and 326–337.

[15] Philippot, *L'Agneau mystique,* p. 97.

Deepening and condensing are the principles of the system that illuminates colors from within like gemstones and captures the diverse textures of things sculpturally. Regarded separately, depth light and density belong to opposite poles. On the axis between transparency and opacity, depth light inclines toward the transparent side and density toward the opaque one. Painted in a single layer, the thin, liquid watercolor technique corresponds to the depth light, and the impasto application of cover-ing paint corresponds to density. Philippot defines density as the visual and tactile quality of the painting material that arises from the relative pigment content in the binder and the greater or lesser homogeneity of the compound. "This is what distinguishes its impasto or liquid quality, a specific form of transparency and opacity, something that one can only describe as the 'specific visual gravity' of the material."[16]

A high visual gravity appears as an enamel-like luster in the paints. Each individual crystalline layer is as dense as each degree of transparency required in the structure permits, and as transparent as the required density can possibly allow. A capacity to refract light, transparency, and density are properties of paints that can be influenced in a variety of ways. By optimizing their variability and exploiting the diversity of their visual effects appropri-ately down to the tiniest detail, van Eyck succeeded in finding the *best way*. His system follows a principle of action in nature discovered by the mathematician Pierre de Fermat in 1662 in connection with the refraction of light. The principle was generalized by Pierre-Louis Moreau de Maupertuis in 1744, and then formulated more precisely by Leonhard Euler and Joseph-Louis Lagrange—and even today, it continues to maintain its universal validity in the field of physics: *"Le principe de la*

[16] Ibid., p. 97.

moindre action."[17] The *minimal principle*[18] is the principle of least effort. But the thriftiness of the medium is not that of the painter. His *best way,* like that of light, is the detour. It takes time, but there is no way of reaching the goal faster.[19] The direct path for light between the thinner and the denser medium would be the longest one. A painter wishing to achieve depth light and density via the direct path would never reach his destination. Modern copyists of the old masters provide vivid examples of this. In almost every museum, one can watch people producing on their easels modern imitations of older paintings using oil paints from the tube. Square inch by square inch: van Eyck or Vermeer, Patinir or Holbein, Dürer or

[17] Max Planck terms this the "crown of the whole system of physics." On this point, see the clearsighted presentation of the philosophical implications of the *principle of least action* given by Ernst Cassirer in *Zur modernen Physik* (Darmstadt, 1994), pp. 180–194.

[18] In physics, it is known as the "principle of least action"—a term, confusing to the layman, that refers to a small action that produces an optimal and consequently large effect. But it is not action in the sense of effect that is implied; in the physical principle, "action" has the meaning of bringing about or influencing. To avoid misunderstandings, we will use the term "minimal principle" here. (It has nothing to do with Ockhamist thriftiness.)

[19] Physicists writing for a popular audience like to describe light as being in a hurry. Cf. Anthony Zee, *Magische Systeme* (Frankfurt, 1993), p. 128. But light hastens slowly: it lengthens the easy way and shortens the hard one. The *teleological* motto for the phenomenon is not "as fast as possible," but "as well as possible." The goal is reached in the most elegant way possible as playfully as in Chinese shadowboxing: the flowing equilibrium of the tai chi fighter diverts the opponent's strength away into the void. This corresponds to the description of the *minimal principle* given by Lagrange: "that namely all of these movements must be such that the amount of total energy is not altered." (Cf. Cassirer, *Physik,* p. 187). What is decisive is therefore not the quantitative minimization, whether of time or of energy; the tai chi movements can be as slow or fast as the *balance of energy flow* allows. Easy though this art of using the most economical movement, imitated from nature, may seem, it is one that is difficult to master. It is not by accident that it originates in a culture in which life is regarded as an intertwining of polar energies that mutually maintain their balance.

Leonardo, from top left to bottom right. Not all of the imitators are bunglers, certainly. But the more precise the copyist is, the worse the result. The "transfer copy" of the original looks as wrong and dead as if it had been produced not by a human being but by an automaton. The outstanding copies and replicas dating from a period when many great painters were not yet signing their paintings disprove the argument that the "hand" of the genius is inimitable and that this alone is responsible for the difference. Comparing enlargements of cross-sections from the original and modern copies would make it clear that the similarity between the paintings is a mere fiction. In enlargements of the cut cross-sections of paint samples, the original would look like a landscape of geological layers of different shapes and colors. Despite all the irregularities in the crystal fragments embedded in the "clinker," these "sediments" would be harmonious in tone at every level, while the paint mixture on one and the same level in the imitation would consist of a single amorphous layer of colored dust, relieved here and there by colored patches. When the material of the paintings is examined under the microscope, it is always found that style and technique are inseparable.

A tiny sample from the blue robe of the Virgin Mary in the Ghent altarpiece reveals van Eyck's genius in using small causes to create large effects. In 1973, van Asperen de Boer investigated three layers in the cross-section. He found a middle level of coarse-grained azurite with very little white lead in an oily medium, enclosed within two thinner layers of white lead with a little azurite.[20] His analysis showed that this "sandwich" arrangement of three levels underneath the concluding ultramarine glaze

[20] Cf. J. R. J van Asperen de Boer, "On a Rational Aspect of van Eyck's Painting Technique," *Studies in Conservation* 18 (1973), pp. 93–95. The middle layer is 45–50 microns thick, while those above and below it are 25 microns.

in an aqueous medium is not only the most economical method of producing a medium dark blue using the relatively expensive azurite,[21] but is also the *best way* of minimizing permeability.[22] Every other arrangement and proportion would have produced higher values. The coloring of the robe is based on a related phenomenon in the blue of the sky, birds' feathers, and butterflies' wings, although van Eyck constructed the transparent dark ground in front of the fine clouding with azurite instead of black. His pigment, which is coarse-grained and irregular in comparison with today's paints, appears under the microscope[23] as finer and more homogeneous than that of all his contemporaries and successors, who used a less complicated version of the layer technique.[24] The question of whether one and the same pigment was used with various grain sizes, depending on the layer, has not yet been investigated. However, if we assume that van Eyck's whole system obeys the *minimal principle,* everything would suggest that a consistent exploitation of the visual effects of various grain sizes would be the core of the secret that has been sought for in vain for so long in connection with the binder.

Among the various possible ways of varying the paints' permeability to light, the use of pigment crushed sometimes more finely and sometimes more coarsely would represent the smallest effective cause. Since the grain size also influences the pigment concentration in the

[21] Even the most expensive of all the pigments, ultramarine, could be limited to the final layer when this azurite understructure was used.

[22] *Permeability* is not the same as *transparency.*

[23] For azurite, the research into particle sizes in the Ghent altarpiece mentioned above found an average size of 4.9 microns, with a standard deviation of 3.1 microns. The size of the most frequent particles lay in a range between 2.5 and 5.0 microns, and the remaining particles were up to 20 microns in size.

[24] Van Eyck was apparently the only painter who mastered the complex layer technique. Cf. van Asperen de Boer, op. cit., p. 93.

medium and the thickness of the layer, it occupies a key position between the poles of transparency and density.

The plasticity of the material in which the grains are embedded also corresponds to the minimal principle. It is not the medium that is new, but the extent of its malleability. What researchers looking for the "x" factor found proved to be a chameleon. Their investigations showed that each pigment is bound differently.

Both in the mental sphere and in the concrete one, everything in van Eyck is conceived from two different sides, between which various levels mediate like layers in puff pastry. In the case of the medium,[25] the opposite poles are termed "fatty" and "lean." A binder containing a balanced mixture of binding elements at the center between the two poles can be developed as needed, either into a fatty or a lean one, by phased modification. In this way, a fatty emulsion could be produced that is familiar to every cook under the term "mayonnaise." This binder was new to the extent that it was the reverse of the emulsions in common use at the time; it was based on oil. The precondition for compatibility between varyingly fatty and lean layers is the way in which they are related by the binder; this relationship has to be all the stronger the closer they are together. At a maximum distance, they can lose it entirely, so that the leanest and fattest layer can manage without a common element, while each has to contain at least one element belonging to the middle emulsion.[26] In this fashion, the rule "fat on lean," which

[25] The English language borrowed the term "medium" from the Latin word for "middle" during the late sixteenth century, as the *Oxford English Dictionary* shows; the technical use of the term "medium" in painting is first found in the nineteenth century. The term "binding medium" emphasizes adhesive properties, while the technical term underlines its mediatory role: the medium holds the particles together and mediates their visual effect.

[26] "Even if the oily phase contains resin, the unusual properties of van Eyck's binder appear to us to be connected above all with the proportion of protein. It seems to us that

applies to every oil technique, can even be reversed, as the blue robe of the Virgin teaches us. The wide range of possible variations allows the bridge that is visually most effective to be built toward every pigment.

The less binder a paint contains, the denser and more enduring it is. Fine, light, and voluminous pigments absorb oil up to 200 percent. Mineral pigments with a high specific gravity[27] can manage with little, above all the leading pigment used in painting, the old form of which vanished during the nineteenth century—white lead. Nine to thirteen percent of binder is sufficient to envelop its roundish, hexagonal crystal. It is strongly birefringent, and brightens other colors without a tinge of blue or red. Since it shortens the drying time of oil, it balances out the tensions occurring during the drying-out process. Together with oil, white lead forms a hard and stable film that gradually saponifies and becomes transparent over the course of time, which is why paintings made using the layer technique increase in beauty as they become older. The sculptural relief in the depiction results from its covering power and body. The high density of its heavy white particles allows systematic minimization of the permeability to a level corresponding to the depth light. At one time it was as useful as it was inexpensive,

the combination of low browning, color depth, and good aging with simultaneous compatibility between the various layers can in fact only be achieved with an oil-protein compound." (Leopold Kockaert and Monique Verrier, "Applications des colorations à l'identification des liants de van Eyck," *Bulletin Patrimoine* 17 [1978–1979], 126.)

[27] To the chemists Kockaert and Verrier, the use of different phases of the reversed emulsion seemed so laborious and elaborate that they thought there must be a trick that would make the complicated theory perfectly simple in practice. They believed it conceivable that all of the pigments were first bound in oil and then thinned on the palette to either lean or fat, depending on their color and covering power. Any painter can prove to himself that with this simple method the medium's homogeneity is destroyed during the second stage at the latest.

and if we overlook its unpleasant toxicity, it could be called the most *courteous* of all the pigments in the sense used in miners' idiom.[28] With its abundance of properties, it was used in painting for centuries to represent light. During the process of rationalization,[29] it became ever poorer. The precipitation of lead salt solutions using carbon dioxide converts it entirely into a *discourteous* fine powder. In the nineteenth century, it had traces of antimony and zinc[30] added in place of the rich trace elements silver and copper. Today, it contains hardly any traces of other elements. It can be manufactured in no time, causing nobody to suffer from lead colic (or "painter's colic") in the process, and it has the same chemical formula as its predecessor, which was begotten in pots, drew its heat from horse manure, and needed four to eight weeks to mature. But the greater the progress, the higher the cost.

At its very birth, modern white lead is already a senile dotard. In oil, it takes on a transparent appearance at once, and the white is correspondingly weak. The body of the seemingly amorphous particles[31] is low. Not surprisingly, therefore, this poisonous paint with its slimy consistency, difficult to paint with, has vanished from artists' studios.

[28] The miner describes a shaft as courteous if it holds rich ore, and as discourteous rock when it is poor or worthless. Cf. Georgius Agricola, *De Re Metallica, Libri XII* (Basle, 1956), trans. Carl Schiffner (*Vom Berg- und Hüttenwesen,* Munich, 1994), p. 84; trans. Herbert C. Hoover and Lou H. Hoover (*De Re Metallica,* London, 1912; rptd. New York, 1950).

[29] The rationalization of white lead production took place in several stages. Cf. pp. 295–303, "White Lead."

[30] For an explanation of the various trace elements and their effects, cf. pp. 293–360.

[31] Under the classical microscope, the uniform particles 1–2 microns in size appear as amorphous spheres and ovals. It is only under the extreme enlargement provided by the electron microscope that they reveal their crystalline form.

Only the discovery of the structural function of the old white lead in van Eyck's layered construction allows us to gauge what has been lost in a paint that once lured the light into its depths and seduced it into lingering in the painting for as long as possible, by diffusing it.

> The ultimate would be: to grasp that
> everything factual is already theory. The blueness of the sky
> reveals to us the basic laws of chromatics. One should seek
> nothing beyond phenomena; they themselves are the theory.
>
> GOETHE

X
Van Eyck's
Lucky Hand

 he imitation of phenomena related to the blue of the sky, of bird feathers, and of butterfly wings draws its life, just as they do, from *structural colors,* even though it cannot manage without blue pigment in the way that nature does. The sky above us is "painted,"[1] like the blue of the eye, without a single trace of blue color. "Extremely fine clouding . . . diffracts the light rays entering, in various ways. The light waves that produce red and yellow are deflected little, while the blue waves, by contrast, are much more strongly dif, fracted . . . One of these primary phenomena that give rise to blue is the bird's feather." Black color particles enclosed in the keratin of feathers, known as melan, ophores, increase the action of the transparent cells over, lying them, "the ultramicroscopic structure of which

---

[1] "If the darkness of infinite space is seen through atmospheric vapours illumined by the day-light, the blue colour appears. On high mountains the sky appears by day intensely blue, owing to the few thin vapours that float before the endless dark space: as soon as we descend in the valleys, the blue becomes lighter; till at last, in certain regions, and in consequence of increasing vapours, it altogether changes to a very pale blue." (Goethe, *Theory of Colours,* pp. 63–64.)

corresponds to the particle size causing the phenomenon of blue to arise."[2]

White plumage and some white butterfly wings work in the same way: their structure determines the wavelength of the light. In white, all the light rays are diffused evenly in all directions by irregularly positioned minute particles, so that the eye observing it receives all the light waves simultaneously.

> This, incidentally, is how the white color of milk is also produced. The particles that . . . create this diffusion of the light may be individual minute particles in the keratin layer, or tiny enclosed bubbles of air. The latter effect is also seen in mammalian hair: if dark pigment is not formed and air is incorporated, then white also appears in mammals. In humans, we are familiar with it as the white hair seen in age.[3]

The most sophisticated color effects in nature, displayed in the shimmering feathers of the peacock, in the metallic sparkle of the wings of the "sky butterfly"[4] or in the iridescent blue-green of parrot fish, are caused by interactions between light waves of different wavelengths in the lattice of the feathers or scales. "When sunlight is split into its different wavelengths, certain types of light known as the complementary colors—yellow and blue, or red and green, for example—can cancel each other out when these pairs act on the eye. In this process, light rays of the same wavelength, however, can intensify their light effect as a result of common action. Canceling some color potentials and intensifying others—this is the phenome-

---

[2] Adolf Portmann, *Kleine Einführung in die Vogelkunde* (Munich, 1966), pp. 25–26.
[3] Ibid., p. 27.

[4] The South American Morphidae were called "sky butterflies" by the Indians.

non physicists describe as interference, and this is what is happening when the color effects in a bird's feathers shine with a particular radiance, often with a metallic hue."[5]

The same principle governs the different lattice arrangements seen in various birds, fish, and butterflies. The dark melanin always absorbs a large part of the light that is allowed to penetrate, thereby increasing the brilliancy of the reflected waves. In sky butterflies, it acts from the underside of the transparent wing membrane, which is covered in brown scales. The blue scales on the upper side derive their color and sheen from the texture of their transparent skin. In all butterflies, each scale is the flat outgrowth of a single cell. A square millimeter of wing contains a tiled arrangement of two hundred to six hundred scales, each "tile" being some 100 microns long and 50 microns wide. Horizontally stacked lamellae form the glittering blue tiled skin in some sky butterflies, while in others, such as *Morpho rhetenor,* the shimmering is caused by thin rows of vertical longitudinal ridges that have a horizontal, cannulated appearance under the electron microscope. The latitude of 0.22 microns between the top and bottom surface of each ridge corresponds to approximately half the wavelength of blue light.[6] The light waves glide down the stairway of ridges and are reflected at each edge. In this way, the brilliance of the blue light reflected increases from step to step.

The enigma of the way in which these phenomena arise was conclusively solved only in the second half of the twentieth century. But the awareness of rich textures and iridescent colors seems never to have been more vivid than in the fifteenth century. Naturally evolved structural colors act on an ultramicroscopic scale that the human hand is incapable of attaining. But weavers of brocade, damask,

[5] Portmann, *Vogelkunde,* p. 27.

[6] Cf. H. Frederik Nijhout, "The Color Patterns of Butterflies and Moths," *Scientific American* 245, no. 5 (1981), pp. 104–115.

and satin are larger-scale relatives of butterflies and peacocks. The texture of the shining materials they produce
resembles the fine moiré pattern of silk that is perceptible
to the naked eye on examining scaly wings[7] and the barbs
of feathers close up. The finest brocade of the period came
to Flanders from Italy, and artists never failed to immortal-
ize the material's transitory splendor in their paintings. In
the world of textiles, the phenomenon closest to that of the
peacock's feathers and the butterfly's wing was produced
in Burgundy, in the renowned "glaze stitch" used for the
liturgical robes of the Order of the Golden Fleece. Their
dalmatics and pluvials shimmered in gold-interweaved
colors, and the eye shapes on wings and feathers were
matched by figurative images on the robes.[8] Two golden
threads were applied to the material, along with colored
silk of greater or lesser thickness, in such a way that iridescent depictions were produced in the play of light and
shadow. It is not recorded how many embroiderers lost
their eyesight in the process, and no one has ever counted
the number of stitches per square millimeter.

"Glaze stitch" was a term borrowed from painting, as
the technique involved letting brilliant grounds shimmer
through, whether needle and thread or brush and paint
were being used. Glaze stitching is painting with needles,
and it witnesses to a conception of painting from which
we have since become estranged. What painting meant
was: working in layers of glaze. Not even when decorating a piece of furniture or wood paneling would it have
occurred to a painter just to carry on applying paint until
the color covered the surface, in the fashion customary

[7] The scientific name *Lepidoptera* for butterflies and moths means liter-ally "scaly wings."

[8] Three pluvials (or copes) of the Order of the Golden Fleece are preserved in the Weltliche Schatzkammer (Secular Treasure-Chamber) in Vienna under inven-tory numbers 19, 20, and 21. (I am grateful to Monique Lévi-Strauss for the explanation of the glaze stitch.)

today. Polychromy was an elaborate technique used right up to the eighteenth century; in it paints with different binders were laid in wafer-thin layers on chalk grounds, which in turn were constructed using multiple layers and had been subjected to a wet polish before being painted— like the grounds used by panel painters and gilders. As well as producing light and dark tones and warm and cold ones, polychromy above all had the effect of creat-ing a play of light on sometimes transparent, sometimes opaque surfaces. Smoothed with agate or roughened with the ball of the thumb, surfaces that were reflective or dull, silky or rough, glittering or powdery were produced, cre-ating the illusion of costly textures such as ivory, porce-lain, and velvet.[9] In the same way, carved and chiseled figures were not simply painted, but were polychromed using a multitude of gossamer-thin layers of paint, and also gilded. The brightly colored, sumptuous splendor of the late Middle Ages may harbor a germ of the kitsch that spread worldwide in the nineteenth and twentieth centuries, but there could be no better training for an artist's eye than to polychrome sculptural works of genius, such as Claus Sluter's *Well of Moses*.[10] The poly-chromed prophets in the sculpture were certainly not as confectionery-colored as we might think. What seems strange to us delighted contemporary viewers: the colorful splendor enhanced by gold—with even Jeremiah's spec-tacles being manufactured from gilded copper. Accord-ing to a statement by Panofsky, the polychromed *Well of Moses* must have had the effect of an outsized *Goldenes Rössl*. This scandalous comparison would have been as

[9] The rediscovery of these com-plex polychroming techniques is owed to a restorer from Lower Sax-ony, Wolfgang Fünders. The old polychrome lacquers have been re-created at Clemenswerth Palace in the Emsland region (designed in the eighteenth century by the architect Johann Conrad Schlaun) following Fünders's formulas. See pp. 358–359.

[10] Since the nineteenth century, these prophets in stone have stood in the garden of the lunatic asylum in Dijon.

incomprehensible to the greatest sculptor of the fourteenth century as to the Parisian masters of the goldsmith's art who created that prodigy of gold, enamel, and
gemstones at the behest of Queen Isabeau.[11] Contemporaries might have been surprised, however, that a depiction of Our Lady with the Christ Child in a floral arbor,
surrounded by childlike saints and King Charles VI at
prayer with his knight, which was intended as a votive
depiction, should be given the same title as a popular
name for inns in Germany. The profane title dates from
the seventeenth century, and since the King's unbridled
brutality was so well concealed in the white-enameled
horse whose rein is being held by the royal groom below
the gallery, the use of the inn name for the piece helped to
conceal the religious motif with its tragic background,
against which the innocent miniature world with its
green-enameled floral meadow appears so sacrilegious.
The Queen's New Year's gift to her mad husband, "with
its bright lustre, as well as the magical healing powers of
sapphires, rubies, and gold," was meant to embody a
"hope that the King might be saved from mental derange-
ment through the intercession of the saints."[12]

In the Neoplatonic tradition, shining articles reflect
the glow of the divine light. All beauty, whether natural
or created by human skill, draws its life from the divine
ideas that shine through it. The splendor of the peacock
and the splendor of the pluvial robe correspond. That
which is unfathomable reveals itself in colorful reflection.
All that shines illuminates—and following this maxim,
no skill was spared in illuminating the world. Whether

---

[11] The *Goldenes Rössl,* produced
around 1400, stands in the Heilige
Kapelle, Altötting (Bavaria). It was
shown at the Bavarian National
Museum in Munich in 1995 (see
next note).

[12] Willibald Sauerländer, "Kin-
der als Nothelfer. Parergon über das
sogenannte Goldene Rössl," in *Das
Goldene Rössl* (exhib. cat., Bay-
erisches Nationalmuseum, Munich,
1995), p. 99.

in manuscripts or fabrics, carvings or sculpture in stone, all earthly things, with their correspondence to celestial ones, were caused to shine forth. A measure of patience inconceivable today was needed to produce these costly treasures, since perfection was the only temporal limitation that counted.

Valéry's "slavish imitation of what is indefinable in things" presupposes the most exact familiarity possible with material effects. From the sphere of craft work, the early Flemings had in front of their eyes the methods of using threads, crystals, enamel, metal, and glass to produce transparency, relief, density, and sheen. To an eye as gifted as van Eyck's, these processes may have revealed the importance of *least action*. In a rabbinical legend,[13] the principle of least action plays the decisive role in transforming this imperfect world into the messianic one:

> To establish the kingdom of peace, not everything must be destroyed that a new world may begin; instead, this cup, that bush, that stone—all such things—have only to be shifted slightly. But as this trifle is so difficult to accomplish and its measure so hard to find, man is unsuited to the task in what concerns the world, and the Messiah must come.

In the painting of the Rolin Madonna, it is Edenic time[14] we have before our eyes. The transformation of the world

[13] The story is related by Ernst Bloch in his story "The Lucky Hand" ("Die glückliche Hand," in *Spuren* [Berlin, 1930; rptd. Frankfurt am Main, 1969], pp. 201–202), where it is ascribed to a "truly cabalistic rabbi." In 1979, Gershom Scholem told me that he himself had invented this story after Bloch had called him names because of his long ears, and had even called him an ass. Thus a trivial occasion gave rise to a legend demonstrating the truly cabalistic intuition of its long-eared inventor.

[14] Bloch describes the lucky hand, the hand with a special knack, as being one that is capable of messianic selection, bringing things out of their scattered state and rendering them "Edenic."

into painting was brought to perfection using the new means of expression through transparent density laid in crystalline layers. But since the measure of the colors was so hard to find, it was the multilayered thought and lucky hand of Jan van Eyck of Bruges that were needed in what concerns painting.

> N*ature, in its deepest sense, is not the epitome of creation, but is itself the creative power from which the form and order of the universe flow. It is here, and here alone, that beauty must compete with truth, and the artist with nature.*   ERNST CASSIRER

XI
Transfiguration of the Rod

 ix steps[1] lead from the garden in the Rolin Madonna to the rampart overlooking the heavenly Jerusalem. The artist is standing there, at the post of the angel of Revelation, at the central point between the human world and the city of God; and this transfigured angel is holding a transfigured rod. The instrument has become more than the symbol representing a court official, since the one who holds it has the power to transfigure symbols and shape them into "physical metaphors for things spiritual."[2] It is not the court valet but the painter who gives the rod its symbolic value—which draws its life from the angel's measuring rod. The hidden[3] meaning

---

[1] The six steps correspond to the six days of creation.

[2] Cf. Panofsky, *Early Netherlandish Painting,* chapter 5: "Reality and Symbol in Early Flemish Painting: 'Spiritualia sub Metaphoris Corporalium.' "

[3] The transfiguration of the angel's yardstick into the court painter's rod seems a perfect example of Panofsky's "disguised symbolism." By contrast, the interpretation

of the rod as a blind person's stick (cf. Hans Belting and Christiane Kruse, *Die Erfahrung des Gemäldes* [Munich, 1994]) appears to be a perfect example of the type of interpretation that refers only to itself. What could seem more appropriate to art historians who have failed to grasp the concept of disguised symbolism than a blind man in a landscape that represents the world?

of the symbol, like everything in the painting, hints at the *visibility of the invisible.* The rod embodies an *inner measure* corresponding to the divine measure; it symbolizes the painter's ability to reconstruct creation on a smaller scale.

In pictorial form, this Renaissance view of the artist's godlike character anticipates the philosophy of Nicholas of Cusa. But the greatness of van Eyck, like that of the philosopher, lies in the way in which this new view of humanity and the cosmos continues to accord with the basic religious ideas of the Middle Ages. The hierarchical order of the celestial and earthly spheres has been revoked, but everything in the sensory world is equidistant from the supersensory one; all things are therefore equally close to God. Although Nicholas of Cusa did not develop a distinct aesthetic theory, the core of his "copulative theology"[4] is the notion of the creative power of man and nature, "from which the form and order of the universe flow." In Cassirer's fine interpretation of an important passage in *On the Spirit,* the human spirit is a "divine seed that comprehends in its simple essence the totality of everything knowable; but in order for this seed to blossom and to bear fruit, it must be planted in the soil of the sensible world."[5]

Painted in 1436 at the earliest,[6] *The Madonna of Chancellor Rolin* is an almost miragelike reflection of the philos-

[4] Ernst Cassirer, *The Individual and the Cosmos in Renaissance Philosophy,* trans. Mario Domandi (New York, 1963; Philadelphia, 1972), p. 45.

[5] Loc. cit.

[6] A dendrochronological examination carried out by Peter Klein in 1983 of the oakwood panels, consisting of three vertical boards glued together, indicated that ca. 1426 was the earliest felling date possible for the oaks "due to the age of the trees," although a felling date of ca. 1431 would be more likely. "Assuming storage of the wood for a period of about ten years in the fifteenth century, the painting would have been carried out in 1436–1441." (Micheline Comblen-Sonkes and Philippe Lorentz, *Corpus, Musée du Louvre,* vol. 2, pp. 78–79. Cf. the incorrect dating by Belting and Kruse with the correct source reference, *Erfindung,* p. 161.)

ophy of Nicholas of Cusa. Since there is no way of perceiving God's existence except through an infinite variety
of individual points of view, the painter is entitled to
place himself at the center of the picture. The world can
only be grasped starting from one's own position.

> Every spiritual being has its centre within itself.
> And its participation in the divine consists precisely
> in this centring . . . Individuality is not simply a
> *limitation;* rather, it represents a particular *value* that
> may not be eliminated or extinguished, because it is
> only through it that the One, that which is "beyond
> being," becomes ascertainable to us.[7]

The world of divine grace and the world of the senses—
which, in accordance with a dualistic tendency in
medieval theology, were regarded as foreign and hostile to
each other—are bathed here in the same divine light.
The one is static and the other dynamic, and both bear
witness to the same harmony and proportion, the sym-
metrical measure marked out by the painter and the angel.
Contempt for the world—the obverse of which was dia-
bolical greed—has vanished both in van Eyck and in
Nicholas of Cusa, since "the mind can come to know
itself and to measure its own powers only by devoting
itself completely and unconditionally to the world."[8]

The closeness to life of the Flemish artist's work, perfectly expressing the reconciliation between the mind and
the world, intellect and sensuous perception, was praised
throughout Europe as a miracle—but not a single painter
from Portugal to Poland, or from Italy to Burgundy, was
capable of *measuring up* to van Eyck. As Panofsky laconi-
cally observes, his technique was "by its very nature inim-

[7] Cassirer, *Individual and Cosmos,* p. 28.
[8] Ibid., p. 44.

itable."[9] Pictures painted as if they were "crystallizations of light itself" are incapable of imitation. The secret of their creation draws its life from their *inner measure*. More painterly than any of the artists of his time, but true to the things themselves nevertheless,[10] Jan was an artist who towered so far above his own century that no one was capable of inheriting his legacy whole—while everyone took fragments of it for themselves. It was a long time before borrowing came to be regarded as theft, and the talented painters of the age rendered back what they had borrowed in transfigured forms. Rogier van der Weyden, the greatest of van Eyck's slightly younger contemporaries, obviously borrowed the pattern of *The Madonna of Chancellor Rolin* for his *St. Luke Painting the Virgin*. Panofsky described the reaction of the master from Tournai to the perfection of the works emerging from Bruges as *"reculer pour mieux sauter"*—a view confirmed by comparing the St. Luke and Rolin Madonnas.

Rogier has shifted all the elements of the shimmering Renaissance atmosphere that were in his model back into the invisible air, strict iconography, and cool light of the Gothic. On a panel twice the size, the Virgin and the figure kneeling opposite her have changed places.[11] It is not

[9] Panofsky, *Early Netherlandish Painting*, p. 303.

[10] Max J. Friedländer regards the history of painting as a path leading from being to appearance: "Artistic representation is essentially determined by whether the painter devotes his sympathies to the absolute thing—i.e., to something independent of conditions of place and light—or to the formal and color appearance in which the thing (accidentally) presents itself at the given point at which it is uniquely perceived. The whole development

of painting might well be regarded as a pathway leading from the former view to the latter . . . Every great painter travels some way along this road. But Jan van Eyck took a gigantic step, up to the point where he succeeded in combining his vivid and lively striving for discovery in relation to existent things with an enraptured devotion to appearance." *Die altniederländische Malerei* (Berlin, 1924), vol. 1, pp. 138-139.

[11] The painting is in the Museum of Fine Arts in Boston, with a replica in the Alte Pinakothek in

the mortal figure of the almsgiver that is present in the little chamber; the saints are once again alone in their own
sphere. The interior, garden, river, and city are set on a
single plane. The perceptual abundance of the world has
been pared down to significant details. The Garden of
Paradise has given way to a lawn with Marian plants, the
Romanesque arcade has been replaced with an oblong,
and the Arcadian landscape is now a distant backdrop of
hills. The lawn and fortress wall occupy the lower half of
the view, and the river and city share half of the remainder, in which a narrow strip of stylized landscape is dominated by a sky filling the remaining four-fifths of the
space.

Only a few human figures are walking along a street in
the nearby town. The pure stream does not reflect any
islands, castles, or bridges. There is nothing in the river's
unvarying rough surface to suggest that it is flowing. The
small, schematically rising waves indicate the unreal
quality of this "water of life,"[12] on which there are no
ships, mill boats, or human beings to cast any shadows. If
the artist's presence is hinted at here at all, it might be in
the similarity of his own features to those of St. Luke; it
was to be another 150 years before the painter's reflection
in his own picture, seen in several of van Eyck's works,[13]
was to return in Dutch breakfast-piece still lifes.

Munich and another in St. Peters-
burg. See Martin Davies, *Rogier
van der Weyden: An Essay, with a
Critical Interpretation of Paintings
Assigned to Him and to Robert Campin*
(London, 1972). On the symbolic
significance of left and right, see
Chapeaurouge, *Symbole.*

[12] "Then he showed me the river
of the water of life, bright as crystal," Revelation 22.1. In the Old
Testament, water—the symbol of

life—signifies the Messianic Age; in
the New Testament, streams of living water symbolize the Holy Spirit.

[13] Concealed in the mirror in
the Arnolfini Betrothal, on the
rampart in the Rolin picture, and
in the armor of St. George in
the Madonna of Canon van der
Paele (cf. *De Vlaamse Primitieven,* ed.
A. Janssens de Bisthoven [Ant-
werp, 1957], plate 156).

In Rogier's version, there are again two figures on the rampart occupying the center of the painting; but here they are closer both spatially and logically to the principal figures, since they belong to the same family—St. Joseph and St. Anne, looking out onto the living water. Their figures do not cast any shadows, and there are no church buildings from which compass directions might be deduced. Like the airless space above, everything is bathed in a uniform light, which obviously emanates from a supernatural source; it was only with the discovery of electricity that floodlighting of this sort became possible in the real world. As in all of the artist's works, *St. Luke Painting the Virgin* reflects the higher power of the divine sphere. Rogier's works testify to a faith entirely rooted in Scholasticism: the truth cannot flourish in natural light. The perfection of nature is not to be found in nature itself, and it therefore forms a distanced background to the bright world of divine grace that is spanned by the mighty vault of heaven. A reference to the Fall of Man—confined to the stonework in van Eyck—is also seen here, carved into the wooden armrest of the throne on which the Virgin is nursing the Christ Child.

It is only in the infant's rapturous face, in the delighted stretching of his fingers and toes, that the picture *St. Luke Painting the Virgin* indicates which direction Rogier took in recoiling from van Eyck. Van Eyck did not describe emotions; they belong to a sphere that is accessible neither to the microscope nor to the telescope.[14] It was to the reproduction of emotions, reflected in facial expressions and gestures, that the solemn artist from Tournai turned.

He shows what it is that takes hold of people and *moves* them. It was not in the St. Luke painting, in depicting dramatic events from the Bible story, that Rogier's art was to reach its apex, but in describing pain and sorrow,

[14] Panofsky, *Early Netherlandish Painting,* p. 182.

repentance and grief, pity and fear, anxiety, horror, and despair. Against the view from Paradise, looking out toward the abundance of the world's life, Rogier sets a reminder of the Last Judgment; against the description of things at rest in themselves, he places the expression of passionate emotion; and against van Eyck's spatial, painterly, and static style, he sets a dynamic, two-dimensional, linear conception of the world.

Nonrepresentational painting adopts "styles" as "subjects." It claims to give a concrete representation of the formal conditions of all painting. Paradoxically the result is that nonrepresentational painting does not, as it thinks, create works which are as real as, if not more real than, the objects of the physical world, but rather realistic imitations of nonexistent models. It is a school of academic painting in which each artist strives to represent the manner in which he would execute his pictures if by chance he were to paint any.

CLAUDE LÉVI-STRAUSS

XII
From the Rainbow to the Earth

 o grasp what stylistic distinctions involve, we need to follow the conception of art theory that Erwin Panofsky expounded in 1925, in his essay "On the Relationship between Art History and Art Theory":[1]

Art—no matter how one defines it, and no matter which of its fields one cares to examine—fulfills its specific task by giving shape to perceptible elements. This means that the products of art must also preserve the "fullness" appropriate to sensory perception, while nevertheless subjecting this fullness to a certain degree of order, and to that extent attempting to confine it by means of this order. Or, to put it differently, it means that in every work of art some kind of balance needs to be achieved between "fullness" and "form" as the two poles of a

[1] "Über das Verhältnis der Kunstgeschichte zur Kunsttheorie," reprinted in Erwin Panofsky, *Aufsätze zu Grundfragen der Kunstwissenschaft,* ed. Hariolf Oberer and Egon Verheyen (Berlin, 1980).

fundamental opposition. Now, this indispensable balance between two opposed principles can only be achieved if the a priori necessity for an antithesis corresponds to the a priori possibility of a synthesis: "fullness" and "form"—as such arising as two opposed principles in which it is not evident, as it were, how they might be able to combine—can and must actually enter into a synthesis, since the purely ontological opposition between "fullness" and "form" has its correlate in (or, to be more precise, is ultimately identical with) the methodological opposition between "time" and "space." The principle of "fullness" corresponds to the phenomenon of "time," and the principle of "form" to the phenomenon of "space." If the opposition between "fullness" and "form" is the a priori condition for the existence of artistic problems, then the interaction between "time" and "space" is the a priori condition for the possibility of solving them.

Thus, if a definition of the work of art may be attempted at all, it might read more or less as follows: regarded ontologically, the work of art is a contention between "form" and "fullness"; regarded methodologically, it is a contention between "time" and "space." And it is only this correlation that renders comprehensible the way in which, on the one hand, "fullness" and "form" can enter into a living interaction, while on the other "time" and "space" can fuse into an individually clear structure.[2]

Panofsky draws out the specifically visual antitheses implicit in this dual problematic of all art, at three levels: the elementary, the figurative, and the compositional. At the first level, the elementary plane of the perceptual, it is

[2] Ibid., p. 50.

the opposition between "fullness" and "form" that appears as the visual and tactile poles; the central point of balance between these values of free space and body is termed "sculptural." An attraction toward the visual pole in the seventeenth-century Netherlands created the "painterly" style, while a shift toward the tactile pole is characteristic of the "stereometric-crystalline" art of the ancient Egyptians. By contrast, at the third level—that of composition—the opposition arising is that between "time" and "space," expressed by the compositional values of "immersion" and "juxtaposition," of fusion and division:

> because, if a genuinely total fusion of several units with one another is only conceivable within the medium of "time," which scorns all division, then conversely, a genuinely strict isolation of several units from one another can only be imagined within the medium of "space," through which not a single movement courses. Consequently, the antithesis expressed by the third conceptual pair could have been characterized no less aptly by the conceptual pair "stillness" and "movement" (being and becoming), except that the concept of "movement" or "becoming" already carries with it the notion not merely of a purely temporal event, but rather of a spatiotemporal one.[3]

At the second, middle level—that of figuration—however, the contention is between depth values and surface values, and this can be conceived *both* "from the opposition between 'fullness' and 'form' *and* from the opposition between 'time' and 'space,' in so far as a specific relationship between depth and surface simulta-

[3] Ibid., p. 52.

neously presupposes a specific relationship between fusion and division, movement and stillness."[4] The absolute antitheses as such cannot be found in any phenomenon; a purely tactile value, being an abstract geometrical structure, would exclude every type of perceptual "fullness"; a purely visual one, being an amorphous light phenomenon, would exclude every type of intelligible form; "and something that is purely surface is as impossible *in concreto* as something that is purely depth; pure 'immersion' would be spaceless time, pure 'juxtaposition' would be timeless space." The extreme poles, unattainable in any form of reality, lie in the realm of the infinite, and it is only the character of the oppositions that is fixed once and for all. But the terminal points of the solutions to problems that are reached lie on a sliding scale in the realm of the finite, "so that a work of art that would have to be described as 'painterly' in relation to the style of the sixteenth century might count as 'sculptural' in relation to the style of the seventeenth century—since the whole scale of values has now shifted toward the 'visual' pole."[5]

The fundamental problems that are involved in the colorless composition of bodies and space also need to be solved for color phenomena. Rejecting the immersion of colors (fusion) in favor of juxtaposition (division) requires surface and tactile values, and is termed "polychromy"; while a preference for the fusion of colors, opting for visual and depth values, is termed "colorism," or in extreme cases "tonality."

> To the extent that it solves the basic problems appropriately, an extremely "polychrome" use of color therefore necessarily correlates with an isolating, flat, crystalline type of spatial and physical composition; while a "coloristic," and particularly

4 Ibid., p. 52.   5 Ibid., p. 54.

"tonal," use of color is just as necessarily found together with a unifying, deep, painterly type of spatial and physical composition.[6]

Panofsky describes the central point of balance between tonality and polychromy as a "harmonious con-cord without refraction of colors." With a characteristic instinct, he regards it as inadequate to characterize color phenomena at only one of the three levels described, and draws attention to this in a long footnote. By mistakenly transferring one of the preconditions for nonartistic expe-rience into the artistic realm, he argues, we regard color as something that has merely been added onto bodies—"attached to them, as it were"—and consequently regard color in the work of art as being neither an elementary nor a figurative factor, but merely a compositional one that in principle does nothing more than add an illustrative aspect to a colorless world that is already "complete." Polychromy, colorism, and tonality are different *solutions* to the problem of "division and fusion," although this does not exclude the possibility that the decisions they represent might in fact be reached for all three of the basic problems.

To assign chromatic values to the figurative and ele-mentary levels omitted in this view, we need to turn our attention to the nature of color perception. As a transi-tional phenomenon between light and darkness, color emerges from the way in which the sense of sight inter-prets the image reaching the retina inside the darkroom of the eye. The 118 million rods on the black melanin base of the retina serve only for twilight vision; 7 million cones serve to receive the display of light in color and to resolve fine details. There are three types of cone, distributed across the retina at various densities. The point of greatest

[6] Ibid., p. 55.

density is the rod-free fovea at the center of the field of vision. The stratification in this tiny[7] center of our sharpest sight differs from that in the rest of the retina, in which cones and rods have more widely branching connections to the nerve cells that are overlaid on them in layers. These transparent cell layers are pushed aside all round in the area of the fovea, forming a ring of dense retina around the resulting shallow pit, into which the light falls directly onto the cones. This more direct connection with the "world" is matched by a more direct connection to the brain: each individual cone in the fovea is linked without branching to a bipolar cell, which in turn is directly connected to a ganglion on the topmost retinal layer.

The spectral sensitivities of the three types of cone in the retinal mosaic correspond to the short blue wavelength of light, the medium green wavelength, and the long red wavelength. All colors can be registered using these three wavelengths.[8] During the next phases of coding, however, the trichromatic interpretation process is converted into an antagonistic four-color system in which the three contrasting pairs blue and yellow, red and green, black and white are opposed. The color opposition corresponds to the spatial variable. The sense of sight perceives things by comparing contrasts, whether using color values or gray values. Even the retinal cells already compare the quantity of light at the center of their receptive field with that of the surrounding field. It is only the *relationship* between the light reflected by an object and the light in its surroundings that allows us to perceive color.

[7] The fovea centralis has a diameter of approximately half a millimeter, and its field of vision at a distance of 2.5 meters is limited to about 25 square centimeters. Cf. David H. Hubel, *Eye, Brain, and Vision* (New York, 1988), and Conrad G. Mueller and Mae Rudolph, *Light and Vision* (New York, 1966).

[8] On the difference between additive and subtractive mixture, see Mueller and Rudolph, *Light and Vision,* index.

At any point on the retina, we can speak of red-greenness, the reading an instrument would give if it were to record the relative stimulation of red and green cones (zero for yellow or white). This value is determined for a particular region, and an average value is determined for the surround; then the ratio is taken. This process is repeated for the yellow-blue . . . and black and white values . . . To any color there corresponds a triplet of numbers, and we can think of any color as occupying a point in three-dimensional space.[9]

Neurophysiological research into the interaction between color and space has confirmed experimentally[10] that "to have color at all, we need to have variation in the wave-length content of light across the visual field."[11]

Color perception requires color differences. The human sense of sight, specialized for perceiving contrast edges, would disregard a world that lacked contrasts of color, space, and time, and that world would remain invisible: its image would touch the retina without being seen.

But we need to keep an eye on the fact that the sense of color is not restricted to the perception of color *tone,* but is also coupled to a sharp-sighted ability to perceive detail, and that light presents colors only when it encounters material objects. Although we are unable to perceive the presence of material in the transparent blue of the sky, we would not see any blue if it were not for the particles of dust and moisture in the air that cloud the darkness of

[9] Hubel, *Eye, Brain, and Vision,* pp. 188 and 187.

[10] A blue speck against a red background vanishes when its borders are stabilized on the retina. "The blue melts away, and all you see is the red background. Stabilizing the borders on the retina apparently renders them ineffective, and without them, we have no color." Ibid., p. 179.

[11] Ibid., p. 178.

space. As one of the "magic tricks" of quantum physics shows, light cannot be perceived unless it touches something.[12] Absolute light and absolute darkness are polar opposites within an infinite field in which there are wavelengths, but no eyesight in which their colors can unfold. Our sight is shaped by the sense of color to such an extent that we are barely aware how great the threshold is that we cross every evening into the sphere beyond color. Even on clear nights with a full moon, the world is colorless, and the eyes of many sharp-eyed creatures[13] perceive it even during daylight as a vivid gray.

In Panofsky's model of the visual sphere, the natural artistry of the *sense of sight* is matched by the artistic nature of the mediation between polar opposites whose theoretical terminal points lie at infinity, since the reality of the eyes is incapable of attaining them. Attached to physical bodies, however, colors belong among finite phenomena. Let us attempt to determine their elementary and figurative poles, therefore, by starting from the central point of balance and continuing conceptually in the opposing directions until we reach extreme solutions. Three-dimensional, sculptural physicality represents the mid-point between the visual and tactile poles—in the

[12] Arthur Zajonc, a specialist in quantum optics, posed the question, "How does light look when left *entirely* to itself?" He constructed a box in such a way that the light from a projector did not touch any objects or surfaces in its interior. The inside of the box could be viewed through an opening, and nothing could be seen in it but the blackness of empty space. "On the outside of the box is a handle connected to a wand that can move into and out of the box's interior. Pulling the handle, the wand flashes through the dark space before me and I see the wand bril-liantly lit on one side. The space clearly is not empty but filled with light. Yet without an object on which the light can fall, one sees only darkness. Light itself is always invisible. We see only things, only objects, not light." Arthur Zajonc, *Catching the Light: The Entwined History of Light and Mind* (New York, 1993), p. 2.

[13] Owls, for example, are almost completely color-blind. The phenomenal vision of these nocturnal birds of prey is achieved by the light-sensitivity of their retinal rods.

former it loses itself in a haze, and in the latter it rigidi-fies into a geometrical contour. In their relationship to color, these opposite poles acquire unequal weights: while color belongs to the essence of the visual, it is an acci-dental property of the tactile. But we need to regard the terms in which the question is posed as abstract points of reference, which take form as such neither in the con-crete world nor in artistic reality. Both wavelengths and geometrical structures have to undergo transformation in the sphere of the visible. It is then, and only then, that they can share in the fullness of the perceptible world. As soon as we turn our attention to their individual em-bodiments, the balance between the opposite poles is once again restored: although the particular colors of concrete physical bodies are subject to the wavelengths of light, the general quality of wavelengths is subordinate to the specific qualities of the material conditions from which it derives its infinite variety of appearances. The color of a geometric structure, being interchangeable, means very little, whereas the red of strawberries is an essential fea-ture of the ripe fruit.

The elementary opposition of colors is expressed in the invisibility or visibility of the materials conveying them. The intrinsic values of colors stand opposed to their rep-resentational values; the former are free, the latter are fixed. No matter what the shade, form, composition, or state of the material to which they are fixed, the former illuminate, while the latter represent, the pure tones that we term warm or cold, active or passive, bright or dark— red, green, blue, yellow, and their primary varieties. Col-ors that represent themselves compete with the glowing colors of the spectrum, which appear indefinitely local-ized.[14] Their ideal lies in the fleeting dispersions of light

[14] Cf. David Katz, *Die Erschein-ungsweise der Farben und ihre Beeinflus-sung durch die invididuelle Erfahrung* (Leipzig, 1911), and Wolfgang Schöne, *Über das Licht in der Malerei* (Berlin, 1954).

in the atmosphere, the blue of the sky, the red of twilight and dawn, and the phenomena of prismatic separation—the finest of which is called the rainbow—and also the luminous effects of crystal lattices and the shimmering of the light diffracting and interfering in grooves, lamellae, leaves, and skins, as well as the hallucinatory colors that the sense of sight deceives us with in floating afterimages. "The physical colors, and in particular those of the prism, used to be termed *colores emphatici,* owing to their special magnificence and energy. On closer examination, however, all color phenomena can be described as hav⁄ing strong emphasis, provided they are presented in the purest and most perfect conditions."[15] The common char⁄acteristic of all apparently incorporeal emphatic colors is *transparency.*

The representational values of colors, by contrast, serve to define boundaries. The corresponding colors are measured from the variety of ways in which they can represent every conceivable type of form, texture, and material condition. The clarity of the localization and modeling requires more or less opaque *density.* Turner's paintings illustrate a painterly and visual extreme, the preference for luminous color phenomena in the atmo⁄sphere, while Mondrian's pattern paintings, at the tactile and linear terminal point of the scale, show how an abil⁄ity to form black lines and blue, yellow, and red oblongs combines the plain representational value of colors with mere colorfulness.

The three⁄dimensional, sculptural physicality that lies at the central point of balance among the elementary color values arises through an interplay between impermeable density and transparency. The reproduction of material qualities that reveals itself to the eye's sense of touch gives

---

[15] Goethe, *Farbenlehre,* p. 187; see *Theory of Colours,* trans. Charles Lock Eastlake (London, 1840; rptd. Cambridge, Mass., 1970), p. 275.

expression to the highest representational value of colors. Although tactile textures can also be constructed without colors, "All kinds of *camaïeu,* or color in color, ultimately mean that a required contrast or some kind of color effect has to be introduced"[16]—even if we are mentally supply/ing the colors as we look at a black/and/white depiction. This translation process is reflected in language in the way in which a nuanced interplay of lively gray values is described as "colorful"—as color itself is an essential characteristic of liveliness.

The colors of the living world vary according to the composition of the material, the lighting conditions, and the distance from which we choose to view them. "Moss/colored," for example, describes a rich mid/green match/ing the general impression of damp moss in a not too shady forest. There are numerous species of moss, among which all the different tones of green are represented; but the cushion of one and the same woodland moss will have a more olive/green effect on the cracked brown bark of a lime tree than on the smooth bluish/gray bark of a beech, and as soon as its detailed structure is examined close up, the moss green becomes transformed into a multiplicity of tones ranging from the brown base of the individual stalks to olive green, ending in the lush green of the bend/ing fronds, with shining greenish/yellow tips. Depending on the climate and time of day, a carpet of moss will appear to show warmer or colder shades; its surface will be denser or looser, more transparent or more opaque; the green light will mix to a greater or lesser degree into yel/lowish, brownish, or bluish areas; and the sheen of the tips of the tiny fronds intertwining with one another will be glassier, oilier, or duller.

Luminous moss, also known as elfin/gold, is quite differ/ent. Tiny and constantly green, it presents the eye with an

[16] Ibid., p. 224 (*Theory of Colours,* p. 334).

illusion of the color's intrinsic value. The chlorophyll grains in this species of moss, which only grows in cavities in cliffs and rocks, are arranged in lens-shaped cells in such a way that the few rays of light that penetrate into the darkness through cracks in the rock are caught as if in a concave mirror and reflected in a shining green,

so that one would think tiny emeralds had been scattered there across the soil. When, filled with curiosity, you reach down to the floor of the grotto to capture a sample of the shining object and inspect what you have brought out on your hand in the daylight, you can hardly believe your eyes. There is nothing there but cold, dull earth and rotten, damp disks of yellowish-gray stone. It is only on closer examination that you notice that the earth and pebbles are partly interspersed and covered with small, matt green dots and fine threads, with tiny moss plants rising here and there in delicate traces that have a pale, bluish-green color.[17]

Compared with the glittering trompe-l'oeil spectacle of this inconspicuous moss species, the familiar green appearances of vegetation seem less enigmatic. But even when we try to reproduce the tactile, hoarfrost texture on the surface of the "simple" leaf of an iris, the overall tone of which can be more or less defined as malachite green, it turns out to consist of a multiplicity of green nuances, ranging from yellowish to bluish-green malachite green, that are inseparable from the material structure of its layers. The bluish-white hoarfrost appearance of the leaf is caused by a gossamer-thin layer of wax that protects it from dew. The sword shape of the iris is created by the way in which the leaves are folded together lengthwise,

[17] Kerner von Marilaun, *Pflanzenleben* (Leipzig, 1888), vol. 1, p. 375.

with the opposed edges growing together. The upright position provides protection against the vertical rays of the midday sun. The hoarfrost appearance varies, depending on the angle at which the light strikes the longitudinal veins of the leafy sheath.

One and the same pigment[18] from the plant world appears in every variety of green; the differences are due not so much to the varying amounts of chlorophyll as to the multiple forms taken by the cell chambers, on the walls of which the chlorophyll grains form first one pattern and then another, and to the outer clothing of the foliage, which provides protection sometimes with hairs, bristles, or spines, and sometimes with varnish or wax coatings.

The intrinsic values and representational values of colors combine in some flowers, yielding snapdragon crimson, geranium red, fiery orange, sulfur yellow, gentian blue, and velvety violet. But the most splendid display of colors is seen in mixed woodland during fall. The fresh green of the leaves withdraws transformed into the interior of the trees; unused residues, in the form of shining yellow grains and various crystals of calcium rich in oxalic acid, are left in the dying foliage. As valuable substances are moved to storage areas in the branches and roots, many trees produce anthocyanin, a pigment that can appear as red, blue, or violet, depending on the presence or absence of acids. The presence of yellow grains alongside acidified red anthocyanin gives the leaf a reddish-yellow appearance. The green of the leaf is thus transformed "now to yellow, now to brown, now to red, violet, and orange . . . and a play of colors arises that is all the more varied the larger the number of plant species that occur together in one place to form a convivial

[18] The involvement of anthocyanins is not taken into account here.

band."[19] When there is a scattering of evergreens as well, the forest is decorated in every color of the rainbow:

> The crowns of the pine trees are bluish-green, the slim tops of the spruces black-green, the leaves of the hornbeams, maples, and white birches a pale yellow; the broad strips of forest stocked with beeches show every gradation from yellow-red to brown-red; the cherry, mountain ash, and barberry are scarlet red, the bird cherry and wild service trees crimson, dogwood and spindle tree violet, the aspens orange, the white poplars and white willows white and gray, the alders a cloudy brownish-green.[20]

The color phenomena that celebrate their triumph in the autumnal forest, in all their ephemerality and change-ability, cannot be reproduced using the yellow, orange, and red of the cadmium palette. The color changes occur inside the fragile tissues of the drying leaves, and in spite of their intensity they are nuanced by body. The old, highly toxic arsenic pigments orpiment and realgar, the genuine varieties of madder paint, the red and yellow earths, are much closer to fall colors than the ultra-yellow, ultra-orange, and ultra-red modern cadmium. The inad-equate representational value of modern pigments has been compensated for using the intrinsic value of color-fulness. In the process, the pigments have sacrificed their enigmatic depth light, at the visual pole, and their density of body at the tactile one. The Doerner technique, in which tactile textures are built up in pure grisaille and overpainted in color, is an attempt to overcome this

[19] Kerner von Marilaun, *Pflanz-enleben*, vol. 1, p. 454.   [20] Ibid., pp. 454–455.

dilemma, and it gives perfect expression to the view that color is merely an illustrative aspect added to an uncolored world.

As Panofsky observes in a footnote, a separate term for the midpoint that lies between depth and surface has not yet been coined. If we follow either the one pole or the other only to the point at which the elementary sculptural quality of bodies is maintained, we can describe linear perspective depiction without impenetrable shadows and unconfining light as "spatiality without dissolving chiaroscuro." Since color arises from the surface of the material, it is threatened, like the bodies, with being dissolved by light, shadow, and distance. The color that belongs to objects themselves is usually termed "local color." "Local colors are the elementary colors, but they are specified according to the properties of the substances and surfaces on which they are perceived. This specification continues to infinity."[21] Local color is thus the color of bodies, but the way in which bodies are determined idealizes the way in which local color is bound to them, to the extent that it takes the color tone standardized according to wavelength, brightness, and saturation and abstracts from the varying play of the light on the transparent and opaque, matt and glossy, smooth and rough textures, just as it abstracts from the shadow effects and light or dark, contrastingly colored or similarly colored influence of the surroundings. Local colors are the chromatic symbols of the world of objects, which distinguish between permanence and changeability, between the constant tone and its accidental variables. They represent the typical yellow of the lemon or the persistent malachite green of the iris leaf as they appear independently of the momentary lighting conditions, temporary states of the material, and changing surroundings. The definition of

[21] Goethe, *Farbenlehre*, p. 226 (*Theory of Colours*, p. 339).

"local color" as "the intrinsic color of an object reproduced in a picture, unaltered by light and shadow or by
adaptation to an overall tone"[22] accords with the general-
ization in surface terms of a color nuance at the flat, figurative pole.

Depth effects require a different type of optics. Spatial
representation modifies colors in the perspective of light
and air as a result of bright and dark tone intervals. Here
we encounter the problem of color refraction. The colors
of the empirical world, which become brighter in light
and darker in shadow, are perceived as constant. A ray of
sunlight on a tabletop, for example, reduces the degree of
saturation of the color, which appears nut brown in dif-
fuse daylight, although the brighter tone does not appear
whiter because of this; and in the same way, in the area of
shadow cast by an object on the table, the very same nut
brown emerges from the darker area.[23] However, every
brightening and darkening of a color in which white,
gray, or black pigment is added is accompanied by a more
or less powerful alteration in the color tone. The stronger
the gray, the more refracted the color appears. "Harmonious concord without refraction of colors" is the term
Panofsky gave to the midpoint between colorism and
polychromy. Tonality goes beyond colorism, which aims

[22] *Der neue Brockhaus* (Wiesbaden, 1958), s.v. *Lokalfarbe.*
[23] The physiologist Ewald Hering (1834–1918), whose theory of
vision anticipated neurophysiological discoveries by fifty years, gives a
clear example of the way in which
our orientation alters perception,
depending on whether we attribute
objective existence to a visual phenomenon or interpret it as a momentary effect of the light. "I am
walking along a path beneath a covering of dense foliage; for a brief
space direct sunlight falls through a
gap in the leaves: at the first moment
I think I see a spot colored white by
spilled lime, but when I look more
closely, I see no more white, but only
light on the grey-brown earth."
Ewald Hering, *Outlines of a Theory
of the Light Sense,* trans. Leo M.
Hurvich and Dorothea Jameson
(Cambridge, Mass., 1964), p. 9;
cited here from Ernst Cassirer, *The
Philosophy of Symbolic Forms,* trans.
Ralph Manheim (New Haven,
Conn., 1955), vol. 3, p. 138.

at a harmonious concord by refracting colors, because the overall tone in it dominates all its coloring. Beyond tonal, ity, the fullness of the colors fuses into a dirty gray or brown,[24] the dull monotony that results from an equal mixture of the three primary colors blue, yellow, and red *alla prima.*

At the other end of the scale, beyond polychromy, the contrasting colors lie directly alongside each other. The *compositional* level, as the term suggests, is the combination of colors, their simultaneous intonation; on its scale, contrasting tones are opposed to similar ones. Just as the color hodgepodge that lies beyond the extreme solution of tonality plunges into a discordant darkness, the enhanced color contrasts that lie beyond polychromy at the other extreme threaten to become canceled out in a harmonious void: to the sense of sight, the equilibrium of their glaring effects elicits the zero value of white. "Everything comes from black only to lose itself in white," wrote the inventor of the ocular clavichord, Louis-Bertrand Castel.[25] But *fine* black is composed of colors that work together without mingling.

In the use of color, the solution lying at the midpoint between fusion and division, immersion and juxtaposition corresponds to the *superimposition* of the layered technique. Along with the number of layers, the scope for achieving balance between the opposite poles increases. In this complex system, the problems of the elementary, figurative, and compositional levels involve different solutions in the individual layers, which—separated from each other level by level, while at the same time being

[24] Depending on the color tone and binder used, a mixture of blue, yellow, and red in equal proportions produces either gray or brown.

[25] Cited after Claude Lévi-Strauss, *Look, Listen, Read,* trans. Brian C. J. Singer (New York, 1997), p. 131. Castel developed his ocular clavichord during the 1820s. See also John Gage, *Colour and Culture: Practice and Meaning from Antiquity to Abstraction* (London, 1993), p. 233.

related to one another in their effects—merge into a syn-thesis in the final picture. The first, "linear" layer of paint in van Eyck's technique forms the basis for the three-dimensional, spatial construction, and at the same time serves to provide chromatic harmony through its coloris-tic orientation: from the depths, the consonance of colors brightened with white lead sustains the fullness of the polychrome details on the surface. In the same way, the density of body and sculptural quality of the lower layers allow a painterly chiaroscuro without dissolving the objects' own form, color, and composition. Transparent clouding allows the colors to remain true to themselves both in light and shadow, and gives life even to the deep-est darkness: "An extravagant abundance of forms not released into visibility is hinted at in the over-dark depths, from which phenomena stream forth eternally changing, as if from a horn of plenty, as soon as the light calls them forth from the richness of the void."[26]

[26] Friedländer, *Altniederländische Malerei,* p. 139.

Part Two

WORLD LANDSCAPE
AND WILD WOOD

The world eternally turns round;
all things therein are incessantly moving, the earth,
the rocks of Caucasus, and the Pyramids of
Egypt, both by the public motion and their own.
Even constancy itself is no other but a slower and
more languishing motion. I cannot fix my object;
'tis always tottering and reeling by a natural giddiness: I take it as it is at the instant I consider it; I
do not paint its being, I paint its passage.

MONTAIGNE

La Nature est un temple où de vivants piliers
Laissent parfois sortir de confuses paroles;
L'homme y passe à travers des forêts de symboles
Qui l'observent avec des regards familiers.[1]

BAUDELAIRE

I

The Sacred in Desolation

ome fifty years had passed since the magnificent marriage of Charles the Bold to
Margaret of York, when after the cere-
mony in Bruges on 28 June 1468 the wedding guests at Sint Jan's hall in Damme
were served a hundred peacocks each day for a week; Burgundy's golden age was a legend, and Charles's dogged
pursuit of the crown, which reached its grisly conclusion
in the mud of St. John's pond at the Battle of Nancy in
1477, on a frozen Epiphany eve, had been consigned to
history. Forgotten was the triumph of the "universal spider"[2] over the death of his rival, in which the south of the
duchy was given away to the French crown, while the
north passed to the Hapsburg emperor, Maximilian; a
new continent had been discovered, the fame of Bruges
had passed away, Portuguese ships laden with pepper and
nutmeg were sailing past the silted-up Zwin and drop-
ping anchor in the harbor on the river Schelde, where the
new capital of world trade was called Antwerp—when,

[1] "Nature's a temple where each living column, / At times, gives forth vague words. There Man advances / Through forest-groves of symbols, strange and solemn, / Who follow him with their familiar glances." (*Poems of Baudelaire: A Translation of "Les Fleurs du Mal,"* by Roy Campbell [London, 1952], p. 8.)

[2] King Louis XI was called "*l'universelle araignée*" because he was so fond of seeing his enemies writhing in the calculated webs he had spun.

from a recollection of Jan van Eyck and Hugo van der Goes, a new genre revealed itself in a painting by Gerard David, the last of the early Flemish painters in the waning days of Bruges.

The two panels of the *Forest View,* each 90 cm × 30.5 cm, once formed the two outer wings of a triptych. We are looking at the very first landscape in Flemish art in which the human figure is not shown.[3] The scene is the *locus amoenus,* the leafy pleasance familiar to poets since antiquity, furnished with shady trees and brooks:

> *Between the clearings, tree trunks moist with dew rose stiff*
> *over wet grass; streams gurgling out from teeming springs*
> *rushed past, glinting with droplets of light. Ivy strands*
> *ran twisting over moss-coated caverns. Undreamed*
> *melodies resounded through the shadows, each bird*
> *calling songs of springtime, humming softly, singing.[4]*

A great-tit has perched on an isolated ivy bush;[5] an ass is resting on the grass in a small clearing in the shade cast by tall trees, each leaf of their foliage gleaming in the sunlight entering from above; a pair of oxen are wading in the clear water of a stream that courses through the wood in three arms; there is sedge lining its banks; swamp irises

[3] Around 1920, the *Forest View* on the outer wings of the altar painting, was sawed off and separated. Until their restoration in the mid-1980s, the two panels were on display in the Mauritshuis in The Hague, on loan from the Rijksmuseum. Violent intrusions seem to be the fate of the triptych. The *Forest View* has been unrecognizable since it was restored; see the postscript at the end of this chapter.

[4] Tiberianus (fourth century A.D.), cited in Curtius, *European Literature and the Latin Middle Ages,* pp. 196–197 (new translation here from the Latin).

[5] The bush has also been considered to be a bramble or vine. An exact identification, in this poorly preserved area of the painting, would be difficult even for a botanist. The shady situation of the forest and the iconography, however, suggest ivy, the tendrils of which bend out into space in a shrublike fashion when there is nothing for them to twine themselves round. See p. 151, note 64.

and reeds are growing between washed-out tree roots in the water; spots of light are dancing on the smooth gray bark of a beech tree; slim trunks are throwing their shadowy reflections onto the cool water, which is mirroring the distant sky; a wooden footbridge leads diagonally across the meandering stream toward the ass in the clearing, set on a tongue of land between the winding course of the stream and the straight moat; brick-red walls are glowing warmly in front of the darkness of the wood; and a tower, house, fortress wall with two gateways, and a wicker fence in front of ivy-clad trees testify to the presence of human beings. And the forest itself speaks of their presence: grazing animals have prevented young undergrowth from springing up between the giant trees; regular grazing of the foliage in the clearing has formed a lawn; the trunks of the copper beeches owe their columnar appearance to timely cutting of the lower branches. Whether there is wilder growth in the more distant forest remains a secret hidden in the darkness that encloses the secluded beech grove like a protective wall.[6]

Since the reforms of the Benedictine Order around 1100, forests with flowing streams had been seen as ideal sites for abbeys, monasteries, and hermitages. The wild wood had become the Western equivalent of the biblical desert. This shifting of scene was due not to an inversion from eroded wasteland to luxuriant growth, but to the loneliness that the forest also represented. The common feature of the two landscapes is desolation hostile to man. "The Lord . . . shall stretch the line of confusion over it, and the plummet of desolation."[7] Whether infertile emptiness or vegetative abundance, deserts and forests are immeasurable, timeless, and impassable. The hermit

---

[6] On the *boschetto adorno,* the pretty wood in the frightful forest, a frequent motif in Romanesque poetry whose source lies in the ancient Vale of Tempe, see Curtius, *European Literature and the Latin Middle Ages,* pp. 198, 202.

[7] Isaiah 34.11.

establishes his cell in the impenetrable undergrowth, and it was *in eremo*[8] that twelve Cistercians and their abbot were instructed to found their monastery. "We have abandoned everything: those are the words that have filled the forests with anchorites."[9] The place for self-chastisement was to be wild, swampy, and remote. The tribulations of clearing, draining, and cultivating fields would satisfy the need for an ascetic life, and a meal of beech leaves would compensate the body. Trees are the guardians of this flight from the world, silent apostles of Christianity. Bernard of Clairvaux praised oaks and beeches as his only teachers. "You will find more in forests than in books; trees and rocks will teach you things no master can make known to you,"[10] the abbot—known as the *doctor mellifluus*[11]—preaches to his pupils. The green, shade-giving trees, based in the earth and pointing to the heavens, are related from their roots to their very tops to the story of salvation. "When the Spirit is poured upon us from on high, the wilderness shall become a fruitful field, and the fruitful field shall be deemed a forest," promises the prophet Isa-

[8] The word "hermit" is derived from the Greek *eremites,* related to the adjective *eremos,* "lonely, solitary, desolate." The form "eremite" also exists in English (used by Milton: "who led'st this glorious Eremite into the desert," *Paradise Regained* 1.8). The instruction to found the monastery *in eremo* simply meant "in a desolate forest."

[9] Peter Damian (ca. 1020–1085), cited after Jacques Le Goff, *The Medieval Imagination,* trans. Arthur Goldhammer (Chicago, 1988), p. 54.

[10] Cited in Georges Duby, *History of Medieval Art* (London, 1986), p. II.58. More soberly than the mystic of Burgundy, who re-garded the accumulation of knowledge as mere vanity, Bernard's Scholastic opponent Abelard described the salutary qualities of nature as follows: "There are forces operating in seeds and plants, in the essences of trees and stones, which can stimulate or tranquillize your souls" (Duby, II.40). An illuminating discussion of the differences between Abelard and Bernard is given by Arno Borst in *Medieval Worlds: Barbarians, Heretics and Artists in the Middle Ages,* trans. Eric Hansen (Cambridge, 1991).

[11] *Doctor mellifluus,* "the mellifluous teacher" (literally, the teacher whose speech flows like honey).

iah, whose view of the forest corresponds to Gerard David's: "Happy are you who sow beside all waters, who let the feet of the ox and the ass range free."[12]

The beauty of the trees acclaims God's purposefulness in arranging all things, and the practical value of their wood proves it. To the glory of the "all in all,"[13] the beams for the abbey roof are made of hard oak, oak bark is used for kindling in the abbey's tannery, and charcoal from beechwood is used to fire up the highest temperatures in the furnaces of the Cistercian glassworks and ironworks. Everything visible is a symbol of things invisible; hidden matters are revealed in woods and waterways. "The source of every spring and river is the sea, the source of all virtue and knowledge is the Lord Jesus Christ."[14] Purity is the greatest virtue in the monastic life, and in the *clear valleys*[15] of Clairvaux its image is called *aube*.[16] So great was the joy over the purifying power and "dependable obedience" of the river Aube that one of St. Bernard's successors in the thirteenth century rapturously proclaimed the little river to be a friend that greets the monks, which excuses itself for sending "half of itself" away on a different course and without grumbling carries out every task required of it. To the Cistercian, the purity of the "beautiful spectacle" of the fish playing "beneath the crystal waves" is never clouded by a single thought of catching a few tasty accompaniments to his beech-leaf dishes

[12] Isaiah 32.15, 20.

[13] Bernard of Clairvaux, cited after Duby, *History of Medieval Art,* p. II.59.

[14] Bernard of Clairvaux, cited after Arno Borst, *Das Buch der Naturgeschichte* (Heidelberg, 1995), p. 246.

[15] *Clairvaux,* or *clairs vaux,* "clear valleys," with "clear" here conveying the sense of brightness and light.

[16] The river Aube has its source near Langres; *aube* is the French for "dawn." "Here is the final hour, the night is far on, the day is approaching, it is already breathing; night is about to pass away," St. Bernard writes in one of his *Sermons on the Song of Songs,* cited in Georges Duby, *Saint Bernard, l'art cistercien* (Paris, 1979), footnote p. 129.

during fasting periods; and the ascetic, condemned to battle with himself, interprets the rushing shoals of trout as
an image of the celestial hosts. Water symbolizes crossing
the boundary between flesh and spirit,[17] and serves a
celestial purpose—it is the only element in the life of the
poor brothers that affords them some relief from the pun-
ishments imposed for their sins. To the "charitable
stream," even the hardest work is effortless, and it expects
no reward other than "being allowed to go free when it has
carefully completed all its tasks. No matter how many
wheels it has set running swiftly, it runs forth bubbling
and seems itself to have been milled and made softer." The
artificially divided river runs tirelessly through the various
mills in the abbey's grounds; it has hardly completed its
work in the cloth mill when it throws itself "impetuously"
into the grain mill, "where it is made to carry out various
tasks and is whirled about to the greatest degree, now
grinding the wheat with the force of the millstones, now
sorting the flour from the bran with a fine sieve."[18]

The way in which the processing of wheat, bran, and
flour in the mill are interpreted is one of the curiosities of
Christian allegory in the poetry and art of the Middle
Ages. By analogy with the "transformation of the
essence" of wheat brought about by milling, the twelfth
century devised the "sacred" or "mystic mill," also known
as the "sacramental mill" or "mill of the Host." The earliest surviving depiction of this is seen in a stained-glass
window in the church of St. Denis, commissioned by the
artistically minded Abbot Suger; and another mill image
from the same century is seen on the capital of a pillar in
Vézelay.[19]

[17] Duby provides a powerful
description of this (*Saint Bernard*, p.
130).

[18] *Patrologia Latina*, ed. J. P.
Migne (Paris, 1841–1864), vol. 185,
pp. 570–572. I am grateful to
Friedrich Kur for this reference.

[19] Cf. Alois Thomas, "Die
mystische Mühle," *Christliche Kunst*
31 (1934).

"Unless a grain of wheat falls into the earth and dies, it remains alone; but if it dies, it bears much fruit,"[20] proclaims St. John's gospel, which opens glorifying the Word: "In the beginning was the Word, and the Word was with God, and the Word was God . . . all things were made through him, and without him was not anything made that was made . . . and the Word became flesh and dwelt among us."[21] This is the Logos of the mystic mill, revolving around the transfigured grain in the Apostolic mill-work. Christian teaching is nourishment, a grain of wheat is the divine Word. The prophet's grain of wheat in the Old Testament becomes the pure flour of the New, from which the bread of revelation is baked—the Host in the miracle of the Eucharist.

"I am the living bread which came down from heaven; if any one eats of this bread, he will live for ever,"[22] Jesus teaches in the synagogue at Capernaum. The roughage of the grain is the burden of death, which he took upon himself. "All flesh is grass," said Isaiah.[23] With the miracle of the virgin birth, the bread became flesh.

At the threshold of the fourteenth century, the poet Barthel Regenbogen[24] described the world as a mill of riddles. Its "well-planned costly building," fashioned in the twinkling of an eye with no need for a single tool, is set in a forest on a hilltop, the "charming form" of which rises out of a lake. "The forest signifies Christianity," the lake is the ocean of creation surrounding the earth, "in which there is many a miracle living"; Jesus, "the noble miller / gave us our life / which is his precious word";

---

[20] John 12.24.
[21] John 1.1–3, 14.
[22] John 6.51.
[23] "All flesh is grass, and all its beauty is like the flower of the field. The grass withers, the flower fades, when the breath of the Lord blows upon it; surely the people is grass." Isaiah 40.6–7.
[24] Regenbogen, a didactic poet and minnesinger, was a rival of the meistersinger Frauenlob in the period around 1300.

Adam is his squire, and the five stones of the mill correspond to the five senses; it is death that gives meaning to
the golden carriage passing through the whole mill—
"this, mortal creatures, mark ye well."[25] Life and death
are mingled in the miracle of the mill.

Another riddling poem of the period also describes a
miraculous mill on a "deep sea"; the nether millstone signifies the Old Testament, and the rotating stone is the
New; the seventy-two wooden chambers in the mill-
wheel are the world's seventy-two languages, the most
precious of which is Hebrew;[26] in its chamber of aloe
wood ("no purer wood was ever formed on Earth"), symbolizing the Virgin Mary, was born the child of the
miller, God the Father.[27]

In the course of time, the symbolism of the mill
changes. The relationship between the Old and New
Testaments moves into the background. The pure flour is
milled from many grains, and the divine wheat grows out
of a single seed. Before the whole matter of the Bible can
be pressed into the wafer of the Eucharist, the fantastic
incarnation from the Word has to take place; before the
bread can become flesh, the Virgin has to give birth to
her child. In the fifteenth century, an immaculate mill
revolves around the incarnation. Without the influence of
the Holy Spirit, the miracles of the conception of a verbal
seed and painless birth would be unthinkable, and what
could illustrate its invisible workings better than the noisy
processes of the water mill?[28] The whole mill building,

[25] *Minnesänger,* ed. Friedrich
Heinrich von der Hagen (Leipzig,
1838), pp. 347–349.
[26] The riddling poem "König
Tirol" is contained in the Codex
Manesse. See also Arno Borst, *Der
Turmbau von Babel* (Stuttgart, 1957–
1963, 1995 ed.), vol. 2/2, p. 840.

[27] Cf. Alois Thomas, "Mystische Mühle," p. 130.
[28] Christian and pagan elements
are combined in the Marian mill.
Ever since the invention of water
mills, their creative and procreative
power has fueled the human imagination; in every period of history,

with all its stones, wheels, and chambers, is now related to the Virgin Mary, and the mystery of Christmas becomes the "guiding star and core of the symbolism of the mill."[29]

The popularity of the Mill of Our Lady during the fifteenth century is seen in the Christmas carol "In Natali Domini," with its clattering refrain:

> *Terit mola farinula,*
> *Dum virgo parit tenera,*
> *Furfurem cribratum partum parit,*
> *Creatura creatorem parit,*
> *Taratantarizate, taratantarizate.*[30]

The symbolism of the Marian mill is clearly seen in a poem by the meistersinger Muskatblüt.[31] The secular millers' saying "I ride and ride unto the mill"[32] symbolizes the immaculate conception; the water is the Holy Spirit, which drives all things through its power and grace,

---

the significance of the mill has oscillated between that of a sacred shrine and that of the Devil's work. In Greek mythology, it was Myles who invented mills and their cult. Demeter, the goddess of wheat-fields, and the virgin huntress Artemis, goddess of birth, were honored as mill goddesses, and Zeus and Apollo also counted among the mill gods. It was in mills that the female demon Alphito, the monstrous goddess of white flour, got up to her tricks. She is one of Hecate's ass-legged Empusae, who also included Lamia, the devourer; these vampire-like beings, able to disguise themselves in many forms, seduce their male victims and steal away their vital forces by sucking out their blood and devouring their hearts. In later times,

Alphito declined into a mere children's bogey.

[29] Alois Thomas, "Mystische Mühle," p. 134.

[30] Daniel, *Thesaurus Hymnologicus* 4.25, cited after Alois Thomas, loc. cit. "The mill is grinding fine flour / While the gentle Virgin gives birth. / A sifted husk she bears, / The creature giving birth to its creator, / Fill the flour in the sacks, fill the flour in the sacks!"

[31] From Upper Franconia, the meistersinger Muskatblüt took part in the Hussite wars of 1420–1430, and his death is dated after 1427.

[32] "*Ich rewt vnd wuel nach einer muel.*" (*Epochen der deutschen Lyrik, 1300–1500,* ed. Eva and Hansjürgen Kiepe [Munich, 1972], pp. 210–213.)

di muel ir billig kennet!
den casten ich lauss wissen dich,
da got sin trait mit grosser arbait
werlich hatt geschuttet . . .
Was ist die gotz barmherczikait,
das ich die muel tu nennen?
maria die vil werde mait,
so muegt ir sie her kennen.[33]

The wide river of Mariolatry had its source in St.
Bernard's *clear valleys.* "I love because I love. I love in order
to love. Love is sublime when it returns to its principle, to
its origin, always going back to draw from its own spring
the waters from which it pours its stream."[34] Medieval
Mariolatry was the religious equivalent of the chivalric
cult of courtly love for the lady. Whether in sacred hymns
or courtly chansons, chivalric romance or mystical speculation, the secular and spiritual minnesingers drew on the
same humanistic sources,[35] describing in the same vocabulary and passionate tones "the same trials, desires, and
hopes of the hero." The earthly knight sitting at the feet of
the *dame sans merci* corresponded to the spiritual knight
kneeling in the dust in front of Our Lady of Mercy. The
tenderest Marian poetry flowed from the pen of the harsh
puritan Bernard of Clairvaux. The equivalent of the
"courtly paradox"[36] for the monks lay in the wealth they
created from their work, asceticism, and poverty. "You

---

[33] "Truly you should know this
mill! I tell of the chamber into
which God with heavy travail
poured his grain . . . What is God's
mercy, that I call the mill? You can
see it is Mary, the noble Virgin."
Loc. cit.

[34] St. Bernard, *Sermon sur le
Cantique des cantiques,* cited in Duby,
Saint Bernard, footnote p. 143.

[35] Duby, *Medieval Art,* II.61,
and Duby, *Saint Bernard,* pp.
149–153.

[36] "Since the love described in
minnesong is not legitimate, it
would be immoral for it to achieve
its goal. The idealization of the
loved one serves the purpose of
removing her far enough to render
her unattainable by her admirer

shall see for yourselves that one can get honey from stones, oil from the hardest rocks"[37]—the abbot would never have dreamed that his prophesy might be fulfilled in a materialistic sense. But the glowing Mariolatry of the holy troubadour survived the decline of the Cistercian abbeys, and its effects continued for centuries.[38] Its symbolism, borrowed from the Song of Solomon, is insistently developed in the Benedictine liturgy:

> I hail thee, Virgin Mary . . . who hast put to flight the powers of evil . . . Thou art the window, the door and the veil, the courtyard and the house, the temple, the earth, lily in thy virginity, rose by thy sufferings. Thou art the closed garden, the fountain of the garden that washes all who are defiled, purifies all who are corrupted and brings back life to the dead. Thou art the mistress of the ages, the hope, after God, of all generations, the king's house of rest and the abode of godhead. Thou art the star which, shining in the East, scatters the shadows of the West; the break of day; the light that knows no darkness.[39]

from the very outset; if the lady were to yield to her lover, she would have to infringe on the values he himself ascribes to her. When the lover praises his lady, he is demonstrating his incapacity to want what he wants. This is what is termed the "courtly paradox." Gert Hübner, "Erotik, Rhetorik und Gesellschaft im Mittelalter," in Rolf Bergmann, ed., *Germanistik und Kommunikationswissenschaft in Bamberg* (Bamberg, 1995), pp. 57–58.

[37] Duby, *Medieval Art*, p. II.127.

[38] The meistersinger Frauenlob (ca. 1250–1318) owed his name ("lady praise") to his song in praise of the Virgin. His sensuous poetry illustrates the relationship between the spiritual and secular forms of courtly love. *"Ey, ich sach in dem throne | ein frouwen diu was swanger | sie truog ein wundercrone | vor miner ougen anger."* ("Ay, I saw upon the throne | A lady great with child | She wore a crown of wonders | In the meadow of my sight.") In another poem, he praises the living bread to which Mary gave birth, which "lit up many a dark, cold heart" so that it "flared up in sundry sweet love" (*"manch finsterkaltes Herz erleuchtete | . . . in mannigfaltig-süsser Minne entbrannte"*).

[39] Duby, *Medieval Art*, p. II.61.

All the paintings of the birth of Christ appear in the light of a day that knows no night, depicting the nocturnal event in an eternal noontide brightness. "In the night of the Lord's birth the darkness of night was turned into the brightness of day,"[40] the *Golden Legend* (*Legenda aurea*) declares.

When the two outer wings of Gerard David's altar painting were still linked in a triptych, the interior of the forest would have opened up to reveal a depiction of the birth of Christ in this "over-bright night." The oxen and ass on the outer panels may be a reference to the scene, but the traditional interpretation of the "gatehouse with tower," in which it is claimed the contemporary viewer would "immediately" have recognized the stable lodgings described in the Christmas story, raises more questions than it answers.[41] Where has the delightful forest disappeared to in the inner painting showing the child in the crib? Why does the stable in the ruined wall bear no resemblance to the brick building in the depths of the forest? At the level of *objects,* there is apparently no continuity between the outer wings and the interior view, and what seems to be such a realistic "gatehouse with tower"[42] proves on closer examination to be inaccessible. No human being could ever have entered either by the tall gate with its pilaster-strip decoration or through the small side gate, because the water flows in front of the arches— running out of the darkness into the light, it starts its branching course through the wood as a living mirror of the azure sky.

Believer or unbeliever, no viewer of the painting in David's time could have had any doubts about the Mar-

[40] Jacobus de Voragine, *The Golden Legend: Readings on the Saints,* trans. William Granger Ryan (Princeton, 1993), vol. 1, p. 40.

[41] Cf. Hans J. Miegroet, *Gerard David* (Amsterdam, 1989), p. 232.

[42] This is the term used in the Mauritshuis catalog, "Schilderijen en beeldhouwwerken 15e en 16e eeuw," *Catalogus 1,* ed. A. B. de Vries (The Hague, 1967), p. 22.

ian significance of the inaccessible gateway,[43] the wall, and the tower. A pure virgin is a fortress: "She is a castle, where a tower stands and is encircled by walls, the two protecting one another."[44] The lonely site, the water-courses, and the building with the gabled roof enhance the castle symbolism with that of the mill.

When we open the *Forest View,* we find two famous forest dwellers on the left inside wing: the unknown donor of the altar painting depicted as St. Anthony, accompanied by a little pig,[45] with St. Jerome and his lion behind. On the right interior wing, there are two famous saints of the mill: the donor's wife depicted as St. Catherine, with sword and wheel; the dean behind her is St. Vincent, who died for his faith like all the saints—according to the legend, sailors dropped his body far out at sea tied to a millstone, "but the corpse returned to the shore faster than the sailors could get there."[46] David depicts the saint with an instrument of his martyrdom and the book of his faith, which taught him how to overcome "millstones."[47]

With the transformation of the allegorical sacramental mill into a Mariological symbol of incarnation during the fifteenth century, the "unreal" depiction of the interior of

[43] "This gate shall remain shut; it shall not be opened and no one shall enter by it." Ezekiel 44.2.

[44] Wackernagel, "Altdeutsche Predigt" 8.13: "In the Mariological symbolism of the Latins and Greeks, the image of the tower, the castle, and the wall is either related to the incarnation of Christ, with the individual parts of the fortress being interpreted as Mary's virtues, which protect her from dangers like the wall and tower; or it is regarded as an image of the protection that Mary offers to people." (Anselm Salzer, *Lexikon der Sinn-*

bilder und Beiworte Mariens [Darmstadt, 1967].)

[45] This attribute of the hermit St. Anthony, the patron saint of domestic pets, refers to the privilege of the Anthonins to breed pigs free of tax; "Anthony pigs" were allowed to roam freely. Cf. Georg Schwaiger, ed., *Mönchtum, Orden, Klöster* (Munich, 1991), p. 51.

[46] Jacobus de Voragine, *Golden Legend,* vol. 1, p. 107.

[47] On the figurative sense of the word "millstone," see Ernest Borneman, *Sex im Volksmund* (Hamburg, 1971), vol. 2, p. 11.9.

the mill gave way to the depiction of a lonely building surrounded by trees at the waterside, recognizable as a mill by its mill-wheel and ass. In Memlinc's work, the motif appears in the background of his painting of the Virgin. The same idyllic mill with an ass appears in his depiction of vanity and unchastity in a single person.[48] The delightful nude is admiring herself in a mirror; she is set in the middle of a triptych between death and the devil. With her uncovered pudenda, the sad but faithful lapdog[49] at her side, and the lecherously posed greyhounds behind her, this vain beauty is under the spell of the *disreputable mill,* whose engines are driven by the desires of the flesh. The ancient Greek word *myllein* means literally "to grind, to press the lips together," and in the figurative sense "to have sexual intercourse, particularly extramarital, to sleep with a whore"; the related word *myllos* meant "female pudenda." It is in this sense of the mill that Job has his wife grinding when he swears his innocence: "If my heart has been enticed to woman, and I have lain in wait at my neighbor's door; then let my wife grind for another, and let others bow down upon her."[50] Even today in vernacular German, "to mill" is equivalent to "engaging in sexual intercourse," and an unfaithful wife is described as a "mill that never stands idle."[51] There must always be an ass with a woman like this; and in the painting, the ignorant creature does not leave us without a lesson. On account of its wild rutting, the ass was a fertility symbol in antiquity—an honor that cost it dearly

[48] *Triptych of Earthly Vanity and Celestial Salvation* (1485 or later), Musée des Beaux-Arts, Strasbourg.

[49] On the interpretation of the terrier often encountered in Flemish painting, which can indicate marital or extramarital relations, depending on whether it is accompanying a faithful or unfaithful mistress, see

Erwin Panofsky, "Jan van Eyck's 'Arnolfini' Portrait," in W. Eugene Kleinbauer, ed., *Modern Perspectives in Western Art History* (New York, 1971), pp. 193–203.

[50] Job 31.9–10.

[51] Borneman, *Sex,* vol. 2, pp. 26.25 and 10.7.

among the Romans: the god Priapus received sacrifices of asses. The ass's sex appears in an obscene passage in Ezekiel, where the prophet describes an unchaste woman who "flaunted her nakedness" and "doted upon her paramours . . . whose members were like those of asses, and whose issue was like that of horses."[52] Balaam's talking she-ass is represented as a good animal, which unlike its angry rider can recognize the angel of the Lord.[53] And Isaiah also praises the ass: "The ox knows its owner, and the ass its master's crib."[54]

All of the virtues attributed to the ass in the fifteenth and sixteenth centuries had vices as their obverse. Depending on whether the animal, used for riding or for bearing burdens, was serving a god or a demon, it could be persistent, patient, obedient, and humble, or stubborn, stupid, sluggish, and indecent. The change in the meaning of every symbol is always based on its opposite meaning. The modest thistle-eater can turn into a pleasure-seeking debauchee at any moment, and the mystic mill can become a disreputable one.

In the work of David, Memlinc's successor in Bruges, no mills are clearly distinguishable in the background. The landscape backdrops of his enchanting little devotional paintings depicting rest during the flight from Egypt sometimes show lonely houses at the waterside in a forest setting, but they never reveal themselves as mills by including an ass or a mill-wheel.

---

[52] Ezekiel 23.18, 20.

[53] Numbers 22.22–35.

[54] Isaiah 1.3. The presence of the ox and ass at the crib is based on this passage in the Bible, although they are not mentioned in the Christmas story itself. "Israel does not know, my people does not understand," Isaiah continues in the third verse. In this way, the ass in Christianity came to represent the Old Testament, while the ox embodied the new revelation. In David's depiction of the birth, the two are lying in common worship at the crib of Christ, just as it is described in the *Golden Legend*. See the detailed note in Panofsky, *Early Netherlandish Painting*, p. 470.

"Nature likes to hide,"[55] and the painter imitates her in concealment. Any awareness of the mill is hidden away in the *Forest View.* The "gatehouse with tower" includes a double representational meaning, since the mill‑castle is a Marian pleonasm; the rhetorical excess is concealed in the forest of symbols.

The quiet, secluded atmosphere of the forest is con‑ structed using the principle of incremental layers of glaze. After Memlinc's simplified layer technique, David attempted to return to the density of the "inventor of oil painting." The warm red tone of the wall in the iridescent green of the leaves also obeys the van Eyck law of color‑ ing: the smallest interval and the greatest contrast.[56]

Painted on the eve of an age[57] in which the dispute on whether the bread and wine, at the moment they are offered to the congregation, *are,* or merely *signify,* the body and blood of Christ[58] was to degenerate into war, the burning of heretics at the stake, and iconoclasm, the *Forest View* emerges as a masterpiece of reconciliation between medieval symbolism and naturalistic "regrowth."[59] "Symbolism transforms the phenomenon into an idea,

[55] Heraclitus, fragment 123, in Kathleen Freeman, *Ancilla to the Pre‑Socratic Philosophers: A Complete Translation of the Fragments in Diels, "Fragmente der Vorsokratiker"* (Ox‑ ford, 1948; rptd. Cambridge, Mass., 1983), p. 33. *"Quae plus latent, plus patent"* is the saying of Bernard of Clairvaux: "That which lies more hidden stands all the more open."

[56] See the excellent monograph by E. Freiherr von Bodenhausen, *Gerard David und seine Schule* (Mu‑ nich, 1905).

[57] Art historians consider the unsigned and undated triptych to have been painted around 1510/1515; cf. Miegroet, *Gerard David,* p. 300.

[58] Cf. Edgar Wind, "Warburgs Begriff der Kulturwissenschaft und seine Bedeutung für die Ästhetik," in *Aby M. Warburg: Ausgewählte Schriften und Würdigungen,* ed. Dieter Wuttke (Baden‑Baden, 1992), pp. 401–417.

[59] Dürer translated *rinascita* with the German word *Wiedererwachsung* (regrowth). The word "Renais‑ sance" is a vegetation metaphor. See also Gerhart B. Ladner, "Vegeta‑ tion Symbolism and the Concept of Renaissance," in M. Meiss, ed., *Essays in Honor of Erwin Panofsky* (New York, 1961), vol. 1, pp. 303–322.

and the idea into an image, in such a way that the idea in the image always remains infinitely effective and unattainable and, even when spoken in every language, remains inexpressible."[60] The light of the clearing in the midst of the dark wood, the well-tended place in the wilderness, eloquent silence, the noontide brightness of the holy night are "harmonies of opposites" and emotive formulas[61] that show the vital energy of traditional topoi. The painter's *savoir-faire de la matière*[62] has canceled out the enigma of incarnation in what is hidden, and incarnated it in what is visible. As in Walter Benjamin's allegory, the symbol has taken up meaning into its hidden, forested interior.[63] The great-tit and the tiny dove flying through the sky; the *two* oxen and the idle ass; the weak, twining ivy; the beeches and the brick wall; the light filtering through the leaves and the crystalline water—everything visible speaks of the open secret.[64]

---

[60] Goethe, *Maximen und Reflex-ionen,* 1113.

[61] Curtius, *European Literature and the Latin Middle Ages,* p. 202. Curtius adopted the concept of polarity and the term "emotive formula" from Warburg, without taking account of the changing function of topoi over the course of history; see Dieter Wuttke, ed., *Kosmopolis der Wissenschaft: E. R. Curtius und das Warburg Institute* (Baden-Baden, 1989), pp. 258–259.

[62] *Savoir-faire de la matière* ("successful reproduction of the material") by analogy with Diderot's *savoir-faire de la chair* ("successful reproduction of the flesh"). In his "Essai sur la peinture," Diderot admires Chardin and connects the art of reproducing "a piece of fabric, a sky, a carnation, a plum with its sugary frost, a peach with its fuzz" with the art of portraiture. Diderot, *Oeuvres* (Bibliothèque de la Pléiade), ed. André Billy (Paris, 1951), p. 1124. In the age of the Enlightenment, the Bible was no longer the key to nature, but itself subject to its laws. *"Rien n'est beau que le vrai"* (Only the truth is beautiful) is the aesthetic motto of the eighteenth century. Even the tiniest and most inconspicuous things point to an *inner* truth, the eternal nature of transient things. In the still life, *savoir-faire de la matière* makes the souls of lifeless objects visible. Cf. Lévi-Strauss, *Look, Listen, Read,* p. 27.

[63] Walter Benjamin, *The Origin of German Tragic Drama,* trans. John Osborne (London, 1977), p. 165.

[64] Ivy, with its "feet that twist and flex" (Ovid, *Metamorphoses*

At the end of his mocking praise of the foolish world, Erasmus lets Folly realize that even pious withdrawal from the world, the mystics' state of being "beside themselves," is very similar to the follies without which humanity cannot exist. The inexpressibility of blissful rapture over the presence of the Creator in his creation "is the part of Folly which cannot be taken away by the transformation of life but is made perfect,"[65] says Folly out of wisdom.

When the fanaticism of his contemporaries came to beggar all description, Erasmus withdrew into a forest of a work—following an ancient tradition, he called his four-volume *Art of Preaching* an *opus sylvanum*. "The elemental, absolute, and incorruptible mysteries of the knowledge of God reveal themselves in the more than luminous darkness of silence."[66]

The depiction of the forest as a place in which everything is echo, connection, and correspondence[67] has a

---

10.100) as a Dionysian decoration in antiquity symbolized the constancy of vegetative energy and the persistence of desire. The source of this symbol of faithfulness and eternal life is a strange reversal: the evergreen climber flowers in the fall, grows during the winter, and in the spring bears its poisonous black berries. Shade, night, and winter coincide with unwilting leaves, twining suppleness, and unexpected fruitfulness. In the clearing with the ass of the Old Testament, the ivy has not yet found its hold on the Christian tree, the true tree of life that the great-tit is proclaiming.

Concerning the *two* oxen, the *Golden Legend* says, "And a few days before Christ's birth, as men were ploughing their fields, the oxen spoke to the ploughmen and said, 'Men will decrease, but the grain

will increase.'" *Golden Legend*, vol. 1, p. 40.

[65] Erasmus, *Praise of Folly*, trans. Betty Radice (Harmondsworth, 1971), p. 207.

[66] (Pseudo-)Dionysius the Areopagite, cited after Duby, *Saint Bernard*, footnote p. 141. In the tradition of Dionysian theology, "the Light of divine origin" can be called, "in its overbrightness, 'darkness'" (*Historisches Wörterbuch der Philosophie* [Basel, 1971–1995], vol. 5, p. 284. Cf. the melancholy attempts by German cultural scholars, confusing "darkness" in a modern way with "obscurantism," to disprove Panofsky's interpretation of Suger. (See Bruno Reudenbach, "Ein Werk der Dunkelheit," *Frankfurter Allgemeine Zeitung*, 3 January 1996.)

[67] In the second verse of Baudelaire's *"Correspondances,"* which

long history. In the light of its tradition, the *Forest View* appears to be the image of a *realm of similarity* in which the widest variety of minds from the most different periods of history can encounter one another:

> *And this our life exempt from publike haunt,*
> *Findes tongues in trees, bookes in the running brookes,*
> *Sermons in stones, and good in euery thing.*[68]

As his life was drawing to its close, St. Bernard came to feel he had turned into a fabled monster (*chimaera*)[69] of his century, and regretted his *vita monstruosa*. "Neither cleric nor layman," he had long since ceased to lead a contemplative life in his monastic habit. Frightened by his own works, he himself no longer understood what he was doing; but he never said a word about the "abyss" into which he had been cast.[70] His last words were, "It is time for this old, fruitless tree to be chopped down."[71]

---

stands as the epigraph to this interpretation of the forest, the sounds correspond to the tones of colors and scents:

Comme de longs échos qui de loin se confondent
Dans une ténébreuse et profonde unité,
Vaste comme la nuit et comme la clarté,
Les parfums, les couleurs et les sons se répondent.

As long-drawn echoes mingle and transfuse
Till in a deep, dark unison they swoon,
Vast as the night or as the vault of noon—
So are commingled perfumes, sounds, and hues.

(*Poems of Baudelaire: A Translation of "Les Fleurs du Mal,"* by Roy Campbell [London, 1952], p. 8.)

[68] Shakespeare, *As You Like It* 2.1, in *The Norton Facsimile: The First Folio of Shakespeare*, ed. Charlton Hinman, 2nd ed. (New York, 1996), p. 208.

[69] In the Middle Ages, *chimaera* had not yet acquired the sense of "illusion," but referred to the fire-breathing monster of Greek mythology, a mixed creature with the head of a lion, the body of a goat, and the tail of a snake. Cf. Jürgen Miethke, "Bernhard von Clairvaux," in *Die Zisterzienser* (exhib. cat., Cologne, 1980), p. 55.

[70] Loc. cit.

[71] Cited after Albert Christian Sellner, *Immerwährender Heiligenkalender* (Frankfurt, 1993), p. 280.

At a hidden level, the ascetic and the libertine correspond to one another.[72] Baudelaire's *"Le Goût du néant"*[73]
reads like an extended echo and reverberation from the
twelfth century, in which a fabulous monster addresses us
at the close of his "monstrous life":

> *Morne esprit, autrefois amoureux de la lutte,*
> *L'Espoir, dont l'éperon attisait ton ardeur,*
> *Ne veut plus t'enfourcher! Couche-toi sans pudeur,*
> *Vieux cheval dont le pied à chaque obstacle bute.*

> *Résigne-toi, mon coeur; dors ton sommeil de brute.*

> *Esprit vaincu, fourbu! Pour toi, vieux maraudeur,*
> *L'amour n'a plus de goût, non plus que la dispute;*
> *Adieu donc, chants du cuivre et soupirs de la flûte!*
> *Plaisirs, ne tentez plus un coeur sombre et boudeur!*

[72] The word "libertine" first
appears in English in Wyclif's Bible
translation of 1382, according to the
Oxford English Dictionary. In the
1540s, the word came to be used
for fanatics and Anabaptists in
northern France. In 1544, Calvin
accused "libertines or spirituals" of
moral dissipation. Cf. *Historisches
Wörterbuch*, vol. 5, pp. 272–273.

[73] *Poems of Baudelaire: A Translation of "Les Fleurs du Mal*," by Roy
Campbell (London, 1952), p. 104:

The Thirst for the Void

*My soul, you used to love the battle's
    rumble.*
*Hope, whose sharp spur once kindled you
    like flame,*
*Will mount on you no more. Rest,
    without shame,*
*Old charger, since at every step you
    stumble.*

*Sleep now the sleep of brutes, proud
    heart: be humble.*

O broken raider, for your outworn mettle,
*Love has no joys, no fight is worth
    disputing.*
*Farewell to all the trumpeting and
    fluting!*
*Pleasure, have done, when brooding
    shadows settle,*

*The blooms of spring are vanquished by
    the nettle.*

*As snows devour stiff corpses in their
    welter,*
*Time wolfs my soul in, minute after
    minute.*
*I've seen the world and everything that's
    in it,*
And I no longer seek in it for shelter;

*Come, Avalanche! and sweep me helter-
    skelter.*

Le Printemps adorable a perdu son odeur!

Et le Temps m'engloutit minute par minute,
Comme la neige immense un corps pris de roideur;
Je contemple d'en haut le globe en sa rondeur
Et je n'y cherche plus l'abri d'une cahute.

Avalanche, veux-tu m'emporter dans ta chute?

POSTCRIPT. In 1985–1987, during restoration in the Mauritshuis, the old overpainting was completely removed from the *Forest View,* and in the process the watercourses on the left panel disappeared along with the brickwork characteristic of the wall.

The process also revealed a second gable roof, a façade rosette in the wall above the small gateway (similar rosettes are used for decoration in Cistercian monasteries; see Georges Duby, *Die Kunst der Zisterzienser* [Stuttgart, 1993], p. 86, fig. 71), and a fantastic, crenellated crown above the tall gateway. The Lombard painter who was active with David in Bruges copied the master's *Forest View* in a "Rest on the Flight into Egypt." The panel, 61 × 53 cm, is in the Durazzo-Palavicini Gallery in Genoa. See Georges Marlier, *Ambrosius Benson et la peinture à Bruges au temps de Charles-Quint* (Damme, 1957), index. In the foreground of a wooded hamlet, the Virgin is nursing the child, while Joseph is taking a nap under a David beech, beside a grazing ass. Behind him are seen the figures of a peasant and a horseman, and there is a farmhouse half-hidden in a copse in the very background. On the right side, a David brook is flowing through a David forest, and on the left there is a winding path linking the hamlet's houses. The first building is the peculiar David one, with tower and crenellated wall, although the little gateway in it, with an open gate, lies directly alongside the large one. Benson's depiction of the Flight moved the restorers in The Hague to regard their predecessors' overpainted watercourses as "pure fantasy," and to interpret the building as a farmhouse. But what would a single farmhouse be doing in the middle of a forest, and what would it have to do with the birth of Christ? The two panels now look as if someone had cut out the central strip of Benson's depiction of the flight, showing the figures, and used the remaining parts as the outer panels of the David triptych—so that the copyist has suddenly become the master. At the time when Benson parted company with David, the master refused to hand over to the Lombard two chests of patterns and sketches. Benson brought a lawsuit against the old painter, and in the end received his sketches. See Hans J. Miegroet, *Gerard David* (Amsterdam, 1989), p. 29. Which opinion was the correct one is a secret that remains hidden in the forest.

... And like a wyvern's trunk was all the rest.
He had two fore-paws, shaggy arm-pit high,
* Whence breast and back and both flanks shimmered off,*
* Painted with ring-knots and whorled tracery.*
Nor Turk nor Tartar ever wrought coloured stuff
* So rainbow-trammed and broidered; never wore*
* Arachne's web such dyes in warp and woof.*

DANTE

II
The Dragon-Slayer
in the Sea of Leaves

hile the first Flemish shoots of the genre "forest landscape" were springing up in the city on the sanded-up Zwin, a very different seed in the forest genre was coming up in Regensburg, on the Danube. Albrecht Altdorfer's subject is not a cultivated forest, but the wild wood. *Silva,* the most ancient face of nature, is "the tireless womb of generation, the first outline of forms, the matter of bodies and the foundation of substance," as Silvestris writes in his *Cosmographia.*[1]

St. George, in black armor on a white horse, has come thundering through a leafy forest in which the trees can hardly be seen for the leaves. The mounted knight looks tiny in this godforsaken wilderness, which wells up over him boundlessly into the darkness. The thick plumes on his helmet merge into the feathering of the rampant foliage; the light traces feverish ripples in the masses of leaves, tossed by the wind in the sultry atmosphere of the primeval forest. There is no sign of a princess, although the dense thickets have opened slightly onto a view of

---

[1] Bernard Silvestre, *Description de l'univers,* 2.47–48, cited after Georges Duby, *Saint Bernard, l'art cistercien* (Paris, 1976), p. 110.

hilly farmland lying under blue mountains on the low horizon. But this pathway into the world has been barred by a flesh-red monster with a crest along its blackish back; with its fin-wings stretched out alongside its bulging-eyed toad's head, the beast is baring its teeth and stretching out its tongue at the white horse. The knight is pausing motionless in the surging yellow-green sea of leaves, as if doubting his own ability to slay dragons.

The military tribune from Cappadocia had traveled far to reach the dragon's realm. The monster lived in Libya in a "pond as large as a lake,"[2] poisoning the town and countryside with its pestilent breath. Two sheep every day were not enough to satisfy its hunger, and it yearned for human flesh. Many sons and daughters of the land of the date-tree had already been sacrificed, and finally the victim's wretched lot had fallen to the king's only daughter—and, filled with missionary zeal, the first of the fourteen auxiliary saints came to her rescue. His lance broke the strength of the winged serpent, but did not kill it outright. "Then he called to the maiden: 'Have no fear, child! Throw your girdle around the dragon's neck! Don't hesitate!' When she had done this, the dragon rose and followed her like a little dog on a leash."[3] When the princess brought the dragon into the town on a lead, the inhabitants of Silena fled in panic and horror and crawled away into the mountain caves to hide. This was the moment for the crusader to convert the heathens from fear of the dragon to fear of God. When he promised to free the country forever from the monster of the lake, the king and all his people—twenty thousand in all, "not counting the women and children"[4]—came flocking to receive baptism. St. George then finally drew his sword and put an end to the dragon, ordering him "to

---

[2] *Golden Legend,* vol. 1, p. 238.   [4] Ibid., p. 240.
[3] Ibid., p. 239.

be moved out of the city, whereupon four yoke of oxen hauled him away into a broad field outside the walls."[5]

For centuries, the only monster in the legend of St. George had been a king or emperor[6] who persecuted Christians and who had the tribune, "a native of Cappadocia"[7] beheaded with a sword after monstrous tortures. In the twelfth century, Crusaders returning from the East embellished the fable of their patron saint with the tale of the slaying of the dragon and rescuing of the Libyan king's daughter. The dragon legend is a chimera that was grafted onto the story in the age of the minnesingers, and it soon completely supplanted the legend of the saint's martyrdom. It was this grafting of ancient dragon-slaying elements onto the Christian rootstock that made St. George's transformation into an earthly representative of the archangel Michael so successful. No champion of the faith seems better suited to appropriating elements of the pagan gods than the great martyr of Cappadocia, who was broken on the wheel, plunged into a cauldron of boiling lead, quartered by horses, had his head studded with sixty nails, and died three times and came back to life three times. Who better to embody the courage of Perseus, the audacity of Cadmus, the strength of Hercules, and the valor of Bellerophon than the intrepid "soldier of Christ" from a land renowned for horse-breeding?

The ancient origins of the saga of St. George and the dragon are suggested by the setting of the story in the *Golden Legend.* "The Greeks give to Africa the name of

---

[5] Loc. cit.

[6] In the sixth century, the legend of St. George was adapted in Byzantium to meet the needs of the High Church. The unhistorical King Datian of Persia was replaced by Diocletian, the notorious perse-cutor of Christians, and the martyr-dom story was put into a courtly and rhetorical form. Cf. *Lexikon für Theologie und Kirche,* ed. Walter Kasper (Freiburg, 1995), vol. 4, pp. 476–477.

[7] *Golden Legend,* vol. 1, 238.

Libya, and they call the sea lying in front of it the Libyan Sea."[8] As they believed, the land in which Atlas[9] bore the vault of heaven on his shoulders was the edge of the world; its situation and climate were favorable to broods of dragons and all sorts of hybrid creatures; in this hotbed of demonic beings, it was the swift-footed, sharp-eyed sileni[10] who most resembled human beings—although they had the ears, tails, and legs of horses. These horse-men are also found in Pliny as music-loving elemental spirits of the wooded parts of the Atlas mountains, in the company of goat-legged friends:

It is said that in the day-time none of its inhabitants are seen, and that all is silent with a terrifying silence like that of the desert, so that a speechless awe creeps into the hearts of those who approach it, and also a dread of the peak that soars above the clouds and reaches the neighbourhood of the moon's orb; also

[8] Pliny, *Natural History,* trans. H. Rackham, W. H. S. Jones, and D. E. Eichholz, 10 vols., Loeb Classical Series (London, 1938–1963), V.i (1), vol. 2, p. 219.

[9] "Mount Atlas . . . is reported to rise into the sky out of the middle of the sands, a rugged eminence covered with crags on the side facing towards the coast of the Ocean to which it has given its name, but shaded by dense woods and watered by gushing springs on the side facing Africa." Ibid., V.i (5–6), vol. 2, p. 223.

[10] Satyrs and sileni are indistinguishable in terms of their outward appearance. They are both elemental spirits of the wooded mountains, related to the centaurs, with equine characteristics in the ears, tail, legs, body hair, and phallus. They tend the mountains, and fresh springs burst up under their hoof-marks. The sileni were originally multiple, but in the fourth century, Silenos appears—the serious, wise, music-loving forest god and teacher of Dionysus, in whose retinue his sons, the sileni, abandon themselves to the hunting of nymphs in Dionysian frenzy. Satyrs and sileni embody unbridled sensual lust and the fertility of untamed nature. In Italy, Silenus merged into Silvanus. (Cf. W. H. Roscher, *Ausführliches Lexikon der griechischen und römischen Mythologie* [Leipzig, 1909–1915; rptd. Hildesheim, 1965], vol. 4, pp. 444–531.)

that at night this peak flashes with frequent fires and swarms with the wanton gambols of Goat-Pans and Satyrs, and echoes with the music of flutes and pipes and the sound of drums and cymbals. These stories have been published by celebrated authors, in addition to the labours performed in this region by Hercules and Perseus. It is an immense distance away, across unexplored country.[11]

As large as a sea and surrounded by fertile land, Lake Triton,[12] fed by the River Triton, was thought to have lain inland from the inhospitable shores of Syrtis Minor, between wooded hills and the desert. The monstrous fauna of this fabulous region included not only Tritonic fish and snake demons, but also the three Graeae[13] and the three Gorgons.[14] The beauty of the mortal Medusa was transformed by Pallas Athene into a winged monster with serpent locks, a snub nose, eyes bulging out of their sockets, a grinning mouth with boar's teeth, and a protruding tongue. One of the epithets of valiant Athena was "Tritogeneia," since she sprang from her father's head in full armor on the shores of Lake Triton, after Zeus had

[11] Pliny, *Natural History*, V.i (7), vol. 2, p. 223.

[12] The legendary Lake Triton seems actually to have existed at one time in the southern Tunisian plain. Shott el Djerid is today's name for the salt lake that remains, much of it covered by the wandering sands. The great plain of the Erg Desert seems formerly to have been a flourishing cultivated area. Today's bare highlands and mountains were once densely forested. Cf. *Paulys Realencyclopädie der classischen Altertumswissenschaft* (Munich, 1939), 2nd series, half-vol. 13, pp. 305–323.

[13] "Graeae" = old women. The three shriveled, gray-haired sisters of the Gorgons, who were blind and toothless, shared one eye and one tooth between them. They lived in a cave in the Atlas Mountains. Perseus stole their prostheses and threw the eye and the tooth into Lake Triton.

[14] "Gorgo" = terrible of gaze and countenance. Stheno, the strong, and Euryale, the far-leaping, were immortal, but Medusa, the Ruler, could be killed. After she had been beheaded, Athena placed the face on her breastplate, the aegis.

swallowed the pregnant Metis.[15] The goddess of war, science, and the arts was the patron of chariots and horses, inventor of bridles, and protectress of dragon-slayers. According to an Attic legend, it was she who beheaded the pregnant Medusa, from whose rump Poseidon's children sprang—the winged horse Pegasus[16] and the warrior Chrysaor.[17] According to other traditions, the invincible virgin was satisfied merely to provide protection while Perseus did the bloody deed.

> *... And as*
> *the son of Danaë flew above the desert sands*
> *of Libya, from the memorable spoils*
> *of serpent-haired Medusa, drops of blood*
> *fell to the earth; and these the ground absorbed,*
> *and then gave life to snakes of varied sorts.*
> *And that's why Libya is snake-infested.*[18]

With Medusa's head in his magic wallet, Perseus flew over Libya, driven back and forth by turbulent winds. From the ethereal heights, he would not have been able to spot the town of Silena—because in antiquity there was no such place. Neither the Greek nor the Roman writers would have dreamt of ascribing mountain and forest demons to a city; the urbanized sileni are pure Crusader fantasy. Silena is a chimeric city grafted onto the legend in the age in which St. George doffed the skin of the martyr and put on the rattling armor of the dragon-slayer. And the metamorphosis of the saint was followed by the muta-

---

[15] "Metis" = counsel, skill, cunning. When Zeus swallowed his first wife, he internalized her wisdom and cunning.

[16] The etymology of "Pegasus" is unclear; one of the possible explanations suggests "white horse."

[17] "Chrysaor" = golden sword.

[18] Ovid, *Metamorphoses* 4.617–620 (p. 134 in the translation by Allen Mandelbaum [New York, 1993]).

tion of the evil monster; in the thirteenth century, the wingless Romanesque dragon snake sheds its skin and reappears as a Gothic dragon with the serrated crest of a lizard and the leathery wings of the bat, that light-shunning creature inhabiting rocky clefts and dark caves. The bat's wings of the demonic serpent seem to have come to the West from China, by Tartar routes.[19] At the time when Jacobus de Voragine was compiling the *Legenda aurea* in Genoa, using a variety of sources for his saints' lives, the Mongol empire stretched from the coast of the Yellow Sea to the borders of Europe. The dragon slain by St. George in his account differs from the ancient ones in its ability to change its element. Half serpent of Mars, half Andromeda's sea monster, it lives first in water and then in the land of mountains and caves. Like the Greco-Roman heroes, the knight finds that dragons cannot be killed at a single stroke. It was in vain that Perseus plunged his blade up to the hilt into the shoulder of the snorting beast, barely managing to escape its frenzied, greedy jaws; it was only when his sickle penetrated a weak spot in the monster's back, covered in shell-like scales, and then its flanks and soft belly, where its massive rump narrowed to a slender fishtail, that the dragon gave up its evil spirit. Cadmus's battle with the dragon also passed through two phases:

> An ancient forest lay at hand: no ax
> had ever violated it. A mass
> of rocks, a grotto forming a low arch,
> stood there among dense shrubs and pliant boughs;
> and from that cave abundant waters gushed.
> That grotto served a serpent as his den—

[19] Cf. Jurgis Baltrušaitis, *Le Moyen Age fantastique* (Paris, 1981), chapter 5. "Tartars" was the name given to the Mongols, because to the West they seemed to have emerged straight from Tartarus.

a serpent that was sacred unto Mars.
He had a golden crest; his eyes flashed flames;
and all his body was puffed out with poison.
He had three tongues that flickered, and his teeth
were set in three rows.[20]

The monster attacks Cadmus's companions; "His fangs
kill some, and some his crushing coils, / and some he kills
with his infested breath."[21] Cadmus throws a well-aimed
rock, and it bounces off the hard scales of the serpent's
hide; but the iron tip of his javelin finds its way into the
beast's innards. Mad with pain, the dragon tears the shaft
out of the wound,

but in his bones the iron tip holds fast.
At that, his wrath can only grow. The veins
along his throat are swollen; his dread jaws
are flecked with white foam; even as they scrape
along the ground, his scales resound; the breath
that issues from his Stygian cave infects
the air. He writhes in giant coils, and then
he stiffens like a towering trunk, erect,
or, like a swollen river, thrusts ahead,
smashing the trees with his onrushing chest.[22]

Holding his spear in front of him, Cadmus pushes back
the monster's thrusting jaws and finally plants the iron
deep into its throat; its neck is skewered to the trunk of an
oak tree.

Beneath the serpent's mass, the oak tree bends;
and at the lashing of his tail, it groans.
the victor looks at the defeated hulk;
but suddenly he hears a voice (although

[20] Ovid, *Metamorphoses* 3.28–34.   [22] Ibid., ll. 71–80.
[21] Ibid., ll. 48–49.

Jacopo Bellini, Paris, Louvre, Cabinet des Dessins

> *he can't tell where it comes from, it is heard):*
> *"Why, Cadmus, do you stare at that slain snake?*
> *You, too, will be a snake at whom men gaze."*[23]

The hero, who has faced the monster fearlessly, freezes in dread at these prophetic words. Horrified, the dragon-slayer recognizes himself in the dragon. But Pallas Athene hurries to him and advises him to scatter the snake's teeth in the ground. Soon the discord-bearing seed begins to germinate:

> *... and from the furrows sprang*
> *spear-tips, then casques with waving plumes, and next,*
> *shoulders and chests, and weapon-bearing arms:*
> *a harvest crop of warriors with shields.*[24]

[23] Ibid., ll. 95–98.   [24] Ibid., ll. 107–110.

From the fourteenth to the sixteenth century, the horse and knight in armor show every sign of being the descendants of the dragon's-tooth seed. In perfect mimicry, the forces of "good" imitate the forces of "evil." Toothed excrescences, scales, spikes, and claws sprout from the armor of both knight and horse; fins grow at the elbow joints, shells at the crook of the knees; dragons spread their bat's wings on helmets; grimacing monkey-devils on the masked visor have bat's wings instead of ears; and the pleated apron of the armor tapers off into claws. Battle helmets show dragon's heads with gaping jaws; toothed crests form the spine of the horse's armor or grow out of its bridle; and the dragonlike shape of the steed's face is adapted perfectly to the horse's anatomy.

The resemblance between the horse and the monster is produced not only by the mask; mettlesomeness is one of the horse's essential characteristics. The dragon's fury, like the horse's, is a Gorgon quality. *Blémma gorgón,*[25] an "eye full of fire" is one of the characteristics of the easily frightened horse, whose eyes bulge out of their sockets when it loses its head; its mettlesome disposition, unpredictable frenzy, foaming at the mouth, rearing up, stamping and neighing with fury are the demonic qualities that the horse shares both with the dragon and with Medusa, the Gorgon.[26]

It was the horror of encountering its own sinister likeness that led to the sowing of the chthonic dragon's tooth-seeds; and the travesty of the dragon represented by Christian knights grows out of a similar recognition: the

[25] Cf. the excellent work by Marcel Detienne and Jean-Pierre Vernant, *Cunning Intelligence in Greek Culture and Society,* trans. Janet Lloyd (Chicago, 1991), p. 190.

[26] Ibid., p. 191: "All this would suggest that in Greek thought the Gorgon symbolized one essential aspect of the horse." The word "dragon" is derived from the Greek *drakon,* meaning "flashing-eyed."

dragon of unbelief can encounter nothing more horrify-
ing than its own mirror image.

"In country districts, the chief obstacle to Christianity
was offered by the tenacious survival of anthropomorphic
cults; here the problem became one of still further
humanizing the divinities of springs, trees, and mountains, in order to rob them of their prestige."[27] Transformed into human beings and placed in an urban setting,
the sileni of the *Legenda aurea* can manage without horses'
limbs; their paganism is the cloven hoof that the Greek
gods of vegetation and husbandry share with the Christian devil. It is no accident that the battle with the dragon
takes place in a land whose inhabitants dwell in forests,
mountains, and caves. "The name George is derived from
geos, meaning earth, and *orge,* meaning to work."[28] The
color of this "martyr of indestructible life"[29] is fresh green,
his saint's day is April 23, the day on which the grazing
season starts and livestock are turned out into the fields in
many regions; the sinister dragon powers have been
tamed, and "the myth changes, but the custom remains."[30]
The festivals and games held in honor of St. George are
Christianizations of the pagan celebrations of spring; on
April 23, Slovenians and Gypsies used to hold processions with a young man dressed in green birch branches

[27] Jean Seznec, *The Survival of
the Pagan Gods: The Mythological Tradition and Its Place in Renaissance
Humanism and Art,* trans. Barbara F.
Sessions (New York, 1953), footnote, p. 13.

[28] *Golden Legend,* vol. 1, p. 238.

[29] "The legend of St. George
belongs to the class of martyrs'
romances of late antiquity, whose
heroes and heroines have been
described as 'martyrs of indestruc-

tible life' due to the hyperbole used
to celebrate and exemplify the
Christian hope of eternal life."
Lexikon für Theologie und Kirche, ed.
Michael Buchberger, Josef Höfer,
and Karl Rahner, vol. 4, 2nd ed.
(Breisgau, 1986), p. 476.

[30] Sir James George Frazer, *The
Golden Bough: A Study in Magic and
Religion,* abr. ed. (London, 1922), p.
126.

from head to foot, "Green George," which ended with him being plunged into water to conjure up rain. The unbridled fertility of the ancient forest and pastoral gods was incorporated into "St. Fearer."[31] As the patron saint of herdsmen, shepherds, and their flocks, ensuring growth, fertility, and invulnerability, St. George, like his cloven-hoofed predecessors, must have secret knowledge of nature's powers. Those who wore St. George thalers as amulets were proof against blows, stab wounds, and bullets; they could never fall from horses, and even the raging sea was unable to harm them. *In tempestate securitas* was the motto on the reverse of the dragon-slaying coin, set under the image of a ship in a storm.[32]

The voyage across the sea of life, together with this Stoic motto, was a familiar Christian emblem that was of ancient provenance: "A new ship / with fresh sails set / is tested by the tempest. / Manliness and steadfastness / are seen in times of trouble"[33] is the moral adapted from Seneca given in the epigraph. Confidence even in tempestuous times[34] is shown by St. George when, confronted by evil, he is not overcome by a storm of emotions. Albrecht Altdorfer has caught the critical moment before the turning point, while the decision to

---

[31] "In Walferdingen every Easter Monday, a prayer against fear is addressed to St. George, using the name 'St. *Ferter*' (=*Fürchter,* fearer)." *Handwörterbuch des Deutschen Aberglaubens,* ed. E. Hoffmann-Krayer and Hanns Bächtold-Stäubli (Berlin and Leipzig, 1930–1931), vol. 3, p. 648.

[32] Ibid., pp. 657–658.

[33] *Emblemata: Handbuch zur Sinnbildkunst des XVI. and XVII. Jahrhunderts,* ed. Arthur Henkel and

Albrecht Schöne (Stuttgart, 1967; rev. ed. 1976), p. 1465.

[34] *Tempestas* = 1) a point in time, a space of time, a season, period; 2) weather, thunderstorm, storm; 3) an onslaught, surge, impetuosity; 4) a stormy time, unrest, a terrible mishap. *Securitas* = freedom from care; 1) unconcern, composure, fearlessness; 2) pejoratively: negligence, carelessness, heedlessness; 3) safety, security, freedom from danger.

slay the dragon is impeded, still being held in the balance. It is nature that reflects the drama of the spirit—in the forest in which battle is done with the dragon—just as it does in the cosmic panorama of his great *Battle of Alexander at Issus.* The "cuteness" of the monster is deceptive; the emotional aspect of the figure is seen in the boundless sea of leaves.

No one either before or since Altdorfer has depicted the dragon-slaying episode in a primeval forest, and no other image of St. George shows the knight paralyzed by fright. In the painted versions of the battle with the dragon, both north and south of the Alps, the scenery is provided by the mountains, rocky caves, city, and lake of the golden legend of St. George, and if the dragon is not dead yet, no fear-struck saint is likely to hesitate before plunging his lance into its throat. In later works, Altdorfer also showed the moment at which the dragon is slain against a more or less classical backdrop.[35]

The ingenious notion of presenting the martyr of indestructible life in the rampant verdure of a forest, held in the spell of the dragon, may have come to Altdorfer from his reading of Jacobus de Voragine. The special element in the Silena story would have been as clear to him as the relationship between "Green George" and the sileni. No one knew better than Altdorfer that the carefree sensuality of the *gens sylvatica,* a people scorning any form of clothing, could be in its element only in the forest; he had a soft spot for forest people both wild and devout, often depicting wild women with or without wild animal skins, wild men with or without loincloths, and families of satyrs, witches, and hermits in forests that show the

---

[35] See the exhibition catalog for the 450th anniversary of Albrecht Altdorfer's death (Berlin and Regensburg, 1988), ed. Hans Mielke, p. 144, figure 68, and p. 116, figure 51.

signs of dying trees.[36] He had a taste that delighted in the limply hanging branches of ailing spruces, bare boughs from which creepers and lichen are hanging down, and the plumelike shoots of trees exhausted by pollarding.[37] Like all the painters of the Danube school, he reveled in flourishes, and everything that was puffy, wavy, feathered, flowing flattered his taste.

At every level at which it can be regarded, Altdorfer's wilderness showing the battle with the dragon represents the opposite pole from David's forest view. The small picture measures only 28 × 22 cm, and it is painted on parchment like a miniature.[38] The use of oil on a ground of this type is unusual; the *alla prima* technique is a break with tradition. Although the yellow-green leaf flourishes are painted into the olive-colored dark areas, the highlights in them have been enhanced afterward; but the painting as a whole is no longer constructed layer by layer, and the completed picture was not based on prior analysis. The painter's brush is free, his calligraphy is lively; his hand has no wish to conceal itself, and art triumphs in the play of lines. Altdorfer has no interest in clear-cut design for leaves and trees; he is fascinated by the cascades of light produced by the wind in the turbulence of the sea of leaves.

On a scale drawn between the poles of his time, Altdorfer stands wholly on the visual and painterly side; fusion and movement are characteristic of his style, and even the intrinsic value of the color is secondary. His for-

---

[36] Ibid., p. 130, figure 61; p. 98, figure 40; p. 74; p. 34, figure 7; p. 142, figure 67.

[37] On pollarding and the decline of the forest from the Middle Ages to the eighteenth century, see Hansjörg Küster's instructive *Geschichte der Landschaft in Mitteleuropa* (Munich, 1995).

[38] The parchment is mounted on limewood; cf. Franz Winzinger, *Albrecht Altdorfer. Die Gemälde* (Munich, 1975), pp. 74–75.

est is not a forest of symbols, not an "image drawn together in the mirror of the mind"[39] that could be identical with the object depicted. Altdorfer's *imaginary* sea of leaves has the emotional value of music, and it is still awaiting a composer capable of reading the score inscribed in its rustling foliage.[40]

[39] Goethe, *Gedenkausgabe,* vol. 23, p. 868.

[40] Rossini would have made a suitable interpreter. It seems to me that a certain satirical element is as unmistakable in this small painting of St. George as in Altdorfer's paintings of satyrs. For the American art historian Larry Silver, by contrast, these paintings show a "Darwinistic heroism in the struggle for survival" ("Forest Primeval: Albrecht Altdorfer and the German Wilderness Landscape," *Simiolus* 13 [1983], pp. 5–43). This Darwinist corridor in the fifteenth and sixteenth centuries was then extended by Simon Schama to lead straight to Nazism (*Landscape and Memory* [New York, 1995]). The *straight* way leads into the dark forest! An undisturbed sense of their own good intentions seems to have concealed from the talented historians Silver and Schama the fact that something of the violence whose roots they seek in the past has crept into their own methodology.

The ancients describe man as being a world in miniature—and the description is certainly a well-chosen one; for, just as man is made up of earth, water, air and fire, so also is the body of the earth . . . Grass grows in the fields and leaves grow on the trees, and each year the greater part of both is renewed. We can say, therefore, that the Earth has bodily life; its flesh is the soil, its bones are the connected layers of rock that form the mountains, its cartilage is tuff, and the arteries of water are its blood. The pool of blood surrounding the heart is like the ocean. Man breathes by the rise and fall of blood in the arteries; and thus it is in the Earth as well, in the rising and ebbing of the seas. The world's life-heat comes from the fire that is spread in the whole Earth, and the seat of its bodily life lies in the glowing embers that stream out of the Earth at various places.

LEONARDO DA VINCI

III
The Inhabited Cloth
and the Garment
of the Earth

 onrad Gesner[1] still believed that dragons were real creatures, and he devoted a long chapter to them in his book about serpents, describing them as giant serpents, with or without crests, whose dragon-nature was evident from the fact that they ate their own kind.

---

[1] The humanist universal scholar, naturalist, and physician Conrad Gesner (1516–1565) helped lay the foundations for modern zoology in his five-volume *Historia animalium* (1551–1587). Edward Topsell's *Historie of Foure-Footed Beastes* (London, 1607; rptd. Amsterdam, 1973) and *Historie of Serpents* (London, 1608; rptd. Amsterdam, 1973) were based on Gesner; dragons are discussed in the *Historie of Serpents*, pp. 153–173.

The Christ Child appears as a friendly dragon-tamer during the Flight into Egypt, as the *Gospel of Pseudo-Matthew* relates. When the Holy Family wants to rest in a cave, many dragons suddenly come out of it. "Then Jesus got down from his mother's lap," commanding the dragons not to harm any of them. He reassures Mary and Joseph with the words "Have no fear, and do not think that I am a child . . . all wild beasts must be docile before me."[2] Lions and leopards as gentle as lambs accompany the fugitives into the desert. On the third day of their flight, the miracle child on his mother's lap turns toward a palm tree, in the shadow of which the fugitives have sat down, and says, "Bend down your branches, O tree, and refresh my mother with your fruit." Obediently, the palm bends its head down to Mary's feet to offer its dates. When they have all eaten of its sweet fruit, the tree remains in its submissive posture until the Son of God says, "Raise yourself, O palm, and be strong, and join my trees which are in the paradise of my Father. And open beneath your roots a vein of water which is hidden in the earth, and let the waters flow so that we may quench our thirst from it."[3] The miracle of the palm tree is thus followed by the miracle of the spring; and when the travelers finally reach Hermopolis, the presence of the divine child in the temple causes the 365 Egyptian idols to fall down. According to later versions of the legend of the Flight into Egypt, the miracles of the dragons, palm tree, spring, and idols were preceded by a miracle of grain:

> The Holy Family had hardly fled from Bethlehem when Herod's soldiers arrived there. They killed the innocent children, and searched for Jesus. Then they hurried to a field at which a farmer was stand-

[2] *New Testament Apocrypha,* ed. Edgar Hennecke, rev. ed. Wilhelm Schneemelcher, trans. ed. R. McL. Wilson (Louisville, Ky., 1991), vol. 1, p. 462.
[3] Ibid., p. 463.

ing. When the farmer had been busy an hour earlier tilling the field and scattering seed, St. Joseph had said to him: "When the soldiers come and ask where we are, give this answer: 'When I was scatter-ing the seeds here, Joseph and Mary came riding past with the child.' At once the seeds sprouted, grew, and formed ears of corn. The ears were ripe when the soldiers drew near. They asked the farmer, "Did a couple with a child flee past here?" He answered, "Yes, when I sowed the field, the ears of which I have just mown, I saw them hurrying toward Egypt." Then the soldiers thought it must have been three months before. They turned back, and the Holy Family was saved.[4]

For centuries, painters depicted the Flight into Egypt as a journey leading into foreign parts, with the figures proceeding from left to right under a bright sky: Mary with the child mounted on an ass, which Joseph is lead-ing by the halter. The Holy Family was granted a rest during its travels for the first time in a painting dating from 1379: against the outlines of a landscape back-ground, Mary is kneeling on the ground and offering the little boy her breast. Joseph, satisfying his hunger with a roll, is holding out a traveling bottle to her, while the ass feeds on a bundle of hay.[5] None of the painters contem-porary with Master Bertram followed the example of his "Rest on the Flight into Egypt." A hundred years were to pass before painters in the Netherlands rediscovered the motif—which very few artists north of the Alps failed to depict, at the beginning of a century filled with refugees

---

[4] The miracle of the cornfield is of a later date than the apocryphal sources. Cf. Karl Vogler, *Die Ikono-graphie der 'Flucht nach Ägypten'* (Heidelberg, 1930), p. 44.

[5] Master Bertram (ca. 1340– ca. 1414), Grabow altarpiece, Kunst-halle Hamburg.

fleeing persecution for their faith. In Gerard David's versions of the "Rest on the Flight," Joseph always appears in the background, as befits his role. If he has not simply fallen asleep somewhere, he is knocking nuts from a tree on the edge of a wood,[6] while the Virgin, oblivious to all around her, is nursing the Christ Child on the grass, or smilingly offering him a grape.[7] Wrapped in a red or blue mantle, she is sitting on the bare earth; her throne is a rocky ledge, and her baggage consists of a willow basket.[8] The painter shows her in full figure or half-portrait in the immediate foreground, in an intimate relationship with the child against a forest background, in a rather northern-looking Egypt. The Madonna and Child occupy a third of the picture's surface area, the remainder of which is shared between trees, rocks, river, mountains, and houses: it is the Virgin who comes first, and then the landscape—but in Joachim Patinir, the relationship is reversed.

Master Joachim shows the world in the immediate distance, in a bird's-eye view from the divine perspective; his "Egypt" is a cosmic panorama.[9] However, as the "good

---

[6] Of all the miracles during the Flight into Egypt, in Flemish painting it is the palm that is first to bow down and submit to secularization. The tree changes and becomes a nut tree—either a sweet chestnut or a walnut, the fruit of which can be knocked down.

[7] The picnic on the Flight into Egypt, with grapes and Joseph knocking down nuts, hangs in the National Gallery of Art in Washington, and various versions of the nursing Virgin on the grass can be seen in Madrid, Oslo, and Rotterdam.

[8] The birth triptych in the interior of David's *Forest View* shows

the open basket containing diapers, rolled up like modern toilet paper.

[9] The original meaning of "cosmos" was not "universe" but "harmonious order and arrangement," the world as a unified whole in contrast to a mere juxtaposition of parts; cf. *Oxford English Dictionary*. "The whole spatial world, and with it the cosmos, appears to be built according to a definite model, which may manifest itself to us on an enlarged or a reduced scale but which, large or small, remains the same . . . Thus, just as there is a magical anatomy in which particular parts of the human body are equated with particular parts of the

landscape painter"[10] had no talent for portraying figures, he borrowed them from his colleagues. "I have sold Master Joachim 4 Christophels on gray paper,"[11] Dürer notes in 1521 in the diary of his journey to the Netherlands. In the Berlin "Rest on the Flight," it was Patinir's friend Joos van Cleve[12] who added the Virgin and Child to the picture.

Adam was created from the dust of the ground, and even the Mother of God is only an earthly woman. She is sitting humbly in a classical Madonna's robe on a green meadow[13] set on a rise. Just as the landscape painter depicts the garment clothing the earth, so the portrait painter portrays the "inhabited cloth."[14] Where the flow-

world, there is also a mythical geography and cosmography in which the structure of the earth is described and defined in accordance with the same basic intuition. Often the two, magical anatomy and mythical geography, merge into one." (Ernst Cassirer, *The Philosophy of Symbolic Forms,* trans. Ralph Manheim [New Haven, 1955], vol. 2, pp. 89, 92.)

[10] Albrecht Dürer, "Tagebuch der Reise in die Niederlande" [Diary of a journey to the Netherlands], in *Schriften und Briefe,* ed. Ernst Ullmann (Leipzig, 1993), p. 54.

[11] Ibid., p. 57. On his first visit to Antwerp, Dürer writes, "Master Joachim has eaten with me on one occasion. Also his apprentice once . . . I have given Master Joachim art for 1 guilder, that he lend me the use of his apprentice and paint; and I have given his apprentice art for 3 pounds." On his fourth visit to the city, he receives as a present from the attorney in Antwerp a "small panel made by Master Joachim, it is S. Loth with

daughters." On his fifth visit, he "made a likeness of Master Joachim in crayon and also did a portrait of him in crayon," and as an honored guest at Patinir's second wedding, praises him as a "good landscape painter." After selling him the four Christophels, Dürer travels to "Mecheln" and then returns for a final visit to Antwerp, before making his way back to Nuremberg. A woodcut by Hans Baldung Grien completes the artists' exchange of gifts: "I have given Green Hans's thing to Master Joachim," reads the diary entry. (*Schriften und Briefe,* pp. 27, 50, 53, 61.)

[12] Joos van Cleve (1485–1540), dean of the Guild of St. Luke in Antwerp (1511).

[13] The green of the meadow, like that of the leaves, has browned over the course of time. See pp. 326–337.

[14] The expression derives from Leonardo da Vinci. Cf. Carlo Pedretti, "Bewohntes Tuch," in *Leonardo da Vinci. Les études de draperies* (Paris, 1989); *Leonardo da*

ing fabric of the blue silk robe and the red cape with the gold-embroidered hem meets resistance, it falls into supple folds and bends; the shadowy areas of the olive-colored silk lining[15] visible at the sleeve and over the Virgin's right knee shimmer red—as if the infant's feet had got caught in the hem, turning out the lining, when Mary lifted him onto her lap to change his diaper. The naked child's gesture of benediction looks like a clumsy imitation of his mother's, and it seems to be directed at the songbird perched on the barren branch of a withered tree with fresh shoots sprouting from its base;[16] the dead wood is putting forth shoots, the spring is bubbling just as the child of miracles has commanded it, and the nightingale's melancholy song has fallen silent as he blesses it—Philomela's sobbing voice[17] will only return again in the

Vinci: Die Gewandstudien (Munich, 1990), pp. 15–21.

[15] The shimmering play of color in this type of silk material was used by Dürer as an example of the way in which shading should not be used. "No matter what happens," he wrote in the chapter on paint, with the exception of iridescent silk material "no paint used in coloring must come out of its nature." (*Schriften und Briefe,* p. 123; see pp. 293–295 below.)

[16] The withered tree putting forth shoots is a familiar Marian motif. "Our Lady of the Withered Tree" was the name of an illustrious society in Bruges, founded to maintain a Franciscan chapel of the same name. Among its members were Philip the Good, Charles the Bold, and, from 1508, Master Gerard David.

[17] The songbird on the withered tree creates a few puzzles. Although a trace of pink madder glaze on the bird's light-gray breast is untypical for a nightingale, all of its other characteristics match the bird. The coloring is too weak for it to be a robin, and its shape is too elongated and its beak too long. A song-thrush, by contrast, has a spotted breast and lighter arches over its eyes. The nightingale used to be known as the "red nightingale" or "red bird." The inconspicuous songbird's brown plumage does indeed have a red sheen, which fades into its light breast. (Cf. Walter Wüst, *Brutvögel Mitteleuropas* [Munich, 1970], p. 340.) Even in antiquity, the nightingale's half-rejoicing, half-sobbing song was linked with love and death. Philomela is changed into a nightingale after killing the son of Tereus, her brother-in-law and violator, and serving him up to Tereus to eat (Ovid, *Metamorphoses* 6.441–670). In Virgil, the nightingale, sitting in the shade of a poplar, laments the

story of the Passion: *"Quand le rossignol a vu ses petits, il ne chante plus."*[18]

The sharp-leafed thistle and the yellow iris at the waterside hint at the path of suffering; earthly life is a pilgrimage from the cradle to the grave, and Christ is the exemplary *homo viator,*[19] the pilgrim whose only home lies in heaven. But the painter would not be a painter if his world-picture could be completely absorbed into that of the *devotio moderna.*[20] Every detail of Patinir's landscapes of

death of her young (*Georgics* 4.511). Even in Pliny's concrete description of natural history, mention of death is not omitted in connection with the bird: it is "not in the lowest rank remarkable. In the first place there is so loud a voice and so persistent a supply of breath in such a tiny little body; then there is the consummate knowledge of music in a single bird . . . the birds have several songs each, and not all the same but every bird songs of its own. They compete with one another, and there is clearly an animated rivalry between them; the loser often ends her life by dying, her breath giving out before her song." (*Natural History* X.xliii [81–83], vol. 3, p. 345.) According to Christian interpretations, the nightingale's song bears witness to the Passion and expresses a yearning for heaven; cf. G. Roth-Bojadzhiev, *Die Vögel in der mittelalterlichen Tafelmalerei* (Cologne, 1985). Johannes Veghe transforms the bird, singing happily in a green tree, into a symbol of the Virgin in her joy over the salvation brought to the world by Christ. Cf. *Wyngaerden der Sele.*

[18] "When the nightingale sees its young, it will cease its song." The French proverb is an accurate reflec-

tion of nature, meaning: once the children arrive, the serious part of life starts. Cf. E. and L. Gattiker, *Vögel im Volksglauben,* p. 88.

[19] *Homo viator* = the pilgrim imitating Christ, a key figure in the *devotio moderna.* The *homo viator* has withdrawn into his inward spirit, both in his own private chamber and on the stony pathways of the foreign parts through which he travels, forever on his way to the Heavenly Jerusalem. See also Reindert L. Falkenburg, *Joachim Patinir: Landscape as an Image of the Pilgrimage of Life* (Philadelphia, 1988). Falkenburg deserves credit for tracing the hidden symbolism, but his Gnostic interpretation obscures his view of the obviously cosmopolitan outlook in Patinir's landscapes.

[20] "The movement's strict, ascetic ideals left no room for the development of independent art." (Peter Eikemeier, "Dieric Bouts, Johannes der Täufer weist auf Jesus hin: 'Siehe, das Lamm Gottes' [Ecce agnus dei]" in *Heft 20 der KulturStiftung der Länder* [Munich, 1990], p. 16. The impossibility of being a *devout modern* and a painter at the same time is shown by the tragic fate of Hugo van der Goes (ca.

the world is certainly related to the events of the salvation story; but at the same time, nature in his devotional pictures has the appearance of bearing an essential relation to man. "We only attend to objects in nature in order to discover and extract all the traits in them that bear an essential relation to our own being; the study of the 'large world' is only used to reflect back the image of the microcosm more and more purely."[21] God made man to serve as the eye and mirror of creation—a mirror "that does not receive the images of things from outside but that rather forms and shapes them in itself."[22] *Saper vedere,*[23] the train-

---

1435–1482). At the peak of his fame (around 1474), Hugo entered the Roode Clooster of the "Windesheim Congregation" near Brussels, where he received the dubious privilege—in addition to the mortification of the senses required of him—of being allowed to record the sensuous world in paintings. He was even allowed to receive highranking visitors, such as the archduke and future German emperor, Maximilian, "because they were all fired by the desire to see his pictures." After five years, this inner conflict between mortifying the senses and bringing them to life ended in insanity. The Brothers of the Common Life were able to prevent Hugo's attempts at suicide only by force, and even the music they provided to soothe his madness, following the example of King Saul, was of no avail against his frenzied self-accusations and his conviction—as a result of the insoluble moral conflict—that he was condemned to eternal damnation. Cf. Rudolf and Margot Wittkower, *Born under Saturn: The Character and*

Conduct of Artists—a Documented History from Antiquity to the French Revolution* (London, 1963), p. 109.

[21] Ernst Cassirer, *Das Erkenntnisproblem in der Philosophie und Wissenschaft der neueren Zeit* (Darmstadt, 1994), p. 161; the quotation refers to Charles de Bouelles (Carolus Bovillus, 1478–1556), whose *Liber de Sapiente* was published in Paris and Amiens in 1510 and 1512.

[22] Another interpretation of Bouelles by Cassirer, in *Individual and Cosmos,* p. 92.

[23] *Saper vedere* = knowing how to see, the perfection of vision. Cf. Cassirer, ibid., p. 158, and Wuttke, *Dazwischen* (index). The feeble sensualism of our own age has projected its own photographic conception of vision onto Netherlandish painting; cf. Svetlana Alpers, *The Art of Describing: Dutch Art in the Seventeenth Century* (London, 1983). In the controversy the book aroused, some aspects of its thesis that Dutch painting represents a content-free reflection of superficiality were overlooked. A pupil of Gombrich, Alpers made

ing of the eye, was one of the ideals of the Renaissance, in both southern and northern Europe.

The azure plumage on the blue-tit's wings, head, and tail gave it its Latin name *Parus caeruleus,* "heaven-tit"; in the still life of the pilgrims' baggage, it has perched on the lid of the artfully woven willow basket. The Virgin's gesture seems to say, "Just sit still and bear witness to the goal of the journey,"[24] while the little bird gazes at the bulging saddlebags looped around Joseph's staff. "Look at the birds of the air! they neither sow nor reap nor gather into barns,"[25] and yet their heavenly father ensures that even saintly pilgrims let crumbs fall to the ground . . .

Date-palm miracles have ceased, however; palms do not grow in this Flemish version of Egypt. The crown of a single red beech is towering up into the sky on the Virgin's right, supplying two of the landscape painter's requirements: an effect of depth and a fine view, unobstructed by branches on the pruned trunk.

The milk for the soup simmering on the fire behind the Virgin has been brought by Joseph from the village of

---

an eclectic selection from among Panofsky's discoveries. (Cf. *Historisches Wörterbuch,* vol. 7, p. 376, s.v. *Perspektive.*) Panofsky's insight that the viewer is openly incorporated into the picture in art from north of the Alps, while in Italian art the viewer's standpoint is set outside of the painting, is taken out of context; Alpers incorporates it into a mechanistic interpretation of painting as a projection of the retinal image. Whether it is Kepler or Locke, Bacon or Huygens, Ptolemy or Mercator—for Alpers, all conceptual structures are merely the sum of their parts, which can be dismantled

and put together again at will, like LEGO bricks.

[24] The affectionate quality of the gesture is clear, but in view of the raised hand of the Mother of God and the kneeling naked child, the witty Surrealist Max Ernst nevertheless came up with the idea of a chastising Virgin putting the Christ Child across her knee to spank it. The painting *La Vierge corrigeant l'enfant Jésus devant trois témoins: André Breton, Paul Éluard et l'artiste* was made in 1926 (oil on canvas; private collection, Brussels).

[25] Matthew 6.26.

thatched houses lying in a bend in the river in the mid-distance on the left of the picture. In the distance, the little man can be seen passing on his way: staff in hand, and leading the ass on a long halter, he is returning to the meadow where Mary is sitting. On the opposite side of the landscape, in a clearing at the edge of the wood, a hind is a distant guest at the Marian idyll.

The deer as a symbol of Christ is derived from the ancient notion that the "gentle"[26] ruminant was hostile to the evil serpent. "Even stags are at war with a snake," Pliny writes in his book on rural fauna, "they track out their holes and draw them out by means of the breath of their nostrils in spite of their resistance. Consequently the smell made by burning stag's horn is an outstanding thing for driving away serpents."[27]

In the early Christian book *Physiologus,* the serpent mutates into a dragon, and the stag into the Lord: "When the dragon flees from the stag into crevices in the earth, the stag goes there and fills the cavities of his belly with spring water, and spouts it into the crevices in the earth, and in this way brings the dragon forth and beats it down and kills it. And in the same way, our Lord kills the great dragon, the Devil, through heavenly water—namely, the divine doctrine of salvation."[28]

The hart's appearance is godlike, and the hind's is pleasing to God. While he proves himself in the battle with evil, her role lies in thirsting and in the quenching of thirst. "As a hind longs for flowing streams, so longs my soul for thee, O God," complains the Levite in exile in Psalm 42. MENS INTENTA DEO[29] is the motto of the hind

---

[26] "Deer also have their own form of stinginess, although the stag is the gentlest of animals," as Pliny writes (*Natural History* VIII.xlix [112], vol. 3, p. 81).

[27] Ibid., VIII.1 (118), vol. 3, p. 85.

[28] *Physiologus,* pp. 43–44.

[29] "Mens intenta Deo" = a mind intent on God.

in the emblem book of Joachim Camerarius;[30] the emblem shows the hind roaming through the landscape and drinking the falling dew of the sun.[31] The *Golden Legend* describes the hind as providing maternal succor to St. Giles, who has sought safety from the "danger of human adulation"[32] by living as a hermit in a cave with a small spring in the wild forest, where God sends him a doe, who "came at certain hours and nourished him with her milk."[33] Royal hunters pursue the animal. When the hermit prays to God to protect the doe for him, the arrow intended for the hind strikes him. This is why St. Giles became the patron saint of nursing mothers and of animals.

In the world of the village at the center of the landscape stage, Patinir provides a spatial juxtaposition of the temporal sequence of the episodes of the flight. In the Flemish Bethlehem behind the little wood with the hind, the innocents are being massacred at Herod's command, and a moment later the pursuers of the Holy Family are abandoning the search on the edge of the village after receiving the true information from the farmer at the miraculous cornfield; as the eye wanders farther to a rock above the Virgin's head, the tiny statue of an idol is seen falling head-first from the top of its vegetative, Hieronymus Bosch–like plinth.

The ease with which the viewer's eye is able to wander about in the painted landscape is also miraculously shared by the refugees themselves. They have covered the path from the spring to the idol in the twinkling of an eye. According to the *Gospel of Pseudo-Matthew,* the pilgrims

[30] The emblem book of fauna by the learned physician, botanist, and amateur zoologist Joachim Camerarius (1534–1598) was published in Nuremberg in 1595. See also Henkel and Schöne, *Emblemata,* pp. 468–469 and clxxxii.

[31] The *subscriptio* for the emblem reads, "With its open mouth, the wandering doe takes in the falling dew; may Thou, O God, moisten our parched souls with Thy dew."

[32] *Golden Legend,* vol. 2, p. 147.

[33] Loc. cit.

quenched their thirst at the miraculous spring, and then continued on their way through the country's scorching heat. Joseph wanted to walk alongside the sea, so that they could rest in the coastal towns, but the Christ Child promised to shorten their way: "What you were intending to traverse in the space of thirty days, you will complete in one day." And at once they perceived the mountains of Egypt and its cities. "And happy and rejoicing they came to the region of Hermopolis,[34] and entered an Egyptian city called Sotinen. And since there was in it no one they knew whom they could have asked for hospitality, they entered a temple which was called the 'capitol of Egypt.' "[35]   •

Like "Silena," "Sotinen" is an imaginary city. The name may have been derived from Sothis, the Egyptian name for Sirius, the Dog Star, which was sacred to Isis. The appearance of the brightest of the stars in the dawn of the month of Thoth,[36] coinciding with the swelling of

[34] Another reading is "Heliopo-lis."

[35] *New Testament Apocrypha,* vol. 1, p. 464.

[36] The period of the Egyptian flood, Achet, and the month of Thoth correspond to the European summer months of July and August. Sothis, the astronomical name for Isis, signals the end of the deadly drought and brings in a new, fruitful period. In the myth, the Mother Goddess succeeds in heal-ing her dismembered husband, Osiris, and conceives with him their beloved son Horus, who is reincar-nated in the kings of the earth. Thoth, the protective god of the moon, the "calculator of the year," is the inventor of the calendar, lord of arithmetic, inventor of writing. Cf. André Pichot, *Die Geburt der*

Wissenschaft (Frankfurt, 1995), pp. 204–205. The ibis and baboon are Thoth's sacred animals; the Greeks compared him to their god Hermes. "His name is said to be derived from the Egyptian word Thoÿth, a col-umn; for the column in Egypt was the bearer of all the knowledge the priests had written upon it . . . Thoth is included in the cabalists' mystical writings as . . . Hermes Trismegistus." (*Vollständiges Wörter-buch der Mythologie aller Völker,* ed. W. Vollmer [Stuttgart, 1851], p. 1037.) On the "thrice great" Hermes and Renaissance Egyptomania, see Jean Seznec, *The Survival of the Pagan Gods: The Mythological Tradition and Its Place in Renaissance Humanism and Art,* trans. Barbara F. Sessions (New York, 1953), and Rudolf Wittkower, *Allegory and the Migration*

the Nile, signaled the beginning of the year. The Egyptian calendar had 365 days, the same as the number of
idols dashed to pieces in the temple, according to Pseudo-
Matthew. In another apocryphal text,[37] the miracle is
restricted to the overturning of a single idol.

Patinir's idol is holding a scepter in its raised right
hand; under the magnifying glass, the falling torso in its
sleeveless gown appears to be a female idol with a pointed
animal head.[38]

The man with a turban and staff on the winding path
leading toward the fortified town inside the picturesque
mantle of cliffs, and the figure with the pointed hat following him at a distance, are taken from one of the
gospels of Christ's childhood. The Arabian one tells of
the healing of the possessed son of one of the priests of
Hermopolis, while Pseudo-Matthew describes the chief
citizen of Sotinen, Affrodosius,[39] who hurried to the temple with his followers and prayed to the Virgin and Child
in front of the 365 smashed idols.

Endless stone steps lead up to the city of Hermes,
Helios, or Isis, with the round temple, which represents
the strong fortress of monotheism after the overthrow of
the false animal gods. *Per aspera ad astra*—the path to

of Symbols (London, 1977), as well
as Edgar Wind, *Pagan Mysteries in the
Renaissance* (London, 2nd ed.,
1967).

[37] *Evangelium Infantiae Arabicum;*
cf. Vogler, *Ikonographie der Flucht,* p.
49.

[38] In another "Rest on the
Flight" by Patinir (Prado, Madrid),
an animal-headed "idoless" is set on
a columnar altar in the open air.
With a quite un-Egyptian degree of
relaxation, she is crouching with a
ball or an egg in her right hand in
front of a fire, while her left hand is
resting casually on her thigh. It
would hardly be surprising if she
were to cross her legs as well. In
front of the altar, pagans are plead-
ingly raising their hands to heaven,
while others are climbing the steps
bringing sacrificial offerings to the
fire—a live goose and a slaughtered
lamb. In the sixteenth century,
"enigmatic" and "Egyptian" were
synonyms.

[39] Another reading is "Affrodis-
ius."

human salvation is one of hardship. The dignity of man lies in his ability to transform himself.

> Inspired by the Cherubic spirit, using philosophy through the steps of the ladder, that is, of nature, and penetrating all things from center to center, we shall sometimes descend, with titanic force rending the unity like Osiris into many parts, and we shall sometimes ascend, with the force of Phoebus collecting the parts like the limbs of Osiris into a unity, until, resting at last in the bosom of the Father who is above the ladder, we shall be made perfect with the felicity of theology.[40]

The sheer cliff towers into the clouds like a broken column supporting the sky, with its rubble lying scattered in the landscape all around. Art historians have regarded a site in southern France as being the source for this bizarre geological formation. A recess in a cliff wall near Marseilles was long considered to be Mary Magdalene's hermitage, where the saintly sinner ascended into heaven, after thirty years of penance during which she received ecstasy[41] seven times a day. Under the name "Tsente Marie

---

[40] Giovanni Pico della Mirandola (1463–1494), *Oration on the Dignity of Man,* trans. Elizabeth Livermore Forbes, in *The Renaissance Philosophy of Man,* ed. Ernst Cassirer, Paul Oskar Kristeller, and John Herman Randall Jr. (Chicago, 1948), p. 230. On the influence that Pico's famous oration, written in 1486, had on Erasmus and other humanists outside Italy, see the introduction by A. Buck to his German edition of the work (*Über die Würde des Menschen* [Hamburg, 1990]); on the great Renaissance philosopher's world

picture and conception of man, see Cassirer, *Individual and the Cosmos,* pp. 115–121.

[41] In Mary Magdalene's harsh wilderness there were no streams of water, no grass, and no trees. "Every day at the seven canonical hours she was carried aloft by angels and with her bodily ears heard the glorious chants of the celestial hosts. So it was that day by day she was gratified with these supernal delights and, being conveyed back to her own place by the same angels, needed no material nourishment." (*Golden Legend,* vol. 1, p. 380.)

Magdalenen ter Spelonken," Sainte-Baume was also known in Flanders as a place of pilgrimage.[42] But although the sites are similar in having castles girdled by cliffs, their outer shape is very different. Patinir's broken pillar of rock has nothing in common with the plateau of hills near Marseilles. It is only the scattered rocks around the mountain pillar and along the shore of the river that seem to have equivalents in reality—the rocky battlements in the valley of the Meuse near the painter's home,[43] to which his fondness for using grotesque cliffs as *repoussoir* is attributed.

Since the time of van Eyck, Bouts,[44] and David, rocky cliffs typify the desert retreat of the saint; they are the cliffs that vanquish the unfaithful, but which the faithful scale in certain trust that God is near: "He bid the cliffs from desert plain to soar, / And from their depths he made clear waters pour."[45] With Patinir and Bles,[46] the cliff

[42] Cf. Robert A. Koch, *Joachim Patinir* (Princeton, 1968), the fundamental study of Master Joachim, as well as Falkenburg, *Joachim Patinir: Landscape as an Image of the Pilgrimage of Life,* and the well-considered reflections of Walter S. Gibson, *Mirror of the Earth* (Princeton, 1989).

[43] Gibson provides an illustration of the rocky battlements of Bayard. Patinir was born either in Dinant or in Bouvignes; the picturesque battlements tower up between the two towns.

[44] Dieric Bouts (ca. 1415–1475). A splendid painting by Bouts was purchased for the Alte Pinakothek in Munich in 1990 with assistance from the KulturStiftung der Länder. A desert motif with a cliff landscape forms the background of the picture, *John Pointing to Jesus, "Behold, the Lamb of God."* Cf. the

description by Peter Eikemeier in *Heft 20 der KulturStiftung der Länder,* pp. 9–23.

[45] "Die Klippen hiess er in der Wüsten springen / und klaren Trank aus ihrer Tiefe dringen." Martin Opitz (1597–1639).

[46] Herri met de Bles (b. 1505/10, d. ?). Patinir's successor may have been his nephew, registered as Free Master Herri Patinir in the Guild of St. Luke in Antwerp in 1535. Bles made his name with depictions of metalworking scenes in imaginary cliff landscapes. In Italy, he was known as "Civetta" (Little Owl), because he "put into all his works a little owl, which is sometimes so hidden away that people allow each other a lot of time to look for it, wagering that they will not find it anyway" (Carel van Mander, *The Lives of the Illustrious Netherlandish*

begins to take on more and more fantastic forms in art. Arrows, cones, needles, battlements, obelisks, pyramids, pillars, horns, and mushrooms; rent asunder, craggy, weathered, and slatelike, with the stone hollowed out to form doorways and arches, towering sometimes in vertical layers, sometimes in horizontal ones, one above the other, next to each other, or rising up individually out of the landscape as if rammed into the earth with a giant's strength.

Cliffs are always cliffs, but one rock need not resemble another.[47] The rock on which one can build is not the same as the "stone of offense" and "rock of stumbling."[48] Only a "brood of vipers"[49] could mistake the divine Rock in the desert—which encircled Jacob and "cared for him, . . . kept him as the apple of his eye," fed him with "the produce of the field," and made him "suck honey out of the rock, and oil of the flinty rock"[50]—for the glowing breccia[51] of the Devil reflecting the conflagration of Sodom and Gomorrah.[52]

Whether it is a mantle of rock or a dangerous cliff, a monument warning of chaos or a pillar of steadfastness,

---

and Dutch Painters, ed. Hessel Miedema, trans. Derry Cook-Radmore [Doornspijk, 6 vols., 1994–1999], vol. 1, p. 137).

[47] "For their rock is not as our Rock, even our enemies themselves being judges," as Moses teaches the Israelites before his death (Deuteronomy 32.33).

[48] Isaiah 8.14.

[49] John the Baptist describes the multitudes who flocked to him in the wilderness for baptism as a "brood of vipers" (Luke 3.7).

[50] Deuteronomy 32.10, 13. In his farewell song, Moses proclaims the name of the Lord: "The Rock" (Deuteronomy 32.4).

[51] "Breccia" is a geological term for a secondary rock formation consisting of fragments of older stone. The angular debris, cemented together, can be produced by tectonic or volcanic movements, and in the early phases of geology the latter form was known as Gluht-Breccien ("ember breccia"); cf. K. C. von Leonhard, Geologie oder Naturgeschichte der Erde (Stuttgart, 1838), vol. 2, p. 37.

[52] Patinir's Burning of Sodom and Gomorrah is in the Boymans van Beuningen Museum in Rotterdam.

the precipitous rock in a gentle landscape creates an effect of fear, either for good or evil. Just as awesome as the petrified power of the Devil is the Lord's rock-firm omnipotence. "God is able from these stones to raise up children to Abraham,"[53] as John the Baptist preaches to the brood of vipers in the desert. He who has "measured the waters in the hollow of his hand and marked off the heavens with a span, enclosed the dust of the earth in a measure and weighed the mountains in scales and the hills in a balance" can also bring stones to life, lifting up the valleys and bringing every mountain and hill low, making the crooked straight and the rough ways smooth,[54] making the wilderness like Eden and the desert like a garden.[55] "Hearken to me, you who pursue deliverance," Isaiah begins his prophecy of the rebuilding of Zion, "look to the rock from which you were hewn, and to the quarry from which you were digged."[56]

The vegetation on the narrow ridge between the abysses of the shaft within the rock and the world beyond it show how undemanding nature is: unbowed by storms, a little tree is stretching into the sky, and grasses and bushes are defying the wind, with their roots clutching the rock. Clouds promising good weather form a fleet passing from west to east through the azure sky along the hazy horizon. In the blue distance on the worldly side, the arms of a River Nile bearing a curious resemblance to the Schelde are flowing into the sea; there are ships sailing into the harbor of a large city with tall towers—with or without the Pharos, it is a Flemish Alexandria, or an Egyptian Antwerp.

---

[53] Luke 3.8.
[54] Isaiah 40.4, 12. The first passage is echoed in the New Testament just before John the Baptist gives his "brood of vipers" sermon (Luke 3.5).
[55] Isaiah 51.3.
[56] Isaiah 51.1.

One half of our physical eyes can see, the
other is blind . . . Nature thus comes to the aid of man by
giving clear-sightedness from the very start to the eye that is
directed forward, toward the external world—opening the
whole world up and presenting it. Only by leaving blind the
eye that looks inward does nature betray man—leaving him
unfinished, so that of his own accord he must convey light
begged from the first eye to the second, until finally he comes to
see with both eyes . . . For—just as our visible eye, set firmly
in its place in the head, only sees with one half of its globe,
while the other half is sightless and left blind—so too the
human intellect, as long as it is bustling actively in the worldly
element and ruled by the senses, is unworthy of its talents,
with one half illuminated and the other half in darkness; only
perceiving what is in the world, and not that which is within
man himself. Imagine, then, that the physical eye could free
itself from its natural position in the head, detach itself from
the individual and make itself independent, as if it were being
held in mid-air by itself. This eye would surely be the supreme
vestige[1] of the thinking capacity for cognition, perfected by
contemplation.

CHARLES DE BOUELLES

IV
Pilgrim Eye
or Reflection of Creation

atinir's epic landscapes are not consistently
constructed. Why restrict yourself to a
single vanishing point? Man was given
two eyes, and a limitless capacity for contemplation. In Master Joachim's work,
one of the viewer's eyes is aligned vertically and the other

---

[1] *Vestigium,* the Latin for "foot-
print, trace, token," is "a mark,
trace, or visible sign of something . . . which no longer exists or
is present" (*Oxford English Dictio-*
nary); the word has been described
as "a metaphor based on an understanding of the life-world" (*His-*
torisches Wörterbuch, vol. 9, p. 1550).

horizontally. All of the vertical objects—trees, bushes, cliffs, buildings, people, and animals—are seen at eye level, but we look down over the horizontal elements of the landscape—fields, meadows, streams, and roads. In this way, we can follow all the details of the flight easily, while at the same time hovering above the land and the water.[2]

This earthly life is a pilgrimage, but the world is a feast for the eyes. The more difficult it is to climb real cliffs, the more the pilgrim enjoys strolling through a picture. Whether the eye wanders along the stony paths, soars with the clouds, lingers at the spring or strays over to the hind in the clearing, roams through woodlands and fields, village and town, or goes leaping over cliffs, rock-hewn steps, and precipices—the journey is effortless. The livelier one's memories of the dog days of life and of hardships suffered in foreign lands, the greater one's relish in the *orbus pictus;* an insatiable enjoyment of beauty is the finest thing the eye has been given.

It was a period in which people regarded themselves as pilgrims in the figurative sense; they were often pilgrims in the literal sense in any case. Some were driven to emigrate by hunger, plague, and political and religious persecution,[3] while for others faith, business, or art was the reason for the pilgrimage. Experience of foreign travel

[2] Friedländer gives a vivid comparison of our situation here to that in the theater: "We are sitting in front of a deep stage, on which the scenery is standing perpendicular, while the floor of the stage rises steeply toward the rear, providing a view from above." Max J. Friedländer, *Von Van Eyck bis Bruegel, Studien für die Geschichte der Niederländischen Malerei* (Berlin, 1916), p. 103.

[3] Cf. Rudolf and Margot Wittkower, *Born under Saturn* (London, 1963). They describe the growing stream of craftsmen from Flanders, Brabant, and southern Germany who fled across the Alps to Italy from the end of the fourteenth century to the beginning of the sixteenth: "Northern tapestry weavers and embroiderers, and even saddlers, furriers, tanners, barbers, and other foreign artisans were to be found in all major Italian cities. Between 1420 and 1450 eight hun-

formed part of an apprentice's training in all of the craft guilds; the apprenticeship years were followed by a period of travel. Journeymen and painters' apprentices traveled the world on foot or on horseback, entering service with a foreign master now here, now there, or settling in towns that were artistic centers in order to prepare the piece by which they would gain from the guild the recognized rank of "master."[4]

Where and with whom Master Joachim served his apprenticeship, and how far away his thirst for learning took him, are not known. Carel van Mander, the Vasari of the north, born twenty-four years after Patinir's death, writes in his *Schilder-Boeck:*

> The grand, celebrated city of Antwerp, which prospers through commerce, has summoned from everywhere the most excellent in our art, who also frequently went there because art desires to be near wealth. Among others this Joachim Patenier . . . went there too . . . He had a certain, individual way of landscape painting most subtle and precise, the trees somewhat stippled—in which he also painted deft little figures so that his works were much sought after, sold and exported to various countries. He had the custom of painting a little man doing his business in all his landscapes and he

dred names are mentioned as members of the confraternity of foreign shoemakers, established in Rome in the later fourteenth century; in the thirty-one years between 1500 and 1531 we find over two thousand names listed . . . Thus during the later fifteenth and sixteenth century the majority of inn-keepers south of the Alps were of German or Flemish origin." (p. 45.)

[4] In the earliest uses of the word "masterpiece" recorded in the *Oxford English Dictionary,* it is borrowed from the German *Meisterstück* in the sense of a "work prepared in order to qualify as a master." In German, permission for a craftsman to prepare a master-piece and seek recognition as a master was termed *Muten.* Cf. Grimm, vol. 12, p. 2796, and Hans Huth, *Künstler und Werkstatt der Spätgotik* (Darmstadt, 1967), p. 10.

was therefore known as "The Shitter." Sometimes you had to search for this little shitter, as with the little owl of Hendrick met de Bles. This Patenier was someone who, in contradiction of his noble art, led a rowdy life; he was much inclined to drink so that he spent entire days at the inn and wasted his earnings in excess until, forced by necessity, he had to devote himself again to the money-making brushes.[5]

The little defecator is only found in two of Patinir's landscapes, which van Mander cannot have known since they were destined for Spain.[6] If the defecators are not merely a legend, they must have crept deeper into the bushes during the course of the centuries—or perhaps they were always hidden in the typical wooden huts that the artist was kind enough to conjure up for them with his brush on this or that cliff.

There is little to choose between a painter known as "Shitter" and a drinker and spendthrift. The legend about his wandering years says more about the recipients of Patinir's art than about Patinir himself. It throws light on the interaction between the world landscape he depicted and the expectations of connoisseurs of his work. Van Mander reveals an image of the Patinir enthusiast of the sixteenth century, for whom even the smallest detail was an opportunity to spin yarns about the Creator of the world and the creator of the landscape. It was still not customary to sign one's paintings at this time; the presence of the work's creator in the picture en passant, either in the form of a little owl or a defecator, was as nat-

[5] Carel van Mander, *The Lives of the Illustrious Netherlandish and German Painters,* ed. Hessel Miedema, trans. Derry Cook-Radmore (Doornspijk, 1994–1999), vol. 1, p. 134.

[6] Cf. Koch, *Patinir,* p. 9.

ural to the viewer of the period as Hitchcock darting through the picture in his films.

Luckily, there is a verbal and pictorial tradition providing information about a Patinir enthusiast who purchased works by the painter during his lifetime. In four of the landscapes, a coat of arms with two black oxen and a motto[7] indicates the identity of the patron, Lukas Rem. Rem was a wealthy merchant, scion of a patrician family of Augsburg, who traveled to Antwerp for the first time in 1508, and was a frequent visitor to the city between 1511 and 1518 both for business reasons and in his capacity as an art lover. He traded in metal, wheat, cotton, spices, and wine. In his diary, the Augsburg merchant conscientiously recorded journeys to his warehouses in Lisbon, Lyons, Cologne, and Antwerp, and pilgrimages to Rome, La Sainte-Baume, and Montserrat, exclaiming "God be praised!" after surviving the perils of foreign lands and noting down ideas about his more or less flourishing business. In passing, he also gives an account of his art purchases. When business was flourishing, he allowed himself "extravagances" in Antwerp, including paintings, jewelry, and costly fabrics; when business was stagnating, he contented himself with purchasing the latest parrots, cats, and other "rare and merry things" in Portugal.[8] Rem chose two mottos for the banner on his coat of arms. One suggests the religious humility of the merchant, while the other points to a pilgrim counting up his credit in future light: ISTZ GVOT GEBS GO (T) (Offer to God all that is good) and POST TENEBRAS SPERO LUC(EM?) (After darkness I hope for light).[9]

---

[7] One of the oxen is St. Luke, and the other has a biblical correspondence to the merchant's surname, after the ancient Hebrew word *reem*, "wild ox." Ibid., p. 10.

[8] Loc. cit.

[9] Loc. cit.

Whether the businessman was traveling by boat on the Rhone as far as Tarascon, to make his pilgrimage on foot from there via Les Baux-de-Provence to Sainte-Baume; whether he was passing through Le Puy toward the Pyrenees; or whether he took the pilgrimage route to Spain from Arles via Montpellier and Saint-Guilhem-le-Désert, his route would always have passed alongside ancient ruins with architecture vying with nature on the peaks or on the edge of wondrous cliffs. The destination of one of Rem's pilgrimages was a famous example of the well-proportioned harmony between Romanesque architecture and mountainous scenery—the Benedictine monastery of Santa Cecilia de Montserrat, founded in A.D. 880 and set at an altitude of 2,300 feet on a 4,000-foot mountain. The art historian Henri Focillon[10] wrote of the monastery that it seemed to have been "raised of set purpose to dominate a convulsive landscape by the force of human intellect."[11] A vivid description of the region of cliffs around the old mountain abbey is provided by a nineteenth-century geologist:

This mountain rises not far from the spot called Cordona, built on the rock-salt masses, in the Spanish province of Catalonia. It has a particularly striking effect, as it towers up straight out of a plain and has strange rock shapes, with sharp, serrated peaks, from which it takes its name; for "Montser-rat" means simply "serrated mountain." At some distance away, its mass resembles the ruins of huge buildings. On a high cliff wall stands the old Bene-

---

[10] Henri Focillon (b. Dijon, 1881, d. New Haven, 1943). The writings of this great French art historian are little read today. Titles such as *The Life of Forms* and *In Praise of the Hand* go against the grain of the time.

[11] Henri Focillon, *The Art of the West in the Middle Ages,* ed. Jean Bony, trans. Donald King, vol. 1, *Romanesque Art* (London, 1963), p. 35.

dictine monastery . . . During the last French war, the monastery was largely destroyed. Higher up one finds the famous hermitages, with steps hewn into the sheer rock leading up to them.[12]

The descriptions of the landscape provided by art-loving pilgrims who commissioned Master Joachim to record their memories of their journeys—in paintings in which meditation on the sacred life is treated as equivalent to meditative contemplation of the world—must have been as Patiniresque as the geologist's portrayal of Montserrat.

Vertical and horizontal views intersect in Patinir's panorama; an east-west axis and a north-south one cross in the middle of the picture. The secular moments of the Flight run horizontally, while the eternal miracles are arranged vertically: time passing away and time standing still.

Time passes away in the twinkling of an eye, but the living stream flows by measure. The journey that by human standards would have taken a month is completed in the eternal measure of a single day; and just as every day, despite its varying events, resembles every other day, all 365 idols of the Egyptian year were subsumed into a single God. He took the measure of time from his prede-cessor, the moon god Thoth, whose month begins with the appearance of the Dog Star.

In the Egyptian pantheon it is the moon god Thoth who, as the measurer, the divider of time, is also lord over just measurement. The sacred ell used in drawing up the plan of temples and in land mea-surement is consecrated to him. He is the scribe of the gods and the judge of the heavens, who has bestowed language and writing on mankind and

[12] Leonhard, *Geologie,* vol. 1, p. 277.

who, through the arts of counting and reckoning, has given gods and men to know what is their due. Here, too, the name for the exact, unchanging measure (*maāt*) becomes the name for the eternal and immutable order prevailing in nature as in ethical life. This concept of measure in its twofold signification has indeed been designated as the foundation of the whole Egyptian religious system.[13]

Orientation in time presupposes orientation in space. In the Latin word *tempus,* the notion of *templum* provides the basis for the concept of a period of time. *Templum* is derived from the Greek root τεμ, "cut," and originally meant simply "bisection, intersection": "according to the terminology of later carpenters two crossing rafters or beams still constituted a *templum;* thence the signification of the space thus divided was a natural development; in *tempus* the quarter of the heavens (e.g., the east) passed into the time of day (e.g., morning) and thence into time in general."[14]

Templum can be the whole canopy of the heavens, or the area for observation of birds marked out by the augur, *hoc omne templum*—the universe or the place from which one observes something, a hill or a wide space, a place of asylum or a grotto, a church or a monastery cell—provided that the area encompassed is an enclosed and consecrated zone, "inhabited by one divine being and governed by one divine will."[15]

As with space, so with time. It is the underlying attitude that determines whether *tempus* will mean duration, an interval, or an expiring period—vanishing or fulfilled

[13] Cassirer, *The Philosophy of Symbolic Forms,* trans. Ralph Manheim (New Haven, 1955), vol. 2, p. 114.

[14] Hermann Usener, *Götternamen* (Frankfurt, 1948), pp. 191–192, cited after Cassirer, *Symbolic Forms,* vol. 2, p. 107.

[15] Cassirer, *Symbolic Forms,* vol. 2, p. 100.

time. Orientation in time and space is a question of point of view. *Contemplatio* also has its root in *templum,* and even the *oltramontani*[16] agreed with Cicero that man is born to contemplate the universe. How else could one explain the fact that the measure of the world is already present in man's inmost being, in the *templum mentis*? What other explanation could there be for the fact that human freedom is based on deficiency?

In homine substantia nulla[17]—in himself, man is without being. Since there is nothing that is purely his, he shares in the characteristics of all other creatures. Following in the footsteps of Nicholas of Cusa, who discovered God in the smallest details, Charles de Bouelles[18] found that every detail of creation is inspired by man. According to Bouelles, there is something human hidden in every being in the world; all things have a few atoms that they share with man. He owes it to himself and the world to discover these, since he was created by nature to go out into the world and investigate the aspects that belong to him in all things, to discover from all beings the indivisible element that determines his own form. Pico della Mirandola's views on the chameleonlike dignity of man were assimilated by Bouelles and developed by him in his *Book of the Sage,* in which the traditional motif of the microcosm is

[16] The Italian artists referred to their colleagues on the other side of the Alps as *oltramontani.*

[17] "In man there is no substance." (Charles de Bouelles, *Le Livre du sage* [*Liber de sapiente*], ed. and trans. Pierre Magnard [Paris, 1982], chapter 19, p. 152.)

[18] Charles de Bouelles (Carolus Bovillus, ca. 1478–1556) was a pupil of Jacques Lefèvre D'Etaples (Faber Stapulenis), who in turn was one of the first pupils of Nicholas of Cusa and editor of his writings in France. Bouelles was forgotten during the centuries following the Renaissance. It was only in 1927 that his *Liber de sapiente,* or *Book of the Sage,* was republished by Raymond Klibansky and appended to Cassirer's *Individuum und Kosmos* (not included in the English edition, *The Individual and the Cosmos in Renaissance Philosophy* (New York, 1963; Philadelphia, 1972). An Italian translation by Eugène Garin was published in 1943, and the bilingual Latin and French edition in 1982.

seen in a fresh light. *"Mundus maximus substantia, scientia nullus: homo scientia amplissimus, substantia pusillus."*[19] It is the deficiency of being that makes knowledge possible. Man is the exception in creation. Brought into being in the abundance of a perfect world, in which every gift, motive, characteristic, place, and form was already allotted, he was intended to take an elevated place beyond the cosmic order as a universal observer, as a natural portrayer and mirror of all things. Mirrors are created in such a way that they need to be placed opposite what they are supposed to reflect. Like a mirror, man is separated from all things. He was left with nothing when he was created; and so that he should be replenished all the more richly with the colorful reflection of life, so that it should stream toward him from every side, he was placed *as if* in the middle of the world.

All forms flow into him himself, as he is drawn toward every shape and species. If he were to be bound to one thing, he would be unable to gain knowledge of it and its substance: for all knowledge and all investigation, every representation of things and every unfolding of their forms traverses the visual diagonal through which that which presents itself to the eye is separated from the power that reflects and looks.[20]

[19] "The world has a maximum of being and a minimum of knowledge; man has an abundance of knowledge and very little being." ("Both are characterized by a maximum and a minimum.") Bouelles, *Liber*, chapter 19, pp. 152–153.

[20] Ibid., chapter 26, pp. 176–179. Man enters the world as a "coarse, rough, confused, imperfect mirror, devoid of all reflection" (pp. 180–181), and remains so until he *transforms* himself in an accurate

mirror of unity in diversity. Bouelles's reflexive cognition of self and world is the exact opposite of the passive mirroring ascribed by Svetlana Alpers to Leonardo, who reproduces "unselectively" (*Art of Describing*, p. 47). Late testimony to the inadequacy of unselective mirroring is found in the third of the splendid *Nine Letters on Landscape Painting*, by Carl Gustav Carus (1789–1869): "Just try it, study natural landscape in a mirror! You will

Human nature is identical with that of the mirror. The true place for both mirror and man is

> the frontal position, at the extreme end, at a distance from and negating all things, in the place of noth-ing, in unreality, beyond all things—where, how-ever, all things must first enter into appearance. For everything lies within the circle of the world and can appear at its center. Where everything exists, it does not appear. Where everything can appear in reality and does so, it does not exist.[21]

Man is neither body nor soul, but the bond between body and soul; the universe is neither man nor world, but the bond between man and world. Neither *exists*; both must first *become.* Nature is that which has already become; culture is that which is continuing to become. The task of man, as the last being to enter creation, is to decide whether he will remain in lethargy like a stone, motionlessly reduced to mere metabolism like a plant and with feelings stirred up by instinct like an animal; or whether he will become human and realize his potential by devoting himself wisely to the world.

see it with all its charms, with all the colors and forms reproduced; but as soon as you hold this mirror image fast and compare it with the impres-sion made upon you by a perfect landscape painting, what do you observe? The latter is obviously infi-nitely far behind so far as accuracy is concerned—not even half of the charm and beauty of natural forms and the brilliance of the colors is ever attained in the picture; but at the same time, you feel that the real work of art is a whole, that it is a small world (a microcosm) to itself and in itself. The mirror image, by contrast, will forever appear only as a fragment, as a piece of infinite nature torn out of its organic context and forced into unnatural constric-tions, and not, like the work of art, as the complete and self-sufficient creation of an intellectual power which is related to us and can be grasped by us. Instead, it is merely a single tone taken from an immeasur-able harmony." (*Briefe und Aufsätze über Landschaftsmalerei,* Leipzig and Weimar 1982, pp. 26–27.)

[21] Bouelles, *Liber,* chapter 26, pp. 180–181.

Will and knowledge may, or rather, must devote themselves to every part of the universe; for only by going through the entire universe can man traverse the circle of his own possibilities. But this complete *openness* towards the world must never signify a *dissolution* in it, a mystical-pantheistic losing of oneself. For the human will possesses itself only inasmuch as it is conscious that no single goal will fulfil it; and human knowledge possesses itself only inasmuch as it knows that no single object of knowledge can suffice for it. Thus, this turning towards the whole of the cosmos always implies the ability not to be bound to any one part. The force of this total conversion is balanced by the force of a total return.[22]

The skill of the sage lies in opposition, and his place lies there where the opposites of art and nature, the senses and the intellect, meet—a point that is subject to constant change, never remaining in the same location. Wisdom is manifested in transition and transformation. Only by adapting himself to changing forms can the sage become the soul of the world, and the world the body of the sage. "Beyond the differences and characteristics of all things, therefore, man prospers in a place that is opposed to all things, at the focus of the world, at the fine center of everything: a universal mediator, who with his energies, nuances, forms, images, and intellectual capacities fills up the remaining vacuum of nature."[23]

Poor in being by his very nature, devoid of reflection and shapeless, man possesses nothing but the core of an original unity, the divine monad, from which he must develop himself in three phases: from the monad, via the dyad, to the triad. Just as he can only recognize the world

[22] Cassirer, *Individual and Cosmos,* p. 86.

[23] Bouelles, *Liber,* chapter 26, pp. 182–183.

from a distance at which he is contrasted with it, he can find himself only at a distance from himself.

"*Peregrinatio Humanae Animae*" is the title of the twelfth chapter of the *Liber de Sapiente*. In Bouelles, the pilgrim does not correspond to the soul that disdains both the body and the world in the *devotio moderna;* the journey of the soul in Bouelles is that of the open-minded sage who reconciles the microcosm with the macrocosm through the virtue of contemplation. His time is fulfilled in the *rediscovered* universe.

The gulf between viewing this earthly life as a pilgrimage and regarding it as a feast for the eyes is canceled out both in Bouelles's cosmos and in Patinir's world landscapes. Neither the Gnostic nor the sensualist interpretation is capable of doing justice to the painter.[24]

"Landscape" in the sense familiar to us today could only be grasped by the human mind once dualism had been overcome. The term emerged from northern European art.[25] The depiction of mountains; woods and rocks; meadows, fields, and villages; rivers, sea, and cities in the background of a painting was originally known as *parerga* (accessory work).[26] But the mere juxtaposition of a series of elements can no more constitute a landscape than placing body parts alongside one another would make up a human being. "Landscape" includes the totality of nature within a special physiognomy of monotonous or contrasting, rough or gentle, harmonious or grotesque regions that reveal to the eye from a sublime distance the invisible interplay of ground, air, waters, plants, animals, people, and the works of man.

---

[24] On the Gnostic view of the cosmos as the epitome of evil, see *Historisches Wörterbuch*, vol. 5, pp. 667–668, under *Malum*.

[25] See *Oxford English Dictionary,* under "landscape."

[26] Cf. E. H. Gombrich, "The Renaissance Theory of Art and the Rise of Landscape," in *Norm and Form: Studies in the Art of the Renaissance* (Oxford, 1966), pp. 113–114.

The way in which "lands" can be converted into land-scape is exemplified in one of the letters of the younger Pliny.[27] In an effort to convey to a friend the delightful appearance of the district around his country estate in Tuscia, Pliny first describes the mildness of the climate and the excellent air, the only wind often being a slight breeze. There are many old people living in this favorable atmosphere, telling tales of olden days:

> If you were to come here . . . you would fancy your-self born in some former age . . . The aspect of the country is the most beautiful possible;[28] figure to yourself an immense amphitheatre, such as the hand of nature could alone form. Before you lies a vast extended plain bounded by a range of moun-tains, whose summits are crowned with lofty and venerable woods, which supply abundance and variety of game; from hence as the mountains decline, they are adorned with under-woods. Inter-mixed with these are little hills of so loamy and fat a soil, that it would be difficult to find a single stone upon them; their fertility is nothing inferior to the lowest grounds; and though their harvest indeed is something later, their heavy crops are as well matured. At the foot of these hills the eye is pre-sented, wherever it turns, with one unbroken view of numberless vineyards, which are terminated below by a border, as it were, of shrubs. From thence extend meadows and fields. The soil of the latter is so extremely stiff, upon the first ploughing it rises in such vast clods, that it is necessary to go over it nine several times with the largest oxen and the strongest ploughs, before they can be thoroughly

[27] Pliny the Younger was the nephew of the writer of the *Natural History.*

[28] "*Regionis forma pulcherrima*" is the wording of the original.

broken. The flower-enamelled meadows produce trefoil and other kinds of herbage as fine and tender as if it were but just sprung up, being everywhere refreshed by never-failing rills.[29]

This opera in the amphitheater of nature concludes with the four seasons of the Tiber, a river that is navigable only in winter and spring, winding through the middle of the fields and transporting the produce of the land to Rome, although in the summer its channel is so low that it can only resume its claim to be a "great river" in the fall.

It is at this point that Pliny introduces a subject with a new temporal and spatial perspective into the picture—and it is only through this that these lands are turned into a "landscape":

> You would be most agreeably entertained by taking a view of the face of this country from the mountains: you would imagine that not a real, but some painted landscape lay before you,[30] drawn with the most exquisite beauty and exactness; such an harmonious and regular variety[31] charms the eye which way soever it throws itself.[32]

Looking down from a sublime distance, the viewer transforms the region into the memory of an amphitheaterlike landscape.

Petrarch's example shows that the perception of landscape implies a new relationship between man and the

[29] Pliny the Younger, *Letters,* with an English translation by William Melmoth, rev. W.M.L. Hutchinson, 2 vols. (London, 1915), Book V.vi, p. 379.

[30] *"Ad eximiam pulchritudinem pictam"*—the original is simply describing an extraordinarily beautiful *image.*

[31] *Varietate* could also be translated "diversity."

[32] Pliny the Younger, *Letters,* p. 381.

world, a specific view of time and space, which was not available before the discovery of central perspective.

On 26 April 1336, the thirty-three-year-old poet climbed Mont Ventoux, his only motive being a "wish to see what so great an elevation had to offer."[33] During the arduous ascent, he soars "on winged thoughts from things corporeal to the immaterial," and takes account of his life:

> The life which we call blessed is to be sought for on a high eminence, and strait is the way that leads to it. Many, also, are the hills that lie between, and we must ascend, by a glorious stairway, from strength to strength. At the top is at once the end of our struggles and the goal for which we are bound. All wish to reach this goal, but, as Ovid says, "To wish is little; we must long with the utmost eagerness to gain our end."[34]

Once he has reached the peak, Petrarch stands "like one dazed," "owing to the unaccustomed quality of the air and the effect of the great sweep of view spread out before me." At his feet lie the clouds, and toward Italy his yearning eyes can see the icy, snow-covered Alps close by. Here he is seized by a fresh notion, which leads him "to a consideration of time rather than place." In his mind's eye, he reviews the last ten years of his life, which he has spent in the "valley of sin." The sun is sinking, and the shadows at the foot of the mountain are growing longer, when Petrarch turns back and looks toward the west,[35] from where he has come:

---

[33] Petrarch, "The Ascent of Mount Ventoux," in *Petrarch, the First Modern Scholar and Man of Letters*, ed. James Harvey Robinson (New York, 1898), p. 308.

[34] Ibid., p. 312.

[35] On the use of the direction of the setting sun to symbolize death, see Cassirer, *Symbolic Forms*, vol. 2, p. 98.

I was unable to discern the summits of the Pyrenees, which form the barrier between France and Spain; not because of any intervening obstacle that I know of but owing simply to the insufficiency of our mortal vision. But I could see with the utmost clear-ness, off to the right, the mountains of the region about Lyons, and to the left the bay of Marseilles and the waters that lash the shores of Aigues-Mortes, although all these places were so distant that it would require a journey of several days to reach them. Under our very eyes flowed the Rhône. While I was thus dividing my thoughts, now turn-ing my attention to some terrestrial object that lay before me, now raising my soul, as I had done my body, to higher planes, it occurred to me to look into my copy of St. Augustine's *Confessions*.

By chance, Petrarch opens his "compact little volume" at the very page on which we read that he was not in a landscape picture after all: "And men go abroad to admire the heights of mountains, the mighty billows of the sea, the broad tides of rivers, the compass of the ocean, and the circuits of the stars, and pass themselves by."[36]

The following passage from Bouelles's *Book of the Sage* sounds like a response to Petrarch's spiritual anguish inspired by one of Patinir's paintings:

Man: do not wither away to become a stone, a plant, or a brutish beast. You are human: remain so. May Being protect you, may life refresh you, may your sensitivity aid you in learning, may your under-standing guide you . . . It is by the senses that you make your pilgrimage through the world; it is by the

[36] Augustine, *Confessions,* trans. E. B. Pusey, book 10; Petrarch, "Mont Ventoux," p. 317. Cf. Wuttke, *Dazwischen,* index.

spirit that you collect yourself within . . . Establish, then, in the spiritual Sinai the contemplation of God, who gave forth the eternal laws; do not look back in fear—for the temptations of the flesh might entice you to return to the jails of Egypt, the vales of ancient servitude, the black shadow of death, the onset of eternal night, and the mire of the Styx.[37]

It was when Leonardo used landscape to show that painting was the victor in the contest between art and poetry that the concept of "landscape" broke free from the *parerga* of the painting's background. Did not the painter, using his mind *and* hands, bring together everything in the universe in a simultaneous "proportioned harmony,"[38] condensed into a single glance and a single moment?

If the painter wants to see fair women to kindle his love, he has the power to create them, and if he desires to see monstrosities to arouse his fear, his amusement and laughter or even his compassion, he is their Lord and Creator. And if he wishes to bring forth sites or deserts, cool and shady places in times of heat or warm spots when it is cold, he fashions them. So if he desires valleys or wishes to discover vast tracts of land from mountain peaks and look at the sea on the distant horizon beyond them, it is in his power; and so if he wants to look up to the high mountains from low valleys or from high mountains towards the deep valleys and the coastline.[39]

Leonardo did not paint pure landscape pictures. Convinced that man is incapable of creating anything origi-

[37] Bouelles, *Liber,* chapter 51, pp. 308–309.

[38] Leonardo da Vinci, *Treatise on Painting,* cited after Gombrich, *Norm and Form,* p. 112.

[39] Ibid., pp. 111–112.

nal except in his children, he praises painting in the *Paragone,* or *Treatise on Painting,* as the *grandchild* of nature, which imitates her works and thereby expresses its love for its "inventor" and "great director."[40] Painting is a science, and those who disdain it love neither philosophy nor nature, as he states at the opening of his theses on the incomparability of painting.[41] When he compares the poet's power to arouse feelings by the power of words, on the one hand, with the painter's power to reconstruct creation in a picture and achieve even stronger effects, it does not imply, as Gombrich holds, that Leonardo regarded the driving force for painting as lying in the sense of self.[42]

The landscapes of the world did not emerge from the omnipotence of the emotions, but from the Stoic position of Bouelles's sage, who animates the world in order to praise creation. Like all humanist scholars of his period, Charles de Bouelles was a pilgrim between worlds. It is not known whether he also saw landscapes painted *alla fiamminga* in the Netherlands or in Spain, in Germany or in Italy. But he owes to the genre his *triadic* contemplation of the pilgrim eye in painting—the pilgrim whose hat is the sky and whose shoes are the earth.[43] With watercolor, brush, quill, and crayon, they drew from life, "for truly, art lies in nature, and he who can draw it out of her has it."[44] From the *parerga* of their travels, they composed their complex visions of the world in oil on wood, in copperplate, or on canvas.

In the hierarchy of genres, this new genre was given the lowest place, although it was immensely popular with

---

[40] Ibid., p. 112.
[41] Loc. cit.
[42] Loc. cit.
[43] "The sky is my hat, the earth is my shoe," is the start of the song of the poor pilgrim in the songbook collected by Achim von Arnim and Clemens Brentano, *Des Knaben*

Wunderhorn (1806–1808; rptd. Munich, 1963), vol. 3, p. 225.
[44] Dürer, *Schriften und Briefe,* p. 198: *"Dann wahrhaftig steckt die Kunst in der Natur, wer sie heraus kann reissen, der hat sie."* (*Herausreissen* = to tear out; [*auf*]*reissen* = to draw, sketch.)

collectors from every class of society both at home and abroad. "There is not a cobbler's house without a German landscape," Vasari wrote in 1548.[45] At this period, the writings of Georgius Agricola first opened the way for a realization that even the shape of the earth is subject to constant change. It is water, wind, and the embers burning within the earth that form mountains, hills, and valleys: "Although all of these changes take place on a vast scale, they usually go unnoticed, since due to the long periods of time they require, they vanish from human memory."[46]

In his great panoramas of the world, the elder Bruegel gave visible shape to these natural forces from a dizzying perspective. Thereafter, painters gradually withdrew once again from the expanse of the world into the safety of the woods. The landscapes produced in the second half of the century give the impression of being a synthesis between David's forest view and Altdorfer's wall of leaves, with a peephole into a distant world with a high horizon added. Magpies, woodpeckers, kingfishers, and owls await the viewer's gaze within the obscurity of the leaves; scenes from the stories of biblical figures, religious penitents, or ancient gods are played out in this or that clearing, if the lush vegetation does not wholly encircle a hunting scene or a solitary angler. And finally, the entirety of the animal fauna enters the earthly paradise in the work of Roelandt Savery, with a natural Noah's ark or the pillared temple of the forest in which Orpheus is singing as he plays his lyre. In the meantime, however, yet another genre had developed out of the outer wings of David's altar.

[45] Cited after Gombrich, *Norm and Form*, p. 110.

[46] Agricola, *De Ortu et Causis Subterraneorum* (Basle, 1546), book 3, p. 36.

Part Three

STILL LIFE
AND THE SOUND OF
RUSHING TIME

It's said that time runs swift; but who has seen it fly?
In the span of the world unmoving doth it lie.

ANGELUS SILESIUS

All good things come from distant parts, the proverb
  Says; and, traveling from far across the sea
In India, tobacco—that noble herb—
  Is evidence of this most certainly.
The New World, sending tribute to the Old,
  This worthy plant in honor does unfold.

It is a herb in which the savages delight
  That's wont to make men fuddled, mad and wild
As foolish as when other lusty things incite
  And please the senses, leaving them beguiled,
Their own flames kindling as our fires they stoke
  Then passing off and vanishing like smoke.

It's murder unavenged for those who crave
  This art that mocks at death in its presumption
And only sends us to an early grave,
  The sick man but a fool for the physician.
The use of this herb he alone should avouch
  Whose body can be brushed off like his pouch.

SIGMUND VON BIRKEN

I
Tobacco Piece
with False Berries

 glass of white wine, a clay pipe, a roll of tobacco with a little pile alongside, a sheet of paper, a burning fuse, and two straw/berries have assembled themselves within the tiniest of spaces. The fuse hanging over the edge of the rummer has been glowing for some 370 years without consuming the hempen cord, while the window of the room in which the little painting[1] was made is still floating in the wine, a triple image of the sun.

---

[1] Georg Flegel, *Smoker's Still Life*, oil on red beechwood, 21.5 cm × 17 cm (Historisches Museum, Frankfurt).

No human shadow clouds the smoker's still life. The painter has made himself scarce, leaving the objects to speak for themselves. Their whereabouts and the reason for their meeting are a mystery. A "tobacco piece"[2] was never set in a niche before.[3] Classics of optical illusion, these painted arch-shaped hollows in the wall produce a deceptive continuity with our own space, while the gifts brought for presentation to the evening's host have canceled out the world's transience through their permanence.

When a world can be revealed within it, the narrowness of the space is pleasing. But what is the world for which the strawberries are intended, and who is the guest for whom the painter has set one solid intoxicant and one liquid one inside the angular niche? The earthenware pipe is leaning on the wall, empty; alongside the roll of tobacco there is a crumbled heap lying ready to fill the pipe, and the glowing fuse is at hand to light it, but what *lout* (the literal meaning of the painter's name, Flegel) has laid the fuse over the rim of the fragile glass, of all places, with its contents ready for us to drink?

The beer tankard is familiar as the "consort of tobacco"[4] in Dutch still lifes, but even in the Netherlands it is sometimes clear wine that is poured for the smoker.[5] Flegel later contrasted this frugal daytime tobacco piece with an appetizing nocturnal one: an apple, vol-au-vents, bread, and a splendid Venetian glass with white wine in it are set on a table in the light of a candle, with the smoker's

[2] Smoker's still lifes were originally termed *toebackje*.

[3] In so-called niche paintings, tobacco utensils are only seen accompanied by powerful *vanitas* elements such as skulls or clocks.

[4] Sigmund von Birken (1626–1681), *Die Truckene Trunkenheit* (Dry Drunkenness) (Nuremberg, 1658; ed. Karl Pörnbacher, Munich, 1967), p. 20.

[5] E.g., in the fine *toebackje* by Karel Slabbaert; cf. Laurens J. Bol, *Holländische Maler des 17. Jahrhunderts nahe den grossen Meistern, Landschaft und Stilleben* (Brunswick, 1969), p. 86.

utensils laid out before them.[6] As the years moved on—
no longer coming toward him, but passing away ever
faster—the painter began to set the time alongside his signature. From 1630 onward, his paintings are dated. The
nocturnal "smoke-drinking piece" (*Rauchsaufstück*) was
painted in 1631, but this daytime niche does not have a
date alongside the ligatured monogram. The painting
combines one early characteristic of Flegel's work and
one late one. At the beginning of his career as a self-
employed still life painter, he devoted himself to the
trompe-l'oeil topic of the "niche," while toward the end
of his career, a monochrome tendency emerges in his
work. The lack of a date and the painting's "topaz coloring,"[7] from which only the strawberries stand out, suggest
that the piece is the forerunner of a series of clay-colored
still lifes that Flegel produced in the eight years before his
death, so that the painting can be dated to the "late
1620s."[8]

The strawberries stand out, both in their coloring and
in terms of content. There is no other smoker's still life in
which the fruit appears—and in fact, it is not really a
fruit. The plant belongs to the Rosaceae family, and in
botany its false berries are termed "receptacles." "In the
strawberry (*Fragaria*), the base of the flower swells into an

---

[6] See the catalog *Georg Flegel 1566–1638*, ed. Kurt Wettengl (Historisches Museum, Frankfurt, 1993), p. 134. The painting does not show a fuse, using the candle instead to represent the element of fire.

[7] Kurt Wettengl, "Die 'Gedeck-ten Tische' des Georg Flegel," op. cit., p. 80. The Flegel exhibition designed by Wettengl and the cata-log of it edited by him, along with his shrewd interpretations of Flegel's still lifes, represent the best possible refutation of all the talk

about the end of art history. Cf. A. Albus, "Kleines ABC prominen-ter Ideen der modernen Art," in *Kursbuch* 122 (Berlin, 1995), pp. 135–146. Wettengl's arguments run from the laying of the table to the humors of medicine, and in what follows here I retrace these argu-ments in order to spin my web of interpretation in the manner of the structuralist Bouelles and the Bouel-list Claude Lévi-Strauss.

[8] Wettengl, op. cit., p. 126.

arching mound, the fleshy receptacle that bears the fruits. The small yellowish grains set on the red surface of the flower base are not actually seeds, but tiny nuts (achenes), each of which surrounds a seed."[9]

In the early seventeenth century, the nutlike nature of the grains and the falseness of the fruit had not yet been discovered, but the special quality of the strawberry did not escape notice in an age that recognized a "natural grace planted by God"[10] in all things: what other berries conceal within their interior, the strawberry reveals. Its seeds are embedded on the outside of the pulp. The mystery of the unfolding of the plant from the seed is applied here to its outer clothing, as it were; and in the hidden sphere, this is what shaped its symbolic meaning. The principle of the false berry is that of inversion. The life that is usually concealed, which germinates within after the outer fruiting body has decayed, appears on the exterior of the strawberry, while the decay of the flesh is concealed within. In both ways, this earth-hugging plant points to distant Paradise: the strawberry appears in Ovid as the nourishment of the Golden Age, in which "Earth of itself . . . offered all that one might need,"[11] while in Heinrich Seuse it is described as "the food of the blessed souls."[12]

By analogy with this embedding of the seed in the pulp, with the seed-children being laid out, the straw-

[9] Kerner, *Pflanzenleben,* vol. 2, p. 429.

[10] "*Von Gott eyngepflantzte natür-liche anmuthung*"—Johannes Kepler, *Tertius interveniens. Das ist Warnung an etliche Theologos, Medicos und Philosophos . . . dass sie bey billicher Verwerffung der Sternguckerischen Aberglauben nicht das Kindt mit dem Badt ausschütten und hiermit jhrer Profession unwissendt zuwider handeln* (A warning to some theologians,

physicians, and philosophers not to throw out the baby with the bathwater by cheaply dismissing stargazing superstitions, thereby unwittingly undermining their own professions) (Frankfurt, 1610); *Gesammelte Werke,* ed. von Dyck/Caspar/Hammer, 1937–, vol. 4, p. 246.

[11] *Metamorphoses* 1.102.

[12] Heinrich Seuse (ca. 1295–1366).

berry was regarded in popular belief as food for the souls of departed children. According to one legend, the Virgin leads the souls of children to pick strawberries in Paradise on St. John the Baptist's day.[13] Medieval alchemists regarded the aromatic fruit as a panacea, and even Fontenelle believed he owed his longevity to it.[14] "The cook is also familiar with strawberries, which make a good mousse, and with their cooling action they are more fitting for those who are sick and feverish more than for those who are in health," Hieronymus Bock wrote in his herbal in 1539.[15]

According to the ancient theory of humors, which held sway for more than two millennia, health was a state in which a balanced mixture of the *quattuor humores* was maintained:[16]

> There are four humors in man, which imitate diverse elements; they increase at different seasons, and rule at different ages of life. Blood imitates the air, increasing in spring and ruling in childhood. Yellow bile (choler) imitates fire, growing in summer and ruling in adolescence. Black bile (melancholy) imitates earth, growing in fall and ruling in maturity. Phlegm imitates water, growing in winter and ruling in old age. If these flow neither too little nor too much, a man will flourish in vigor.[17]

[13] Cf. Manfred Lurker, *Symbolik*, p. 177, and, in the *Wörterbuch der deutschen Volkskunde*, ed. O. A. Erich and R. Beitl (Stuttgart, 1974), p. 179: "Yet another type of 'berry offering' is when children leave a berry that has fallen to the ground lying where it has dropped. In Bohemia, for example, they say this is for the 'poor souls.' "

[14] Bernard de Fontenelle (1657–1757).

[15] Hieronymus Bock (1498–1554), *Kräuterbuch*. "Die Köch seind der Erdbeeren auch gewar worden, machen gute Müslin, gebüren den kranken, hitzigen Menschen mehr dann den Gesunden, um der Külung willen."

[16] *Quattuor humores* = four liquids. The word "humor" is derived from the theory of the temperaments.

[17] Pseudo-Bede, *De Mundi Constitutione*, 1135, cited after Raymond

The four elements are inhabited by four qualities: fire by heat, air by cold, water by wetness, earth by dryness. The humors in man, the four character types, ages of life, and seasons are all tempered in two ways: blood, the sanguine type, childhood, and spring are considered warm and wet; yellow bile, the choleric type, youth, and summer are warm and dry; black bile, the melancholy type, maturity, and fall are cold and dry; phlegm, the phlegmatic type, old age, and winter are cold and wet.[18]

Illness is defined as a predominance or scarcity of one or the other of these qualities. By applying the opposite element, the physician aims to restore harmony in the balance of the humors. The treatment is based on nutrition, attempting to readjust the "dyscrasia"[19] of wet and dry, warm and cold, sweet and sour, bitter and salty, pungent and dull substances in the body through a wise choice of

Klibansky, Erwin Panofsky, and Fritz Saxl, *Saturn and Melancholy: Studies in the History of Natural Philosophy, Religion and Art* (London, 1964), p. 3.

[18] The link between the cosmic elements and the "bodily humors"—blood, yellow bile, black bile, and phlegm—and their connection with the four seasons led to a division that was then referred back to the view of the elements. A fourteenth-century *Kräuterbüchlein* (herbal) states, "the first part is the summer, which has a dry and warm nature and resembles fire. The second is spring, which is warm and wet and resembles air. The third is winter, which is cold and wet, like water. The fourth is fall, which is cold and dry, like earth . . . All of God's creatures have their nature from these four, then he is known as 'microcosm.' " (*"Daz erst tail ist der sumer, der ist trockner und haizer natur und geleichet sich dem feur. daz ander ist der lenz, der ist haizer und fäuchter und geleichet sich dem luft. daz dritte ist der winter, der ist kalter und fäuchter natur, als daz wazzer. daz vierd ist der herbst, der ist kalter und truckner natur, als die erde . . . von den vieren habent ir natur alle geschepht gots, und der mensch hat aller der natur iegleichs ain teil an ime, etliches mer, etleichs minner; wan er aller vier an im hat, so haizet er microcosmus."*) Cf. Grimm, vol. 11, pp. 78–79. As with all theories, there were various schools of thought regarding the humors, with disputes over which was the correct system; cf. *Saturn and Melancholy,* pp. 10–11.

[19] From the Greek word for "bad mixture"; "a bad or disordered condition of the body, originally supposed to arise from disproportionate mixture of the 'humours' " (*Oxford English Dictionary*).

counteracting foodstuffs. The classification of dishes, drinks, and medicines according to the crasis theory—which was attributed to Hippocrates, systematized by Galen, and canonized by Avicenna—was as familiar in the seventeenth century as the three corresponding precepts:

> The first is to maintain a certain diet in eating and drinking, and to observe well the conditions of the place and time, of the body, and also of the dishes and drinks themselves, which is to say: *quantitas, qualitas, substantia, modus, ordo, & mensura.*[20] The second commands avoidance of anything rotten. The third forbids the use of any things that are damaging to nature in themselves and which can weaken the heat or wetness introduced, which is to say: excessive lying awake, worry, trouble, tiredness, and then too much of dry or warming substances, which cause the body to dry up.[21]

Just as the natives of America welcomed as gods those who were about to destroy them, the white men welcomed tobacco—which came to Europe in the sixteenth century—as a divine plant that was a panacea for every ill. The fresh leaves were used as plasters for wounds, and their juice was used as a balm and tincture, in ointment or tablet form; initially, the cured leaves were sniffed in powder form, and finally their smoke was "drunk,"[22] in imitation of the Indian "swallowers." In the enthusiasm that followed its discovery, the power to cure any type of afflic-

---

[20] I.e., quantity, quality, substance, mode (method of preparation), order (sequence), and measure.

[21] Sigmund von Birken, *Trunkenheit*, p. 134.

[22] The word "smoking" for the consumption of tobacco came into use only toward the end of the seventeenth century; before that, "drinking" or "boozing" was used.

tion was ascribed to this member of the nightshade family. Tobacco could dispel catarrh and phlegm, and strengthen the vital spirits as well as the powers of memory, "by purifying and emptying its house—that is, the brain, the fortress and capital of phlegm (as Hippocrates calls it)—of coarse fumes, so that it can then be filled with the ideas of things."[23] In addition, the "sacred wound salve and tobacco herb" could heal open wounds, boils, asthma, rheumatism, cough, women's disorders, poisonous bites of rabid dogs, toothache, headache, and stomachache. In particular, over a long period its reputation for working miracles against the plague encouraged the spread of tobacco.

Due to its pungent taste, burning the mouth and "disturbing the senses," tobacco was regarded as being warm and dry in nature, like the choleric. Three types were distinguished, and they were associated with different *humores,* classified as cold or hot, which gave the choleric herb a melancholic tendency.[24] Phlegmatics and old people were regarded as benefiting from tobacco, while there was no doubt of its injurious effect on youths and those with a choleric temperament, who were already heated to start with. "Tobacco, in our Age, is immoderately growne into use; And it affects Men with a secret kinde of Delight; In so much, that they who have once inured themselves to it, can hardly afterwards leave it," Francis Bacon wrote in 1623.[25]

The "smoke-drinking addiction" first appeared in Spain, England, and Holland. The ranks of the herb's foes swelled in proportion to those of its enthusiasts. What to some was a "miracle confection," the "noblest

---

[23] Sigmund von Birken, *Trunkenheit,* p. 139.

[24] Ibid., p. 97.

[25] Francis Bacon (1561–1626), *History Naturall and Experimentall, of Life and Death* (London, 1638; STC 1158), pp. 192–193, a translation of the Latin original, *Historia Vitae et Mortis* (London, 1623; STC 1156), pp. 220–221.

medicinal herb," a "pleasure-herb," the "salvation of the whole world" was to others a body-destroying "hell's herb," whose devilish origin could easily be recognized from its stench and the "bellows cheeks" of the "smokepots," "tobacco-heads," "puff-war heroes," "pipe-chewers," "pipe-milkers," and "snot-mouths" who used it.[26] The engraved title page of Sigmund von Birken's *Dry Drunkenness* declaims,

What is it all you puffers do? Is smoking drinking?
The pipe is made of dirt, and all that's left is ashes.
What is tobacco? Death. Flee, flee this herb, concealing
A viper within—or it will have you in its clutches.[27]

At the same time, one writer regarded the deadly effects of tobacco as being a punishment for the annihilation of the Indians: "I have, said the Devil, fairly revenged the Indians on the Spaniards, for the violence they did to them; for by putting tobacco in the Spaniards' heads, I did them more damage than the King of Spain did to the Indians with all his Columbis, Pizarris, Cortesiis, Alkmeiris, and other tyrants."[28]

The puffing fashion first came to Germany along with the English auxiliaries sent to the Winter King, Frederick V, in Bohemia at the start of the Thirty Years' War. When the tobacco trade began to flourish during the

[26] These terms for tobacco and smokers are all taken from Johann Neander (see this page, above) and Sigmund von Birken (*Wunder-Confect, fürnembstes Arzney-Kräutlein, Erfrölichungs-Kraut, Heil aller Welt; Höllenkraut; Blasebalg-Backen, Rauch-döpfe, Krauthäupter, Schmauchkrieg-Helden, Pfeifenbeisser, Pipenmelker, Rotzguschen*).

[27] Sigmund von Birken, *Trunk-enheit*, p. 200: *"Was macht ihr Schmäucher ihr? was Trinken, ist der Rauch? | Die Pipe, komt vom Koht. Was überbleibt, ist Aschen. | Was ist Tabak? der Tod. Flieht, flieht vor diesem Strauch, | der eine Schlange deckt! Sie wird euch sonst erhaschen."*

[28] Johann Michael Moscherosch (1601–1669), cited after Karl Pörnbacher, afterword to *Truckene Trunkenheit*, p. 211.

1620s, Spanish, Flemish, Dutch, and Wallonian *Tubacks-kremer* ("tobacco merchants") settled in the German cities, taking the place of the spice merchants, confectioners, and apothecaries who had formerly sold the drug wrapped in little packages. The tobacco merchants soon became known as "tobacconists" (*Tabakisten*),[29] and the districts around Frankfurt, Hanau, and Nuremberg became renowned for tobacco growing.

A eulogy of tobacco by the Bremen physician Johann Neander was published in 1622, becoming the most successful tobacco book of the first half of the seventeenth century. The occasional lampoon was probably also appearing by this time, but the full-blown dispute over the plant, which had already occasioned a pamphlet of invective in England in 1602, broke out in Germany only around the middle of the century.

If the estimated date of the painting is correct, the "Tobacco Piece with Strawberries" was painted in around 1628. Frankfurt had not yet become a theater of war. The unscrupulous condottiere from Bohemia,[30] whose motto "War feeds war" elevated plunder and pillage into a principle, had been appointed generalissimo of the Baltic and Oceanic Seas, and his army of mercenaries was busy laying waste to Brandenburg, Pomerania, Mecklenburg, and Jutland. In Flegel's home country of Bohemia and Moravia, horrific punishment followed the collapse of the republic of Estates based on the Dutch model. One hundred and fifty thousand emigrants—dispossessed nobles and a people deprived of all the freedoms of the Estates—fled from the prospect of forcible re-Catholicization.

---

[29] Cf. Wettengl, *Flegel* catalog, p. 74. Tobacco growers and manufacturers were also known as "tobacconists" in English (*Oxford English Dictionary*) and *Tabakisten* in Ger-man (cf. Alexander Dietz, *Frankfurter Handelsgeschichte* [Frankfurt, 1925], vol. 4, p. 58).

[30] Albrecht von Wallenstein (1583–1634).

Flegel was an old man by now. A self-portrait of 1630 shows the sixty-four-year-old with a long beard over his ruff; with wrinkled forehead, he is looking with a half-skeptical, half-melancholy gaze from the frame of a medallion leaning on a sandglass. Two of his seven children had followed in his footsteps professionally, probably serving their apprenticeship with him. One, an "apprentice painter," died at the age of nineteen in 1616 and the other, an "artist" aged about twenty-one, died in January 1623. The entries for them in the register of deaths place the two strawberries lying under the coffin-shaped arch of the niche here in the light of the souls of the departed.[31]

Death made Flegel the successor of his own artistic heirs. As he goes to meet it, the painter has brought for those who have gone before him an offering of smoke, wine, and berries. In Hippocrates, the aphorism *Vita brevis, ars longa*[32] is used to introduce a skeptical observation: life is short, and the art of humoral medicine requires a great deal of time. For Flegel's sons, the physician's art was of no avail. It was only in art that its balancing forces were able to unfold: in the *Smoker's Still Life,* a tobacco piece with strawberries, a remembrance of the apprentice painter and the young artist has remained alive.

---

[31] It is only very rarely that we are able to find traces of the lives of the discreet painters of still lifes in their paintings. We know nothing about a great painter such as Clara Peters, although she left a self-portrait in the convex mirrors of the magnificent goblets in her wonderful still lifes. See Pamela Hibbs Decoteau, *Clara Peters* (Lingen, 1992), p. 113. If we knew nothing about the trial for heresy to which Torrentius was subjected, we would only be able to interpret the painter's *Still Life with Bridle* as an allegory of temperance. Cf. Zbigniew Herbert, *Still Life with a Bridle: Essays and Apocryphas,* trans. John and Bogdana Carpenter (London, 1993), pp. 82–112.

[32] "Life is short, art is long." The passage in Hippocrates reads, "Life is short, science is long; opportunity is elusive, experiment is dangerous, judgement is difficult" (*The Medical Works of Hippocrates,* trans. John Chadwick and W. N. Mann [Oxford, 1950], p. 148). See also Seneca, *De brevitate vitae* 1.

"Water, earth, air, and fire, and the other parts of this creation of mine, are no more instruments of thy life than they are of thy death," Nature says in Montaigne. "Why dost thou fear thy last day?"[33] It was a timely question for Flegel, over sixty years old. In the smoker's still life, we can see his answer with our own eyes. If we listen closely, we will see the stillness in the sound of rushing time.

[33] *The Essays of Michel de Montaigne,* trans. Charles Cotton (London, 1913), vol. 1, p. 83.

*G*o out of this world," says nature, "as
you entered into it; the same pass you made from death to life,
without passion or fear, the same, after the same manner,
repeat from life to death. Your death is a part of the order of
the universe, 'tis a part of the life of the world. Shall I
exchange for you this beautiful contexture of things? 'Tis the
condition of your creation; death is a part of you, and while
you endeavour to evade it, you evade yourselves."

MONTAIGNE

II
The Fuse
Forever Passing Away

oney-colored, the wine is glinting through
the green glass. Three of the senses are
needed to judge of its quality in color,
bouquet, and taste. Taken at the right time
and in moderate quantities, wine is
praised in the Bible as the water of life;[1] but the demonic
effects of excessive consumption were summed up by Fischart in a rhyme:

I truly think that with the wine
He's drunk the holy ghost divine
In the shape of a raven all white.[2]

[1] "Wine is like life to men, if you
drink it in moderation. What is life
to a man who is without wine? It has
been created to make men glad.
Wine drunk in season and temper-
ately is rejoicing of heart and glad-
ness of soul." (Ecclesiasticus
[Sirach] 31.27–28.)

[2] "*Da hat er, denck ich, bey dem
Wein | den heiligen Geist genommen ein |
in einer Gstalt eins weiszen Raben.*"
(Johann Fischart [1546/7–1590];
cf. Grimm, vol. 28, p. 848.)

⁄ 223 ⁄

It is a question of temperament[3] whether wine gladdens the heart, puts cares to flight, soothes melancholy, reveals truth, brings lost words swimming to the surface, unlocks every window of the mind "to make the understanding fly"[4]—or instead makes one dull and stupid, stirs up envy and resentment, greed and anger, makes the tongue behave as if it were walking on stilts[5] and torments the mind with illusions. What matters is whether the drinker's temperament matches that of the drink. "We have so many instructions on how to cultivate wine properly, but none on how to drink it properly. It only grows well when protected by a gentle sky; and equally, those who drink it are best to have gentle souls,"[6] wrote Lichtenberg—at a time when the theory of the humors was already almost forgotten. Only the term "dry" for wines in which the sugar is completely fermented recalls today the old theory in natural science that regarded all liquids that were acidic, bitter, and astringent as "dry." Humoral medicine saw the essence of things as lying not in their general state but in their power to mediate between the macrocosm and the microcosm. The temperature affects whether wine is sweet or acidic, but wine is always regarded as dry. Its choleric nature in youth and its melancholic nature in maturity are assigned to the realms of the earth and the air. Just as black bile produced the "most varied mental conditions," "wine, according to its temperature and the amount drunk, produced the most varied emotional effects, making men cheerful or sad, or garrulous or taciturn, or raving or apathetic."[7]

---

[3] *Temperamentum* means "correct mixture" and "proper measure."

[4] Fischart, loc. cit.

[5] Ibid., p. 847.

[6] Georg Christoph Lichtenberg, *Schriften und Briefe,* ed. Franz H. Mautner (Frankfurt, 1983), vol. 1, p. 525. The letter is not included in the selection translated into English in his *Aphorisms and Letters,* trans. Franz Mautner and Henry Hatfield (London, 1969).

[7] Klibansky, *Saturn and Melancholy,* p. 30.

The self-consuming element that wine arouses creates an effect of inversion, following the principle "wine lives on wine"—according to a proverb, at the first glass it is the man who drinks the wine; at the second, it is the wine that drinks the wine; and at the third, it is the wine that drinks the man.

The reason why the heating or inflammatory effect of wine is linked to its "airy" nature in humoral medicine can be appreciated only when we recall the natural processes by which it is produced, from the vineyard to the barrel—processes that at one time were perfectly familiar, when every child was able to watch them with his own eyes. The age of pictorial emblems was still at home with the wealth of allegory[8] that encompassed bending the twigs, cutting, peaking, binding the grapes, raking, fertilizing, weeding, picking, pressing the wine, fermenting it, and burning the dead vine wood in winter, as well as the vine's panicled inflorescences known as "lights," the "tears" of the sprouting vine, the "bud-wool" of the shoots, the "knots" of the stems, the "rape"[9] of the grapes, the pips, and the "frost" on the berries that holds their yeast.

The vine flourishes in stony, well-drained soils that warm up quickly. The proportions of clay, silicate, calcium, and iron oxide in the earth give the wine its characteristic taste, and the warmth of the sun completes the ripening process. At the grape harvest in September, the winepress follows, with the cellarman succeeding the winegrower. The metamorphosis of must into wine is

---

[8] "Thus the great allegorical current of the Middle Ages, far from shrinking, flows on in an ever widening channel," wrote Jean Seznec in his cheerfully melancholic book on the emblem-loving sixteenth and seventeenth centuries (*Survival of the Pagan Gods,* p. 103).

[9] *Rape* (substantive 6) in the *Oxford English Dictionary,* "The stalks of grape-clusters, or refuse of grapes from which wine has been expressed, used in making vinegar."

accomplished by fermentation, a process that resembles rotting.[10] The yeast particles break down the glucose in the grapes, and that is converted into alcohol and carbon dioxide—producing effervescence and a rise in temperature. A careless cellarman may find the carbon dioxide release bursting the barrel. After the first purification, the wine is separated from the yeast, which is left behind as an inedible sediment—the separation process not being accomplished without leaving a residue.

Fully fermented and clarified, the wine is a child of the fall, just like the melancholic. The bitter residues match the image of black bile, just like the barrel that bursts in unfavorable conditions. The "airy" nature of wine is seen in its effervescence; it is this that kindles fire in the drinker. Like the element of air, wine wavers between hot and cold, depending on its variety, its age and purity; and just as "noble melancholy"[11] is distinguished from the common type by the link between its earthy firmness and warm-blooded vivacity, so too a nobler wine is distinguished by the link between earthy dryness and airy heat, through which in the course of time its subtle body develops: "The older it grows, the drier and hotter it becomes," writes Dryander; and Guarinonius declares that fully fermented wine is "much nobler and more special, just as all that is dry in nature is more noble than what is moist."[12]

Even the best wine can never be wiser than its drinker. The drinking customs of the age are seen in a harsh light in a remark in the *Book of the Sage:* "So many mugs and amphorae of wine are drunk, one is tempted to think the

<hr />

[10] Cf. "Das Wesen der Gärung und der Fäulnis," in Dannemann, *Naturwissenschaften,* vol. 4, pp. 227–228.

[11] Cf. Klibansky, *Saturn and Melancholy,* pp. 122–123.

[12] Johann Dryander (1500–1560), *Der gantzen Arzenei gemeyner Inhalt, wes einem Artzt, bede in der theoric vnd practic zusteht* (Frankfurt, 1542), folio 36 recto. Hippolytus Guarinonius (1571–1654), *Die Grewel der Verwüstung menschlichen Geschlechts* (Ingolstadt, 1610), p. 637.

reproduction of the human race serves no other purpose than to dry out the vineyards."[13]

It is only in measure that noble wine can contribute to the harmony of the *quattuor humores,* to a concordance of mind and morality. These, too, draw their inspiration from the cosmos. Clarity of mind is like fire, its purity like air, its firmness and capacity to receive impressions are like earth, and its flexibility is like water. So far as morality is concerned, the mind has sweetness in place of blood, "in place of red bile bitterness, in place of black bile grief, in place of phlegm equanimity. For the doctors say that the sanguine are sweet, cholerics bitter, melancholics sad, and phlegmatics equable. Thus in contemplation lies sweetness, from remembrance of sin comes bitterness, from its commission grief, from its atonement equanimity."[14]

Just as air mediates between the heat of the sun and the earth, mature wine can help relieve bitterness and grief in well-tempered equanimity. To remove the residues of bitter feeling, a little tobacco is harmless in old age. But the dual heat of wine and tobacco seems poorly balanced by the two moist, cool strawberries.

"Look not to the wine, as it glitters in the glass,"[15] is an ancient admonition. In the enigmatic reversal of this in the deceptive painting, the balancing takes place at another level, behind the painter's back.

There are twelve professions represented in the painting (if we disregard traders).[16] A stonemason has carved

[13] Bouelles, *Liber,* chapter 16, p. 134.

[14] Cf. Klibansky, *Saturn and Melancholy,* p. 107.

[15] This saying, quoted by Bouelles in his *Book of the Sage* (*Le Livre du sage*), p. 132, is by the Neo-Latin poet Ludovicus Pictorius Bigus (1454–1520), whose *Christiana Opuscula,* published in Modena in 1498, is dedicated to Giovanni Francesco della Mirandola.

[16] Stonemason, bricklayer, glassblower, winegrower, cellarman, tobacconist, papermaker, farmer, hemp-dresser, rope-maker, pipe-baker, gardener.

the stones for the niche, a bricklayer has set them in place. In a forest cabin in Hesse or in the Spessart mountains,[17] a glassblower has given the rummer its bulging shape with his breath, and has fused the berries onto the cylindrical stem. We have met the winegrower in the vineyard, and the cellarman at his barrels. The tobacco has probably come from Strasbourg and has been cured, piled, rolled, and pressed into bales in Frankfurt.[18] The paper for the wrapper in which the "tobacco merchant" sold his wares has been made by a papermaker out of old rag, and the "fimble hemp" grown by the farmer has been hackled by the hemp-dresser[19] into threads, from which the rope-maker has twisted the cord for the fuse. The fine white clay of the "smoke-flute" has been fired by a "pipe-baker" in a mold that stamped the tendril pattern on it, and even the two strawberries have attained their "noble" form through garden cultivation.

The materials of the niche, pipe, and glass belong to the mineral kingdom, while those of the other five objects belong to the vegetable kingdom: stone, clay, and quartz sand belong to the body of the earth, while strawberry, vine, tobacco herb, hemp, and flax have their roots in it. Fire was the decisive element in creating their shapes. The strawberries have ripened in the natural fire of the sun, and the glucose that warms the wine as it decomposes is owed to the sun. The tobacco pickle made of wine, salt, and spices[20] is reduced on the flame in the kitchen, while the pipe is baked in the kiln and the glass is taken from the furnace. Hemp is roasted before it is twisted, and even the water in which the rags are rotted in the barrel for paper-making is heated.

[17] Cf. Wettengl, *Flegel-Katalog,* p. 74.

[18] Cf. Dietz, *Handelsgeschichte,* vol. 4, pp. 56–57, and Sigmund von Birken, *Trunkenheit,* pp. 106–107.

[19] On hemp and hemp-dressing, cf. Grimm, vol. 10, pp. 431–432 (*Hanf, Hänfer*).

[20] Birken, *Trunkenheit,* pp. 102–103.

The objects have received their shapes in antithetical ways: in the strawberry, the flower base swells up from *within* through *cold moistness,* and ripens through *natural* warming from the *outside* to become a *soft* fruit. The berries of glass are created in *dry* form, through *artificial* fire from *outside,* and *harden* through *natural cooling* from *within.* In the grape, the fruit is harvested when the leaves from which the grapes drew their nutrients have already fallen, while in the tobacco herb the formation of fruit is arrested so that all the nutrients are drawn into the leaves. In contrast to the *hot*-blown *liquid* of molten glass, which receives its shape through *internal* pressure and *discontinuous* heat,[21] the *hard* earth of the pipe is molded by *external* pressure when *cold,* and is baked using *continuous* heat. The *wet* fibers of the paper pulp *stick together* when they are ladled by the papermaker, while when the hemp is hackled, the *dry* fibers are *combed apart.* The *spicy* and *salty* sauce or pickle in which the dry tobacco leaves are fermented is added from the *outside,* while the ferment for the *"noble rot"* and *sweet* fermentation of grape juice comes from *within.*

[21] "The glassblower starts his operations with a *tube,* which he first closes at one end so as to form a hollow vesicle, within which his blast of air exercises a uniform pressure on all sides; but the spherical conformation which this uniform expansive force would naturally tend to produce is modified into all kinds of forms by the trammels or resistances set up as the workman lets one part or another of his bubble be unequally heated or cooled. It was Oliver Wendell Holmes who first shewed this curious parallel between the operations of the glassblower and those of Nature, when she starts, as she so often does, with a simple tube. The alimentary canal, the arterial system including the heart, the central nervous system of the vertebrate, including the brain itself, all begin as simple tubular structures. And with them Nature does just what the glassblower does, and, we might even say, no more than he. For she can expand the tube here and narrow it there; thicken its walls or thin them; blow off a lateral offshoot or caecal diverticulum; bend the tube, or twist and coil it; and infold or cramp its walls as, so to speak, she pleases." (D'Arcy Wentworth Thompson, *On Growth and Form: The Complete Revised Edition* [Cambridge, 1942; rptd. New York, 1992], pp. 1049–1050.)

Three things are set before the eye for consumption: wine, strawberries, and tobacco. The rummer is the drinking vessel, the pipe is the smoking tool, the wrapper is the envelope for the tobacco, the fuse is the den of fire, the raw fruits are lying on bare stone—and in the painting they are all encased within the niche.

The glass is as fragile as the clay pipe, and the paper wrapper is hardly more durable than the fuse. Paper slowly decays in damp air, while the fuse is consumed quickest in fire. The more durable the object, the more transitory its abode; savage minds on each side of the ocean correspond to one another.[22] To the painter, who immortalized the tamed fire of the fuse, the everlasting niche must have seemed the appropriate place for ephemeral berries.

Dryander's *Arzney Spiegel,* or *Mirror of Medicine,* reflects the ephemeral body and everlasting temperament of the strawberry:

> The fruit of the strawberry . . . carries much moisture, strong oil and *sal essentiale,* and although its temperament is cold and moist, its sweet and winelike scent seems also to give it a fleeting warmth. Thence, too, if it is not eaten on the same day on which it fully ripens, this fleeting scent passes away, and it rots. In the hot summertime, the berries are otherwise a pleasant dish, particularly for those who are choleric and hot in nature. The berries quench thirst, assuage the heat of the liver and kidneys, purify the blood, assuage bile, promote the passage of urine and stone, and incite sweat . . . And since they bear the signs of leprosy upon them, they are praised as excellent against the latter by Ramundo

---

[22] Cf. Claude Lévi-Strauss, *L'Origine des manières de table—Mythologiques, III* (Paris, 1968), p. 405.

Lullio.[23] But they are not healthy for a sick and cold stomach, and are harmful to those with dropsy . . . they provide very little nutrition, and they easily upset the stomach and then cause fever.[24]

The digestibility of the strawberry is a question of the stomach, which Galen described as the kitchen of the human body:

On the other hand, Galen teaches that nothing can feed the body unless it is first prepared in the stomach, as if in a kitchen; and this is the highway of nutrition, that it passes through the mouth to the stomach, as if into a pantry. From there its very essence is received by the liver, where it is turned to blood, and flows to all the members as foodstuff; which does not happen with smoke. Then again, he teaches that procreation and nutrition are of one and the same material (*"generationis & nutritionis eandem esse materiam"*). But a man is not generated from smoke, and thus smoke is incapable of providing him with nutrition. Moreover, since water cannot provide nutrition, so much the less can smoke, which is far thinner and more incorporeal.

Much more in the same vein could be said; and equally, much could be answered to it. Although smoke itself cannot be touched, it rises from touchable things, and is transformed into things that can be touched, such as soot or haze. Moreover, tobacco smoke contains a herblike power, which is agreeable to the mind, heart, and stomach, strengthening these and putting fresh life into them. Then again, man has two natures: a physical one, which is fed

---

[23] Ramon Llull, or Raymond Lully (ca. 1235–1316).

[24] Johann Dryander, *Artzney Spiegel. Gemeyner Inhalt derselbigen* (Frankfurt, 1547), folio 34 recto.

by earthly and watery matter, and a spiritual one, which is fed by fiery and airy matter—as Galen teaches.[25]

Strawberries, wine, and tobacco are spicy, and their quality is first recognized by the nose. The strawberry's winelike scent is as fleeting as smoke. Its full red color conveys a mental impression opposite to that of white wine and black tobacco; just as its freshness in taste is equally distant from the noble rottenness of wine and the burning decay of tobacco. In the *triangle of the humors,*[26] the strawberry represents water, winter, old age, and the phlegmatic temperament, and forms the apex above the airy wine and the fiery tobacco. At the temporal level of ripening, the elements are shifted. Just as the strawberry quickly acquires from the sun a "fleeting warmth," an airy quality, the airy warmth and moistness of the young wine slowly acquires earthy dryness and fiery heat, while in the course of time the hot and dry tobacco loses its spiciness to the air. The transformation of tobacco is accomplished as it burns within its own element, so that in terms of the duration of its taste and its form, it is as distant from the wine as from the quickly rotting straw/berry, whose place it now takes in the triangle. In the con/text of orientation and procreation, the opposites form a circle. The creeping growth of the perennial strawberry plant is *horizontally* oriented, with runners spreading radi/ally; the upright growth of the annual tobacco plant is *vertical;* and the vine lies at the midpoint between these, since as a climbing semishrub it winds itself *spirally* around the stake. Vine and tobacco spread by seed, while

[25] Sigmund von Birken, *Trunk/enheit,* pp. 117–118.

[26] A borrowing from the culi/nary triangle in Lévi/Strauss, *L'Ori/gine des manières de table,* p. 406; see also *Le Cru et le cuit—Mythologiques, I* (Paris, 1964) and *Du Miel aux cen/dres—Mythologiques, II* (Paris, 1967; index: *cru, cuit, pourri*).

strawberry spreads by both runner and seed. The ephemeral strawberry is thus linked to life in two ways: the seeds develop from the rotted fruit, while the mother plants form a carpet on the forest floor with their daughters. In cultivation, the runners are removed, so that all of the plant's strength goes into the fruit. In the making of white wine, the grape seed is not used, and is left behind during pressing;[27] in tobacco growing, it is necessary to prevent seeds from forming. In tobacco, the buds are not allowed to develop; in the grape, the seeds are not allowed to develop; while the twice-guaranteed fertility of the strawberry is halved. On the way from nature to culture, it is life that is controlled in the strawberry, while it is death that is controlled in wine and tobacco: fermentation processes are equivalent to rotting. Fire is the opposite of fermentation, and this is the element that is controlled during the burning of tobacco.

The wine, strawberries, and tobacco are intended as a trompe-l'oeil of insatiable contemplation, and when seen from the humoral point of view, it is the mind rather than the body that they feed. The path of intellectual nourishment in the *Book of the Sage* gives the impression of being an unnatural deviation from Galen's highway of physical nutrition. For the powers of cognition, it is not the stomach that is the "kitchen," but the heart. Evidence at the intellectual level requires symmetry on the physical level. Bouelles agrees with the theory of the humors to the extent that in Galen, too, the "human mind-soul" resides in the heart and rules "the rest of the psyche . . . from the left cavity."[28] In Bouelles's system, the three modes of the mind—cognition, memory, and contemplation—correspond to the mouth, stomach, and heart. Cognition corresponds to the ingesting mouth, and memory to the

<hr/>

[27] Must is not added to white wine.

[28] *Hippokratische Schriften*, part XVI/68.

"collecting, fixing, and preserving stomach"; while the "assimilative, ordering contemplation"—which sends back to the cognitive power that which has been taken in, linked to memory, and conceptualized—is held to corre⁄ spond to the heart, because it "cooks, digests, and trans⁄ forms" what has been received from the stomach, and returns it to the organism in the blood.[29]

> Just as no natural nourishment can fall into the bowl of the stomach without passing through the mouth, and therefore there is nothing in the stom⁄ ach that has not been in the mouth, so too nothing can be cooked in the heat of the heart that has not beforehand spent some time in the hollow of the palate[30] and the basin of memory; and likewise, there is nothing in the inner memory that was not beforehand in the external cognition, and nothing in contemplation that was not beforehand in cogni⁄ tion and memory. The mouth receives its nourish⁄ ment from no other organ preceding it; it grasps it with the teeth itself. The stomach obtains every⁄ thing it receives from the mouth. The heart, finally, owes to the one and to the other—mouth and stom⁄ ach—what it burns and digests.

Transferred to what Bouelles terms "the organs of the soul," the allegory reveals its meaning:

> The power of cognition does not receive intelligible form from any other part of the soul going before it. Memory is only filled with this form, even satu⁄ rated, through the power of cognition, while contemplation starts from both the one and the

[29] Boulles, *Liber,* chapter 10, p. 106.
[30] *Palato, palais* = "palace."

other—from the power of cognition and from memory.[31]

Three modalities and three organs of the soul correspond to three types of food: that of the senses, that of the imagination, and that of reason. The first comes from the world, the second from the body, and the third is independent—in it, the drama of the sensory world and physical imagination is brought to completion.

The senses, too, "shine" in three ways, in "astonishing symmetry and proportion." There are therefore not five senses, but six—three dominant and three subservient. The hands "create for the eyes writings, colors, and every type of painting. The mouth provides for the ear voices, their sound and every form of harmony. The sense of smell penetrates with diverse scents the brain, the seat of imagination and its illusions, and flatters it pleasantly with their sweet aroma."[32] Hands, mouth, and nose are the vassals, which serve their lords—vision, hearing, and brain—with colors, voices, and scents. The sixth sense in this system is the power of imagination, inventiveness, or fancy.

This triple structure is enclosed within a quadruple one. The literal influence of the large cosmos on man's small one is reflected in the four stages through which existence passes. The element of earth is equivalent to existence, and is reflected in the mineral kingdom; the element of water is equivalent to life, and is reflected in the vegetable kingdom; the element of air is equivalent to emotion, and is reflected in the animal kingdom; the element of fire is equivalent to understanding, and its image is seen in the kingdom of man. Just as the sensory world recognizes itself in the human mind, so too earth, water, and air are conceived in the light of fire. Because it

[31] Boulles, *Liber,* chapter 10, p. 108.
[32] Ibid., chapter 30, p. 202.

encloses the other spheres within the arch of the heavens, effects every transformation in nature, is set in opposition to the earth at the utmost distance, and remains constant within change, fire in Bouelles is regarded—in a Hera- clitean and Stoic tradition—as being the Logos of cre- ation, to which the origin of every shape is owed. The world has developed from the original rational divine fire, and all things return to the "ever-living Fire, kindled in measure and quenched in measure."[33] Man has brought down fire to Earth from the heavens, and has thus inverted the natural order. Rational fire and fiery reason are assimilators; their technique is called the "art of oppo- sites,"[34] *inversion* is their principle of life.

It is through the power of cognition that "the great chain of being"[35] is brought forth from the darkness and chaos of its original identity into the light of oppositions, where it appears in its "concert of opposites."[36] When opposites coincide, things change their places and run back through the sequence of contradictory correspon- dences in the reverse direction. The process termed "antiperistasis"[37] by Bouelles was brought to perfection in a structuralist form by Claude Lévi-Strauss:

> The fundamental opposition, the source of the myr- iad others . . . is precisely the one stated by Hamlet, although in the form of a still over-optimistic choice between two alternatives. Man is not free to choose

[33] Heraclitus, fragment 30, in Kathleen Freeman, *Ancilla to the Pre-Socratic Philosophers* (Oxford, 1948; rptd. Cambridge, Mass., 1983), p. 26.

[34] "The art of opposites": *Ars oppositorum* by Charles de Bouelles was first published in an anthology in Paris in 1511. *L'Art des opposés*, ed. and trans. Pierre Magnard (Paris, 1984).

[35] Ibid., chapter 7, p. 84.

[36] Heraclitus, fragment 8: "That which is in opposition is in concert, and from things that differ comes the most beautiful harmony." (Free- man, *Ancilla to the Pre-Socratic Philosophers*, p. 25.)

[37] Cf. Bouelles, *L'Art des opposés*, chapter 6, pp. 75–76: "Antiperista- sis" is the term used for the cycle and inversion of opposites.

whether to be or not to be. A mental effort, consubstantial with his history and which will cease only with his disappearance from the stage of the universe, compels him to accept the two self-evident and contradictory truths which, through their clash, set his thought in motion, and, to neutralize their opposition, generate an unlimited series of other binary distinctions which, while never resolving the primary contradiction, echo and perpetuate it on an ever smaller scale: one is the reality of being, which man senses at the deepest level as being alone capable of giving a reason and a meaning to his daily activities, his moral and emotional life, his political options, his involvement in the social and the natural worlds, his practical endeavours and his scientific achievements . . .[38]

The elementary opposition that produces all the others brings us back to the "tobacco piece," the banquet of the sage.[39] At the end of his *Art of Opposites,* Bouelles leads the reader through a "labyrinth" of varied and quadratic oppositions—into which we shall now follow him, taking with us the strawberries, tobacco, wine, and fuse.[40]

The red strawberry rots, and its corruption is linked to the element of water. The fermented tobacco is burned in fire. The fermented wine oxidizes in the course of time, its corruption being effected by air. The strawberry decomposes in the open, while the tobacco meets its end in an open vessel and the wine in a closed one. What remains of the wine is the oxide; what remains of the

[38] Claude Lévi-Strauss, *The Naked Man,* vol. 4 of *Mythologiques,* trans. John and Doreen Weightman, University of Chicago Press ed. (Chicago, 1990), p. 694.

[39] "His passive intellect is the table laid out for the joys of the mind." (Bouelles, *Liber,* chapter 6, p. 130.)

[40] Bouelles, *L'Art des opposés,* pp. 172–173.

tobacco is the ash; and what remains of the strawberry is the seeds. The inversion of visible life and hidden death in the illusory berries is reflected as a symbol in the mirror of the human mind: on the symbolic scale, the strawberries are brought into Paradise for the souls of the children. "What is revealed reveals itself to all the world and conceals itself in secret, while what is hidden is concealed from the world, but known to be revealed in secret."[41]

In the pipe, tobacco is the life of the fire, which in the end is buried by the dead (the ash), and the fire is the death of tobacco, which makes ash into the death of death: literal resurrection to life out of a double negation, which has a converse side; fire transforms what nourishes it into ash as the smoker transforms the tobacco, but the fire eats the body of the tobacco, while the smoker swallows the soul of the herb, as it were. The question of whether his own soul will ascend invisibly to heaven in death, like the smoke that visibly mixes with his breath in life, or whether the Devil will swallow his soul in the form of smoke after it has been exposed to the fires of purgatory, like the tobacco in the smoking-vessel, cannot be resolved by any pipe-milker in this world—and this is the basis for the contradictory symbolism of tobacco. "Life is the life of life and the death of death, while death is living death, and dead life."[42]

Oxidized wine turns brown and becomes undrinkable once the air has penetrated into the bottle through the crumbling cork; if the time has been missed to drink the mature wine, it is sooner or later spoiled. Once it has become oxidized, "inflammation" is lethal. The production of the wine requires an "inflammation" to be overcome—as it cools after the warming caused by deoxidation. The period of maturity is completed in the

---

[41] Ibid., p. 174.   [42] Loc. cit.

corked bottle, in which the wine mingles with a suitable amount of the element from which it has been separated.

The wine matures in the course of time, and oxidizes as time goes on; once it has reunited itself with the element that escaped so swiftly during fermentation, it instantly loses its earthy and fiery body, and turns brown; its "eternity" is sealed not in a measureless bond, but in a measured one. Mature wine is called *firn* in German, a word derived from *fern*, "far"—"because what stands at a distance in space must also do so in time."[43] Like the mature wine painted by Flegel, cooked in the kitchen of the heart à la Bouelles and transformed into blood, it unites beneficially with its element and ascends to the realm of the illusory berries: *vivitur ingenio caetera mortis sunt,* "we live in the mind, and all the rest belongs to death."[44]

In tiny whitish-red bars, the glowing heat runs across the space-time of the fuse in the smoky topaz tones of the still life. In the burning part of the snaking hemp, the texture is still visibly intact, while the burnt part is hidden in the black beyond the glow. At discrete intervals, the dead part of the fuse drops away from the glowing line, momentarily interrupting the continuous link with the ash. The fuse is forever passing away, and in the coincidence of opposites it, too, has become a symbol of the *vita brevis.*

Lunte, the German word for "fuse," originally meant "rag, scrap." In Luther's translation of the Bible, Queen Esther thought as little of the crown on her head as

---

[43] Cf. Grimm, vol. 3, p. 1675. The adjective *fern* for "old" survived in the word *fernyear* (yesteryear) in Middle English (Chaucer, *Troilus and Criseyde,* v. 1176, "fare wel al the snow of ferne yere!").

[44] Cf. Dieter Wuttke, *Der Humanist Willibald Pirckheimer—Namengeber für ein mathematisch-naturwissenschaftliches und neusprachliches Gymnasium? Ein Beitrag zur Überwindung der "Zwei Kulturen"* (Nuremberg, 1994), p. 68.

worthless *Lunten,* "rags";[45] in his *Table Talk,* Luther mentions the torn and crushed *Lunten* used to make rag paper in the paper-mill.

Twisted and soaked, rags can be made into a wick—the German word for which, *Docht,* goes back to the Old Norse *þáttr,* "braid of a cord; span." A pharmacopoeia of 1572 throws light on the "wick" aspect of the fuse: ". . . what happens to the heart is like the wick of a torch—burning brightly at first, but becoming harder and more scorched, gaunt, and fragile the longer it lasts, losing its strength from moment to moment."[46]

The word *Lunte* for "fuse" first appeared in the sixteenth century in Dutch, and soon spread to other languages. As a means of igniting explosives, the fuse serves the purposes of war. The German expression *Lunte riechen,* to smell a fuse (i.e., a rat), associates the word with a sense of danger, since it is only the acrid smell made when it burns that betrays the sniper in his hideout.

The earliest meaning of *Lunte* links the word to Middle Dutch *lunderen,* "to do something useless, waste time with inappropriate things, be indecisive." In a synecdoche, rags (*Lumpen*) can take the place of the *Lump* or the rogue *Lunterus,* whose life is as torn and ragged as his clothing.

In every case, rag (*Lunte*) is a fabric that has lost its value through wear and tear in the course of time, but that can serve a new purpose when it is torn and pounded or twisted and soaked to form a span of cord—although it preserves something of its dubious, torn existence: paper, wick, and ragged life all lack durability.

Compared with the long hempen cord from which it is cut, the fuse is only a short span, in the spatial sense.

[45] Cf. Grimm, vol. 12, p. 1307 (the passage is in the apocryphal part of the Book of Esther, *Additions to the Book of Esther* 14.16 in *The New Oxford Annotated Bible with the Apocrypha*).

[46] Grimm, loc. cit.

Soaked in a lead oxide solution and ignited, it can be used to pass on a flame, while the fuse itself is consumed and passes away slowly but surely in the process. Fire is concentrated in the smallest space, burning through the soaked hemp as it is consumed as slowly as possible, span by span. Just as the piece of hemp, as part of the whole cord, represents only a short span, so too the whole of the fuse appears long in relation to the one section of it that is glowing. In the tiny fire of a fuse, time is stretched out to the maximum compared with the short time span of a great blaze; but equally, time appears minimized in the single moment that the fuse glows. The constancy of the fire in the fuse is owed to the principle of taking up precisely the amount of space, fuel, and air needed to ensure that it neither flames up nor dies out.

As the trigger for explosives, the fuse initiates destruction; as a dispenser of fire for peaceful purposes, it embodies transience and the cycle of life. The glow is continuously connected to the ash, without being buried by it; the ash drops away discontinuously, without releasing flames. In the fuse, the whole and the part coincide. "The whole is whole as a whole, a part made up of parts. The part is part of the whole and the whole of the parts."[47]

Non sine igne is a motto seen on emblems, since sacrifices and works of art can never be "without fire."[48] *Vita brevis, ars longa* is the fundamental opposition between life and art, which can only coincide in the work: the more the artist sacrifices of his life, the longer his work will survive.

All things at the right time and according to measure—this is what the fuse, tobacco, wine, and strawberries are telling us. All things pass away through the element dominating their temperament, and they rise up

[47] Bouelles, *L'Art des opposés*, p. 172.

[48] Cf. Henkel and Schöne, *Emblemata*, p. 132.

again out of it. "Life returns in the footsteps of death, just as light returns in the strides of the night."[49]

No insight is capable of stilling the thirst for knowl-edge, and the eyes insatiably drink in color and texture from the likeness of objects. Nor are the sense organs that are ever open—the nose and the ears—left hungry in Flegel's deceptive image. In his *trompe-nez,* there are bitter and sweet, acrid and sweet scents playing with fire,[50] while the sixth sense feigns the likeness of voices speaking in the niche: the quiet fire in the loud wine, the tones sounding from the mute pipe, the rustling snake of the tobacco and the crackling snake of the hemp, the ringing glass and the crunching seed coat of the two false berries.

The art of opposites forms the basis for all of the arts, and if we had not recognized the maximum of tamed earthly fire in the fuse, and the minimum of celestial fire in the painted reflection of sunlight that penetrates win-dow, rummer, and wine without consuming them, the coincidence of transience and permanence within a fragile glass could not have crossed the threshold of awareness.

[49] Bernard of Clairvaux, cited after Georges Duby, *Die Kunst der Zisterzienzer* (Stuttgart, 1993), p. 154.

[50] The German word for play-ing with fire, *kokeln,* is connected with *gaukeln* and *Gaukelspiel,* "illu-sion," as well as with the English word "giggle."

As then the Tulip for her morning sup
Of Heav'nly Vintage from the soil looks up,
Do you devoutly do the like, till Heav'n
To Earth invert you—like an empty Cup.[1]

OMAR KHAYYÁM

III
Batavian Harlequinade, or the Florimaniacs' Delight

n imaginary bouquet—no vase has ever contained one like this. Tulips, sulfur rose, sweetbrier, damask rose, nasturtium, morning glory, mallow and carnation, star of Bethlehem, scilla, iris and hya-cinth, pansy, columbine, and fritillaries are seen in unwithering flower. A florilegium stretching for a whole garden season, from March to October, is on view—the whole drama of florescence, set against a dark back-ground. In their fringed, striped, checked, mottled, and spotted vestments, the protagonists look like figures from the commedia dell'arte.

Four varieties of tulip dominate the scene. The princi-pal role is played by Superintendent,[2] caught at the moment its petals unfold. A common housefly is sitting on the shining atlas silk of its pink-mottled petals, and has been witnessing to imminent decay for some 340 years.[3]

---

[1] Translated from the Persian by Edward Fitzgerald.

[2] *Tulipa* hybrid *schrenkii* × *stel-lata.* I am grateful to Sam Segal (private communication) for pro-viding the old names of the tulips. With regard to the star of Bethle-hem, my identification differs from

his; he regards the flower as *Ixia candida.* Whether it is an iris or a lily, the plant with the orange-colored stamen seems to be a lost species awaiting rediscovery.

[3] Johannes Goedaert (1617–1668) painted the picture around 1660. Cf. Laurens J. Bol, "Johannes

Alongside Superintendent: an ivory-colored, brown-mottled tulip called General of the Generals of Gouda.[4] The eye of a dark Spanish iris is glowing brightly above the oval tulip bud of White Flannel Coat,[5] which is opening the vermilion-hemmed tips of its garment next to a Latour tulip,[6] the bloom of which, with a crimson varnish on a shell-white ground, recalls precious Chinese porcelain. The bonnet of a columbine, the common aquilegia,[7] is partly hidden by the fine tulip, and the laughing face of a *Viola tricolor* is looking out from between the grander tulips.

The bumblebee, a lazybones only out for its honey, has alighted on the rose for all eternity, while in the darkness an Orange Tip butterfly is flying toward its caterpillars' fodder plant.[8] Nasturtium, "nose-tormentor," was the botanical name as well as the common one for the small Indian cress from Peru, before Linnaeus renamed it *Tropaeolum minus.*[9] Alongside the spectacular tulips, the

Goedaert, schilder-entomoloog," in *Oud Holland* 74 (1959), 1–19.

[4] *Tulipa* hybrid *biflora* × *stellata.*

[5] *Tulipa* hybrid *biflora* × *schrenkii.*

[6] *Tulipa* hybrid *clusiana* × *schrenkii.*

[7] Aquilegia is called columbine in English because the five anthers above the sepals resemble doves cooing with their beaks together. In *Flora von Deutschland,* ed. F. L. von Schlechtendal (Gera-Untermhaus, 1880), aquilegia is called "harlequin flower" owing to the resemblance of the individual spurs to a fool's cap (index).

[8] *Anthocharis cardamines* was also formerly known as *Kressenfalter,* "cress butterfly." Cf. F. Berge's *Schmetterlingsbuch,* 3rd ed. (Stutt-gart, 1863), p. 66. Goedaert's depiction differs from the usual appearance of the Orange Tip. By chance, it resembles one of the butterflies from Nabokov's universe: *Zegris eupheme,* formerly known as *Anthocharis eupheme.* Cf. ibid., plate 10, and Dieter E. Zimmer, *A Guide to Nabokov's Butterflies and Moths* (Hamburg, 1996), p. 153 and figure 11. Since a butterfly native to Russia and Spain is unlikely to have found its way to Middelburg, Goedaert's insect seems to be a hybrid butterfly proclaiming, from the seventeenth century, the great Russian writer's arrival.

[9] *Nasturtium indicum,* the "Indian cress," was changed to *Tropaeolum* because the colorful columns of large nasturtiums wind-

other flowers in the painting seem to have rather small blooms compared with today's garden forms. Whether they are chances of nature like the fritillaria, or playful cultivated forms like the striped damask rose,[10] almost all have colored patterns. Fresh and pristine, the patterned flowers glisten in the clear light, while the rose leaves, marked by the brown colors of fall, are being nibbled by a spiny caterpillar.

The monochrome play of yellowish and reddish ochre tones in the olive-colored foliage forms a melancholy contrast to the cheerful polychromy of the company of flowers. Dewdrops are glittering on the weary green, and two exotic shells with mother-of-pearl effects are lying empty, half in shadow, half in the light, whose reflections on the edge of the *Nautilus pompilius* correspond to the calices of the nocturnal hyacinth.[11]

On the other side of the Chinese vase with its bamboo decoration, a nimble blue-tit is tearing apart a moth of the owl family, *Noctua pronuba,* called *Hausmutter* (house-mother) in German and Dutch. In Dutch, the blue-tit is called *pimpelmees,* and a drinker is called a *pimpelaar*— because like the bird, the "pimpling" man is also blue.[12] The incessant ding-a-ling of bells, the repetitive song of blue-tits, and the tearful lamentations of the drinker are all combined in the onomatopoeic word. The intoxication of tulipomania came as a bolt from the blue, and some of the Batavian harlequins caught up in it ended like the housemother in the painting.

ing round stakes reminded Linnaeus of the *tropaeum,* the victory sign of the Roman legionaries that was decorated with their enemies' weapons—the leaves are like shields, the flowers like bloodstained golden helmets. The Spanish destroyers of Inca culture thus acquired a Roman bearing in the name of the flower from Peru . . .

[10] *Rosa damascena versicolor,* "York and Lancaster Rose."

[11] Above it, the metallic blue of a dragonfly has sunk beneath the blushed varnish of a later restoration.

[12] Cf. Grimm, vol. 13, p. 1858, s.v. *Pimpelmeise* and *pimpeln.* In Dutch, *pimpelen* means "to drink, tipple."

The Dutch love of tulips has lasted through the centuries; Haarlem is still the heartland of tulip bulb production. But the magnificent striped, mottled, and hemlined skirts, and the martial names the tulip hybrids used to have, are long gone. Texas Flame, Sweetheart, Angélique, Dreaming Maid, Dutch Princess, or African Queen are the varieties familiar today. The sex assigned to tulips has also changed. In the seventeenth century, the upright tulips were regarded as male, and the varieties were categorized into aristocratic classes. The most sought-after red and pink mottled ones had the foremost place; they were rare and precious. *Ex minimis patet ipse Deus,* "God reveals himself in the tiniest things"[13]—no one had yet realized that the tiny cause of the bizarrely mottled rarities was a virus.

A Flemish nobleman brought the tulip to Europe from the Orient; Gesner gave the first scientific account of the plant; and in 1576, the great Fleming Carolus Clusius, court botanist in Vienna, described the enigmatic varieties of the cultivated turban-flower.[14]

"I grow weak when the sun is hidden," the tulip confesses in an early emblem by Camerarius.[15] As the plant made its way from the gardens of princes to those of commoners, the variety that came to light was the underground stock market bulb of the celestial speculator. The

[13] On this motto for a tulip garden in an engraving by Adriaen van de Vennes, *Zealand Nightingale* (*Zeevsche Nachtegael,* Middelburg, 1623), see Sam Segal and Michiel Roding, *De Tulp en de kunst* (Zwolle, 1994), p. 10.

[14] The Flemish nobleman who brought the tulip to Europe was Ghislain de Busbecq, the Hapsburg ambassador to the court of Süleyman the Magnificent in Constantinople. The word "tulip" is derived from the Turkish *tülbent,* "turban," the symbol of the Sultan's lordly dignity. The mottled virus tulips are known today as Rembrandt tulips. But the monster turbans with which the painter burdened his biblical figures recall Flaubert's description of Bovary's cap, rather than the Oriental-Dutch hybrids.

[15] Cf. Henkel and Schöne, *Emblemata,* p. 311.

sun god of idolatrous worship soon became "the hard cash of the *a priori.*"[16]

"A fool and his money are quickly parted," is an emblem motto from as early as 1614 over a mottled pair of tulips shown in front of their sprouting, moneybag-shaped bulbs.[17] No flower was better suited to the whims of the goddess Fortune than the tulip's polychrome cups, whose markings, colors, and shape are sometimes faithful, sometimes fickle. The origins of the Dutch tulip trade seem like a conspiracy between Fortune and the god of thieves at the expense of poor Clusius. His tulip collection, established in Vienna and expanded in Frankfurt, was the botanist's only possession of any value when he took up an appointment at the University of Leyden in 1593. The tulips flourished magnificently in the new botanical garden. It took the thieves only a single night to dig the precious flowers up. After their haul had been scattered across the seventeen provinces of the northern Netherlands, Clusius was hailed as the founder of the Dutch tulip-growing industry.[18]

The latent tulipomania became manifest at the end of 1634. Inns were turned into stock markets, "where the drinkers, instead of using cards and dice, now exhila-

---

[16] Alfred Sohn-Rethel, *Das Geld, die bare Münze des Apriori* (Berlin, 1990).

[17] In Roemer Visscher, *Sinnepoppen* (Amsterdam, 1614). Cf. Segal and Roding, *De Tulp,* p. 18.

[18] Cf. William Curtis, *Curtis's Flower Garden Displayed,* ed. Tyler Whittle and Christopher Cook (Oxford, 1981), p. 20. In 1575–1576, Clusius planted 1,500 seeds and bulbs, brought from the Ottoman Empire by Busbecq, in the new imperial garden in Vienna.

The story of the theft in Leyden has all the qualities of legend. Even while he was still in Frankfurt, Clusius complained in a letter to Camerarius that people were stealing tulip bulbs from his garden. Cf. *Das Camerarius-Florilegium* (Erlangen, 1993), p. 9. In the legend of the Leyden theft, the tulip seems to express the cruel fate that befell the great botanist of the sixteenth century. Cf. Whittle and Cook, loc. cit.

rated themselves with playing tulips."[19] The bulbs were no longer traded individually, but by weight, and prices were quoted by the grain, the goldsmith's smallest unit of weight. If it pays, even the devil has a weakness for the tiniest things—and so the harlequins learned to abstract from tulips as well as thalers.

Many of those who wished to purchase a rare bulb received, instead of the bulb itself, only a certificate to show that they had entered into a contract for such a bulb; and in turn they were able to sell this paper at a higher price. The sums involved consequently rose to unbelievable levels. The main fraud lay in the fact that the bulb allegedly bought or sold often existed only in the imagination of the two mutual swindlers involved . . . The parties doing business agreed on fixed-term delivery. On a given day, the transaction was to be realized at a set price; if this fell through, it was not the tulips, but the difference between the sums that was paid. In this way, the trade came to involve quantities of bulbs so great that all the gardeners in Holland would not have been able to produce them in the space of ten years.[20]

It was in the seventeenth century that the superstitious belief in paper promises of imaginary quantities of gold[21] yielded the first flowers of addiction. A vivid example of the insanity of abstract exchange is provided by an

[19] M. von Strantz, *Die Blumen in Sage und Geschichte* (Berlin, 1875), p. 281. See also Simon Schama, *The Embarrassment of Riches: An Interpretation of Dutch Culture in the Golden Age* (London, 1987), pp. 350–365.

[20] Strantz, *Die Blumen*, pp. 279, 282.

[21] Cf. Sohn-Rethel, *Das Geld*, p. 34.

invoice for goods in kind published in a pamphlet against tulipomania in 1636. A single bulb of the variety Viceroy at this point cost 2,500 guilders, a sum almost equivalent to the total of the following "rabble of commodities":[22]

160 bushels of wheat	448 guilders
320 bushels of rye	558 guilders
Four fatted oxen	480 guilders
Eight fatted pigs	120 guilders
Twelve fatted sheep	120 guilders
Four tuns of beer	32 guilders
Two tuns of butter	192 guilders
One thousand pounds of cheese	120 guilders
One bed with accessories	100 guilders
Several articles of clothing	80 guilders
One silver beaker	60 guilders

Before the collapse of the tulip stock market in 1637, the rarest bulb came to cost as much as the most expensive buildings along Amsterdam's canals, as Maria Sibylla Merian recalled in the preface to her flower book of 1680:

A flower called *Semper Augustus* by the tulip-dealers was sold for 2,000 Dutch guilders; which in 1637 could no longer be purchased for any sum whatsoever, for there were only two of the sort, one in Amsterdam and one in Haarlem. It was also said that someone had a garden of tulips for which (including the flowers) he had been offered 70,000 guilders, and he had not accepted this but had wished to keep his garden with its flowers. People commenced to enter into this trade so much—for in the beginning it yielded very well—that the weavers

[22] On the Marxian concept "rabble of commodities," see Sohn-Rethel, loc. cit.

even sold their looms and invested the money in flowers; and many people sold fine, expensive houses, country estates, and all that they had, even borrowing great sums of money at interest and risk- ing it on such flowers that had neither scent nor taste; but that they delighted greedy hearts for a short time with their fleeting beauty.[23]

If all is vanity, so too is the moral that all is vanity.[24] It was not vanity but wisdom that Merian saw in the delight of those florimaniacs who were not led astray by mere paper flowers:

For nature, with her sweet ornaments, can accom- plish so much in great enthusiasts that they regard the contemplation of such flowers as being worth more than all their treasures together; and would rather diminish their wealth, than lessen their plea- sure. And this may be held against them the less, because there lies in these colorful masterpieces a secret tendency, not to make blind those who have eyes to see—but to bring sight to those whose eyes are blind.[25]

When the painter and entomologist Johannes Goedaert in Middelburg painted the *Flowers in a Wan-li Vase with Blue-Tit* on the island of Walcheren, tulip prices had long since settled back to normal and were again graded according to the old ranks. After the fatal tulipomania, the fritillaria fever that followed was kept within bounds. Clio, Merveilleuse, Serpentino, and

[23] Maria Sibylla Merian, *Neues BlumenBuch—Allen Kunstverstän- diger Liebhabern zu Lust, Nutz und Dienst, mit Fleiss verfertiget* (Nurem- berg, 1680); facsimile reprint, ed. Helmut Deckert (Leipzig, 1968), p. 0 [sic].
[24] Vladimir Nabokov, *Strong Opinions* (London, 1973), p. 193.
[25] Merian, loc. cit.

Viperino were names of the noble rarities among the "dice-boxes," as forgotten today as the carnivalesque car-nations in the gardens of Dutch and Walloon weavers.[26]

While the artists of the time were displaying their vir-tuoso painting styles in magnificent, spreading flower bouquets, Goedaert continued unwaveringly, and with artistic strictness, to paint his imaginative and scientifi-cally accurate botanical portraits. He brought to perfec-tion a tradition of which, in the field of panel painting, he was the last representative.[27] It had begun with Ambrosius Bosschaert at the start of the century, and was continued by painters who were masters of the art of erasing every trace of themselves in their own paintings in order to bathe flowers, insects, birds, lizards, snails, and shells in the light of an unfading delight.[28]

[26] *Fritillaria,* "dice-box," named for the checkered pattern of the flower's corolla, either because of a checkered pattern used on dice-boxes or because *fritillus* was thought to mean "chessboard" (*Oxford English Dictionary*). On the history of the *fritillaria* fever, see Christabel Beck, *Fritillaries* (Lon-don, n.d.). On carnations in weavers' gardens, see Whittle and Cook, *Curtis's Flower Garden Displayed,* p. 182.

[27] It continued on parchment and paper in botanical and entomo-logical works, such as that of Maria Sibylla Merian.

[28] "Those familiar with the Dutch flower painters of the seven-teenth century and their pupils among all the peoples of Europe will know that they were capable of stripping everything insignificant from the parrot tulip, buttercup, and fire lily with the same magnificent intellectual eye . . . the painted flower immortalizes the impression that the real one might make on the enraptured eye only for a single sec-ond. It does not thereby make an already existing external phenome-non external once again, but bathes the fading form in the light of an unfading delight." (Rudolf Bor-chardt, *Der leidenschaftliche Gärtner* [Stuttgart, 1968; rptd. Nördlingen, 1987], p. 265.)

> It takes a long time for a world to
> vanish—but that's all it takes. FONTENELLE

IV
Toad's View of a Snuffler

 very floral still life has to have an insect, even if it is only a fly. For a painter wishing to deceive the eye, the fantastic trompe-l'oeil achieved by insects was the supreme pattern to follow. Not only are the various textures of the plant world imitated by insects down to the finest detail; the resemblance to reality in these tiny creatures, which have been bewitched and turned into flowers, leaves, bark, or branches, is further intensified by signs of decay—with simulated damage such as tears or spots, and moldy, rotten, or dried-out patches. As long as painters still proudly claimed *Natura sola magistra* as their motto, they were able to learn this skill from Nature, the supreme illusionist—because in paintings, as in life, it is the tiny flaw that lures the enchanted gaze into beauty's trap.

For thirty years, Goedaert pursued the drama of insect metamorphosis. His hedgerow theater was the island of Walcheren, his box seat was a house with a sea view on the outskirts of Middelburg, his traveling stage was the island with its contrasting harmonies of undulating dunes, rough grasses, wild herbs, crooked trees, and flat fields surrounded by hedges and stretching away between scattered farmhouses, gardens, meadows, and woods to dissolve into the soft light on the horizon.

Pan or Proteus was the title of the mystery play of meta-morphosis, whose secrets were to remain hidden for many years yet.[1] It is only today that we understand the hormonal processes that lead to the complete imago of the butterfly emerging from the formless pulp of decomposed larva inside the pupa—confirming what the seventeenth century saw in this process: the miracle of resurrection from decay. In the rich storehouse of Baroque emblems, the one that most inspired the imagination of painters, researchers, and poets was that of the imago slipping out of the chrysalis and unfolding. In the emblem book *Silene Alcibiadis, sive Proteus* by the Zealand poet Jacob Cats,[2] a butterfly emerging from its chrysalis on a dune embodies the transforming power of love. *Amor elegantiae pater* is the motto alongside.

As the greatest artists of transformation in the animal world, insects reveal the One that is present in the Many, the principle of "the whole in the part." Exploring the arcana of insect life lay in the tradition of the Renaissance humanists, following on from Pliny. "We marvel at elephants' shoulders carrying castles, and bulls' necks and the fierce tossings of their heads, at the rapacity of tigers and the manes of lions, whereas really Nature is to be found in her entirety nowhere more than in her smallest creations."[3]

This was the inspiration for Goedaert to write and illustrate his work *Metamorphosis et Historia Naturalis Insectorum,* the first independent study of insects in the history of entomology.[4] Amor was the father of his artistic sense; his urge to conduct research was grounded in his faith;

[1] On the topic of Pan and Proteus, see Edgar Wind, *Pagan Mysteries in the Renaissance* (London, 2nd ed. 1967), pp. 191–217.

[2] Amsterdam, 1618. Cf. Henkel and Schöne, *Emblemata,* p. 912.

[3] Pliny, *Natural History,* trans. H. Rackham, W. H. S. Jones, and D. E. Eichholz, 10 vols., Loeb Classical Series (London, 1938–1963), XI.i (4), vol. 3, p. 435.

[4] The *Theater of Insects* by the Scotsman Thomas Mouffet had already been published in 1634, but was primarily a compendium of insect illustrations taken from earlier

and his learning gave him the freedom to trust the accuracy of his own eye.[5]

More than 150 colored engravings of maggots, worms, caterpillars, larvae, pupae, cocoons, butterflies, flies, bees, bumblebees, crickets, grasshoppers, and other invertebrates illustrate the three small volumes of his book on metamorphosis. "There is no reason to reproach ourselves that we are dealing merely with miserable little animals," he writes in his own defense, in the preface addressed to the "most learned reader," because the description and history of these creatures clearly show "that GOD has set nature's greatest miracles within the tiniest things." He notes with pride that he has only described what he has learned by experiment and from his own experience, "which, although it is also the teacher of fools, is at any rate the surest way to that certain knowledge of natural science that we must begin to acquire." The glass cases in which he kept his caterpillars, worms, and other insects made it easier for him to observe and precisely depict each stage of their metamorphosis. "I gave to each the food appropriate to its species, and painted them from life before metamorphosis began," he observes in explaining his methods,

> and I also recorded the exact time and form of the metamorphosis, and using my own colors painted the new creatures that emerged from them. Sometimes, I went out at night with a lantern to catch insects that do not come out by day. Or I dug up the

writers. Cf. Paul Smart, *The Illustrated Encyclopedia of the Butterfly World* (London, 1976), p. 85.

[5] In addition to the Bible, Goedaert quotes ancient and modern specialist literature: Aristotle and Pliny, Boxhorn, Dodonaeus, Rondelet, and Aldrovandi; and the classics of humanist learning: Seneca, Cicero, Horace, Pindar, Ovid, Aesop, Augustine, and Erasmus. Cf. L. J. Bol, "Johannes Goedaert," p. 3.

earth and brought home with me those that are rarely seen.

To the question of why even scholars, "refraining from carrying out their own experiments and failing to think for themselves," had remained in error regarding the origin and nature of insects, he responded in the same style as Nicholas of Cusa, Pico della Mirandola, and Bouelles:

> Man was created in the image of God, at the very end of creation, as a microcosm and compendium of the universe. Although he did not sustain immense misery when he fell from grace, he did acquire immense ignorance. Nevertheless, there lies within us still a light of nature, with whose aid— through careful observation and diligent examination of creatures—and thanks to those works of God which are visible, we can grasp and capture with our understanding that part of God that is otherwise invisible.[6]

Research into arthropods was in the air. One year after Goedaert's death, Jan Swammerdam's *General Natural History of Insects* was published in Utrecht. What had remained invisible to the naked eye during vivisections and autopsies conducted for the glory of God was rendered visible using the magnifying glasses and microscopes of Middelburg's lens makers. With devout skill and limitless patience, the brilliant microscopist Swammerdam dissected the "unfathomable arts and master-

---

[6] From the preface to the 1662 Latin edition published in Middelburg, which was translated from the earlier Dutch version (ca. 1660) by Goedaert's friend, the physician and theologian Johannes Mey.

pieces of the great Architect."[7] The scissors, knives, and lancets he used to master the divinely fashioned crea-tures were so small they had to be sharpened under a magnifying glass.

The conscientiousness of the researcher was one thing; the conscience of the chiliast was another. Writing his final work, Swammerdam was half blinded by spending so much time looking down the microscope, and exhausted by the vain effort to reconcile his insatiable thirst for knowledge with his search for salvation. He describes the life of the mayfly as an "image of human life," and confesses he has succeeded in completing the book only after suffering a thousand fears, pangs of con-science, and scalding rebukes from his God-fearing heart, with sighs, sobs, and tears.

On folding back the bee's coat, Swammerdam discov-ered a heart, brain, trachea, stomach, and intestinal system. To depict the inconceivably fine vessels, he used tiny glass needles to blow colored liquids into them. The *Bible of Nature* illustrates his astonishing discoveries in magnificent engravings: the bee's sting—a perfect arrow with a barb, beneath fluttering bands of muscle; the ovaries of the queen bee—two fanned-out sea anem-ones over the coral stump of the entrails; the course of a nerve in the mayfly's larval body—a delicate chain within pinnate gills and the spiral rings of branching air channels.[8]

"Every stroke from the hand of Apelles," the tireless dissector wrote in his anatomy of the rhinoceros beetle, "is nothing but a clumsy blot compared with nature's del-icate lines. The tissue of any man-made fabric must hide

[7] Cf. Dannemann, *Naturwis-senschaften*, vol. 2, p. 177.

[8] The *Bible of Nature* was pub-lished in 1737 by the anatomist Boerhaave, who purchased Swam-merdam's manuscripts after his death.

itself for shame compared with the texture of a single trachea. Who can depict such a thing? What wit is capable
of describing it? Who could have the diligence to study it
sufficiently?"[9]

It was the age of the open-air still life. The impulse not
to depict flowers and fruit in the form of a *nature morte* on
a stone plinth any longer, and instead to portray the life of
plants together with all the living creatures of the forest
floor, dune, or field, came from Marseus van Schrieck in
the second half of the century.[10] Marseus was a wanderer
all over Europe, nicknamed "Snuffler" by his colleagues
in the league of Netherlandish painters in Rome because
he was always snuffling about looking for snakes,
amphibians, lizards, frogs, toads, insects, and fungi. His
paintings present the deathly fauna and flora of evil
against the background of the dark forest—nature as an
opera or a baroque tragedy, offered up to his revered frogs
from their own perspective.

Parasites, stranglers, constrictors, predators, and killers
are at work in the kingdom of decay. Who will fall victim
to whom? That is the question. A proud tulip, banished
along with a feathery star ipomoea to the half-light of the
musty underwood world, is being forced by a four-lined
snake to bow down in front of a goat's-beard mushroom,
on which a hawk-moth caterpillar with its bright tail-
horn has taken up a rigid, sphinxlike pose. Rest or threat?
is the riddle the caterpillar sets the tulip, whose stalk leaf
has caught in the sticky cap of the boletus hiding in the
shadow.[11]

As well as the nameless boletus and the coral fungus,
other figures on the scene in the Snuffler's painting

[9] Cf. Dannemann, *Naturwis-senschaften*, p. 379.

[10] Otto Marseus van Schrieck (ca. 1619–1678).

[11] The hawkmoth family (also known as sphinx moth) is called Sphingidae after the sphinxlike pose the caterpillars adopt either at rest or when threatened.

include delicious Caesar's mushrooms, from a family that has some highly toxic species, and a fallen *Russula*.[12] Greek antiquity regarded fungi, which spring up overnight from damp moss, as the jokes of nature. Homer believed they were the fruit of the bond between heaven and earth, since they tend to appear after thunderstorms. Dioscorides attributed their poisonous nature to the fact that they appear in the vicinity of snakes' lairs and near trees that bear deadly fruit: "These fungi have a soft, sticky surface, and they rot and decay as soon as they are removed from the ground. Edible mushrooms taste neither pleasant nor sweet; and excess consumption, if the body cannot digest them, can lead to injury and attacks of suffocation, provoking the disease known as frenzy."[13]

What to the mycophile is a "miracle" is merely a "callosity of the earth" to the mycophobe. In Pliny, the two attitudes coincide. On the one hand, fungi are "choice eating," while on the other, they are poison-bearers arising out of the mud. "How chancy a matter it is to test these deadly plants!" To Pliny, the enigma of their poisonous nature seemed insoluble—as was the enigma of their hybrid quality, in which it was unclear "whether they are alive or not."[14]

Even in the sixteenth century, Mattioli believed that the poisonous nature of some fungi could be identified from the shimmering discolorations produced when they break open: "When they are broken open, they turn first green,

[12] In the shadows of the painting, the boletus cannot be precisely identified. The painter has placed his signature on the fallen *Russula*: "OTTO MARSEO 1662." Cf. Gian Casper Bott, *Stilleben* (Bilderhefte des Herzog Anton Ulrich-Museums, Brunswick, 1996, no. 10), p. 52.

[13] *Materia medica*, vol. 4; cf. Severino Viola, *Die Pilze* (Munich, 1972, 1977), p. 9.

[14] In the sixteen books that Pliny devotes to the vegetable kingdom, fungi are dealt with in only a few pages: *Natural History* XIX.xi–xiv (33–38), vol. 5, pp. 441–445; and XXI.xlvi–xlvii (92–99), vol. 6, pp. 359–65.

then blackish-red, and eventually dark blue and finally black . . . This is a circumstance that requires a strong person who is not sensitive and will not take fright at the malignancy of these changes when he sees them."[15]

Three men from the Netherlands—a poet, a pastor, and a botanist—were the intrepid authors of the first books on mushrooms to throw light on the "theater of fungi."[16] But the "private life of fungi" long remained in the dark, feeding the imagination.[17] "Almost everywhere in the world, these fructifications are associated with either thunder and lightning, or the devil, or madness."[18] *Amanita caesarea,* the delicacy most sought after by Roman mushroom-lovers, which can be eaten raw, is seen in the painting of the forest floor, serving as cradle and nourish-ment for the bluebottle; soon this parasitic fruit of rotten-ness will itself fall prey to rottenness.

The tulip has had to swallow its humiliation, while the rival adders are singing a rousing aria of discord.[19] In the meantime, a yellowish-green *Coluber* snake is darting its tongue out of hungry jaws at the *Bufo bufo.* Coil, throttle, and swallow is the method of the race of snakes. Defense-less victims are devoured alive. Mice, birds, lizards, frogs,

[15] The commentary on Dios-corides by Pietro Andrea Mattioli (1500–1577) of Sienna, published in Venice in 1548, went through more than sixty editions in various languages right up to the eigh-teenth century.

[16] The three fearless students of fungi were: the poet Adriaen de Jonghe (1511–1575), in his work *Phalli ex fungorum genere* (Delphis, 1564); the cleric Frans van Sterbeeck (1631–1693), in *Theatrum fungorum* (Antwerp, 1675); and the botanist Carolus Clusius, in *Fungorum in Pannoniis observatorum brevis historia* (Antwerp, 1601).

[17] The reproductive system of fungi was identified only in the mid-nineteenth century. *La Vie privée des champignons* by the French mycolo-gist G. Becker was published in Paris in 1952.

[18] Claude Lévi-Strauss, "Mush-rooms in Culture," in *Structural Anthropology,* trans. Monique Lay-ton (Harmondsworth, 1978), vol. 2, p. 224.

[19] *Avaler les couleuvres* (to swal-low snakes) means "to swallow one's anger, accept offenses, and hide the pain they cause."

and toads are their favorite dishes, and young adders can practice with smaller prey, such as beetles and grasshoppers. Like all the snakes, adders have forked tongues and often shed their skin.

"Awake, be on your guard! Deception lurks in dark corners on every side. Take care you are not caught; be sober and watchful!"[20] The toad is apparently deaf to this warning, with which Camerarius explains the emblem of a snake between grass and herbs. As the epitome of ugliness, the toad itself embodies malice, lust, miserliness, and insatiability—vices that are hard to reconcile with soberness and watchfulness. In fact, the warty beast from the family of the Discoglossids (toads with disk-shaped tongues) is both gluttonous and watchful at once. Its prey consists of earthworms, slugs, wasps, bees, spiders, beetles, and every type of insect. It spurns butterflies, as the dust on their wings sticks to its slimy tongue and makes them difficult to swallow. The extreme mobility of its goggle eyes is matched by the agility of its tongue, which it thrusts at the victim it has spotted from its hiding place. It is the stomach that rules the toad's behavior, according to Alfred Brehm, who gives a vivid description of its hunting technique:

> Suddenly, its eyes start to glitter, and it rouses itself from its seeming torpor and moves toward its prey at a speed utterly in contrast to the rest of its nature. As soon as it reaches the right distance, it stops in its course, glares straight at its victim like a pointer dog in front of the quarry—only the twitching at the tips of its toes reveals its excitement—and then shoots out its tongue to catch the victim and throw it down its wide-open gullet, swallowing it and storing it in

[20] Cf. Henkel and Schöne, *Emblemata*, p. 631.

the stomach almost simultaneously . . . And immediately after this, the toad is sitting there motionless
in its lurking posture again, peering all around.[21]

The natural foes of this agile but ungainly hunter are
the toad blowfly and the adder. It is helpless against the
insect, but it knows how to impress the snake: it swells
itself up and wobbles back and forth on outstretched
legs, while its ears and the glands on its body exude a
milky secretion containing a strong toxin.[22]

In the painting, the toad, with its body clearly swollen,
is busy licking its mouth with the sticky flap of its
tongue.[23] Its gluttony seems to have overcome it in the
middle of its display dance, while its bigmouthed mate
remains hidden in the deep shade behind the boletus. A
lizard—sleek competitor for the sluggish toad's prey—is
beside itself with fury as it watches the discoglossid relish-
ing the delicacy it has just snatched from under the
lizard's snout—a deceiver never likes to be deceived.
In emblems, the lizard embodies malicious deception,
malevolence, jealousy, and lust for revenge.[24]

The cruel opera being played out around the beautiful
tulip is a drama of dark passion. The distant rumble of
thunder has drowned out the little grasshopper's rustling
and chirping. Nothing matters to the three adders but the
toads. The figurative meaning of "toad" in Dutch and
German—money, bucks—seems to be connected with
the animal's insatiable greed, which was regarded as

[21] *Brehms Tierleben,* vol. 1, p. 211.

[22] Cf. Ludwig Trutnau, *Euro-
päische Amphibien und Reptilien* (Stuttgart, 1975), p. 123.

[23] Marseus depicted a toad with
an extended column of tongue and
a butterfly sticking to the end of it in

a forest-floor still life now in the
Staatliches Museum in Schwerin.
See the illustration in Erika Gemar-
Koeltzsch, *Holländische Stillebenmaler*
(Lingen, 1995), vol. 3, p. 923.

[24] Cf. Henkel and Schöne,
Emblemata, pp. 663–664.

unclean.[25] A rhyme by Hans Sachs invokes a reverse economics:

> And then the toad came waddling up
> and wanted to go with the fox as well.
> The fox said: no one can fill your belly,
> The whole of the earth would never suffice you.
> You spare what's good and you guzzle what's bad.[26]

The large king dragonfly, with its giant faceted eyes, has the best view in this shadow kingdom of the toads. The dragonfly's Latin name, *Libella,* means "balance, scales," the name given to damselflies in the eighteenth century. *Libella* refers to the insect's horizontal flight, in which the "fickle dragonfly" inscribes invisible geometric shapes in the air. Before the large damsel was given its royal name, the less courteous terms used for the insect were "horse-stinger" and "devil's darning-needle." It is the most talented of the predators shown in the painting. "Devil's darning-needle" is the name still given to the dragonfly family by Brehm, who describes the "large devil's darning-needle," with its different-sized pairs of wings, as "the true master of the air."

Dragonflies live exclusively by predation. The impetuous ones with unequal wings, in particular, take the role in the insect world that the falcons have among the birds. Flying at breakneck speed, they catch up with their victims and snatch them into the

---

[25] *Kröte* (toad) was Luther's translation of "lizard" in Leviticus 11.29 (*crocodillus* in the Vulgate): "And these are unclean to you among the swarming things that swarm upon the earth: the weasel, the mouse, the great *lizard* according to its kind . . ."

[26]
"Nach dem watschlet daher die Kröt
Und wolt auch mit dem Fuchsen gan.
Der sprach: niemand dich füllen kan,
Des ganzen Erdrichs will dir zrinnen
Du sparst das Gut und frisst das Arg."
Cf. Grimm, vol. 11, p. 2416.

air. Usually they do not even take the trouble to con/sume their victims in a safe place, but immediately start eating the prey, tearing it apart as they fly—so that whole body parts, broken/off wings, the head or a leg of a beetle or fly, drop to the ground, and even before finishing its meal the murderous drag/onfly, racing to the hunt, is already on the lookout for fresh victims.[27]

The moral interpretation given to the dragonfly in emblems is based on a different perspective. Although the damsels are warriorlike, with their metallic armor, they devour the vermin of the Devil, such as blood/sucking mosquitoes, flies, and beetles, and are thus doing battle for the good. In a miniature by Joris Hoefnagel, three dragonflies are depicted as the highest creatures, repre/senting the element of fire.[28] In one of the finest illumi/nated manuscripts, a blue/gold darner is seen spreading the glassy net of its wings in the context of a song of praise to Christ and his virgin mother: a damselfly cruci/fix set above a pear and a carnation, on which a small ich/neumon fly is sitting with its long death's sting.[29] On a page of the emblem/book that Jakob Hoefnagel pro/duced from miniatures by his father, the front legs of a king dragonfly are seen grasping the title of the emblem, emphasized with capitals, at the center of the inscription:

Dedit mihi Dominus   *ARTE*   *mercedem meam*
Et in illa laudabo   *nomen eius*[30]

[27] *Brehms Tierleben,* vol. 2, p. 64.

[28] Cf. Thea Vignau/Wilberg, "Hortus Philosophicus: The Hu/manist's View of Nature in the Era of Erasmus," in *Center 15* (National Gallery of Art, Record of Activi/ties and Research Reports, June 1994 to May 1995; Washington, D.C., 1995), p. 116.

[29] Cf. the facsimile edition of the *Mira Calligraphiae Monumenta* by Georg Bocskay, illuminated by Joris Hoefnagel (1542–1600) (London, 1992), folio 76, p. 205.

[30] Ibid., p. 43.

"The Lord has given me ART as my reward, and through it I shall praise His name." The dragonfly's body glitters like a piece of jewelry, now that it has risen into the air with whirring wings out of its ugly aquatic pupa. As with the moth and the butterfly, the dragonfly's ability to undergo metamorphosis points to the vanquishing of death. Freed from the greed of its caterpillar phase, the large peacock moth in its brown, furry jacket, with its white collar and the magnificently patterned costume of its wings—with the black eyes on it circled in cinnamon-color, white, amaranth red, and black paint—is flying around the flowering Blessed Mary's thistle.

The various items in Marseus's paintings are shown true to life, but the combination of them depicted is entirely imaginary: sun-loving garden hybrids and flow-ers of the field are blooming in a shady wood; snakes are chasing butterflies; dragonflies and nocturnal moths are on the wing at the same time.[31] Although it makes no sense in nature, it reflects the human world all the more clearly. No one was more familiar with the behavior of insects and reptiles than the Snuffler. He reared them in terrariums on his small property at the gates of Amster-dam, where he could observe them and sketch them in peace and quiet, and he was a precise observer of other aspects of nature as well. It was no accident that he dis-covered the secret of the ichneumon fly, and passed it on to Swammerdam.[32]

[31] Cf. Bol, *Holländische Maler,* p. 336, fig. 303, and p. 338, fig. 305.
[32] "Nothing more annoying can happen to an insect lover than when, with tremendous effort, he manages to raise caterpillars so far that they are about to metamorphose, or have already pupated—and instead of the longingly awaited butterfly, quite different creatures emerge. For ex-ample, even the finest and most perfect caterpillar is often attacked now by many, now by a few, mag-gots, which settle in it and then eat their way through it and kill it; and instead of the butterfly, what comes out of some pupae is nothing but smaller or larger ichneumon flies . . . How this could come to pass has baffled many people, and

These dramatic forest scenes with animal protagonists were imitated, with variations, by many painters. Jan Davidsz de Heem created bouquets of flowers and arrangements of fruit that, left in a grotto by an absent-minded lover, are visited by tiny insects on the ground. His pupil Abraham Mignon, the teacher of Merian, added a lighter note to the genre. With field flowers burst-ing with health and the joyous throng of tiny creatures in his sunlit still lifes of undergrowth, he presents nature as a magnificent feast.[33]

Elias van den Broeck preferred to compose his reptile and insect scenes around thick-fleshed cacti and agaves seen in pale moonlight—the nocturnalia of a somnam-bulist.[34] In his biographies of Netherlandish painters, Jakob Campo Weyerman reports in 1729 that the "velvet-trousered Seigneurs" of Antwerp had chased Elias van den Broeck off to Amsterdam because they despised his method of sticking real butterflies onto pic-tures instead of painting them. These "peevish children" had not considered, Weyerman scoffs, that "the stuck-on

even Swammerdam says he would have nothing proper or trustworthy to declare about it, if Otto Marsilius (a famous painter of flowers and insects) had not reported observing caterpillars being stung by gnats, which laid the eggs in them from which these worms came; and it is quite credible that the ichneumon flies . . . emerging in this way from insects of a quite different type, have—along with various other worms that live on decayed car-rion—given rise to the erroneous opinion that through decay, one creature can arise from another quite different one." (August Johann Rösel von Rosenhof, *Der Insecten-*

Belustigung [Nuremberg, 1746], "Sammlung der Hummeln und Wespen," part 2, p. 18.)

[33] Jan Davidsz de Heem (1606–1684); cf. Gregor J. M. Weber, "Stilles Leben am Erdboden," in *Kunst und Antiquitäten* 1/2 (1993), 27. Abraham Mignon (1640–1679); one of his finest forest-floor paintings is in the Musée des Beaux Arts in Brussels.

[34] Elias van den Broeck (ca. 1650–1708); cf. Bol, *Holländische Maler,* fig. 308, p. 342. A *Forest Floor with Cacti and Exotic Beasts* is held by the Staatliches Museum in Schwe-rin (inv. no. 73).

butterflies were more beautiful and more natural than painted ones, as they not only preserve the full markings, but also last longer than painted ones."[35]

As ephemeral as the life of the butterfly is the colored dust of its wings. The faded phantoms of formerly glorious butterflies, which as time goes on begin to look like holes in the painting, show that those long-departed velvet-trousered critics were right. Almost all the painters of the forest-floor genre used the slap-on method—and foremost among them was the Snuffler.[36] They also cheated in depicting lichen and mosses. Why bother painting those complicated structures, when you can simply stick a piece of moss or lichen onto the coarse-grained oil paint?

In contrast to Goedaert, who perfected the miracle of incorporating modern natural science into the older forms of art, Marseus moved with the times. Alongside the enamel glaze of the many-layered *Flowers in a Wan-li Vase with Blue-Tit,* his smooth depictions of forest floors create an effect of charming miniature stage sets.[37] In Goedaert's cheerfully melancholic flower portrait, tulipomania appears as a harlequinesque instant within an eternity of delight in nature's eye-opening masterpieces; while the creatures in this horrific-comic tulip opera, in

---

[35] *De Levens-beschryvingen der Nederlandsche Konst-schilders en Konst-schilderessen* (The Hague, 1729–1769), vol. 3, p. 211. See also Weber, "Stilles Leben," p. 27.

[36] See the vivid microscopic photographs of old and new impressions of butterflies' wings in Weber, "Stilles Leben," p. 29.

[37] In comparison to a stage set, his forest floors are tiny, but in comparison with their natural models, the figures on this underwood stage are fairly large: the female toad in the painting is 14 cm wide if we take into account perspective foreshortening, so that it is slightly larger than the real amphibian, which is 13 cm long. Since the Snuffler was concerned more with dramatic effect than with density, his paintings are mostly large format. I am grateful to the restorers and Antje Maack, of the Herzog Anton Ulrich Museum, for measuring the toad.

the darkness of devouring allegory, are entirely absorbed in their roles as portrayals of human madness. On the model of the meanings given in the emblem, Marseus looks for the particular as an example of the general, while Goedaert sees the general in the particular, "not as a dream and shadow, but as a living revelation, directly before one's eyes, of what is unfathomable."[38]

The Snuffler patrolled the woods with the eye of a collector of nature's curiosities, while the author of the theory of metamorphosis, roaming the woods and dunes of Walcheren, used structure to sharpen his sense for the life that lies in the detail.

In the seventeenth century, the price of a painting was still determined by the time required to paint it. The longer the art took, the more valuable it was. To regard this as overrating the handicraft aspect of the work would be a misjudgment of this method of estimation. It was an age that recognized an artist's talent by the degree of difficulty he had to overcome, by the measure of perfection to which he had submitted himself. The velvet-trousered art lovers, with their low view of the slap-on and press-on methods, would have agreed perfectly with the view Karen Blixen puts into the mouth of the divinely gifted cook in one of her novellas: "It is terrible and unbearable to an artist . . . to be encouraged to do, to be applauded for doing, his second best . . . Through all the world there goes one long cry from the heart of the artist: Give me leave to do my utmost!"[39]

When we look back on the history of art, the butterfly-hunting adders of the underwood world reveal themselves as artists straining for effect, who have relinquished

---

[38] Goethe, *Gedenkausgabe, Naturwissenschaftliche Schriften*, part 2, p. 705.

[39] Isak Dinesen, "Babette's Feast," in *Anecdotes of Destiny; and, Ehrengard* (New York, 1993), p. 59.

the love of detail in favor of chiaroscuro, who have given up the deep visual weight of the time-consuming layer technique in favor of a faster, shallow *peinture;* and who have abandoned the wish to vanish, like God, out of their own creation, in favor of a desire to parade a flaunting manner.

Part Four

VIEW WITH TEN
LOST COLORS

You can blow the trumpet of the
Last Judgment once; you must not blow it every
day.   EDGAR WIND

> The majority of those who are alive today, crossing the arena exhilarated or deafened by their own noise, should not forget that there is a vast audience watching them from the gallery. The dead can give no orders, they can't sue us to assert their sleeping rights; it is our word alone that counts. But their silence asks: "We played for you on the flute, we sang laments—did you hear nothing?" Our sense of humanity should be strong enough, and our imagination vivid enough, for us to answer: "Because the pace of our games is faster than yours, we nearly forgot the more reflective rules of your game. But you are right, we need to be told: you can only gain your own history for yourself if you speak to those who have gone before, and take account of those who are to follow."
>
> ARNO BORST

I
Return of the Butterfly

e have come a long way from the Stoic philosophy that promised moral dignity to the people of the seventeenth century.[1] In a world of mere use-values, absolute dedication to a cause that demands renunciation and brings no reward is bound to look like a poor investment. Festivities, art, and even waste are measured by their use-value, and it is puzzling for us to read that medieval peasants were willing to ruin themselves "because, no matter how poor they were, they had no choice but to offer their bride a cape of red cloth on their wedding day."[2] The end of the century that invented the industrial-scale production of corpses witnessed the triumph of a belief that immortal bodies can be created.

[1] See the important work on this by Ernst Cassirer, *The Myth of the State* (London, 1946), which he finished shortly before his death in New York in 1945. On the revival of Stoic ideas in the seventeenth century, see pp. 218–219.

[2] Georges Duby, *Saint Bernard, l'art cistercien* (Paris, 1979), pp. 14–15.

For the time being, the scalpel is still needed to ensure eternal youth. We believe happiness is at our disposal; we want to be artists, incarnate divinities, or divine devils who can take the places left vacant by the gods of whom (according to Theodor Adorno) all that has survived is their envy.

"Because the instantaneous sensation means more to us than the sustained imaginative pursuit, we fall into that typically Romantic predicament which Wordsworth, in 1800, called a 'degrading thirst after outrageous stimulation.' "[3] We may have rid ourselves of the Devil, but who could doubt that he has bequeathed us the spirit of banality as the legacy of his unreality?[4]

In one of his scrapbooks, Lichtenberg notes that for most people, a lack of belief in one thing is based on blind faith in another.[5] "Big bang" is our term for the story of creation; the angels' capacity for bilocation has been passed on to electrons in an expanding universe; the heavenly hosts of light waves take two million years to travel to the nearest galactic cloud in Andromeda; the Great Attractor has risen up to become the god who suffers no other gods beside him; Maxwell's demon has visited Sacred Entropy upon us, and there are demonic quanta in a negative state producing holes in nothingness. The myths we have eliminated are returning to haunt us from the celestial realms of scientific rationality.[6] Since this sphere is as inaccessible to the layman as the supralunary one formerly was to mortals, we have come to depend on popularizations. As we can no longer dis-

[3] Edgar Wind, *Art and Anarchy*, 3rd ed. (London, 1985), p. 41.

[4] Cf. Borges, "A Comment on August 23, 1944," in *Selected Non-Fictions*, ed. Eliot Weinberger (New York, 1999), pp. 210–211.

[5] Lichtenberg, *Schriften und Briefe*, vol. 1, p. 508 (L 670).

[6] Cf. Claude Lévi-Strauss, *Histoire de lynx* (Paris, 1991), pp. 10–11.

tinguish between mystifications of things unimaginable and utter nonsense, we have lost our sense of what is inconceivable.

Redeemed from faith, we damn and deify.[7] It would be hard to idolize something more unreal than the present age, except perhaps the stillbirths of permanent innovation. We scorn the salon painters of the nineteenth century in exactly the same way that the twenty-first will mock our own colossal trumpery, whose spiritual kinship with totalitarian kitsch escapes us only because we behave like Clever Hans in the fairy tale.[8] Fear of committing misjudgments has never saved anyone from misjudgment; on the contrary, it appears to prove incontrovertibly that we are denying our own reasons for *wanting* to be deceived.

To believe that the present age must be immune to error since all the information there could possibly be simply rains down whenever we press a button is to fall victim to a double illusion. First, no one can absorb more information than the short span of life permits, and second, the quantity and the effortless ease of reception mean stupidities multiply incomparably faster than the fruits of thought that are hidden deep in the jumble of information.[9]

We are prisoners of a technological universe in which the progressive impoverishment of the natural world runs parallel with an ever poorer cultural world. Blind to the magnificence of the world of animals and plants—inexplicable in terms of use-value—we are inclined not to imitate nature's artfulness, but to transfer her merciless

---

[7] Cf. Odo Marquard's introduction to the article *Malum* in *Historisches Wörterbuch,* vol. 5, pp. 654–655.

[8] He leaves all the thinking to his mother and is always getting everything wrong by applying the advice appropriate in the previous situation to a new one. See *The Fairy Tales of the Brothers Grimm,* trans. Mrs. Edgar Lucas (London, 1909), pp. 217–222.

[9] Cf. Stanislaw Lem, "Zu Tode informiert," *Der Spiegel* 11 (1996).

dictates to the realm of culture—thereby indulging in what Panofsky refers to as "insectolatry."[10]

The superstitious notion that genius can be weighed in gold could only have deployed its fatal power through the divorce between art and science, mind and nature, head and hand. In today's art market of yesterday's latest styles, it recalls the era of the tulip fraud. According to a saying of Valéry's, "Nothing leads more certainly to perfect barbarity, than an exclusive attachment to the pure spirit."[11]

Pure abstraction reflects the real abstraction of bucks, the "toads" of Marseus's painting, and the fate of the painter Mark Rothko illustrates the kind of snakes you have to swallow when the only standard of evaluation you use is the cash of the "rich bastards" against whom you think you are painting.

Convinced that "interesting painting" expresses not what you see, but rather what you think, the Abstract Expressionist Rothko did his utmost to mystify himself in his giant murals. Commissioned to paint the walls of an expensive restaurant, he resolved to "ruin the appetite of every son of a bitch" among the "richest bastards in New York," using his paintings to make them feel "they are trapped in a room where all the doors and windows are blocked up, so that all they can do is butt their heads forever against the wall." But a trial meal at the Four Seasons showed him that the bastards had not the slightest intention of looking up from the expensive delicacies on their plates to spare a single thought for his last judgment on them in paint.

Furious, he returned his cash advance and signed a contract with some other bastards: "the greatest contract ever signed by a living artist." One million dollars was the price for the reverse side of self-mystification: the

[10] Erwin Panofsky, *Meaning in the Visual Arts* (Harmondsworth, 1970).

[11] Cf. Edgar Wind, *Art and Anarchy*, p. 20.

humiliation of self-betrayal. Feeling he had sold his soul, Rothko took his own life a year after signing the contract.[12]

Where there is nothing greater than the ego, art must inevitably be mistaken for life. By what standard could a work be judged, in a community of artists that combines a belief in the "healthy truth that *I am here*" with the hard view of the contemporary age that even the "greatest genius" can never leap beyond the boundaries of its epoch?[13] Those who bow down to such dogmas must be permitted every liberty. Freed from all restraint, each is at once his own tyrant and the slave of his own time.

It is not from a loss of the center that the fine arts are suffering, but from a fixation of the center. Only the ephemeral half of Baudelaire's definition of *modernité* has been left over;[14] and a hemiplegic modernity is not modernity. Cut off from the immutable, it has lost its spirit. Without a grammar, it can never be decided whether someone stands above grammar or below it.[15] Those who have never mastered any rules are incapable of transforming them. The disorder of a lack of rules is identical with rigidity. Whether figurative or abstract painter, video

[12] All quotations are from Jack Flam, "The Agonies of Success," *New York Review of Books* 40, no. 20 (2 December 1983), pp. 36–39 (review of James E. B. Breslin, *Mark Rothko: A Biography*).

[13] Extracts from Wassily Kandinsky, *Über das Geistige in der Kunst* (Munich, 1912) and *Aufsätze von 1923 bis 1943*, in Walter Hess, *Dokumente zum Verständnis der modernen Malerei* (Hamburg, 1956), p. 94.

[14] "*La modernité, c'est le transitoire, le fugitif, le contingent, la moitié de l'art, dont l'autre moitié est l'éternité et l'immuable.*" ("Le peintre de la vie moderne," in *Oeuvres complètes*, ed. Claude Pichois [Paris, 1976], vol. 2, p. 695.) "What is transitory, fleeting, and contingent can never emerge without separating itself from what is immutable and eternal." Baudelaire's requirement that modernity should become *antiquité* not in opposition to other epochs, but in the specific ways appropriate to each period, cannot be fulfilled when one half of it has been scotomized. The absolutization of novelty breaks novelty's promise; instead of *becoming* antiquity, this type of modernity wants to *be* antiquity.

[15] On this point, see Albus, "ABC prominenter Ideen," p. 146.

artist or performance artist, every producer is condemned by the absolutization of innovation to a lifetime of peddling the same old trick. If he goes about hawking two, then even that will become his trademark. "Corporate identity" is the slogan for self-marketing. The arbitrariness of a powerful man such as Rolin could be resisted with skillful trickery; the stock exchange only reacts to butterflies that set off tornadoes.

After the victory of representation over what was represented, painting swallowed its object and went on to display itself alone. Since its rules were now formulated at only one level, its repertoire was soon exhausted; and Marcel Duchamp, the first to recognize this, set up the ready-made over its grave. The great pessimist could never have dreamed that his "inexorable negations," imitated on a mass scale on the ghost train of art, would turn into their own opposites.[16] The healthy truth of "I am here" took out a subscription to shock. In the boundless dungeon to which art has willingly consigned itself, the interpreters have ever since been kings. Their interest in promulgating the art of artlessness is clear: since not everything that is artless can be art, they alone have authority.[17]

Painting began with the visibility of the invisible, and ended with the invisibility of the visible. "Without a program or commentary, the eye is no longer satisfied; it has abdicated as an organ of enlightenment."[18] The fine arts have become the servants of the servile ear.

---

[16] Hans Platschek, *Von Dada zur Smart Art* (Frankfurt, 1989), p. 130, and *Engel bringt das Gewünschte* (Frankfurt, 1987), pp. 67–82.

[17] On this point, see the study of the art scene by Tom Wolfe, *The Painted Word* (New York, 1975). It was impossible to dismiss Wolfe's acute observations of this status-oriented world as philistine or reactionary, and in consequence *The Painted Word* was silently ignored.

[18] Cf. Chapeaurouge, *Das Auge*, p. 153.

The way in which theory has entwined itself around art reminds one of the method of manufacturing Emmentaler cheese on the principle: first take the holes, and then put the cheese round them. No matter whether the theoretical dough swelling up around the holes has been mixed in the dull cauldron of political correctness or in the sublime crucible of metaphysics—unless form and content interfuse, there can be no question of art.

Nothing living can absolutize itself in the flowing stream of time without drowning in it as a corpse of illusion. But we might at any rate take the trouble to learn from history.[19] We have lost our belief in progress, but we still pay tribute to its puppet, "the spirit of the times." We would never dream of mistaking totality for truth any longer, but the negative side of this sophism is still the deadliest heirloom of Hegelian philosophy.[20] In reversed conditions, world history is once again to become the Last Judgment, and no one in *thrownness* shall ever come up out of the stream of time.

Faced with the Gorgon's head of progress, it has become impossible for art to progress. Just as the lame weaver dreams he is weaving, the blind painter dreams the blue of blue. If it is not with fear that he guards his creative dream against knowledge, then it is with force. When Soviet astronaut Yuri Gagarin announced in 1961 that the cosmos was black, Jean Tinguely, who happened to have heard this ancient discovery being confirmed on the radio, was indiscreet enough to pass it on to Yves

---

[19] On 3 November 1933, Heidegger, as the rector of the University of Freiburg, told his students: "Let not theorems and ideas be the rules of your being; the Führer himself and he alone is German reality and its law, today and for the future." Cf. Alfred Grosser, *10 Leçons sur le nazisme* (Paris, 1976, 1984), p. 95. Precisely because it is a matter of distinguishing between politics and art, artists cannot share the misjudgments of those whom they would rightly be accused of serving.

[20] On this point, see Cassirer, *Myth of the State*, pp. 342–360.

Klein. "A moment's silence, and then Yves Klein grabs Tinguely by his shirt and punches him full in the face with his fist."[21]

Those who run with the pack dream it is the avant-garde.[22] Contradictions can do no harm to dreams; dreams live on them. The illusoriness of the art world can be measured by the fact that the contradiction that defeated Rothko has long since been absorbed; those who show society its own ugliness at the same time think it completely natural to court its favors and strive for recognition from it. In the hell of use-values, the consumption of horror is booming.

In contrast to his imitators, Duchamp knew the distinction between fame and celebrity.[23] Asked whether he

[21] *Süddeutsche Zeitung* magazine, 20 October 1995: interview with Jean-Christoph Ammann, director of the Museum of Modern Art in Frankfurt. Ammann, spilling the beans of the museum world, tells the story of the thick-as-a-fist black eye with enthusiasm for this brave defense of an artistic concept. To ignorant observers who thought they could splash paint around in exactly the same way, he responded: "Very good, congratulations. Perhaps you can even do it better, but was it originally your idea?" On "the fear of knowledge," see Wind, *Art and Anarchy,* pp. 47–62, and Wuttke, *Aby M. Warburgs Methode,* pp. 12–13.

[22] On this point, see Hans Magnus Enzensberger, "Aporien der Avantgarde," in *Einzelheiten* (Frankfurt, 1962), pp. 290–315. The rigidity of the present age can be seen in the fact that in the nearly forty years since the publication of "Aporien der Avantgarde," not only has no one in Germany pursued Enzenberger's analysis further, but, in addition, if anyone were to take notice of it on the art scene today they would still be outraged by it. "Reality is always anachronous," writes Borges ("Two Books," in *Selected Non-Fictions,* p. 209), and due to the information jumble mentioned above, it is more so today than ever.

[23] The use of words such as "celebrity" and "prominence" illustrates the blindness that identifies life with work, and in its exclusive focus on the present moment regards fame as equivalent to success. The inappropriateness of such words in qualitative contexts becomes clear when one looks at the significance they can acquire in inhuman conditions. See Primo Levi, *If This Is a Man,* trans. Stuart Woolf (London, 1962), pp. 72–73, and *The Drowned and the Saved,* trans. Raymond Rosenthal (New York, 1988), pp. 88–104.

realized he was one of the most famous artists in the world, he answered,

> I don't know anything about that. In the first place, ordinary people have never heard of me, although most of them know Dalí or Picasso, or even Matisse. Secondly, I think when someone is fa-mous it is impossible for him to realize it. Being famous is like being dead: I don't think the dead realize they are dead. And thirdly, if I was famous, it is not something I would be very proud of; it would be a clownish kind of fame due to the sen-sation that was caused by *Nu descendant un escalier.* Although of course I expect that when that kind of vileness continues for more than fifty years, there must be something more to it than just scandal.[24]

The interviewer asked what this "something more" might be. "It. The thing that has no name." Descending a staircase, the naked Muse says a moving farewell to painting . . .

The god of the arts, like Nicholas of Cusa's, has no name, and could never be accommodated in a church. As painting began to disregard the need to reconcile what is perceptible with what is intelligible, the scholars and writers who were not afraid to think against the grain of their times continued to exercise the art of the opposing statement. A love of detail and a grasp of structure have remained alive in their works. If they had not freed them-selves from their contemporary age, they would not have been able to perceive the visibility of the invisible and

[24] Platschek, *Smart Art,* p. 130. Moved, and without bothering to look for the bottle rack in the cellar, the Muse left the building, ensuring that—until she is rediscovered—the art of painting will remain hidden in the creations of writers and philosophers. See below.

would not have been what they were in the eyes of their contemporaries: outsiders and heretics.

Dürer remarks that a good painter is "inwardly full of figures, and even if he could live forever, he would always be able to pour forth, from those inner ideas of which Plato writes, something new in his work."[25] It was not painters, but Goethe, the scientific poet, and D'Arcy Thompson, an artistic polyhistor of Baroque stature, who beheld the ideas of creation. The one succeeded through pure contemplation in drawing the metamor- phosis of plants into the web of words; the other managed to decipher the geometric language of the book of nature, so that his webs of coordinates, modeled on Dürer's *Geometry* and *Treatise on Proportion,* captured the transfor- mations of fish and crustaceans, the metamorphosis of the crocodile's skeleton, the pelvic bones of dinosaurs and bird fossils, and the skulls of extinct rhinoceroses, right down to their most recent memento mori.[26]

The short book by the much admired poet and much smiled-at naturalist was published in 1790, and the long one by the mathematician, physicist, and classical scholar, whose bel canto style was thought embarrassing and whose hypotheses were not understood in his time, was published in 1917. The latter developed the science of which the first had been the godfather: morphology.

If you wish the Whole to refresh your heart,
You must glimpse the Whole in its smallest part.[27]

How far Goethe was from his contemporaries' habits of thought can be seen from the misunderstood depiction of

[25] ". . . inwendig voller Figur, und obs müglich wär, dass er ewiglich lebte, so hätt er aus den innern Ideen, davon Plato schreibt, allweg etwas Neus durch das Werk auszugiessen." Dürer, *Schriften und Briefe,* p. 119.

[26] See the illustration on p. 377.
[27] "Willst du dich am Ganzen erquicken, / So musst du das Ganze im Kleinsten erblicken." (Goethe, *Werkausgabe letzter Hand,* vol. 2, p. 228.)

his ur-plant, produced two years after his death. The drawing by the botanist Pierre-Jean-François Turpin looks like a vegetabilic anticipation of Bovary's cap.[28]

It was only in the twentieth century that the full implications of Goethe's research for comparative morphology were recognized. D'Arcy Wentworth Thompson's *On Growth and Form* is now regarded as the "the finest work of literature in all the annals of science that have been recorded in the English tongue," and its bel canto singer—who agreed with Jean-Henri Fabre, "that wise student and pupil of the ant and the bee," that numbers are *la clef de voûte de l'Univers,* and like him did not believe in God but *saw* him—became one of the forerunners of catastrophe theory and chaos research.[29]

> The waves of the sea, the little ripples on the shore, the sweeping curve of the sandy bay between the headlands, the outline of the hills, the shape of the clouds, all these are so many riddles of form, so many problems of morphology, and all of them the physicist can more or less easily read and adequately solve: solving them by reference to their antecedent phenomena, in the material system of mechanical forces to which they belong, and to which we interpret them as being due. They have also, doubtless, their *immanent* teleological significance; but it is on another plane of thought from the physicist's that we contemplate their intrinsic harmony and perfection, and "see that they are good."[30]

[28] See the illustration on p. 378.

[29] The first quotation (the words of Peter Medawar) is in the introduction to the abridged edition of D'Arcy Weatworth Thompson, *On Growth and Form,* ed. J. Tyler Bonner (Cambridge, 1961), pp. ix–x; the second is from Thompson, *On Growth and Form: The Complete Revised Edition* (Cambridge, 1942; rptd. New York, 1992), p. 1097. It was Medawar who described Thompson's style as *"bel canto."*

[30] Thompson, *Growth and Form,* p. 10. Lichtenberg anticipates this

The dispute between Aristotle and Plato, between the old way and the new, becomes pointless for one who can distinguish different levels and who has grasped that the whole is not only more than the sum of its parts, but *always* something very different from the parts, although it does not appear in them differently: as the harmony and balance of their interplay.[31]

Completely "engrossed by the peculiar beauty which is manifested in apparent fitness or 'adaptation'—the flower for the bee, the berry for the bird," Thompson, as a critical teleologist, was convinced it was too easy to assume that "fortuitous variation" and the "survival of the fittest" would provide "a sufficient basis on which to rest, with the all-powerful help of natural selection, a theory of definite and progressive evolution."[32]

As the translator of Aristotle and author of a *Glossary of Greek Birds* and a *Glossary of Greek Fishes,* an aviary and aquarium of every bird and fish mentioned in classical Greek literature, Thompson succeeded in fusing modern science with antiquity. He is a good example of the way in which the question of the avant-garde, in no

topic in a brief mental sketch: "When considering the surfaces of bodies, the following should not be forgotten: the process of melting, the grinding of glass until it is dull, the way that oil suppresses the waves of the sea, and color changes and color as such." (*Schriften und Briefe,* ed. Wolfgang Promies [Munich, 1971]: "Sudelbücher II," J 1802.)

[31] See *Growth and Form,* p. 10, footnote. A good example of the phenomenon of two irreconcilable theories proving to be equally valid because they belong to different levels has recently been provided by the neurophysiology of the process of vision. The dispute between Helmholtz and Hering (red, green, and blue versus red-green, yellow-blue, black-white) was a wild-goose chase. Helmholtz had grasped the cone principle of vision, and Hering the antagonistic measuring processes at the subsequent levels of the optic nerve. See David H. Hubel, *Eye, Brain, and Vision,* pp. 170–174. The dispute over inherited and acquired characteristics has also been resolved by neurobiology; v. loc. cit.

[32] *Growth and Form,* pp. 3 and 8.

matter which of the liberal arts, can only be answered from a distance. It is no accident that from posterity's point of view, those who are able to discern the tradition's inventiveness and who are aware of what they owe to it are so often regarded as modern.[33]

In the introductory chapter of *On Growth and Form*, the modern traditionalist or traditional modernist recalls the ancient Hebrew view that "God made 'every plant of the field before it was in the earth, and every herb of the field before it grew,' " and, with the generosity of spirit deriving from his classical education, concludes that this is a common and at the same time noble view, as "it brings with it a glimpse of a great vision, and it lies deep as the love of nature in the hearts of men."[34]

Just as not all art is art, not all science is science. Distinctions are drawn between soft and hard, pure and applied. It is with the latter that the blame lies for the fall from grace implicit in the divorce between mind and nature. One of the greatest verbal artists of the twentieth century believed that the hallmark of the reduction of science to mere use-values can be seen in the ephemerality of the various illusions generated by flickering screens all over the world—that everything in nature can be reduced to "bits"; that immortal bodies can be cloned out of nothing in the laboratory; and that humanity is about to solve the enigma of life. The more genuine scientific knowledge one has, said the novel-writing lepidopterist, the greater one's sense of mystery becomes. If we did not respect the solitude of the Russian émigré, who dismissed every attempt at classification, we might imagine him in the company of D'Arcy Thompson and his Cusanian/Bouellian predecessors—discussing together the sharp-sightedness of the animal that wears a

[33] See the article "Modern, die Moderne" in *Historisches Wörterbuch*, vol. 6, pp. 54–55.

[34] *Growth and Form*, p. 4.

coat of *petit-gris,* or the Cinderella shades of the miraculous spiral of color.[35]

"Of how it is that the soul informs the body, physical
science teaches me nothing; and that living matter influences and is influenced by mind is a mystery without a
clue," Thompson wrote in 1917.[36] Trying to explain life
using chemistry is to clarify *obscurum per obscurius,* as one of
his talented successors, the mathematician René Thom,
wrote.[37] The topologist established the canon of form-
creating elementary catastrophes, seven in number: the
fold, the cusp (from *cuspis,* a point or spike), the swallow's
tail, the elliptical umbilicus (from the Latin word for navel), the hyperbolic umbilicus, the butterfly, and the para-

[35] *Petit-gris,* literally "small gray,"
means "fell, gray hide," the winter
fur of the Siberian squirrel, *Sciurus
vulgaris varius.* (*Sciurus* means "shading itself with its tail.") The larger
American variety of the shade-tail is
the *grand-gris* leitmotiv haunting
Nabokov's *Pnin.* The resourceful lit-
erary nutcracker Michael Maar
revealed how this "King and
supreme cracker of nuts . . . leapt
out through the foliage of the neigh-
boring novel" *Lolita* into *Pnin*
(*Frankfurter Allgemeine Zeitung,* 4
October 1994). Thompson mentions the size of the squirrel's eye in
Growth and Form (p. 53). On Cinderella shades, see *Pnin* (Harmondsworth, 1960), p. 80. On the
spira mirabilis, see part one, chapter 5
above, footnote 22. In the seventeenth century, Jakob Bernoulli
wrote, "Just as the infinite series
submits to a finite sum / And what
seems boundless to you yields to a
boundary, / So in this humble body
is concealed a trace / Of the infinite deity, and what is narrowly
bounded becomes boundless." The
fleeting shape of a miraculous spiral
of color can be glimpsed in August
Strindberg's *Blue Book:* "The colors
of the spectrum only display light in
declining degrees of strength on
each side of yellow, the strongest,
which lies in the middle. The colors
of the prism begin with red and
close with violet, because the transition from blue, the penultimate in
the scale, and red, the first, is violet.
Those, therefore, who expect to find
a color beyond violet on the outside
of the rainbow, and who believe
they have even seen it in pho-
tographs of the spectrum, are probably waiting in vain, unless they are
waiting for red-blue or blue-red!
Or black! *Lavender gray,* says
Helmholtz." (Italics added; *Blaubuch,* rptd. from the first German edition of 1908 in *Die Republik,*
nos. 61–67, ed. Petra and Uwe Net-
telbeck [Salzhausen-Luhmühlen,
1983], p. 349.)

[36] *Growth and Form,* p. 13.

[37] René Thom, *Prédire n'est pas
expliquer: entretien avec Emile Noël*
(Paris, 1991), p. 102.

bolic umbilicus. "Catastrophe" means "sudden turn, over-turning." Since morphogenesis appears to be the result of a conflict—between different centers of attraction, or be-tween different areas of the same center—it was this "over-turning" that gave the topological art of opposites its name. The hypothesis of a philosophy 2,500 years old, which reemerged in *On Growth and Form,* received its brilliant confirmation in Thom's *Structural Stability and Morpho-genesis:* that of the pre-Socratic philosophers Anaximan-der and Heraclitus. The mathematician and philosopher of nature translates *logos* as "form." According to his lucid interpretation of the obscurities of Heraclitus, the unity and stability of objects are owed to their formal structure.

> There are simulating structures of all natural exter-nal forces at the very heart of the genetic endow-ment of our species, at the unassailable depth of the Heraclitean *logos* of our soul, and . . . these struc-tures are ready to go into action whenever necessary. The old idea of Man, the microcosm, mirroring World, the macrocosm, retains all its force: who knows Man, knows the Universe.[38]

The search for perfection and the unattainability of this goal are identical in Thom's philosophy of overturning. *"La vie n'a pas le temps d'attendre la rigueur"* is an aphorism of Valéry's quoted in his book.[39] He provides support for the view that it is impossible to exhaust the soul's sense of form by quoting the "dark one": "No matter how far your path might carry you, you could never reach the bound-aries of your soul, its form is so deep."[40]

---

[38] René Thom, *Structural Stabil-ity and Morphogenesis: An Outline of a General Theory of Models,* trans. D. H. Fowler (Reading, Mass., 1975), pp. 324–325.

[39] Ibid., p. 280.
[40] Heraclitus (544–483 B.C.) was nicknamed "the dark one" because of the profundity of his teachings. My version of fragment

Why did the *techné* of the old masters live on among the artists of language? Why does the layer technique—which, according to the laws of van Eyck's coloring, the smallest interval and the greatest contrast, allows the maximum of detail to be depicted within suspended time—reappear in the work of Proust, in which the eternal rises up from the depths of the soul through an uneven cobblestone?

Why do the shades of Nabokov's unique universe—quartz pink, oatmeal color, paradise green, lavender blue—crystallize in the convex mirror of his art against the dark foil of life, following the motto of Flemish painting technique: to be as transparent as the greatest possible density allows? Why does van Eyck's "ample-jowled, fluff-haloed" Canon van der Paele come to life again in Nabokov's *Pnin,* painted in minute detail—"the knotty temple, the sad, musing gaze, the folds and furrows of facial flesh, the thin lips, and even the wart on the left cheek"—when not a single contemporary painter, even if he is still capable of depicting a nail and its shadow, is able to create the illusion of skin that breathes?[41]

Why is "craft" a taboo word in the fine arts, while in literature it has continued to be a requirement that is taken for granted? Cassirer published a succinct answer to this question five years before the world premiere of that total work of art in the field of politics, "The Destruction of Humanity." All life and all creativity, the courteous philosopher writes, is linked to the fundamental phenomenon of polarity—which is not the same as duality. This

45 follows Thom's version; in Freeman the translation reads, "You could not in your going find the ends of the soul, though you travelled the whole way: so deep is its Law (*Logos*)." (Kathleen Freeman, *Ancilla to the Pre-Socratic Philosophers,* p. 27.) In fragment 115, Heraclitus says that "the soul has its own Law (*Logos*), which increases itself"; according to Thom, this would refer to the inexhaustible capacity of its form to transform itself.

[41] *Pnin,* p. 129.

is seen most clearly in language, which on the one hand strives to achieve individual expression, while on the other it can arise only through an objective, supra-individual medium of forms.

> The productive art of the individual (the great artists of language) is never demonstrated by an abandonment of this medium, but is seen in the way in which they discover, behind the merely conventional formula, the form of the original productive energy. But it is in appearance alone that they seem to be the creators of form here . . . It is not *they* who create "language," but language that creates in them and through them . . . The individual, like "life," cannot possess itself in any other way than by passing beyond itself into the world of forms, by *abandoning* itself to it. It is only through the renunciation represented by impersonal form that the individual can *gain* itself—it must stake its life, in order to gain the realm of the mind.[42]

All true creators of language, from antiquity to the present day, have known that they are *weaving the apparel of the godhead.* But they do not weave it with their hands.[43] The separation of head and hand is less of a creative problem for them. They do not produce status symbols, and the costly fabric of their texts is incapable of being used as a physical veil for anyone's scruples. The value of their manuscripts in bucks or "toads" only emerges posthumously, and manuscripts are too inconspicuous to decorate the temple of physical abstraction. Why should

[42] Ernst Cassirer, *Nachgelassene Manuskripte und Texte,* ed. John Michael Krois (Hamburg, 1995), vol. 1, p. 218.

[43] Their manual skills are a different matter. They only need a "lucky hand" in the figurative sense, so that the decline of manual skills in a factory-made world cannot become a creative problem for them.

they let anyone buy up their thirst for knowledge, what would happen to them if they gave in to the temptation to sign that declaration of the bankruptcy of the imagina⁄ tion that postulates that everything in history could only have happened in precisely the way it did? The past is not fixed and established; every age needs to transform it and reimagine it afresh. "Unlike Orpheus we win our Eury⁄ dice by looking back and lose her by looking ahead."[44] To find the viewpoint from which that of the past that was endowed with gifts for the future can arise once again, distance is required.

"Do not forget: books are the creation of solitude and the *children of silence,*" Proust warns.[45] Like the velvet⁄ trousered critics and Blixen's Babette, he was convinced that for anyone devoted to an ideal, the greatest beauty must be perceived as lying in those things that present him with the greatest difficulty, "which is as it happens an instinctive morality to counterbalance our vices and weaknesses."[46] In the eyes of the asthmatic author of the *Search for Lost Time,* with the long breath of its meander⁄ ing sentences, the whole art of living lies in "using those persons who cause us suffering as a mere step, crossing which we gain access to their divine form—and thus populate our life joyfully with divinities."[47]

Techné is a question of the love of wisdom (philoso⁄ phy); the profession of the artist is one of morality. "Dilettantism has never created anything," because the

---

[44] Jean Paul Richter, *Horn of Oberon,* p. 29.

[45] Marcel Proust, *Against Sainte⁄ Beuve and Other Essays,* trans. John Sturrock (Harmondsworth, 1988), p. 99. The double meaning in French of *silence*—"stillness, calm" and "quiet, abstaining from speech"—is not clear in translation.

Since Proust contrasts the *enfants du silence* with the *enfants de la parole,* it is the absence of speech that is intended here.

[46] Ibid., p. 101.

[47] Proust, "Le Temps retrouvé," in *À la recherche du temps perdu,* ed. Pierre Clarac and André Ferré (Paris, 1954), vol. 3, p. 899, footnote.

dilettante does not wish to counterbalance his vices and weaknesses, but to declare that they are art.[48]

The best school for aesthetics we could possibly visit is still that of Jean Paul Richter, who said—looking backward far into the future—"It follows from the lawless, capricious spirit of the present age, which would egotistically annihilate the world and the universe in order to clear a space merely for free *play* in the void, and which tears off the *bandage* of its wounds as a *bond,* that this age must speak scornfully of the imitation and study of nature."[49]

There can be no doubt that the twentieth century also had its gifted painters; but no one has overcome the stagnation of painting, and no one has been able to hold back the decline of the profession. Their works can only be mimicked, since "The reflection does not reflect itself."[50] As long as painting turns its back on nature, it will never be able to regrow. For the time being, we can only exercise our eyes with the aid of the poets and philosophers. A description of morphogenetic fields in perceptual terms is found in Strindberg's *Blue Book* under the heading "The Cyclamen, Illuminating Great Disorder and Great Coherence." We follow the playwright as he takes a walk in the woods above the Danube. A carpet of ivy is spread in the temple of Nature, and in its midst the trompe-l'oeil of its pattern suddenly opens up:

> The leaves had angled themselves toward the sun, which was barely able to penetrate the tree's foliage. After I had contemplated the ivy for a while, I noticed a cyclamen in the midst of it. And then I noticed still more, and finally I could see just as many cyclamens as ivy leaves. I had not seen the

[48] Proust, *Against Sainte-Beuve,* p. 70.

[49] *Horn of Oberon: Jean Paul Richter's School for Aesthetics,* p. 15.

[50] Ibid., p. 38. Jean Paul continues: "If we were completely aware of ourselves, then we would be our own creators, unlimited."

cyclamen straight away because this species, *europaeum*, has a dark green pattern on the middle of the leaf, with a whitish-gray outline around it, so that the dark green on the inside forms the shape of an ivy leaf . . . I had often observed in the plant world nature's manner of drawing a sketch before executing it, and I noticed here with the cyclamen that the red color for the flower was already in readiness in the leaf stalk and applied on the palette of the leaf. I therefore wondered whether the white guilloche pattern on the upper side of the leaf might not be the sketch for a new form . . . The ivy leaf is a mathematical figure termed cissoid, discovered by Diocles. It is characterized in modern geometry as follows: a curve that constantly follows the perpendicular line drawn between the vertex of a parabola and its tangent. Or thus: a line imitating the contour of an ivy leaf by approaching its asymptote. / The cyclamen leaf, again, forms a caustic figure, which as is well known arises through the refraction of rays in a concave mirror, or by rays falling through a transparent hemisphere, a cone or cylinder. / When one sits on a porch where the rays of sunlight pass through thick foliage, countless ellipses are seen on the floor. These are caused by the fact that the cone of light passing through the gaps in the foliage is transected by the floor in such a way as to form ellipses. They are therefore conic sections. What is happening, then, under the dense foliage in the forest? It is almost impossible to calculate this, but that need be no obstacle to the notion of conceiving in advance some idea of the play of lines arising in all the conic sections, to which the parabolas and hyperbolas also belong, and which have an intimate connection with the cissoids and the caustic lines.[51]

[51] Strindberg, *Blaubuch*, pp. 369–370.

In the same way that the cyclamen reflects the ivy in the *Blue Book,* the mackerel reflects the waves of the sea and teaches us mackerel art: "The mackerel has the breaking of the waves marked out so sharply on its back that a marine painter could copy it and transfer it in perspective to a canvas in order to reproduce the waves."[52]

The way in which the perfection of a freshly emerged butterfly, with every scale on its wings, is reflected in the mind of a poet and physicist is seen in Lichtenberg's "Comparison of the Painting on a Butterfly's Wing with a Masterpiece of Mosaic Work":

> Our solar system is infinitely small compared with the immensity of immeasurable space, just as the greatest human art dwindles to nothing under even the most favorable comparison with the eternal works of nature. If any of these were to be removed from the larger whole, it would leave a gap no greater than that of a grain of sand purloined from the shore of the ocean; and when we compare the greatest masterpiece of mosaic art with the wing of a butterfly—of which nature forms thousands in a single hour of summer and melts them away again unnoticed and unadmired by us—the mosaic is but worthless child's play, even if only surface is compared with surface.

An unnamed English naturalist had counted 931,808 colored scales on a single square inch of a peacock butterfly cut from its pupa just before metamorphosis, and Lichtenberg compared this with the 868 mosaic stones in the finest neo-Roman painting.

> Against this, our imbecilic eye needs to use magnifying glasses to perceive the miraculous arrangement hidden within the scales of the butterfly's wings, the

[52] Ibid., p. 372.

colored lines of which thousands regard as being their whole purpose. When the beauty of the final effect is broken down by enlargement, a different beauty emerges again from beneath its cover—the beauty of the individual parts, their form and fibers; and here, too, new beauties would appear yet again if our glasses were capable of drawing back the curtain that veils them.[53]

Painting was able to claim its place as the art of arts only as long as it still encompassed the seven liberal arts within it; as long as the painters, in the contest of the arts, gave their utmost to breathe life into the world. Without their learning, without their counterbalance of morality, a new peacock butterfly can never spread forth its wings from the subverted profession. Look back at painting's multilayered lepidopterous phase. The Lunar Orbiter sent back its images of our blue star from the immeasurable, lifeless reaches of space. If we had fully grasped this star's uniqueness, we would look with different eyes at the fly that has finished its morning wash and is strolling over apple-green waxy skin around a globe with a stalk. Perhaps then we might have regained the intensity of gaze that distinguished a van Eyck or Rogier, Patinir or David, Flegel or Goedaert. We should take up from them—not to do the same as they did, but to have a share in the same: in perfect creation, in the imitation *according to* creation that is the form of our immortality.

[53] Lichtenberg, *Schriften und Briefe,* vol. 2, pp. 228 and 230. What the imbecilic eye saw through Lichtenberg's magnifying glass is today known as the Julia constant or Mandelbrot constant. The physicist worked on dendrites, and described their development in his essay *De nova methodo naturam ac motum fluidi electrici investigandi* (Göttingen, 1778), in which the fractals that are still known as Lichtenberg figures are illustrated. (I am grateful to the mathematics enthusiast H. M. Enzensberger for the reference to Mandelbrot.)

II
Of Lost Colors

rom white lead to alabaster, the pigments listed below are still available, or have now become available once again. As building blocks for producing depth light and density in an oil medium, they are more or less useless in the forms commercially available today. On the way from depth painting to surface painting, what was lost along with the art of how to build up a painting in multiple layers was the knowledge of the laws according to which light is diffracted and refracted, depending on the grain size and shape of the body of the paint. Those wishing to emulate the high visual weight of early Netherlandish painting would not only have to grind their pigments themselves, but would also have to manufacture them themselves according to the old formulas.

"In all things there is light and dark," writes Dürer in the drafts of his *Treatise on Painting,* "that bends and diffracts from the eyes. If this were not so, all things would appear flat, such that one would recognize nothing but the mere differences between the colors." Sublime painting, which gives the eye the illusion of body, avoids the mixing of colors.

> You must paint something red in such a way that it is red throughout—and the same with all of the colors—while at the same time it appears sublime. The same applies to shading, that it may not be said

one has fouled a fine red with black. Take care, therefore, that you shadow each color with a color that competes with it. For example, when we use a yellow color: if it is to remain in its own nature, you must shade it with a yellow that is darker than the main color . . . No matter what happens, a color must never lose its nature by mixture with black.[1]

When the greatest painter of the seventeenth century created his still life views of people, smooth painting of fine detail was as much in keeping with the times as the emphasis on brushwork, and allowing details to vanish away in chiaroscuro was as familiar as the mixing of paints. Vermeer knew how to use "Chinese patience" to erase every trace of its creation from a painting.[2] As with van Eyck, the secret of his art seems to lie in the grain size of the paints within the layered structure. His pigments were as full-bodied as they could possible be. Even the coarsest ones were still not coarse enough for him. The rich texture of the *petit pan de mur jaune* mentioned by Proust in the *View of Delft* is owed to the addition of quartz sand to lead-tin yellow.[3] Similar material effects, although different visual ones, can be created by adding alabaster or calcite. The quartz, gypsum, or calcite crystals, transparent in the oil medium, alter the play of light without interrupting the color tone.

Many of the important paints used in older art, such as the yellow, green, red, and brown earths, madder, and

[1] Lichtenberg, *Schriften und Briefe,* vol. 1, pp. 122–123.

[2] Cf. Jean-Louis Vaudoyer, "Le mystérieux Vermeer," *L'Opinion,* 30 April/7 May/14 May 1921, pp. 515 and 543. "That is how I should have written," says Bergotte as he gazes at the *View of Delft,* ". . . I should have laid more layers of paint over one another, I should have made my words richer in themselves, like this little piece of yellow wall." (Proust, *A la recherche du temps perdu,* ed. Jean-Yves Tadié [Paris, 1987–1989], vol. 3, "La Prisonnière," p. 692.)

[3] *Vermeer en plein jour,* ed. Jørgen Wadum (The Hague: Mauritshuis, 1995), p. 14.

stone black, are not included in the list below. When peach stones are packed airtight in aluminum foil, it is easy to calcine them in burning embers and pound them in the mortar.[4] Earths can also be obtained in the raw state. Rose madder, from the root of the madder plant, is a vegetable pigment, an extremely fine-grained glaze paint. However, the pigments listed in this chapter have been selected for their relevance to that quality that cannot be captured by the raster screen of our oculocidal four-color world: the raw shape of their crystalline bodies.

In his book on painting, Pliny says of the famous painter Apelles that he used great deliberation "so that the brilliance of the colours should not offend the sight when people looked at them as if through muscovy-glass and so that the same device from a distance might invisibly give sombreness to colours that were too brilliant."[5]

Colored reflections have nothing in common with glaring, garish colorfulness; light should contemplate itself layer by layer, grain by grain.[6]

WHITE LEAD

Flake white, shell white, snowflake white, silver white, Krems white, Cremnitz white, Venetian white, Venetian

[4] For larger quantities of peach stones, it is best to fill a metal can as tightly as possible and punch two or three air holes in the lid.

[5] Pliny, *Natural History,* trans. H. Rackham, W.H.S. Jones, and D. E. Eichholz, 10 vols. (London, 1938–1963; Loeb Classical Series), XXXV.xxxvi (97), vol. 9, p. 333. Muscovy-glass (*lapis specularis*) is the same as alabaster. This passage in Pliny might have provided the inspiration for van Eyck to develop

his depth effects. Whether alabaster was mixed with his white lead has not yet been investigated. He enhanced the visual beauty of rose madder, from the root of the madder plant, by mixing it with aragonite (a form of calcite with a rhombic trellis structure). Cf. Coremans, *L'Agneau mystique,* p. 69.

[6] I am grateful to Wolfgang Fünders, Georg Kremer, and Evert Thielen for their advice on paint and painting technique.

shell white, Dutch shell white; Latin: *cerussa, cerosa, album, album plumbum, albus, glaucus, leucos, minium album, psimithium, psimithin, simity.*

CHARACTERISTICS. *Color:* warm, pure white. *Material appearance:* round grains. The raw material consists of heavy, hard, shell-shaped flakes with shiny fracture surfaces. *Chemical composition:* $2PbCO_3 \times Pb(OH)_2$ = basic lead carbonate.

PHYSICAL PROPERTIES. Strongly birefringent crystalline particles with a slablike appearance and a hexagonal outline under the electron microscope. *Refringency index:* $\varepsilon = 1.94$ $\omega = 2.09$. *Density:* 7.0. *Toxicity:* grade 3 toxin; inhaling the dust of the pigment for extended periods can be life-threatening.

The production of white lead has been known since antiquity. Pliny[7] describes the process in the thirty-fourth book of his *Natural History*:

> *"Psimithium"* also, that is cerussa or lead acetate, is produced at lead-works. The most highly spoken of is in Rhodes. It is made from very fine shavings of lead placed over a vessel of very sour vinegar and so made to drip down. What falls from the lead into the actual vinegar is dried and then ground and sifted, and then again mixed with vinegar and divided into tablets and dried in the sun, in summertime. There is also another way of making it, by putting the lead into jars of vinegar kept sealed up for ten days and then scraping off the sort of

[7] Gaius Plinius (A.D. 23–79), also known as Pliny the Elder and Plinius Secundus.

decayed metal on it and putting it back in the vinegar, till the whole of it is used up.[8]

In the Middle Ages, the white flowers of thin sheets of lead were sometimes produced using vinegar and sometimes using urine vapor.[9]

In the seventeenth century, the process known as *loogen* is described in Holland, the Dutch being famous for their outstanding "shell white," which they called *schelpwit, schulpwit,* or *schilferwit.*[10] The glazed lower part of conical clay pots was filled with vinegar, and spiralshaped rolledup strips of cast lead rested on jutting ledges of clay above it. The pots were stacked in several layers among rotting horse manure or used tanning bark, which gave off heat and carbonic acid, and were left for several months for the crystallization process to take place. The hard flakes of socalled lead chalk were then tapped off the corroded spirals, whose shelllike shape had decomposed into caked flowers. In this state, the concave flakes were "flake white"—the best form of white lead, since it was guaranteed unadulterated. Before use, it had to be ground with water, carefully washed and dried, and then wetground again.

Although white lead may tend to blacken in an aqueous binder, manuscript illuminators also regarded it as an

[8] Pliny, *Natural History* XXXIV.liv (175), vol. 9, pp. 253–254.

[9] Cf. Heinz RoosenRunge, *Farbgebung und Technik frühmittelalterlicher Buchmalerei* (Munich, 1967), and the same author's contribution to *Reclams Handbuch der künstlerischen Techniken* (Stuttgart, 1984), vol. 1, pp. 98–99.

[10] The Dutch used the terms *schelpwit, schulpwit,* or *schilferwit* for the unadulterated raw material that the painters had to prepare themselves, while the pulverized material blended with chalk or alabaster was termed *lootwit.* Cf. T. Goedings, "Een ZeventiendeEeuwse Verklaring voor het Woord Schulpwit," in *IIC Mededelingenblad* 1 (March 1989), 7–12.

indispensable pigment. "We need it in one way or another for almost every color, and for this reason it is compared to butter, which improves every dish," writes Gerhard zur Brügge in his book on the art of illumination.[11]

Robert Dossie's *The Handmaid to the Arts,* first published anonymously in 1758 and revised in 1764, praises Italian flake white in particular:

White flake is lead corroded by means of the pressing of the grape, and consequently, in fact, a ceruse prepared by the acid of grapes. It is brought here from Italy, and far surpasses, both with regard to the purity of its whiteness, and the certainty of its standing, all the ceruse or white lead made here in common. It is used in oil and varnish painting for all purposes where a very clean white is required . . . White flake is usually had of the colour-men in a prepared state, under the name of *flake white,* being levigated and mixed up with starch, and most frequently with white lead, or much worse sophistications. Whoever, therefore, would be certain of using this pigment pure, should procure the white flake in lump as it is brought over, and levigate it themselves, washing it over also."

For coarser work, Dossie recommends the less expensive English lead white, which is "the corrosion or rust of lead formed by means of vinegar."

[11] Gerhard zur Brügge, *Illuminir- oder Erleuchterey-Kunst,* trans. Johann Langen (Hamburg, 1678), pp. 9–10. The long title translates: *The Art of Illumination or Lighting, or the Proper Use of Watercolors, Wherein Their Correct Grounds and Perfect Use, Both for Painting and Illuminating, Are Briefly Demonstrated. First Shown Forth by the Excellent Illuminator Gerhard zur Brügge and Now Again Expanded and Improved for the Use of Enthusiasts, with Remarks on Applying and Painting with Watercolors by Wilhelm Goeree.*

Notwithstanding the low price of white lead, yet, being consumed in great quantities, it is for the most part adulterated by the manufacturers of, or whole⟋sale dealers in it. The common sophistication is with chalk or powdered talc, as being the cheapest ingredients with which it can be mixt without changing too much its appearance. This in a lesser degree is of no great moment, as they only diminish the quantity of body or covering matter in the paint; but when in a greater proportion, they not only pro⟋duce a great loss, by rendering a larger quantity nec⟋essary to do the same work, but deprave the paint highly with respect to its other qualities.[12]

In his manual for "staffage painters," the Parisian painter, varnisher, and paint dealer Jean⟋Félix Watin also observes that "flake or shell white is without doubt the finest white for painting." The French merchant could not understand why the best flake white commercially available, which had formerly come from Venice, was now entirely in the hands of the English and Dutch. Not content with that, they were even taking "lead and vine⟋gar from France, and then bringing the manufactured flake white back here."[13] It would be so much simpler with this process, now so "easy and simple," to set up fac⟋tories in "other places"—which he points out would be all the more profitable, as the pigment serves, as it were, as the ground for all colors, since it is mixed with all the other paints.

If Watin had lived to see the way in which his dream of paint manufacturing was realized during the nine⟋

[12] Robert Dossie, *The Handmaid to the Arts* (London, 1764), vol. 1, pp. 131–133.

[13] Jean⟋Félix Watin, *Der Staffir⟋maler, oder die Kunst anzustreichen, zu* *vergolden & zu lackiren,* trans. from 2nd, extensively revised French edi⟋tion (Leipzig, 1774; rptd. Aichstet⟋ten, n.d.), pp. 13–16.

teenth century, he would not have recognized his flake white. Mass production of the pigment, precipitated with carbonic acid from sugar of lead, was first carried out in France and Germany. The result was a powder that was whiter than any Dutch or Venetian shell white ever was; and in this production method, all that was left of the pigment's former virtues was its drying effect on the oil and the film-stabilizing role of lead oleate.

J.-G. Vibert, a genre painter and instructor in painting technique at the École des Beaux Arts in Paris, stood out in the struggle against the flood of inferior pigments that swamped the market during the second half of the nine-teenth century. He saw to it that the Société des Artistes Français set up a commission to monitor quality, and founded a research laboratory at the École. In 1891, he published his lectures on painting technique under the title *La Science de la Peinture*. The work went through nine editions in its first year; in its appendix, the author dis-cusses "good and bad paints," particularly *"blanc de plomb ou blanc d'argent."* He complains of the inferiority of the precipitated pigment, which lacks all consistency and is as poor as all the other paints—but which the artist has to live with, as all the small old-fashioned firms that used to produce good-quality paints have been swallowed up by large industrial companies. "To obtain paints suitable for use in art nowadays, painters would have to make them themselves, which is impossible, or they would have to agree to commission purpose-made products—which, we hope, will soon become possible."[14]

Vibert's hope that tube paints could be improved was as vain as his pious wish that painters would realize they had no need to be ashamed of mastering their craft. Those with a sense of shame were perfectly well aware of why a "blush" rose to their cheeks when their technique

[14] J.-G. Vibert, *La Science de la Peinture* (Paris, 1891), p. 281.

was compared with that of their old masters. Vibert, by contrast, was already incapable of gauging how distant his "science" of painting was from the examples he recommended—Rubens, van Dyck, Leonardo, and Michelangelo.

Still, a great deal more lead-bearing water was to pass under the bridge, unnoticed by the painting technicians and artists of the time, before the laboratory method drove out every other method of production. In 1839, the "chamber process," a clinical version of the old pot and horse manure procedure, was introduced in Germany. The lead sheet was exposed to steam, acetic vapor, and the gas of carbonic acid in a closed chamber. This chamber white[15] was not as fine as the former flake white, nor was it as ugly as the new laboratory paint. However, the Dutch *loogen* process continued to be used by smaller firms in various European countries for a long time yet. Gentele's *Textbook of Paint Manufacture* of 1880 describes the production of white lead down to the smallest detail. Horse manure and used tanning bark were still being employed to produce heat through a process of slow decomposition that forms carbonic acid at the same time.

There is a fundamental difference between types of bark. Soft bark from young trees heats up much more and is better. The bark of soft wood also heats up more than that of oakwood, and the bark of willows, which is formed like soft straw, proves best. *Manure and oakwood bark* are used in *Holland, manure* is mainly used in *Germany, oakwood alone all over England, spruce bark in the Northern countries, willow bark* only in *Petersburg.* When appropriately used, however, all materials give good results.[16]

[15] The famed Cremnitz white was produced in a similar, but not quite as sterile, fashion.

[16] J. G. Gentele, *Lehrbuch der Farbenfabrikation* (Brunswick, 1880), p. 116.

Around 1900, there were still ten companies producing white lead in Rotterdam, which in the seventeenth
century had been one of the three centers for the flourishing *loogen* process.[17] The rock-hard white lead shells with
the shiny fracture surfaces that used to be known as flake
white were therefore still in existence. But lead chalk was
no longer sold in its raw form. Whether in the tube or as a
loose pigment, what was sold was "white lead"—lead
chalk powder, ground with water "extremely fine"[18] in
mechanically operated stonemills, and blended with
cheap filling materials.

The difference between white lead and flake white,
familiar to every staffage painter in the eighteenth century,
had been forgotten. Those chemists and paint manufacturers who still knew what was involved preferred to keep
it a secret. No one could have afforded the expense of
preparing the material by hand.

The best white lead was now thought to be Cremnitz
white from Klagenfurt in Austria. The beauty of the paint
lies in its whiteness, which depends not only on the way in
which it is produced but also on the quality of the molten
lead. Cremnitz white owes its fame to the excellent lead
from Villach, and a chamber process as time-consuming
as the old Dutch method.[19]

Today we know that the old flake white contained a
much larger proportion of silver and copper than the
white lead produced in the nineteenth century from overseas ores. The traces of zinc and insoluble antimony in
the later form, which were not present before 1850, are
thought by experts to be due to the different origins of the
lead.[20]

[17] Cf. Goedings (note 10 above), p. 11.

[18] Gentele, *Lehrbuch*, p. 121.

[19] Ibid., pp. 135–139.

[20] Cf. Rutherford J. Gettens, Hermann Kühn, and W. T. Chase, "Lead White," in Ashok Roy, ed., *Artists' Pigments: A Handbook of Their History and Characteristics* (New York, 1993), vol. 2, pp. 67–81.

The soft powder sold today contains such minimal traces of other elements that the origin of the lead can no longer be identified. Chemical analyses are only capable of identifying the company's "trademark"—the tiny difference that reveals the producer. The only form of white lead available today, either in Europe or anywhere else, is precipitated laboratory white lead, which can be recognized by its tiny amorphous particles of 1–2 microns. As soon as European Union laws come into force, even this degenerate version of the former flake white will cease to exist.

In oil, white lead covers, gives body, and is stable. It passes on its drying effect to the other paints and brightens them, without creating bluish or reddish tinges, as its successors in zinc and titanium do. For centuries, artists used this well-behaved pigment, the density of which was revealed even in the finest layers. The good state of preservation of many old paintings is due to its stabilizing function in the film of paint; and the beauty of the paintings is still growing as they increase in age, as the basic lead carbonate saponifies in the oil.

LEAD–TIN YELLOW

Lead stannate yellow, canary yellow, massicot, masticot.

CHARACTERISTICS. *Color:* bright lemon yellow and warmer shades. *Material appearance:* small particles with a glassy quality and a shell-shaped fracture surface. *Chemical composition:* Pb_2SnO_4 = lead stannate (lead-tin oxide).

PHYSICAL PROPERTIES. This artificial mineral pigment is strongly birefringent and has a tetragonal crystal system. *Refringency index:* $\omega = 2.29$ $\varepsilon = 2.31$. *Density:* 9.00. *Toxicity:* grade 3 toxin.

Known to painters south of the Alps as *giallorino* or *giallolino*, "little yellow," lead-tin yellow was given the same name north of the Alps as yellow lead oxide[21]—"massicot" or "masticot." Both north and south, it was a popular pigment from the fifteenth to the seventeenth century. The lemony and warmer variants of "little yellow," with its superb covering, lightfast quality, and body, is seen in works of art from Giotto to Tintoretto, from the Maître de Flémalle to Vermeer, from Dürer to Flegel. Gradually supplanted in the eighteenth century by Naples yellow, lead antimoniate, it was forgotten in the nineteenth. It was rediscovered and identified during studies of old paintings at the Doerner Institute in 1941, and is now being produced once again for restorers' needs. Only two formulas for the paint have survived, both preserved in a fifteenth-century Italian manuscript known as the Bolognese manuscript.[22] *Giallolino* is a fusion of Saturn red and the Jupiter ore known to miners as hermaphrodite: red lead and stannic oxide, mixed at a ratio of 3:1, are calcined at 650–800°C. The lower temperatures yield warmer tones, and the higher ones cooler tones. The requirement for binder in lead-tin yellow lies between 15 percent and 25 percent, and it has the same drying effect on oil as white lead.[23]

Gerhard zur Brügge counts massicot among the "noblest paints" in the art of illumination:

Masticot is a very good yellow paint, although one kind falls out higher than the other, and it is mostly mixed with the green paints, as it is only rather mea-

[21] Yellow lead oxide, which is produced by heating white lead to about 300°C, is a rarely used pigment that discolors to reddish or brownish when exposed to light. Cf. H. Kühn, "Farbmaterialien," in *Reclams Handbuch*, p. 27.

[22] Ibid., pp. 16–17.
[23] Cf. Hermann Kühn, "Lead-Tin Yellow," in Roy, *Artists' Pigments*, pp. 83–112.

ger and thin. But it is sometimes used to lay on clear summer weather in the fading of the air, which has to be gradually reduced as one moves down towards the mountains. Thus it also serves to highlight far-off bushes, sunlit valleys or plains against the hills, as shall be explained below in the laying on of landscape.[24]

Which massicot is meant here—pure yellow lead, or the lead-tin hermaphrodite—remains Gerhard's secret.

ORPIMENT

Auripigment, orpment, common orpiment, yellow orpiment, arsenic yellow, yellow smelter's fume, Chinese yellow, king's yellow; Latin: *auripigmentum, arrhenicum, arsenicum citrinum.*

CHARACTERISTICS. *Color:* light to dark sulfur yellow. *Material appearance:* medium-sized, irregular flakes with a resinous, mother-of-pearl sheen, with a slightly shell-like fracture; fracture surface diagonally striped, often with a fibrous structure. Watin writes of the raw material, "It must be in fine chalk-like pieces of a golden yellow color, and as shiny, and must be able to be split into flakes or thin slabs easily."[25] *Chemical composition:* As_2S_3 = arsenic sulfide.

PHYSICAL PROPERTIES. Orpiment has a monoclinic system, and is found with small, flaky, columnar, slablike, short-prism crystals, granular to dense, also kidney-shaped, spherical, clustered, stalklike, radial,

[24] Gerhard zur Brügge, *Illuminir- oder Erleuchterey-Kunst,* p. 17.
[25] *Der Staffirmaler,* p. 31.

rough, in lodes of ore, sprinkled in clays, marls, around volcanos and in hot springs—usually accompanied by its reddish sister material, realgar, which gives the yellow a reddish tinge when it is added to the pigment. The translucent to opaque malleable flakes glitter on the perfect fracture surfaces like mother-of-pearl. The infernal stench of sulfur and arsenic is mainly emitted when it is heated; when the pigment is cold, the smell is more like that of garlic. To obtain the brilliance and covering power of the luxuriant yellow, the strongly birefringent pigment tended to be used in a coarse-grained form. The lightfast color was used in book illumination, panel painting, and in watercolor and oil media. Theoretically, the sulfur pigment is not compatible with paints that contain lead or copper.[26] In an aqueous binder, the bright yellow surface appears "never quite smooth, at times glimmering with tiny, sparkling points."[27] *Refringency index:* $\alpha = 2.4$ $\gamma = 3.02$ $\beta = 2.81$. *Density:* 3.4–3.5. *Toxicity:* grade 1 toxin; although synthetic arsenic sulfide is one of the deadly poisons, the natural form is regarded as generally nontoxic, since the arsenic it contains is not bound to oxygen.

> *The lustrous gold of words has poison in its ground*
> *And orpiment therein, it harms those who are sound.*[28]

The orpiment of the Baroque poet Friedrich von Logau must have been the arsenic sulfide produced by sublimation or precipitation, known as king's yellow. The artificial pigment contains arsenic, As_2O_3, the notorious poison. It is only when arsenic is bound to oxygen that the

---

[26] In an aqueous medium, it can form black lead sulfide or copper sulfide.

[27] Roosen-Runge, *Farbgebung,* p. 86.

[28] *"Der Worte güldner Glantz hat Gift zu seinem Grunde | und Operment steckt drinn, es schadet dem Gesunde"*— Friedrich von Logau.

body can break it down; but still, few are likely to follow Pliny's recommendation to rub *arrhenicum* into the nose to remove polyps.[29] "The best," writes the friend of the Roman emperor, "is of a colour of even the finest coloured gold, but the paler sort or what resembles sandarach is judged inferior. There is also a third class which combines the colours of gold and of sandarach. Both of the latter are scaly, but the other is dry and pure, and divided in a delicate tracery of veins."[30]

In Pliny's book on painting, *arrhenicum* is listed as a color under the name *auripigmentum*. The brilliant yellow was used in Egypt, and particularly in China, long before our time. There are orpiment beds in Yunnan and the Caucasus, in Anatolia and Kurdistan, in Naples and in the Banat region, in Transylvania and on St. Andrew's Mount in the Harz mountains in Germany, but the mineral is never found in large quantities. The relative rarity of the stone and the tricky qualities of the pigment, which does not bind easily with other paints, explain why this brilliant yellow is listed in every treatise on painting from Cennini to Mayerne, but is only rarely used in panel paintings after the fourteenth century. In the fifteenth century, it was replaced by lead-tin yellow, which had fewer problems and was available in limitless quantities. Boltz von Ruffach describes

A fine golden yellow. Take orpiment, and grind it well enough on a stone with goat's gall or cattle gall. Place it in a small clean bowl, put in good saffron, and if needed pour in good white wine, neither too much nor too little. Set it on the flame, and bring it to a decent boil, until it thickens. Then take it up, and let it cool, and use it. It is very fine, and golden

---

[29] *Natural History* XXXIV.lvi (178), vol. 9, p. 257. [30] Ibid., XXXIV.lvi (178), vol. 9, pp. 255–256.

in color, it is always thinned with gall tempered with wine. Always keep this in a little glass.[31]

Boltz considered that caution was undoubtedly needed when handling "*auripigmentum,* which is called orpiment," a "paint that is fine, but requires care":

When you grind it, bind your mouth and nostrils, that you may not smell the steam and dust. Grind it well on a stone, with a pure thin parchment‑paste water, or gum water, whichever you wish. And take care never to lick a brush with this paint on it, for it is harmful. If you wish, grind it with distilled wine, temper it with it, and put a little lump of gum in, this makes it strong.[32]

Gerhard zur Brügge also cautions against the paint he calls "orpment or yellow smelter's fume":

Yellow orpment is a fine paint, but poisonous, so that when using it one should keep it away from one's mouth. It is ground with old urine, and then allowed to dry, and mixed with gum water when it is to be used. It is used to lay on silken and atlas ladies' dresses, and it can be deepened with moun‑tain brown and saffron, and the deeper parts with furnace black or lamp‑black. But as it is poisonous, it is not well to use it for heightening. One can even leave it unused altogether.[33]

No matter how poisonous the stinking arsenic yellow is, it is advisable to cover the mouth and nose when grind‑

[31] Valentin Boltz von Ruffach, *Illuminir‑Buch* (Basle, 1549; St. Annaberg, 1690), p. 44.

[32] Ibid., pp. 41–42. For further instructions on the use of orpiment, see under "Realgar," below.

[33] Gerhard zur Brügge, op. cit., p. 18.

ing it with old urine. This expensive paint is now being produced from the mineral once again in small quantities, for restorers.

REALGAR

Arsenic orange, ruby sulfur, red orpiment, red smelter's fume, red arsenic, red sulfuret of arsenic, rosaker, sandarac; Latin: *sandaraca, risigallum, resegale, arsenicum rubrum.*

CHARACTERISTICS. *Color:* orange-red. *Material appearance:* as for orpiment. *Chemical composition:* As_2S_2 = red arsenic sulfide.

PHYSICAL PROPERTIES. The pigment derived from the flame-red to ruby-red prismatic crystals has the same characteristics as orpiment. *Refringency index:* $\alpha = 2.46$ $\gamma = 2.61$ $\beta = 2.59$. *Density:* 3.5–3.6. *Toxicity:* grade 1 toxin.

This brilliant red sister color to orpiment has only rarely been used in European painting. In its synthetic form, realgar is used more often as a poison against rats and mice—and this is the origin of its name, derived from the Arabic *rahg al-far,* "mouse dust," "mouse poison," which became *rahg al-gar* by a slip of the pen, and thence *realgar.*[34]

In Dioscorides[35] and Pliny, the mineral is called *sandaraca.* Pliny describes the qualities of sandarac as follows:

It is found both in goldmines and silvermines; the redder it is and the more it gives off a poisonous scent of sulphur and the purer and more friable it is, the better it is. It acts as a cleanser, as a check to

[34] Cf. Dietlinde Goltz, *Studien zur Geschichte der Mineralnamen in Pharmazie, Chemie und Medizin von* den Anfängen bis Paracelsus (Wiesbaden, 1972), p. 241.
[35] Ibid., p. 158.

bleeding, as a calorific and a caustic, being most remarkable for its corrosive property; used as a liniment with vinegar it removes fox-mange; it forms an ingredient in eye-washes, and taken with honey it cleans out the throat. It also produces a clear and melodious voice, and mixed with turpentine and taken in the food, is an agreeable remedy for asthma and cough; its vapour also remedies the same complaints if merely used as a fumigation with cedar wood.[36]

Paracelsus regarded natural red arsenic sulfide as a weak poison, and therefore considered it unusable as a medicament. In his view, the virtue of poisons lay in the fact that "one poison overcomes another," and he therefore considered yellow arsenic to be of little value in medicine, and thought red arsenic "worthless."[37]

Boltz von Ruffach uses the pigment he calls *Rüschgäl* to shade orpiment and other light yellow colors.

In the Mayerne manuscript, Cornelis Janson, the Dutch portraitist and painter of historical scenes, discusses red and yellow arsenic sulfide under the heading "Of Orpiment," describing them as two types of paint used to produce a gold color.

They first have to be ground in water, and when they are dry, they are easily mixed with a little oil, either on the palette or, if more is needed, on the stone, but they are never ground well with oil. The best oil for mixing, and to make it dry, is oil boiled with litharge.

Yellow ocher is a ground for this, if it is not too bright, but English ocher is . . . more suitable, has

[36] Pliny, *Natural History* XXXIV.lv (177), vol. 9, p. 255.
[37] Hans Lüschen, *Die Namen der Steine* (Thun, 1968), p. 178.

more body, is browner and serves better for the gold ground. Orpiment is good on any paint except verdigris; but no paint can be put onto orpiment, for it kills them all, whether it is laid on top of the other paints or mixed with them, except for yellow ocher or similar yellows, to break the shadows; but the shadows are best made with other paints, with this orpiment only being used for highlights.[38]

There has never been any shortage of stable red pigments. A multitude of red earths, minium, and vermilion can always be mixed with yellow to make a fiery color; it is not surprising, therefore, that the difficult sandarac is rarely encountered in art. The ancient name for the mineral went out of use in the eighteenth century. "Sandarac" is now used only for a golden resin exuded from North African conifers and old juniper trunks.[39]

VERMILION (CINNABAR)

Mountain vermilion, orange vermilion, vermily, Chinese vermilion, English vermilion, scarlet vermilion; cinnabar, cinoper, sinoper, sinnopite, sinople; Latin: *vermiculum, cinnabaris, minium, cenobrium.*

CHARACTERISTICS. *Color:* depending on the stone, fire red, coral red, cherry red. *Material appearance:* irregular, unevenly fractured splinters, sometimes tiny, sometimes very large, with clearly visible edges. *Chemical composition:* HgS = mercury sulfide.

PHYSICAL PROPERTIES. The mercury ore cinnabar, known to mineralogists today as cinnabarite, is

[38] Cited after Ernst Berger, *Quellen für Maltechnik,* p. 337.
[39] Cf. Lüschen, *Die Namen der Steine,* p. 309.

found in a small-grained to finely grained crystalline form, often as an earth, coarse and sprinkled. The crystals can be split into perfect prisms, and have a vivid, diamantine sheen, sometimes morello red,[40] rarely transparent, usually with translucent edges or quite opaque; the scarlet-colored earthy mass has a dull appearance. Cinnabar is found accompanied by pure mercury, pyrite, stibnite ("gray antimony"), and marcasite, often in seams with opal, chalcedony, quartz, gypsum, calcite, dolomite, and realgar, near active volcanos and hot springs, and as an impregnation in sedimentary rocks, in fissures and faults. At the highest density, the birefringent particles have a misty transparency when thinly applied; otherwise, the paint is renowned for its covering power and body.[41] *Refringency index:* $\omega = 2.819 \, \varepsilon = 3.146$. *Density:* 8.1. *Toxicity:* the stable HgS bond has so far proved nontoxic.[42]

κιννάβαρι (*kinnabari*) is the Greek word, derived from the Persian, for mercury sulfide—known in English as cinnabar, or more often vermilion. The earliest mention of the mineral is in the oldest of all European lapidaries, the *History of Stones* by Theophrastus (ca. 372–ca. 287 B.C.), a pupil of Aristotle. He reports that *kinnabari* had been known in Greece since the sixth century, and that it may have been used in Asia Minor long before that. A few centuries later, Pliny writes on *cinnabaris* in his book on painting, but—as had already been the case in Dioscorides—the word is now no longer used to refer to cinnabar, but to a pigment derived from red Indian resin that is still known by its older, mythological name: dragon's blood. For many centuries, from Pliny to

---

[40] Due to the admixture of carbonic and bituminous matter.

[41] Cf. Roosen-Runge, in *Reclams Handbuch,* p. 78.

[42] Kurt Wehlte, *The Materials and Techniques of Painting,* trans. Ursus Dix (New York, 1975), p. 106.

Lohenstein,[43] the legend circulated that dragon's blood was shed during the titanic battle between an elephant and a dragon: "Cinnabar is the mixture of dragon's blood and elephant's blood when they fight each other," Lohenstein's novel *Arminius* informs us. In Pliny, too, it is in connection with a tragedy that the paint and the legend appear: "Nowadays when purple finds its way even on to party-walls and when India contributes the mud of her rivers and the gore of her snakes and elephants, there is no such thing as high-class painting," the Roman scholar laments[44]—invoking the immortal works of famous Greek painters such as Apelles, who was able to restrict himself to four paints.

As if there were not already enough confusion over cinnabar or vermilion, Dioscorides and Pliny prefer the term *minion* or minium for the mercury pigment—a word also used for red lead (Pb_3O_4).[45] In the labyrinth of ancient cinnabar terms, words are constantly changing their meaning. It is as if something of the strangely capricious metal that the pigment contains had communicated itself to those naming it, so that the terms form an amalgam now with one red and now with another, like the "living silver" of the god who was known to the Greeks as Hermes and to the Romans as Mercury.[46]

"Some mistakenly believe," writes the innocently confused Dioscorides,

> that *kinnabari* is the same as what is called *minion*. For *minion* is obtained in Spain from a special stone, mixed with silver sand, not otherwise known. In the

[43] Daniel Casper von Lohenstein (1635–1683), author of several Baroque tragic dramas and novels, including *Arminius.*

[44] Pliny, *Natural History* XXXV.xxxiii (50), vol. 9, p. 299.

[45] The red lead also known as Saturn red is the familiar antirust paint known today as minium.

[46] The word "quicksilver" was originally an AngloSaxon adaptation of Pliny's *argentum vivum,* with "quick" having its old sense of "living."

furnace, it acquires the most radiant and fiery color. In ore mines, it gives off a choking odor. The workers in such places therefore cover their faces with bladders so that they can see without inhaling the air. Painters use it for precious wall decorations.[47]

In its pure, unbound state, mercury—which was known to the Greeks as *hydrargyros*—is as fleeting and perilous as the water snake Hydra, the many-headed monster with a poisonous dog's body, whose heads grew back double when they were chopped off. It was vanquished by Hercules with the aid of fire.[48] Mercury's contradictory quality perfectly reflects the duality of Hermes. He is the god of wisdom *and* of deceptive guile, closest relative of the sun *and* the moon, oriented eastward *and* westward; as Psychopompos, he conducts departed souls into the underworld *and,* having led the sun into the sky, bears the children of the gods to their wet-nurses. What could better embody the impossibility of forcibly unifying the dual nature of Hermes than a metal in which the deadly effects of boundless division are so vividly seen when one tries to grasp it in a single piece?

In nature, virgin quicksilver only appears sparsely, in the shape of tiny, reflective pearls in scarlet or often liver-colored earthy rock, or between delicate, morello-red crystals. The first description of the distillation of *hydrargyros* from the ore in which it is most commonly found— the cinnabar referred to as *minion*—again comes from Dioscorides. The volatility of the "water silver" makes it easy to separate it from sulfur by roasting the ore. The steam, piped into clay chambers, condenses on the walls and is collected as distilled mercury.

[47] Cited after Lüschen, *Namen der Steine,* pp. 348–349.

[48] *Hydrargyros* = "water silver"—hence the abbreviation Hg for the element mercury.

In Pliny's time, the best Spanish minium mines were owned by the Roman state, which controlled mining and banned local processing of the mineral. Under careful guard, ten thousand pounds of raw minium annually were transported to Rome under seal. Artificial cinnabar does not seem to have been known in antiquity, and since the ore is usually found with a more livery than coral-red color, finely colored stones were extremely precious. According to Pliny, a pound cost 70 sesterces—a colossal price that was set by law to prevent arbitrary increases. The pigment was used in painting, as well as for writing on parchment. In wrestling matches, the victors rubbed minium, which was also used as a medicament, into their bodies. Like common salt, cinnabar is one of the miracles of chemical metamorphosis. Every day, we improve the taste of food using a seasoning that combines two poisons: chlorine and sodium. Similarly, the deadly poison of mercury becomes harmless when it is stably bound with sulfur.

Sulfur and mercury always fired the imagination of the alchemists. "Cinnabarine and red sulfurous vapors"[49] filled the spherical vessels used in the art of Hermetic refining. All metals, it was thought, were composed of the fiery element inhabiting sulfur, and the moist element that moves mercury. The mystic "marriage" of the elements mercury and sulfur (the "loving couple" in the Hermetic vocabulary), in the "nuptial chamber" of the retort, lies at the center of the purification theories that spread into the West through Moorish influence. Out of the fiery-moist fusion of mercury (thought of as female) with sulfur (regarded as male), there emerged the hermaphroditic image of the cinnabarine guild: a body of

---

[49] Leonhard Thurneysser, *Vel Magna Alchymia, das ist ein Lehr und Unterweisung von den offenbaren und verborglichen Naturen . . . allerhandt wunderlicher Erdgewechssen* (Berlin, 1583).

mercury with a soul of sulfur, with two heads and a dual sex. The importance of mercury in producing the "philosophers' stone" can be seen from the multitude of secret names it was given, reflecting mercury's changeable nature: "white bird," "philosophers' water," "our water," "froth of the poisonous dog," "tailed scorpion," "poisonous snake," "sweat of bodies," "reviver of the dead." With its ability to dissolve other metals, mercury was regarded as the "reviver" of metals. In particular, when mercury was fused with gold and silver, it provided dishonest practitioners among the learned pioneers of chemistry with a convenient conjuring trick in their "transformation of metals"—since evaporation of the mercury solvent leaves a residue of pure gold or silver.

"Do not make gold, make medicine!" Paracelsus urged the alchemists, teaching them that one poison can overcome another. Nothing could come of the "stone of stones," "king of kings," or the "philosophers' stone"; but it was no accident that the nimble messenger of the gods, Mercury, was also the protector of travelers, mer-chants, and thieves. The futile search for the golden elixir of youth—shown in alchemical emblems as a red lion wearing a crown and with a raised paw—was based on the mercurial "dragon": the synthesis of vermilion. The dragon originally came from China, where the red pig-ment also seems to have played a role in the art of embalming; and the formula for vermilion was brought to the Islamic world by the Arabs before reaching the West as the "red dragon," the alchemists' *materia prima,* from Arabic esoteric doctrines.

Two paths lead to vermilion: one dry and one wet. The early method of producing vermilion, which was practiced from the eighth century to the eighteenth, used fire—the dry way. Mixing mercury with molten sulfur at a ratio of 5:1 produced the black mercury sulfide called "Moor" or "Ethiopian mineral." Heated in clay retorts, the pulverized Moor sublimates and precipitates on the clay walls. The transformation of the black into red is purely physical, as the heat rearranges the crystalline structure and the black cubic system becomes a red hexagonal one.

The bluish-red sublimate is collected from the cooled, broken vessel, and has to be ground for a long time with water and then again ground dry for a long period. Only then does it develop the brilliant red and its peculiar sheen:

> It is very necessary that vermilion should be extremely well levigated, as it both contributes to its brightness and spending further in the work; and this can scarcely be effectuated by mills without the subsequent use of the mullar and stone, though it has been usual for preparers to pass it off as it comes out of the mill; but whoever would have vermilion in perfection, especially for painting carnations or mixing with white, should improve its fineness by washing over.[50]

This recommendation also applies to natural vermilion, and loses its relevance only when the pigment is produced using the wet method. The modern process (as might be expected) is simpler and cheaper, and produces a vermilion that could not have been made even with the patience of a Cennino Cennini. "Know," Cennino told the painters of the fifteenth century, "that if you ground it every day for twenty years, the colour would still become finer and more handsome."[51]

When it is produced the easy way, the pigment still has the beauty of its tone, but its body is left behind. The uni-

[50] Dossie, *Handmaid to the Arts,* vol. 1, pp. 47–48. "Carnations" is used in its older sense of "flesh tints" here (not the flower).

[51] Cited after Daniel V. Thompson, *The Materials and Techniques of Medieval Painting* (London, 1936), p. 104.

form particles are so tiny that their strongly birefringent properties cease to be effective. Vermilion's capricious vice—it sometimes converts into black metacinnabar when exposed to sunlight in an aqueous binder—occurs more often with the manufactured pigment from England and Germany than with the dry pigment formerly produced mainly in Holland, which had to be carefully washed, levigated, ground, and dried. The vermilion layers in older paintings were usually protected by a madder varnish against relapsing into "Moor."

Elaborately sublimated vermilion is barely distinguishable from the natural form even under the microscope. Indicators of the difference are traces of accompanying minerals, as well as the long splinters of crystal—only visible through the use of extreme enlargement (with scanning electron micrography)—that are characteristic of the columnar structure of lumps of sublimated vermilion.[52]

In the twentieth century, all that survived of the three types of vermilion was the mere outward appearance. Instead of the paint susceptible to blackening, we now have a bodiless cadmium red, an ultrared pigment that lacks mercury and sulfur.

The word "vermilion," used synonymously with "cinnabar" in English since the Middle Ages, is derived from the Latin *vermiculum,* the scarlet worm. Originally, *vermiculum* referred to the color carmine, which is obtained from alkermes or kermes, the scarlet grain insect later known as cochineal. When the worm name *vermiculum* was transferred to artificial cinnabar in the Middle Ages, the ancient confusion over the names of red colors repeated itself once again.

"Miño" is the name of a river in Spain that the

[52] Rutherford J. Gettens, Robert L. Feller, and W. T. Chase, "Vermilion and Cinnabar," in Roy, *Artists' Pigments,* vol. 2, pp. 159–182.

Romans called Minium. Whether the pigment was known as *minium* in antiquity because the river bore vermilion sand with it, or whether it was the river that took its name from this, we cannot know. But vermilion has been mined since ancient times in the town of Almadén—in the Spanish province of La Mancha—which was called Sisapon under the Romans. Neither Idrija in Carniola nor Monte Amiata in Tuscany has ever been able to match Almadén. Despite centuries of mining, the barren region with its bare, rocky ridges still has the world's richest deposits of vermilion.

There are few traces left today of the elaborate methods of producing vermilion[53]—the protracted washing, grinding, and levigation of both the sublimated and natural pigment—except for an idiom used in German: *mach keinen Zinnober,* "don't make cinnabar," don't make a fuss. The cinnabarine fusspot does not appear in the Grimms' *Historical Dictionary,* the thirty-first volume of which, from *Z* to *Zmasch,* was published only in 1956, giving five columns for the wealth of different meanings of the word *Zinnober.* The word appears in German literature referring to paint, makeup, and medicine, as a simile and a metaphor, sometimes conveying radiance and beauty, sometimes coarseness and ugliness. The flickering glints of its alternating meanings are seen in the scolding of the alchemists, "Paracelsists . . . with their imp *daemonio,* cinnabarine devils, murderous tinctures"; in the old equation of drunkenness with cinnabar in the sermons of Abraham a Sancta Clara; in the sweet cinnabar-red cheeks of Stieler's "armored Venus" and Heine's "dimple in cinnabar cheeks, where roguishness secretly giggles"; in Brentano's "Purple and cinnabar reveal / How truth stands and where it goes; / When the basilisk all glaring /

[53] Genuine mountain cinnabar and sublimated vermilion are now being produced once again by the Kremer company for restoration purposes.

Out of false appearance crows."[54] Finally, the word takes on the nasty *and* attractive, loutish *and* dignified, ridiculed *and* admired figure of the goblin "Little Zaches, sur-named Zinnober" in the tale by E.T.A. Hoffmann. The changeling Little Zaches meets a tragicomic end, being sublimated into a minister; and there the irretrievable loss of cinnabar is clear.

MALACHITE
natural and artificial

Mountain green, earth green, copper green, mineral green, azure green, iris green, verditer green; Greek and Latin: *molochites, chrysocolla, viride azurinum.*

CHARACTERISTICS. *Color:* light, cool green in watercolor techniques, dark emerald green when bound in oil. *Material appearance:* a coarse powder consisting of irregular, splintered crystal fragments that have a fibrous structure, with a splintery and shell-like fracture and silky, glassy, or greasy sheen. *Chemical composition:* $CuCO_3 \times Cu(OH)_2$ = basic copper carbonate. *Toxicity:* grade 3 toxin.

PHYSICAL PROPERTIES. Finely prismatic hair-shaped to needle-shaped crystals in radiating tufts and fibrous fans are less frequent than grape-shaped or kidney-shaped, agatelike striped aggregates. Frequently found in copper mines in many parts of the world, often accompa-nied by the closely related azurite and other cuprous min-erals such as chrysocolla and cuprite, which confirm the pigment's natural origin when they are found as traces in

---

[54] *"Purpur und Zinnober weiset | wie es mit der Wahrheit steht; | wenn der Basiliske gleisend | aus der falschen Schminke kräht."*

it. The finer the grain of the pigment, the weaker its color; very finely grained pigments appear almost color‑less. Malachite is one of the paints that combine body with transparency. In an oil medium, strong depth light creates a dark emerald green. *Refringency index:* strongly birefringent. $\alpha = 1.6$ $\beta = 1.8$ $\gamma = 1.9$. *Density:* 4.

From China to Egypt, malachite was already known as a pigment thousands of years ago. In the thirty‑seventh book of his *Natural History,* Pliny describes the stone as follows: "Malachite is an opaque stone of a rather deep green shade and owes its name to its colour, which is that of the mallow. It is warmly recommended because it makes an accurate impression as a signet, protects chil‑dren, and has a natural property that is a prophylactic against danger."[55] The belief in the green mineral's pro‑tective power gave it the name "scare stone," which was used right up to the eighteenth century. In 1780, the disbe‑liever Adelung could still write that " 'scare stone' is a name for malachite among the common people, as it is supposed to be good against sudden frights."[56]

The varying appearances of malachite have meant that since antiquity, and even in more recent mineralogy, it has often been confused with other stones. In its prismatic, diamantine needle form, it is confused with emerald; as a dense, earthy aggregate, it is confused with the bluish‑green, equally clustered but amorphous chrysocolla, a term that has been reserved for copper silicate since the nineteenth century. According to Pliny, chrysocolla is found in India, where the gold that contains the stone is "dug up by ants."[57] Since Pliny describes it as resembling

[55] Pliny, *Natural History* XXXVII.xxxvi (114), vol. 10, p. 257.
[56] Johann Christoph Adelung (1732–1806), cited after Lüschen, *Namen der Steine,* p. 316. The Ger‑man word is *Schreckstein.*
[57] *Natural History* XXXVII.liv (147), vol. 10, p. 285.

gold and being rectangular, he cannot have been referring to chrysocolla here, which is otherwise identical with malachite in the *Natural History.*

In the early treatises on painting, the pigment was rarely called malachite. Cennino Cennini calls it *verde azzurro,* and Valentin Boltz von Ruffach refers to it in his book on illumination of 1549 as "flake green": "Flake green is made of ore stones, and one form is finer than the other. It is a heavy material like lapis lazuli. Do not grind it too hard, or else it will lose its green color; temper it with egg white distemper or parchment paste, in which a little honey may be mixed."[58]

The close relationship between the pigment and azu-rite may be one reason why there are very few references in the literature on painting to malachite, which was in use up to the seventeenth century. The two paints are pro-duced and used following the same rules, so that those who knew about azurite would realize malachite was the same thing, only green. Formulas for one pigment made those for the other unnecessary. The instructions on using gold in painting apply equally to silver, and just as silver took second place to expensive gold in such descriptions, so the green stone took second place to the rarer blue one.

The "light pale green color" that Boltz calls "moun-tain green" was probably an artificial malachite[59] also known as "verditer green." The terminology for the arti-ficial minerals was even more muddled than for the nat-ural one. The basic copper carbonates that research has shown were used in Italian paintings of the early Renais-sance are thought to be artificial, due to the spherical par-ticles found; but it has not yet been possible to reconstruct

[58] *Schiefergrün.* Boltz von Ruf-fach, *Illuminir-Buch,* p. 84.
[59] On this, see Frederike Ellwanger-Eckel, *Herstellung und Verwendung künstlicher grüner und* *blauer Kupferpigmente in der Malerei,* published by the Institut für Muse-umskunde, Staatliche Akademie der Bildenden Künste in Stuttgart (Stuttgart, 1988).

them from any of the old formulas.[60] Precipitation of copper nitrate solutions onto calcium carbonate is thought to be involved—a method of producing copper green that was discovered accidentally, according to de Mayerne: "Verditer green is itself a green color, as bright as meadow green or sea green. I have been told that this color was discovered unexpectedly by someone or other who precipitated strong king's water[61] (*aqua regalis*) onto white lead (others say onto chalk), which at once turned green. Others have told me that it is the aquafortis used when separating copper, silver, and gold."[62]

But there was also a naturally "precipitated" copper green that was sold as a pigment. Agricola, who describes it, calls it *chrysocolla:*

> Since all solidified juices and earths, if abundantly and copiously mixed with the water, are deposited in the beds of springs, streams or rivers, and the stones therein are coated by them, they do not require the heat of the sun or fire to harden them. This having been pondered over by wise men, they discovered methods by which the remainder of these solidified juices and unusual earths can be collected. Such waters, whether flowing from springs or tunnels, are collected in many wooden tubs or tanks arranged in consecutive order, and deposit in them such juices or earths; these being scraped off every year, are collected, as *chrysocolla* in the Carpathians and as ochre in the Harz.[63]

[60] Cf. Rutherford J. Gettens and Elisabeth West Fitzhugh, "Malachite and Green Verditer," in Roy, *Artists' Pigments,* pp. 183–202.

[61] "King's water" (*Königswasser*) is nitric acid, so termed because it dissolves gold, the "king" of metals.

[62] Cited after Berger, *Quellen für*

Maltechnik, p. 143. "Aquafortis" was "the early scientific . . . name for the nitric acid of commerce" (*Oxford English Dictionary*).

[63] Georgius Agricola, *De Re Metallica,* trans. Herbert C. Hoover and Lou H. Hoover (London, 1912; rptd. New York, 1950), p. 584.

It is difficult to distinguish between naturally precipi-tated and artificially produced "chrysocolla," so that we will probably never know which of these was the source of the round particles of the malachitelike pigment used in early Renaissance paintings.

Paler and less stable than genuine malachite, verditer green seems to have been used less frequently than the equivalent artificial blue. Copper-green pigments with a different structure, such as copper sulfate, copper chlo-ride, and copper phosphate, were often called "verdigris"; this is actually a misnomer, but as it is traditional, they are discussed here under this term.

Whether they used the term "verditer green" or "verdi-gris," the painters of the fifteenth and sixteenth centuries on both sides of the Alps had at their disposal copper-green pigments, of both natural and artificial origins, which have baffled researchers. The green paint in the Ghent altarpiece, interpreted by Coremans as malachite, is now regarded as artificial after the most recent analyses, owing to the grainy form of its particles. It has not yet been possible to reconstruct the pigment.[64] The various classical methods of synthesizing pigments may well have been kept secret by the various studios. However, it may also be a "forgotten" pigment of natural origin that is involved.

Watin mentions a green color that he calls "mountain green" or "Hungarian green,"

a greenish mineral that is found in small grains like sand in the mountains of Kernhausen in Hungary. It must have the appearance of a fine dark Saxon green, once it has been pulverized. To be used, it needs to be ground, whether for oils or watercolors;

[64] Cf. *Bulletin de l'Institut Royal du Patrimoine Artistique* 22 (Brussels, 1988/89), 41–46.

and it must be used carefully, as it makes the colors darker.[65]

The *Handmaid to the Arts* lists malachite under the name *terre verte*. In a German translation of Dossie's manual published in Dresden in 1792, a footnote informs the bewildered reader that "earth green" (*Erdgrün*) or "mountain green" is

a kind of copper green that is called malachite when it is solid and hard, and can be polished; but when it is earthy, soft, and can be crushed, it is given the name mountain green. It is found in metal mines along with silver and lead, and also on stones that contain metal. It may be of the same kind as that which naturalists call natural verdigis [*Grünspan*].[66]

Dossie's commendation of this green pigment at the end of his section on it can be quoted in full:

Terra verte is a native earth, which in all probability is coloured by copper. It is of a blue green colour, much of that teint which is called *sea-green*. What we have in common here is not very bright, but being semi-transparent in oil, and of a strong body in water, and standing equally well with the best pigments, it is very much adapted to answer some purposes in both kinds of painting, though it is not so generally used by those to whom it would be serviceable as it merits. Mr. d'Acosta says, in his book of fossils, that there is a kind which is very bright, and is found in Hungary; if it could be procured

---

[65] Watin, *Der Staffirmaler*, p. 25.
[66] *Praktisches Handbuch für Künstler* (Dresden, 1792), vol. 1, p. 119.

here, it would certainly be a very valuable acquisi-
tion to oil painting, as the greens we are forced at
present to compound from blue and yellow are sel-
dom secure from flying or changing.

Terra verte, as brought from abroad, is of a very
coarse nature, and requires to be well levigated and
washed over; but no other preparation is necessarily
previous to its use. The only method of distinguishing its goodness is by the brightness and strength of
its colour.[67]

VERDIGRIS

Vert de Grèce, salt green, copper green, rust of copper,
Montpellier green, Spanish green; Latin: *viride hispanicum,*
viride graecum, aerugo, viride aeris, flos aeris, viride salsum, iarin.

CHARACTERISTICS. *Color:* depending on its composition, mainly bluish-green and greenish-blue nuances,
but also a yellowish garish green and deep spruce green.
Material appearance: basic verdigris was sold in large,
coarse lumps, which produced a bright blue-green powder with an acidic smell when they were crushed and
ground. *Chemical composition:* the multitude of different
types of verdigris can be divided into two groups: basic
and neutral copper acetate. Neutral verdigris has the formula: $Cu(CH_3COO)_2 \times H_2O$. *Toxicity:* poisonous.

PHYSICAL PROPERTIES. The coarse, irregular,
glassy particles are well visualized under the microscope;
the transparent crystals of basic verdigris have the appearance of fine bundles of needles, and those of the neutral
form have slablike flowers with rhombic and hexagonal

[67] *Handmaid to the Arts,* vol. 1, pp. 118–119.

surfaces, growing together in clusters and sometimes forming twins; both types are strongly birefringent. *Refringency index:* $\alpha = 1.53$ $\gamma = 1.56$. *Specific gravity:* 1.9.

The painters' verdict on this artificial mineral pigment, familiar since antiquity, was that it was appealing to the eye but unstable and hostile to other paints. The oldest formula for making copper green is found in Pliny, who calls verdigris *aerugo:*

> Some people put the actual vessels, made of white copper, into vinegar in earthenware jars, and nine days later scrape them. Others cover the vessels with grape-skins and scrape them after the same interval, others sprinkle copper filings with vinegar and several times a day turn them over with spattles till the copper is completely dissolved. Others prefer to grind copper filings mixed with vinegar in copper mortars.[68]

In the first half of the twelfth century, Theophilus Presbyter describes the production of "salty green," a basic copper chloride with the formula $CU_2(OH)_3Cl$, the structure of which is equivalent to that of atacamite,[69] which was not then known:

> But if you wish to make a green paint, take a piece of oakwood, as long and broad as you like, and hollow it out in the shape of a small box. Then take copper, make it into thin strips, as broad as you like, provided they are long enough to cover the width of the hollowed-out wood. After this, take a shallow

[68] Pliny, *Natural History* XXXIV.xxvi (111), vol. 9, pp. 209–210.

[69] Atacamite, leek green or grass green to emerald green, has the formula $Cu_2Cl(OH)_3$, and is mainly found in South America and Australia.

dish of salt, crush it together hard, and place it in the fire. Cover it with coals overnight, and next day grind it carefully on the dry stone. Once you obtain soft twigs, place these in the hollow of the wood in such a way that there are two parts below the open‑ing and one part above it, brush pure honey onto both sides of the copper strips, scatter the ground salt onto them, and lay them continuously next to each other on the wood. Cover this with another piece of wood suitable for the purpose, so that none of the vapors can be lost. Then, have a hole drilled in the corner of this wood, through which you can pour in warm vinegar or warm urine, so that it is filled to one third, and then block the opening. You should put the wood in a place where you can cover it with manure on all sides. But after four weeks, lift the lid, scrape off what you find on the copper, and keep it. When you put the wood back again, follow the same order as described above.[70]

In the reconstructions of this salt green carried out in the 1960s by the art historian Heinz Roosen‑Runge, using both vinegar and urine, it was found that urine produced a fuller verdigris.[71] *Non valet in libro,* warned the manu‑script illuminator Theophilus—because the fine, salty kingfisher green corrodes parchment over the course of time. Other medieval formulas describe brushing the copper plates with soap or egg yolk, with either vinegar or urine being applied to them; or a combination of honey and cream of tartar is recommended. Depending on the ingredients and the extent of their effect, brighter or darker, colder or warmer green tones were produced.[72]

[70] Cited after Ellwanger‑Eckel, *Kupferpigmente,* pp. 12–13.
[71] Roosen‑Runge, *Farbgebung,* vol. 2, p. 98.
[72] Ibid., vol. 1, pp. 90–91.

A warning against this volatile pigment, "which is obtained with the help of salt," is given by Leonardo da Vinci in his *Treatise on Painting.* "Even when it is ground with oil, the green that is prepared with copper evaporates with all its beauty if it is not varnished at once."[73] To "enhance the beauty of copper green," Leonardo recom‑ mends that the pigment should be mixed with "camel's aloe,"[74] a plant resin with a yellow to yellowish‑brown color:

> If the verdigris is mixed with camel's aloe, the same green increases its beauty, and saffron would assist in this even more; but the latter evaporates. The goodness of this camel's aloe is seen if it dissolves in warm spirits, for it dissolves better warm than when it is colder. And if you have finished your work with simple verdigris and then varnish it finely with this aloe dissolved in spirits, it will give a very fine color. The aloe can also be ground with oil, either alone or together with the verdigris, and the same with any other color you wish.[75]

In the twelfth book of *De re metallica,* describing the extraction of soda, saltpeter, alum, vitriol, sulfur, and bitumen, Agricola mentions the production of a sub‑ stance he terms *chrysocolla:* "Native as well as manufac‑ tured *nitrum* is mixed in vats with urine and boiled in . . . caldrons; the decoction is poured into vats in

---

[73] Leonardo da Vinci, *Traktat von der Malerei,* nach der Überset‑ zung von H. Ludwig, neu hrsg. von Marie Herzfeld, Jena 1909.

[74] The hard brown, bitter‑ tasting "resin" extract of the aloe plant is obtained by boiling and thickening the juices the plant exudes. In the *Wörterbuch der Natur‑ geschichte* (Weimar, 1825–1838), horse aloe (*Rossaloë*), which is iden‑ tical to camel's aloe, is defined as the residue of the fine extract of *Aloë soccotrina* and *Aloë vulgaris.*

[75] Leonardo, *Traktat,* p. 103.

which are copper wires, and, adhering to them, it hardens and becomes *chrysocolla*."[76]

Just as the English word "verdigris" is a corruption of *vert de Grèce,* the German equivalent *Grünspan* is a corruption of *Spanisch Grün.* In Boltz von Ruffach, the color is called "Greek or Spanish green," and his formula for producing it reads:

Take copper sheeting, brush this with purified honey, and hang it in a glazed pot over strong vinegar that is good and old, making it hot beforehand. Let it stand in a warm place well covered, four or five weeks, the longer the better. Uncover it, and scrape the green bloom cleanly off the copper sheets. Hang it inside again as before, and keep taking off the green *flores* as long as it still produces any green.[77]

According to Boltz, the "green *flores*" are ground with vinegar and tempered with gum arabic.

The basic verdigris produced in wine-growing regions using the marc of grapes—traditional in the south of France since the twelfth century—was renowned. A formula given in an "arts and crafts manual" of 1696 recalls the old procedure:

Imitating the very best French and Rhenish verdigris. Place wine marc and copper sheets layer by layer over each other, in a wooden vessel of good oakwood, and pour over it one part of strong vinegar, and three or four parts of boys' urine, scatter on top some ground alum and saltpeter, let it stand thus and dry. Then moisten it again with boys' urine,

[76] Agricola, *De Re Metallica,* p. 560.
[77] Boltz, *Illuminir-Buch,* p. 46.

and let it dry again; and repeat this often and much until the copper sheets are wholly corroded, and the whole mass together has been turned into a fine verdigris. *Quod in massam panis forma conglobatum, corioque in volutum ad nos transferatur.*[78]

In the eighteenth century, the center for verdigris manufacturing was Montpellier. The work was carried out by women[79]—who were probably able to manage without boys' urine. When alternating layers of wine marc and copper sheets ferment, acetic acid forms to produce the green blooms.

The Mayerne manuscript includes a strong warning that verdigris is incompatible with other pigments:

> Verdigris (which is used for varnishing) is so hostile to all other colors that it spoils them all, particularly ash blue; even when one works with a brush . . . that has been cleaned in oil which has been in contact with verdigris, or when one places paints on a palette on which it has been, everything is spoiled; those wishing to work with verdigris must therefore use a different brush, palette, and oil for cleaning it.[80]

In his description of the accidental production of "verditer" when cleaning silver with king's water, de Mayerne mentions another way of precipitating copper green, using "aquafortis"—a method of production he describes earlier in the manuscript: "Make sure what can be used to precipitate the blue-green color that is given off

---

[78] *Kunst- und Werckschule, Anderer Theil* (Nuremberg, 1696), cited from the later edition of 1760, p. 185.

[79] Cf. Hermann Kühn, "Verdigris and Copper Resinate," in Roy, *Artists' Pigments*, pp. 131–158.

[80] Cited after Berger, *Quellen für Maltechnik*, p. 101.

with the filtration water and is called *verditer*. I do not know whether, if chalk is added, the color may be absorbed thereby and acquire body, or something differ-ent. Try the powder of unburned alabaster,[81] dissolved chalk, powdered talc, chalk of Briançon."[82] In Agri-cola's description of solutions used to separate silver from gold, special praise is given to a form of aquafortis made from one pound of verditer and three-quarters of a pound of vitriol; another is made from orpiment, vitriol, limestone, alum, and potash. Detailed formulas for green paints consisting of copper vitriol, potash, and other ingredients resembling Agricola's aquafortis, which chemists term copper sulfates, are first found in the eigh-teenth and nineteenth centuries, although the equivalent pigments can be found in paintings from the fifteenth, sixteenth, and seventeenth centuries.[83]

"Distilled verdigris" precedes the aquafortis green in the Mayerne manuscript. Basic verdigris is one thing, and its neutral "child," the purified and crystallized verdigris, is another. According to de Mayerne, this served for var-nishing "on white and black, or on masticot, as well as all other colors," and it was embedded in varnish due to the pigment's volatility. The drying effect of the "distilled verdigris" was welcome, and it was therefore added to the poorly drying black paints. Formulas for producing this pigment were traditional until the discovery of chromium oxide green.[84] The *Handmaid to the Arts* gives the following instructions:

Crystals of verdigrise, called distilled verdigrise. Distilled verdigrise is the salt produced by the solution of

[81] V. "Alabaster," pp. 355–360.
[82] Cited after Berger, *Quellen für Maltechnik*, p. 107.
[83] Cf. Ellwanger-Eckel, *Kupfer-pigmente*, pp. 5–6.

[84] Chromium oxide green was discovered in 1838, and was mass-produced from 1859 onward.

copper, or common verdigrise, in vinegar. The crys-tals thus formed are of an extreme bright green colour, and in varnish, where they stand perfectly well, they have a very fine effect. In oil they hold their colour well enough to answer many purposes, where colours are not required to be greatly durable; but in paintings of consequence they cannot be depended upon, being apt to turn black with time.

The crystals of verdigrise may be prepared in the following manner. Take of the best verdigrise four ounces, and of distilled vinegar two quarts. The verdigrise being well pounded, let them be put into a circulating vessel, that may be formed of a matrass, (which is a round bodied glass with a long straight neck) and a Florence flask, which must have its neck inverted into the matrass, the thick end being broken off. This circulating vessel must be placed in a gentle sand-heat, or other warm situa-tion, where it must continue, being frequently shaken, till the vinegar has dissolved as much as it can of the verdigrise. Remove the verdigrise and the vinegar then into a proper glass for decanting the fluid, when it shall become clear, from the sediment; and when it has stood a due time to settle, let it be carefully poured off and evaporated to about half a pint, which may be best done with a sand-heat, in a glass body or cucurbit, having its neck cut off to a wide mouth. It may be set to shoot in the same ves-sel, or in a glass receiver with a wide neck; and, when the crystals are formed, they must be taken out, and carefully dried in the shade.[85]

The French advisor for "staffage painters" of the same period devotes only a single sentence to the dissolution of

[85] *Handmaid to the Arts,* vol. 1, pp. 113-114.

raw basic verdigris in distilled vinegar, vividly describing its blooming or "shooting" in thinly split rods, "which give the crystals, clustering together, almost the shape of a grape. The fine crystals, which are quite dry, have a high color, and a velvety appearance, are the ones preferred."[86]

The initial bluish tone of the painted color changes within a few weeks into a warmer green. This alteration is more marked in the basic verdigris than in the neutral one, which is why painters came to prefer the latter.

When one examines older paintings, scarcely any confirmation can be found for the bad reputation this poisonous pigment has. The properties of verdigris do not look nearly as harmful as the literature on painting techniques suggests.[87] There is a strange disparity between theory and practice. Theoretically, verdigris is incompatible with pigments that contain either lead or sulfur; in practice, verdigris was always mixed with white lead and lead-tin yellow, and it has survived the centuries without any recognizable damage. The blue of the sky that Watteau painted using verdigris and ultramarine is still shining unchanged.[88] Mixtures of verdigris with the arsenic sulfides orpiment and realgar have even been identified in paintings by Tintoretto.[89] The pigment's surprising stability matches the term used for it in Italian: *verde eterno.* Since copper is the metal of Venus, crystallized verdigris is also called *cristalli di Venere.*

The noticeable browning of formerly grass-green and leaf-green meadows and trees in some Dutch and Italian paintings of the fifteenth and sixteenth centuries has puzzled researchers. It is probably due to photocatalytic reactions in the dark green copper-resinate glazes. Copper

---

[86] Watin, *Staffirmaler,* p. 23.
[87] Cf. Kühn, "Verdigris," in Roy, *Artists' Pigments,* pp. 131–147.
[88] Rutherford J. Gettens and George L. Stout, *Painting Materials* (New York, 1966), p. 169.
[89] Kühn, op. cit., p. 145.

resinate is a transparent color formed from verdigris and resins, a fine neutral emerald green.[90]

Mayerne calls it "pleasant green," and his formula states: "Venetian turpentine 2 oz., turpentine oil 1½ oz., mix this and add 2 oz. verditer to it. Set it on hot ash and let it boil slowly. Test whether the color pleases you on a glass. Strain through a linen cloth." Another variant of the formula gives a "translucent green . . . that is applied to a ground of gold and silver." For this purpose, verditer ground raw on marble is used in the same quantity, and at the end a "nut-sized piece of *terra merita* (curcuma, turmeric)" is added. Then "let it boil lightly, until you can see that your green has become pleasant. Strain it slowly through a piece of linen. To use it on wood, the wood should be gilded."[91]

Only a few formulas for making copper resinate have been handed down to us. By the time of the Mayerne manuscript, the translucent resinate green was only rarely used.

In his *Inleyding tot de hooghe Schoole der Schilderkonst* (Rotterdam, 1678), the trompe-l'oeil painter Samuel van Hoogstraeten, a pupil of Rembrandt's, expresses regret that none of the greens available are of the same good quality as other paints: "Green earth is too weak, verdigris is too hard, and ash green is too unstable."[92] Whatever this "ash green" was, the confused nomenclature for copper-green pigments indicates the difficulty of distinguishing between the components of green. Of all the older paints, green is the most enigmatic. The headaches caused by its problematic application in painting are evident in this. What are we to think of Leonardo's verdigris bound in oil, which could be wiped off with water?[93]

---

[90] Restorers wishing to imitate it using modern pigments take a mixture of Prussian blue, madder, and Indian yellow.

[91] Cited after Berger, *Quellen für Maltechnik*, p. 157.

[92] Ibid., p. 377.

[93] Leonardo, *Traktat*, p. 103.

How are we to explain the discrepancy between theory and practice regarding mixtures with incompatible pigments? Various copper compounds have been identified in paintings in addition to the carbonates—phosphates, nitrates, chlorides, and sulfates; were they natural or artificial in origin? Obsolete procedures used in the art of separation, exhausted mines, and forgotten pigments are possible explanations. Knowledge of the pigments formerly in use was preserved not by painters, but by the mineralogists of the nineteenth century. A pigment that came from Russia was found to be natural chromium-oxide green. Since chromium was discovered only at a late date, no one has made a search for the element in older paintings; and if no one looks for something, it will not be found.[94] A dictionary of natural history published in 1826 describes one "highly green" natural chromium oxide from the Tyrol, and another "intimately mixed with chalcedony" from the mountains near Le Creusot in the Département Saône et Loire in France:

> When compounded with these siliceous and silicon clay components, it has the following characteristics. Its specific gravity is 2.6; it is found coarse, with an earthy or irregular fracture, is partly semihard, partly soft to crumbly, apple-green, verdigris to siskin-green and leek green, greenish-gray in powdered form, matt and opaque, insoluble in acids, and it stains borax glass a fine emerald green.[95]

The vivid names for various shades of green used to include *Gänsekotgrün,* "goosedung green," equivalent to the French *caca d'oie.* The Grimms' dictionary also gives

[94] I am grateful to Georg Kremer for the information about natural chromium green.

[95] *Wörterbuch der Naturgeschichte,* vol. 3, pp. 112–113.

Gänsdreckfarbig, "goosedung-colored," and *Gänsedreck-farbe,* "goosedung color," illustrated with a quotation from Schiller's *Intrigue and Love:* "Your Highness is wearing a *merde d'oie* beaver coat." Miners called the yellowish-green crust of arsenic-iron sinters, sprinkled with silver, "goose-dung" or "goosedung ore."[96]

The wealth of green tones is reflected in the multitude of names for them. Siskin, frog and parrot, grass, leek, reseda and mignonette, iris, olive, almond and apple, sea and moss, jade, turquoise and emerald, bottle-green and celadon have served to distinguish them. The richly layered depiction of woods, pastures, and meadows in older landscape paintings earned the name Paradise green. Whether it was composed of the blooms of copper or forgotten pigments, it is testimony to the successful fulfillment of the artist's task of reconstructing in panel painting the green garment in which the kingdom of earth clothes its dust.

AZURITE
natural and artificial

Mountain blue, blue bice, copper blue, sky blue, azure, ash-blue, chessylite, chessy copper, mineral blue, sanders blue, bice, Bremen blue; Latin: *armenius, lapis armenius, caeruleum, quianus, azurium citramarinum.*

CHARACTERISTICS. *Color:* cool, lighter or fuller glaze blue, depending on the grain size. *Material appearance:* fairly large, irregular crystalline debris with shell-shaped, almost irregular fracture and glassy sheen. *Chemical composition:* $2CuCO_3 \times Cu(OH)_2$ = basic carbonate of copper.

[96] Cf. Lüschen, *Namen der Steine,* p. 223.

PHYSICAL PROPERTIES. The small to medium-sized monoclinic slablike and columnar crystals are found growing onto or into one another in stepped structures, or as spherical, clustered, bulbous groups; more rarely, they are found singly. Azurite is also found in a coarse form, sprinkled, settled, in the rubble of narrow tunnels, in stalactitic forms, sometimes covering the walls of caves, so that hollow spheres and lumps arise, with glandular surfaces on the interior. Groups of crystals like coarse masses often form radiating, stemlike precipitations. Traces of the accompanying minerals malachite and cuprite affect the pigment's color tone. The strongly birefringent particles are translucent to transparent, and turn pale if ground too fine. The strong depth light of the pigment gives it an almost black appearance when bound in oil. The addition of white lead provides the blue with covering power. *Refringency index:* $\alpha = 1.73$ $\beta = 1.75$ $\gamma = 1.83$. *Density:* 3.7–3.9. *Toxicity:* weakly toxic.

"Azure, a deep blue, sky-blue paint: a foreign word only in use since the last century, from the French *azur,* English *azure,* serving the poets for a rhyme on *nur, spur, flur,*" stated Jacob and Wilhelm Grimm's *Dictionary* in 1854. By that time, azurite had already long since ceased to be used in painting. The word "azure" has the same root as "lapis lazuli"; the *l* in *lazuli* was regarded as representing the Arabic article (*"al azur"*) or the Romance article (*"l'azur"*), and consequently dropped.[97] Azurite was often confused with lapis lazuli, or thought to be identical to it. In Pliny, the pigment is called *armenium,* from the origin of the stone. But it is clear from the context that his Armenian blue does not represent lapis lazuli, which also came from Armenia:

[97] The *Oxford English Dictionary* even cites two uses of "lazurite" for "azurite" in the seventeenth century, from medieval Latin *lazur,* "lapis lazuli."

Armenia sends us the substance named after it Armenian. This also is a mineral that is dyed like malachite, and the best is that which most closely approximates to that substance, the colour partaking also of dark blue. Its price used to be rated at 300 sesterces per pound. A sand has been found all over the Spanish provinces that admits of similar preparation, and accordingly the price has dropped to as low as six denarii.[98]

The sites in which azurite is found are generally the same as those for its close relation, malachite, but it occurs in smaller quantities, so that the blue copper pigment has always been more precious than the green one. In antiquity, the blue stone was mined on Sinai. In the Middle Ages, English, Spanish, Italian, and German types of azurite were known, and the latter is mentioned by Cennini as *azzurro della Magna;* in the Bolognese manuscript, it is called "German" or "Teutonic azure."[99] The principal source of supply in the sixteenth century seems to have been Hungary. In the nineteenth century, particularly splendid dark blue crystals were found in the red sandstone of Chessy, near Lyon.[100] The gradual disappearance of the pigment during the second half of the seventeenth century is connected with the occupation of Hungary by the Turks. In the eighteenth century, the new, rich pigment known as Parisian, Berlin, or Prussian blue replaced the expensive, flashing blue mineral pigment.

The preparation of the pigment is similar to that of malachite. Selected fine lumps of azurite are crushed,

[98] Pliny, *Natural History* XXXV.xxviii (47), vol. 9, p. 297.

[99] *"Azurrum almaneum sive Teothonicum"*—Roosen-Runge, in *Reclams Handbuch,* pp. 95–96.

[100] The oldest document attesting to copper mining in Chessy dates from 1414. The famed azurite stones known as "chessylite" were discovered in 1812, and were excavated until the "blue mine" was exhausted in 1839.

washed, ground with water, levigated, and strained. The finer the grain, the weaker the color appears. "On the other hand, to allow a good, thin application of the paint, the pigment grains need to be ground as finely as possible. To obtain a pigment size that is technically optimal for painting—i.e., fine, as well as a brilliant blue tone," late medieval formulas recommend the trick of soaking the azurite in an alkaline solution of potash or sal ammoniac, and then grinding the pigment with egg yolk and washing it out with alkali, wine, or water. "The result was a very brilliant blue color tone, closely resembling lapis lazuli."[101]

In water-based techniques, azurite's relatively large crystal grains have a splendidly glittering appearance, and manuscript illuminators therefore remained faithful to the pigment longest. In the edition of Gerhard zur Brügge's *Illuminator's Art* expanded by Wilhelm Goeree in 1677, natural blue copper carbonate is called "sky-blue, *ascus*," and the "excellent illuminator" gives the following advice on how to use it:

> Sky-blue, which is also called *ascus,* is a very beautiful color, which is found in various kinds, both very light and darker. One must always strive to find the most beautiful, richest, finest, and that which is least sandy. For the most outstanding and special works, some enthusiasts therefore use what is called ultramarine; but since this is very dear, especially when it is very beautiful, and as it is not found everywhere, one can achieve just as much with the best sky-blue. Since it is always found in a fine form, sky-blue or *ascus* must not be ground too

[101] Robert Fuchs and Doris Oltrogge, "Das Blau in der mittelalterlichen Buchmalerei— Quellenschriften als Basis naturwissenschaftlicher Farbuntersuchungen," in *Blau: Farbe der Ferne* (exhib. cat., Heidelberg Kunstverein, 1990), p. 107.

much, or it will lose its fine color, as do many paints of this type, such as red lead, massicot, smalt, and the like. It must therefore only be mixed with gum water; and put a little white lead with it, which makes it smooth, for it often falls out rather rough . . . However, it should also be noted with sky-blue that one cannot grind it too much or mix it with other paints, one must use it pure. For if it is not applied cleanly, it becomes slightly greenish, especially when one wishes to use it separately; but white can often prevent this.[102]

The method of refining azurite mentioned above was still familiar to the painters of the sixteenth and seventeenth centuries. De Mayerne advises that the pigment, which he always refers to as *"cendrée,"* ash-blue, should be filtered from alkaline solution using grainy ash or soft soap, and he mentions the origin of the *"lapis armenus"* used in one of his refining experiments—Schwaz, in the Tyrol.[103] The city was famed for its copper and silver mines, which came into the possession of the Fugger family in 1515.

Lazure stone or azure stone? Ash-blue or ultramarine ash? Mountain blue or azure blue? The confusing similarity between the names for azurite and those for lapis lazuli must have been very convenient to crooked traders. Confusion with the incomparably more expensive pigment "from overseas," ultramarine, would always have been a rewarding business.

Equally, those who traded in blue verditer were able to profit from the term "ash-blue," taken from the French, since the name was transferred from natural blue copper carbonate to the artificial one. "Sanders blue" is a corruption of *bleu de cendres,* and it refers to common verditer.

[102] Gerhard zur Brügge, *Illuminir-oder Erleuchterey-Kust,* pp. 12–13.

[103] Cf. Berger, *Quellen für Maltechnik,* p. 129.

Numerous formulas for the production of artificial copper blue have been handed down since the Middle Ages. These mostly involve copper sulfate solutions, which turn dark blue with the effect of sal ammoniac (ammonium chloride), and yield a relatively stable pigment when bound with chalk.[104]

The *Nuremberg Art Book* (*Nürnberger Kunstbuch,* late fifteenth century) recommends the following method of production:

> Item, if you would make good lazure, take one part of calx of egg-shells, the eighth part of salammoniac, the sixth part of copper flake,[105] and grind all these with one another with good strong wine vinegar and lay it in a copper vessel and pour on good wine vinegar, so that it goes a good half finger's breadth above these matters, and close it well with bread dough or with wax or dough that is well prepared with salt or with wheat, and close it so that no vapor may come out, and set it in warm horse-manure or in a cellar, this will make a good lazure.[106]

The Bolognese manuscript (mid–fifteenth century) contains a slightly different formula:

> *To make artificial azure.*—Take of sal-ammoniac 1 part, of verdigris 2 parts, of ceruse ½ a part, grind them well together, and make them into a paste with oil of tartar,[107] and put the whole into a glass vase luted in the manner of the philosophers; and when

---

[104] Cf. D. V. Thompson, *Medieval Painting,* pp. 151–152.

[105] *"Kuppherschlag,"* the material that falls off when knocking the copper.

[106] Cited after Ellwanger-Eckel, *Kupferpigmente,* p. 25.

[107] Oil of tartar, "old name for a saturated solution of potassium carbonate" (*Oxford English Dictionary*).

the lute is dry put it into the oven while the bread is baking, and when the bread shall have been baked 7 times, the process will be completed.[108]

The Mayerne manuscript lists various formulas for azure, of Italian and English origin:

Take flaky soap-stone[109] and a new pot, and put therein one layer of soap-stone, one of sal-ammoniac, and another of powdered verdigris, and fill the vessel layer by layer, then seal up the vessel as best as may be with clay putty, bury it in fresh manure, surround it with unslaked lime, and let it stand twenty days. Dig it out, and you will obtain the finest azure.[110]

Another Italian formula is based not only on copper but on silver as well:

Take a newly glazed pot, put into it two ounces of sal-ammoniac and two ounces of verdigris, both well powdered, and pour onto this as much vinegar as you think good. Then take a square plate of the finest silver, that has a small hole in the middle of it, so that it can be hung with a brass wire about four fingers above the vinegar; and close this with a second pot and seal it up together with the first, so that no vapor can come out. Fix the said brass wire in the upper pot, and place the two vessels surrounded

[108] Mary Philadelphia Merrifield, *Original Treatises, Dating from the XIIth to XVIIIth Centuries, on the Arts of Painting* (London, 1849), vol. 2, p. 392.

[109] "A massive variety of talc," *Oxford English Dictionary.* A later collection of formulas (*Kunst- und Werckschule,* p. 392) recommends the ingredient "soap-stone, or Our Lady's ice."

[110] Cited after Berger, *Quellen für Maltechnik,* pp. 219–221.

with unslaked lime in manure, and after 14 days open the said vessels and you will find the plate covered with azure; remove this with great care, and close the vessels again; after eight days repeat this, and if there is not enough vinegar, add some more, and you will see an excellent and well‑tested secret.[111]

In the Middle Ages, azure produced using silver was regarded as the most valuable artificial blue. Attempts to produce a blue bloom on modern silver proved fruitless; Thompson calls this puzzling process "the silver‑blue mystery."[112] The multitude of silver‑blue formulas that have survived from the Middle Ages suggests that the tale was not invented, however. More recent investigations have confirmed the suspicion that the blue color was due to the silver's copper content. The silver used in the Middle Ages was only slightly purified of its natural copper impurities.[113]

The *Trier Painters' Book* (*Trierer Malerbuch*) from the second half of the fifteenth century includes a silver‑blue formula that is less complicated than the above "well‑tested secret" from Italy:

Item, if you wish to make a good azure, take equal parts of cream of tartar and sal‑ammoniac, and grind them well together and pour common urine into it, which should be well purified by heating over the fire, and much good vinegar, and then take silver sheets and the sal‑ammoniac and the cream of tartar that you have ground and spread it on the

[111] Ibid., p. 221.
[112] Thompson, *Medieval Painting*, p. 154.
[113] Cf. Fuchs and Oltrogge, in *Blau: Farbe der Ferne*, p. 110.

sheets, and hang these over the vinegar, and bury them in horse-manure 14 days long or more, in this way good azure is obtained.[114]

Silver must still have contained copper in the seventeenth century, since de Mayerne wrote in the margin of his manuscript, "is wrong; I've tried it," when formulas were useless—but he did not add any comments on silver-blue.

Boltz von Ruffach produces artificial copper blue using verdigris and sal ammoniac, calling this "bastard azure":

Take two parts of burnt eggshells, as much as you like, and sal-ammoniac one part, pound them together in a mortar, and then grind in one part of verdigris, as much as the amount of paint you want, and grind it well with vinegar on a stone. Put it together in a good new pot, and seal as well as can be at the top, that no vapor may come out. Set it in a warm place one month long, then open it, and thus you will obtain a sweet little color.[115]

A few variants of this formula are collected in the *Kunst- und Werckschule,* published in Nuremberg in 1696, including many "silver mysteries." In one, "little sheets of the very finest silver" in a solution of salt, rock alum, and vinegar "in a new pot" are buried in wine marc; in another, the silver sheets, previously treated with "filtered juice of lemons and long aristolochia," are exposed to vinegar vapor in an airtight vessel and after ten days (the anonymous author assures us) "you will find the sky-blue you desire."[116]

---

[114] Cited after Fuchs and Oltrogge, p. 111.
[115] Boltz, *Illuminir-Buch,* p. 52.
[116] *Kunst- und Werckschule,* pp. 122–123.

Blue blooms of silver are no longer found in the *Hand-maid to the Arts* in 1746, and the dangerous instructions in the Mayerne manuscript and the anonymous Nuremberg writer for making "artificial azure" with mercury are no longer mentioned either. In any case, the alchemical mercury–sulfur–sal ammoniac concoction only produced blue smoke, and no pigment at all.[117]

Dossie recommends producing verditer and *"bleu de cendres,* or sanders blue" from copper-saltpeter solutions. The two formulas he gives are preceded by a long warning:

Verditer is the mixture of chalk and precipitated copper, which is formed by adding the due propor-tion of chalk to the solution of copper, made by the refiners in preparing the silver from the *aqua fortis,* in the operation called parting, in which they have occasion to dissolve it, in order to its purification. Verditer is, when good, a cool full blue, but without the least transparency either in oil or water. It is of a moderate degree of brightness, and would have consequently a considerable value in the nicer paintings, where it would supply the place of ultra-marine, or at least of the ultramarine ashes, if it could be depended upon. But in oil it is very subject to turn greenish, and sometimes black; and in water, where it is safer, it is yet not always found to hold. For which reasons it is rejected, except in paper-hangings and other coarse work, or in var-nish, where this objection to it ceases.

Verditer is only to be had at a cheap rate from the refiners, who are at no expense in the making of it, but that of the chalk and labour, as they could find no other use for the solution of copper made by pre-cipitating the silver from the *aqua fortis,* in one of

[117] Cf. Fuchs and Oltrogge, p. 112.

their most common operations, were they not to apply it to this.[118]

In 1858, another unstable form of verditer was discov‑ered—copper hydroxide, $Cu(OH)_2$, known as Bremen blue. No verditer was able to hold its own against the inexpensive and stable blue pigments that were now available to artists. The particles of modern verditer syn‑theses are small, more regular and rounder than those of the natural mineral, and the color corresponds to that of finely ground unimproved azurite. It would be worth testing the characteristics and properties of copper azures produced using older formulas.

ULTRAMARINE
from lapis lazuli

CHARACTERISTICS. *Color:* Depending on the com‑position of the stone and the care with which it is extracted, ultramarine has the appearance of a more or less deep sapphire or cornflower blue. *Material appearance:* transparent particles of varying sizes, mostly flat, with a splintered corner outline and a shell‑shaped to uneven fracture. *Chemical composition:* Only approximations can be given for this multilayered mineral pigment. Mineralo‑gists consider that a formula more or less as follows can be given: $(Na,Ca)_8(AlSiO_4)_6(SO_4,S,Cl)_2$ = sulfur‑containing sodium‑calcium‑aluminum silicate.[119] The blue color is created by the sulfur radical compounds enclosed within the silicate lattice.

---

[118] *Handmaid to the Arts,* vol. 1, pp. 88–89.
[119] Cf. Joyce Plesters, "Ultramarine Blue, Natural and Artificial," in Roy, *Artists' Pigments,* pp. 37–65.

PHYSICAL PROPERTIES. The semiprecious stone lapis lazuli has a cubic crystalline system, and is therefore one of the unirefringent minerals. Its glittering elements consist of the strongly birefringent particles of calcite embedded in it, ingrown quartz grains, and veins of pyrites. Rarely, it is found crystallized into rhombic dodecahedrons, and usually it is found in coarse form as a contact mineral in marble and granulite. The dark blue stone is opaque, with a matt to oily sheen, and the trans-parent pigment particles shine like glass. *Refringency index:* 1.5. *Density:* 2.4. *Temper:* 5.5. *Toxicity:* nontoxic.

The blue stone was already known at an early period in Egypt and in ancient Mesopotamia. Its Babylonian name was *uqnû,* and if the Assyriologists are right, it was used not only as a jewel, but also as a paint.[120] The Babylonians believed there were male and female *uqnû,* a distinction also familiar in classical antiquity. In Pliny, the dark blue stones are regarded as the male ones.[121] The Greeks and Romans, who preferred to use lapis lazuli for gems rather than as a pigment, referred to it as "sapphire." Pliny's remark that *sappiri* are never transparent, and that gold "glistens as dots" within them, makes it clear that his blue stones, "rarely tinged with purple," are identical to our lapis lazuli. The best *sappiri* are found in Persia, Pliny reports.[122]

The valuable commodity probably came to Persia from the Hindu Kush, reaching Italy by Venice. The term "lapis lazuli," with its magic formula quality, also derives from Persia: *lazuli* is the Latinized form of *lāzhward,* the Persian word for "blue."

The earliest paintings using pulverized lapis lazuli date from the sixth century A.D., and decorate the walls of

[120] Cf. Goltz, *Geschichte der Mineralnamen,* pp. 89–90.
[121] Pliny, *Natural History* XXXVII.xxxix (120), vol. 10, p. 263.
[122] Loc. cit.

cave temples in the northeast of Afghanistan, not far from the famous lapis lazuli mines of Badakhshan, which Marco Polo visited in 1271. The opaque "sapphires" have been exported from this barely accessible region on the upper reaches of the Oxus, on the northern side of the Hindu Kush, since time immemorial.

The color from beyond the sea, the precious ultramarine painstakingly wrested from the stone, a pigment treasured above all others by the painters of the Middle Ages and the Renaissance, was of the finest blue, with the depth light and sheen of a jewel. "Ultramarine blue is admired as the most precious," writes Boltz von Ruffach, lamenting that it is little used, and only rarely, in the "High Dutch" lands (Germany). Dürer was an exception to this rule. "Know that I use the very finest paints I can obtain," he writes in November 1508 to his commissioning patron, the Frankfurt cloth dealer Jakob Heller, complaining that he requires as much as 20 ducats to pay for ultramarine alone. "If you were to purchase one pound of ultramarine," the painter tells the merchant and patron of the arts, "you could hardly manage it with 100 florins. For I can hardly buy a single fine ounce for less than 10 or 12 ducats."[123]

The procedure involved in producing a paint out of the hard mineral is as long and wearisome as the process of transporting the blue stones from the Hindu Kush— which is why the pigment was at times more expensive than gold. It is no surprise that a material as precious as this should also have had healing powers ascribed to it. A medical prescription from England, noted by de Mayerne, describes "the right way of extracting the tincture from lapis lazuli." The English apothecary advises employing a poor painter for the long hours needed to grind the hard stone, "since the profit would cover the

[123] Dürer, *Schriften und Briefe,* p. 88.

costs." His instructions end with a description of the benefits of ultramarine: "It is the diamond among the colors, owing to its imperishable virtues. It is also beneficial for the brain, and thus very favorable against madness, giddiness, pounding of the heart, melancholy, and other diseases of the spirit."[124]

Numerous formulas for ultramarine have been handed down, from the time of Cennini to Bouvier, but they all follow the same principle, using different pastes. Cennini processes raw lapis lazuli, while other writers calcine the stone and sometimes quench it with vinegar water. Calcination not only makes the powdering process easier, but it can also be used to test whether the semiprecious stone is genuine; in contrast to azurite, lapis lazuli maintains its blue color when it is fired and never becomes crumbly in the way that azurite does.

Whether it is raw or calcined, the stone pounded in the mortar has to be ground for many hours. "The smaller it is ground, the better it is; and it cannot be ground too small. And this is the noblest part of the whole art," states the *Kunst- und Werckschule.*[125]

Dossie, the expert author of *The Handmaid to the Arts,* says that the following method of preparing the pigment is best:

Take the *lapis lazuli,* and break it into very small pieces, or rather a gross powder. Put it into a crucible, and cover it securely, to prevent the coals from falling amongst it. Calcine it then with a strong fire for an hour if there be any large quantity, or less time in proportion, and quench it, when taken out of the fire, in vinegar; stirring them well together, and suffer it to remain in that state for a day or two. Pour off

[124] Cited after Berger, *Quellen für Maltechnik,* pp. 239, 241.
[125] *Kunst- und Werckschule,* p. 111.

then the vinegar, except what may be necessary for moistening the calcined *lapis lazuli* in grinding, which operation it must then undergo, in a mortar of flint or glass, till reduced to the greatest degree of fineness those means may effect. But, if it appear yet too hard to be easily ground, give it another short calcination, and quench it a second time in vinegar. The vinegar must then be washed off from the powder, by the putting it to several successive quan⁄ tities of clean water; each of which must be poured off when the *lapis lazuli* has been well stirred about in them, and is again settled to the bottom. It must then be ground on a porphyry stone, with a muller, till it be perfectly impalpable, and then dried; in which state it is duly prepared to mix with the fol⁄ lowing cement.—Take of Burgundy pitch,[126] nine ounces,—of white resin, and Venice turpentine, six ounces,—of virgin wax one ounce and a half,— and of linsee[d] oil one ounce and a quarter. Mix them together by melting in a pipkin over the fire; and suffer them to boil till they acquire so stiff a consistence that, being dropt into water while of this boiling heat, they will not spread on the surface of it, but form a roundish mass or lump. The cement being thus formed, may be poured out of the pipkin in the water, and made into cakes or rolls for use. Of this cement, take an equal weight with that of the calcined *lapis lazuli,* and melt it in a glazed earthen pipkin; but not so as to render it too fluid. Then add it to the calcined matter by very slow degrees, stirring them together with an ivory spatula till the whole appear perfectly mixed. Being thus mixed, heat the composition to a something greater degree, and cast it into a large bason full of

[126] Burgundy pitch = the resin of the spruce tree, or colophony.

cold water. When it has cooled to a consistence to bear such treatment, knead it well like the dough of bread, with the hands rubbed over with linseed oil, till all the parts be thoroughly incorporated with each other. Then make the mass into a cake, which may be either kept till some other convenient time in cold water, or immediately proceeded with in the following manner. Put the cake into an earthen dish or bason, the bottom of which should be rubbed with linseed oil, and pour on it water of the warmth of blood. Let it stand a quarter of an hour; and as the water softens the cake, it will not loose the finest part of the calcined matter; which, on gently stir-ring the water, but without breaking the cake or separating it into lesser parts, will be suspended in the water; and must be poured off with it into another vessel. The quantity of water must then be renewed, and the same operation repeated a second or third time; and as the mass appears slack in affording the colour, it must be moved and stirred, in the manner of kneading, with the ivory spatula, but not broken into fragments or small parts; and when so much of the colour is extracted as to render it necessary for the obtaining of more, the heat of the water must be increased to the greatest degree. The quantities of the calcined matter (which is now the ultramarine) that were first washed off, and appear of the same degree of deepness and bright-ness, may be put together, and the same of those of the second degree, the last washings making a third. The water being then poured off from each of these parcels, put on a lixivium formed of two ounces of salt of tartar, or pearl-ashes, dissolved in a pint of water, and filtered through paper after the solution is cold. This lixivium must be put on boiling hot, and the ultramarine stirred well about in it, and then the mixture set to cool. The powder being subsided, the clear lixivium must be poured off, and clean water put in its place, which must be repeated till the whole of the salts of the lixivium are washed away. The ultramarine must afterwards be dried, and will be then duly prepared for use . . .

The other method I have proposed to give differs from the above only in the using virgins wax and the best white resin melted together in equal quantities, instead of the more compound cement; and this gives up the colour, on its being infused with warm water, much sooner than the other.[127]

The final section discusses "ultramarine ashes," a pigment consisting of the residue of lapis lazuli in the paste.

. . . as the coloured particles which remain are mixt with those of another kind contained in the *lapis lazuli,* whether earths or metalline substances, these ashes must of course be much less valuable than even the worst ultramarine. Sometimes, nevertheless, when the operation of the extracting the colour from the calcined *lapis lazuli* has not succeeded well, a considerable share of the ultramarine is left behind with the recrement, and greatly enhances the worth of the ashes; and indeed, as it is certain that what colour they possess, when genuine, will never fly, they always bear a good price.[128]

Only acids and acidic vapors can affect ultamarine's miraculous stability. They corrode the pigment, causing the color to turn gray and fade. This has been termed "ultramarine disease," and it is similar to a phenomenon

[127] Dossie, *Handmaid to the Arts,* vol. 1, pp. 71–76.

[128] Ibid., vol. 1, pp. 79–80.

known to restorers as "blushing," caused by clouding of the varnish or binder.

Synthetic ultramarine was discovered almost simultaneously in Toulouse, Tübingen, and Meissen. When manufacturing of it began in the early 1830s, one kilogram of natural ultramarine cost between 6,000 and 10,000 francs in Paris. The artificial form undercut this colossal price by nearly a hundred percent—thereby sealing the fate of what had formerly been the proudest of paints. Both painters and apothecaries were saved a great deal of work, and no one needed to worry anymore whether the blue purchased at such a massive price was really genuine.

A hundred years later, the Dutch forger van Meegeren was to be exposed by a few grains of modern cobalt blue, with which the genuine ultramarine he used had been blended without his knowledge. The fatal cobalt particles formed part of the mosaic of evidence that finally put him behind bars, even though he had spared neither effort nor expense in obtaining the blue that Vermeer preferred.[129]

The ultimate azure pigment, from which all the azures and lazures first took their name—genuine ultramarine—has recently come into production once again. At the Kremer company, in the Algäu region of Bavaria, the pulverizing of the stone is done not by poor painters, but by electric ball mills. Even so, the color is dearer than gold, just as it always was: a kilogram today can cost more than $15,000. The price of the ultrablue industrial product, which is not as stable and is less translucent, with its tiny, regularly spherical particles lacking glittering elements, has by contrast fallen substantially. A kilogram of artificial ultramarine currently costs around $10 to $15.

[129] Simply managing to get hold of the pigment, at a time when it had long since disappeared from the market, demonstrates the forger's resourcefulness.

"Old alchemists will be my witnesses, who have never either by chance or by experiment succeeded in creating the smallest element which can be created by nature,"[130] Leonardo da Vinci wrote in 1508, in a polemical pamphlet against the foolish art of conjuring gold. He contrasted the alchemical mercury-sulfur trick[131] with the gold-veined lapis lazuli, the beauty of the color of ultramarine, which is "unaffected by the power of the fire." In the eyes of the Renaissance painter and researcher, no chemical bond created by man, no matter how commendably useful it might be, could measure up to the elementary things accomplished by Nature.

Long before the synthetic form supplanted natural lapis lazuli, the Baroque poet Barthold Heinrich Brockes sang the praises of both the color and the stone, in a collection entitled *Earthly Delight in God:*

> *As lapis lazuli does show,*
> *Delight with use can be combined—*
> *Where these two hand in hand do go,*
> *To suitable avail entwined.*
> *From the selfsame stones we treasure,*
> *Which bring us all both joy and pleasure*
> *We draw forth the ultramarine,*
> *The color rare, the hue so fine.*[132]

ALABASTER

Gypsum, mineral white, terra alba, lady's ice, specular stone, selenite, moonstone, gypsum spar, atlas spar, silk

[130] Cited after John Gage, *Colour and Culture: Practice and Meaning from Antiquity to Abstraction* (London, 1993), p. 141.

[131] See under "Vermilion" above, p. 311.

[132] *"Noch bezeugen Lasulsteine, | dasz mit Lust der Nutzen auch | in denselben sich vereine | durch vernünftigen Gebrauch. | Diese Steine sind es eben, | die uns viel Vergnügen geben, | woraus wir Ultramarin, | die so rare Farbe, ziehn."*

spar; Latin: *selenites, lapis specularis, glacie divae Maria, diaphanes, aphroselenus, gypsum lamellare.*

CHARACTERISTICS.   *Color:* white in an aqueous medium, colorless and transparent in an oil one. *Material appearance:* flexible, glittering flakes with sharp edges, a soft, irregular fracture, and reflective glass sheen. *Chemical composition:* $CaSO_4 \times 2H_2O$ = calcium sulfate.

PHYSICAL PROPERTIES.   Gypsum has a mono-clinic crystal. The columnar, slablike, needle-shaped, or lens-shaped crystals have a glassy sheen on the crystal surfaces and a mother-of-pearl sheen on the perfect fracture surfaces. Double crystals with arrowhead shapes, deriving from fused lenses, were found mainly in Montmartre in Paris. Bushy and star-shaped fusions of imperfect ovals form what are known as "gypsum roses." In an aqueous medium, the pounded particles of the pigment always reflect the light at an angle of $30°$, while in an oil medium they are completely transparent. Both in the white state and the transparent one, only a slight addition of colored pigment is sufficient to color the particles. *Refringency index:* birefringent $\epsilon = 1.53$ $\omega = 1.62$. *Density:* 2.3–2.4. *Toxicity:* nontoxic.

In antiquity, the reflective crystal of gypsum was regarded as the stone of the moon goddess, and was therefore given the name *selenites.* Dioscorides[133] devotes three sentences to it in his work on pharmacology:

The stone selenite, which some called moon-foam, because it is found at night when the moon is waxing, arises in Arabia; it is white, transparent, and

[133] The Greek physician Dioscorides wrote the five books of *De materia medica,* about A.D. 40. The fifth is devoted to wine and to the minerals used in medicine.

Aragonite

Cerussite, the natural equivalent of synthetic flake white

Cerussite crystals

Cerussite triplet

Orpiment from Turkey

Orpiment from Banská Bystrica, Slovakia

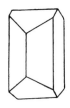

Orpiment crystal

Realgar crystal in marl

Realgar crystal

Cinnabar from Szlana in Hungary

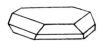

Cinnabar crystals

Mercury on earthy cinnabar

Malachite from Siberia

Malachite twin

Malachite on brown iron ore

Malachite crystals on limonite

Malachite from Siberia

Pure copper with dendritic growth

Pure copper in granular quartz

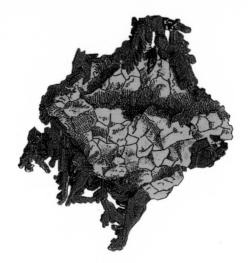

Pure copper

Chromite with chrome ochre

Azurite on sandstone

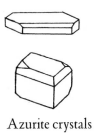

Azurite crystals

Azurite from Chessy

Copper indigo on copper silicate

Lapis lazuli

Lapis lazuli from Tartary, with pyrites

Lapis lazuli from Siberia

Pyrite crystals

Alabaster

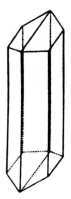 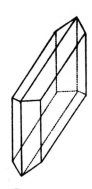 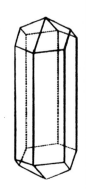

Gypsum crystals

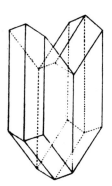 

Twin

Fractured piece of a twin of
lens-shaped crystals

light. Scrapings from it are given as a drink to those with the falling sickness, and women wear it as an amulet for protection. It seems that when it is put on trees, it encourages the formation of fruit.

Pliny regarded the belief in the stone's miraculous affinity to the moon with a certain skepticism: "The 'selenitis,' or 'moonstone,' a transparent, colourless stone with a honey-coloured sheen, contains a likeness of the moon, and reproduces, if the report is true, the very shape of the moon as it waxes or wanes from day to day."[134] In his book on painting, Pliny praises Apelles as the "artist of artists," and compares the visual effect of his paintings with that of the mirror-stone:

His inventions in the art of painting have been useful to all other painters as well, but there was one which nobody was able to imitate: when his works were finished he used to cover them over with a black varnish of such thinness that its very presence, while its reflexion threw up the brilliance of all the colours and preserved them from dust and dirt, was only visible to anyone who looked at it close up, but also employed great calculation of lights, so that the brilliance of the colours should not offend the sight when people looked at them as if through muscovy-glass and so that the same device from a distance might invisibly give sombreness to colours that were too brilliant.[135]

In vessels for ointments, in miniature sculptures, or pearls, the fine-grained, translucent white form of gyp-

[134] Pliny, *Natural History* XXXVII.lxvii (181), vol. 10, pp. 311–313.

[135] Ibid., XXXV.xxxvi (97), vol. 9, p. 333. "Muscovy-glass" was a term used both for mica and talc. The German translation of Dossie's *Handmaid to the Arts* (1792) translates "powdered talc" as "*Marienglas*" (alabaster).

sum spar is called "alabaster." The terms *Fraueneis* and *Unsrer Lieben Frauen Eis* ("Our Lady's ice") are found in German from the fifteenth century onward; "moonstone" fell out of use for the substance only toward the end of the eighteenth century, as interest in the miracle-working stone was gradually waning. As the age of Enlightenment advanced, it came to be the accepted view that alabaster was most definitely not the dew of heaven that had curdled in the moonlight—as had been thought in the age that believed in miracles. The name "moonstone" was left vacant, and was borrowed by a type of feldspar that shows a surging gleam of milky light when it is polished. Even today, however, mineralogists use "selenite" for the finely fibered form of gypsum crystals, which due to the silky sheen of their honey-colored parallel aggregates were also known as "atlas spar" or "silk spar."

The thin flakes of gypsum were used for a long period for sparkling decorations on devotional images and music boxes: "The virgins in the nunnery make all sorts of ornaments out of the flakes, and commonly lay these over their pictures and shrines."[136]

Since the Gothic period, alabaster has principally been used in coating and casting. De Mayerne mentions "unburnt alabaster" as a base for "verditer"; 140 years later, the German translation of Dossie's *Handmaid to the Arts* uses *Marienglas* (alabaster) to render his "powdered talc." By the time of Bouvier's widely read *Handbook of Oil Painting* of 1828, alabaster appears only as a degreasing agent in the production of drying oil. The glittering pigment then vanished altogether. The marvelous alabaster coatings used in palaces and churches in the nineteenth century were replaced by easy-care paint. Alabaster was rediscovered in 1983 by Wolfgang Fünders after two hundred years of oblivion, during the

[136] *Zedlers Universal-Lexicon* (Halle/Leipzig, 1732–1754), vol. 8, p. 1564.

reconstruction of polychrome coatings on the walls and ceilings of the palace and hunting lodge of Clemenswerth, and the role it played has yet to be fully investigated.[137]

Gypsum crystals occur in caves and fissures in the weathering zone of beds of ore. "As a result of modern extraction methods, which start in the solid gypsum rock at a greater depth, below the weathering zone, the recovery of alabaster has ceased here. In any case, it can only be obtained manually."[138]

The raw material for the pigment, which is now being produced once again for restoration work, comes from Cyprus. Ground in a stonemill and sieved into medium-sized or fine grains, alabaster is available today once again. But—since nothing is ever the same as it used to be—even this pigment differs from the old one. The processing of the crystals to produce a paintable powder should really be carried out only by pounding, since milling causes the reflective fracture surfaces in the pigment grains to turn matte.

Anyone wishing to obtain the characteristically strong light reflection of alabaster and the depth effect that the pigment can create would have to order it *coarsely* milled and then pound it in the mortar himself.

Forgotten by artists, alabaster inspired the imagination of the Romantic poets. Chapter 38 of Jean Paul Richter's *Flegeljahre,* or *The Awkward Age,* is entitled "Marienglas," and opens with a description of its reflective effects: ". . . the Romantic journey into such blue days—in such conditions, and as such a sudden gift—was, for him, to

[137] Clemenswerth, in the Emsland region in north Germany, was designed and built between 1734 and 1737 by the architect J. C. Schlaun of Münster.

[138] Wolfgang Fünders, "*Aktuelle Befunde zu Verwendung 'vergessener'* Pigmente in niedersächsischen Raumfassungen," in *Restaurierung von Kulturdenkmälern: Beispiele aus der niedersächsischen Denkmalpflege* (Hamelin, 1989), p. 44.

pass into the brightest sun of happiness, where sparkling light scatters and one seems entirely covered with shining glints." The gypsum ("lady's ice") crystallizes in a quite different climate in a poem by Clemens Brentano, hope-lessly in love:

> Thirst; love; a dream desert—there on the hill
> Shines the ray of dawn, the gleam of shepherd's fire.
> Where thirst saw the crystal waterfall's spill,
> Love found the rubble of the lady's ice.[139]

[139] "*Durst, Liebe, Wüstentraum, dort scheint am Hügel | Der Morgenstrahl, ein Hirtenfeuer weiss. | Wo Durst gewähnt des Wasserfalles Spiegel | Fand Liebe ein Geschiebe Fraueneis.*" (Clemens Brentano, *Werke* [Munich, 1968], vol. 1, p. 625.)

The illustrations following page 356 are taken from *Das Mineralreich in Bildern* by J. C. von Kurr (Stuttgart/Esslingen, 1858).

GLOSSARY
IN PLACE OF THANKS
INDEX

GLOSSARY

ALLA PRIMA or direct painting: spontaneous painting in a single layer and at one session. The quickest way of creating an effect, with paint, sketch, and modeling all being applied at once. In the older layered technique, only the concluding touches were applied to the painting *alla prima*.

AMORPHOUS (mineralogy): lacking a crystal structure.

ATMOSPHERICS: components of the atmosphere that have physical and chemical effects.

CALCINATION: transformation of substances, their color and/or texture, by means of fire.

CANADA BALSAM: a thick, clear turpentine from the balsam fir tree of Canada. It is used to embed microscopic color samples.

CHROMATOGRAPHY: a process of chemical analysis in which mixtures of substances, such as the binder used in painting, can be reduced to their constituent parts using the varying ability of their components to cling to specific absorbent materials.

CISSOID (mathematics): an ivy-leaf curve, a flat curve of the second order.

COAT (German *Fassen*): to cover with metal or paint; to polychrome sculptures, pieces of furniture, paneling, and the back of panels used for painting, with a many-layered polished chalk ground prepared wet with linen balls and/or stems of the horsetail plant.

DISTILL: derived from Latin *distillare,* "to drip or trickle down." A fluid mixture is boiled, and the steam that it gives off cools and condenses, and drips off to be collected. The various boiling points of the substances the mixture contains allow them to be separated.

EMBLEM: derived from ἔμβλημα. Before becoming generalized in English to mean "symbol" or "type," the word meant anything inserted, whether a scion or a mosaic, inlaid work in wood, or something thrown into a speech. It is used, particularly in the Baroque period, for "a drawing or picture expressing a moral fable or allegory."

GRAFT CHIMERA (botany): graft chimeras consist of tissue combinations of two genetically different plants. They can arise during grafting, and are not hybrids produced sexually.

GUILLOCHE: "To decorate with intersecting curved lines on high-quality paper or metal, ivory, or wood."

IMPRIMATURA: a wash or glaze of pigmented oil or gum that has an isolating effect, which is applied to the ground before or after the underpainting.

INTERFERENCE COLOR: a color arising when light passes through, dependent on the density and birefringency of a crystal. It is caused by interference between two polarized waves.

ISOLATING VARNISH: an unpigmented layer of painting oil, paste, or emulsion over a ground, intended to prevent the color binder from being absorbed into the ground.

LEVIGATION: grinding a substance in water, with subsequent sedimentation: the finer particles in the powder float, while the heavier ones separate to the bottom.

MULLER: a conical or punch-shaped instrument made of glass or stone, used to grind pigment and binder on a rough stone or glass slab.

PARAGON: "a pattern or model of excellence," an evaluative comparison in the contest of the arts.

PRECIPITATE (chemistry): to separate a substance out of a solution and deposit it in a solid (powdery or crys-talline) form.

REPOUSSOIR: an object in the foreground of a pic-ture, which enhances the effect of depth.

SPECIFIC GRAVITY: the weight of a substance in relation to its volume; the density of a body in comparison with the density of water.

SUBLIMATION: conversion of a solid substance into vapor by heating and resolidifying it on cooling, without it passing through the fluid phase.

TEMPE: a wild and romantic erosion valley on the Peneus River between Mount Ossa and Mount Olympus in Thessaly; in poetry it is used to mean "delightful valley, forest vale."

TRANSPARENT CLOUDING: shadowing in the purely visual color structure caused by overlaying of transparent layers.

UNDERPAINTING: laying out the composition on the painting surface, in contrast to sketching, in which the composition is prepared in a form external to the painting.

VISIERUNG: "to sketch out and measure, to represent artistically in the correct proportions." The draft sketch of an art work, which usually accompanied the contract between the artist and the commissioning patron. In the Middle Ages and the Renaissance, this was known as Visierung. The shorter form visir is also found: "The inte-rior of the Town Hall is to be painted according to Dürer's visir" (Hampe, Nürnberger Ratsverlässe, vol. 1, p. 201, no. 1319).

The Madonna of Chancellor Rolin,
from G. Josef Kern, *Grundzüge der linear-perspektivischen
Darstellung in der Kunst der Gebrüder Van Eyck
und ihrer Schule* (Leipzig, 1904)

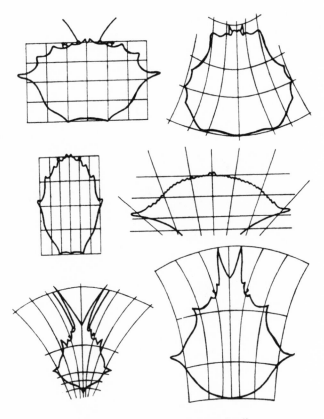

"Carapaces of Various Crabs,"
from D'Arcy Wentworth Thompson, *On Growth and
Form: The Complete Revised Edition* (Cambridge, 1942;
rptd. New York, 1992), p. 1057

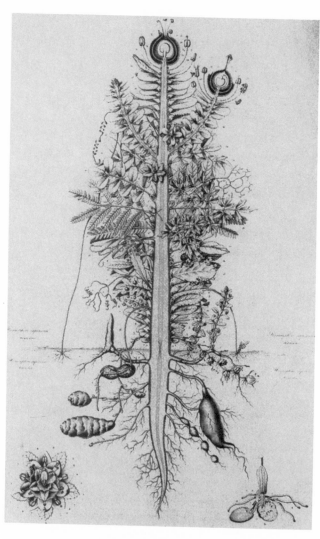

"Ur-plant," after P. J. F. Turpin, 1837;
from Karl Mägdefrau, *Geschichte der Botanik*
(Stuttgart, 1973)

IN PLACE OF THANKS

There were four friends in the galaxy of those who gener-
ously enriched *The Art of Arts* with their knowledge and
ideas—my guiding stars. Encouragement to write a book
on painting originally came from Hans Magnus Enzensberger, during a visit to the Maastricht art fair at the
beginning of March 1993. His trust in me, and the reas-
surance he provided during my three-year journey into a
distant age, gave me the confidence to complete the work
to the best of my ability. The core around which it crystallized was a desire to understand why I had been unable
to progress artistically myself in my painting, and the
hope that at the end of my voyage into enigma the gateway to art would once again open up.

The realization that the morality of the profession is
inseparable from that of life, no matter how inadequately
we are able to live up to it, cannot be drawn from books
alone; I had a living link between humor and *humores*
before my eyes in the form of Monique and Claude Lévi-
Strauss. The experience of the steadfastness of their
word, the balance of their courteous distance—from
which alone closeness can come at a distance—protected
me on a rough path.

At the end of 1994, the star of a new friendship rose
for me in Bamberg, and quickly joined the constellation.
At all times—and by return of post—Dieter Wuttke,
with the calm reflectiveness of a scholar in the humanist
tradition, answered nine hundred ninety-nine questions
and one final one as well, and provided me with generous
praise, gentle criticism, and wise wit through all the
proofs of the spirit till I reached the end of the journey.

Chatoillenot, 1 October 1996

INDEX

ILLUSTRATION CREDITS

ENDPAPERS

Friedrich Brentel, *Paradise*: Private collection.

COLOR GATEFOLDS

The Madonna of Chancellor Rolin: Courtesy of the Louvre, Paris. © Photograph by Erich Lessing/Art Resource, New York.

The Betrothal of the Arnolfini: Courtesy of the National Gallery, London. © Photograph by Erich Lessing/Art Resource, New York.

St. Luke Painting the Madonna: Courtesy of the Hermitage, St. Petersburg. © AKG Photo, London.

Forest Landscape: Courtesy of the Maurithuis, The Hague.

Triptych of Earthly Vanity and Heavenly Salvation: Courtesy of Musée des Beaux-Arts, Strasbourg. © Photo Les Musées de la Ville de Strasbourg.

Forest with St. George: Courtesy of the Alte Pinakotech, Munich. © Art Resource, New York.

Rest on the Flight: Courtesy of the Staatliche Museen zu Berlin, Preussischer Kulturbesitz, Gemäldegalerie, Berlin. Photograph by Jörg P. Anders.

Smoker's Still Life: Courtesy of the Historisches Museum, Frankfurt. © AKG Photo, London.

Flowers in a Wan-li Vase with Blue-Tit: Private collection, Middelburg.

Forest Floor: Courtesy of the Herzog Anton Ulrich-Museum, Braunschweig. Photograph by B. P. Keiser.

Rider on Palfrey with Fantastic Harness: Courtesy of Louvre Départments des Arts Graphiques, Paris. © Photograph R.M.N., Paris.

A NOTE ABOUT THE AUTHOR

Anita Albus is a writer and artist based in Munich and Burgundy. Her publications include a translation into German of portraits of nineteenth-century characters by Jules and Edmond de Goncourt under the title *Flashlights,* and she has illustrated *The Passionate Gardener* by Rudolph Borchardt and *The Jealous Potter* by Claude Lévi-Strauss. She is also the author of *The Garden of Songs, Hushaby, etc., The Botanical Drama,* and *Love Bonds.*

A NOTE ON THE TYPE

The text of this book has been set in a typeface called Poliphilus. This face is a copy of a roman type that Francesco Griffo cut for the Venetian printer Aldus Manutius in 1499. It was cut by the Monotype Corporation of London in 1923, six years earlier than Bembo, the celebrated and widely used revival of the Aldine type used for Pietro Cardinal Bembo's 1495 treatise *De Aetna*. Thus it appears that before Bembo was cut, the Monotype Corporation had already designed a roman based on another Aldine type—that of *Hypnerotomachia Poliphili*—which was actually Griffo's second version of his roman.

The italic of Poliphilus is called Blado. The italic was cut especially to accompany Poliphilus and was based on a formal italic of the calligrapher and printer Lodovico degli Arrighi—the formal italic having been known as Vincentino. It is named after the Roman printer Antonio Blado, who printed many books in this font, using it as an individual type and not as a subsidiary to the roman.

Composed by North Market Street Graphics
Lancaster, Pennsylvania

Printed and bound by Quebecor Printing
Fairfield, Pennsylvania

The Art of Arts

REDISCOVERING PAINTING

Anita Albus